More Praise for *Control Your Destiny or Someone Else Will*

"The rules for succeeding in business in the nineties have changed radically from those in the eighties. *Control Your Destiny or Someone Else Will* superbly defines those changes and explains how Jack Welch engineered one of the most successful transformations of a corporate culture in American business history. Anyone at any level in business will profit from this account of the renaissance of GE."

—Benjamin M. Rosen, Chairman of the Board,
Compaq Computer Corporation.

"The deal-by-deal commentary of *Control Your Destiny or Someone Else Will* makes fascinating reading for anyone who likes thinking about why corporations like behaving the way they do. . . . There is at least as much to be learned here as from reading Peter Drucker, John Kenneth Galbraith or Michael Porter."

—David Warsh, *Boston Globe*

"*Control Your Destiny or Someone Else Will* is an inspiration. Its possibility-thinking message—that we can face the facts and take responsibility for our own lives—is just what we need in these times of tumultuous change."

—Dr. Robert Schuller, Founding Pastor, Crystal Cathedral Ministries

"It isn't just GE that brings good things to life, it's life that Jack Welch brought to GE. *Control Your Destiny or Someone Else Will* is an utterly fascinating look into a business that the pundits tell us no longer exists: an American company that is healthy, flexible, creative, and run by a brilliant leader. The rough times ahead—the challenges that confront all of us in business—may be less burdensome in light of this extraordinary account of how Jack Welch turned GE around and created an astonishingly strong ecology for growth and viability. *Control Your Destiny or Someone Else Will* is terrific—it's a shot in the arm, and a totally involving read."

—Harvey B. Mackay, author of *Sharkproof*
and *Swim with the Sharks Without Being Eaten Alive*

"Messrs. Tichy and Sherman include a guide to [Welch's] revelations, the 'Handbook For Revolutionaries,' showing how executives can do with other companies what Mr. Welch did for GE."

—Toronto *Globe & Mail*

"The book explains how companies and individuals can face accelerating change and intensifying competition and win."

—*Fortune*

"The January 1, 1900, *Wall Street Journal* reported that the top twelve companies of the time were:

American Cotton Oil Company	National Lead
American Steel Company	Pacific Mail
American Sugar Refining	People's Gas
Continental Tobacco Company	Tennessee Coal and Iron
Federal Steel	U.S. Leather
General Electric	U.S. Rubber

Only General Electric remains. Why? *Control Your Destiny or Someone Else Will* explains. For those who wish to be long-run survivors, the answers are vital."

—Lester C. Thurow, former dean, Sloan School of Management, Massachusetts Institute of Technology, and author of *Head to Head*

"The volume by academic Tichy and journalist Sherman is the first scholarly attempt to pin down the secret of GE's success. . . . Tichy and Sherman give a helpful, clear account of all these developments, illustrating their case with interesting case studies of individual businesses which have been turned around."

—*Financial Times*

"One of America's astute young change agents meets one of America's most vibrant CEOs, and the result is a powerful book. Revolution is just the right term for the changes at GE. This is a fascinating story with widely applicable lessons."

—Rosabeth Moss Kanter, Professor, Harvard Business School, and coauthor, *The Challenge of Organizational Change*

"A third of the increased earnings has come from increased productivity. General Electric now has about the same growth in efficiency as its overseas competitors. . . . But getting to that point . . . has been a desperate struggle. . . . That struggle is told in a new book about Welch and General Electric—*Control Your Destiny or Someone Else Will*."

—Houston Chronicle

"A remarkable, accurate, and refreshing story of the dramatic change and redirection of one of the world's most successful companies. Jack Welch's leadership can serve as a valuable tutorial for business managers who are attempting to drive change."

—Lawrence A. Bossidy, Chief Executive, AlliedSignal, and
former Vice Chairman, General Electric

"Noel M. Tichy and Stratford Sherman tell a remarkable tale. . . . This book is full of managerial gems such as 'change before you have to,' 'don't manage—lead,' and 'if you don't have a competitive advantage, don't compete.' The authors insist that although Jack Welch is a remarkable leader, anyone can revolutionize a company for the better."

—Industry Week

"Managers discuss cultural change frequently, but seldom achieve it. This has become increasingly clear to me as we struggle to make our company a more dynamic, competitively effective enterprise. *Control Your Destiny or Someone Else Will* explains how General Electric's strong and unyielding leadership got GE focused on a simple, yet powerful vision. This book—and the 'Handbook for Revolutionaries' that accompanies it—is filled with practical tools for change."

—William L. Weiss, Chairman of the Board, Ameritech

"What Tichy and Sherman supply is an explanation of the strategy and its execution that alternately made Welch the most feared and respected leader in American business. . . . The book serves as a primer on how American companies need to restructure their focus on global economy and just how daunting that task is in the face of a company's bureaucracy. . . . [It] also serves as description of how a company's bureaucracy can derail the ideas of leaders. . . .

Finally, the book explains why the massive restructuring of American business must continue despite employee dislocation, to enable the U.S. to be more competitive in global markets that threaten to undermine our core industries."

—*Pittsburgh Post-Gazette*

"More insight per square inch than any business book I've read in years. Everyone should read it."

—Herbert J. Siegel, Chairman of the Board, Chris-Craft Industries

"If Jack Welch didn't write the book on corporate restructuring, it's only because Noel M. Tichy and Stratford Sherman beat him to it. *Control Your Destiny or Someone Else Will* is not only the title of their fascinating book but one of the mottoes of the man who put GE through the wringer a full decade ahead of everyone else. . . . The authors cite Mr. Welch's work at GE as a successful model of how business will adjust to changes in the market-place. . . . Mr. Welch has redefined the process, shifting power from the managers to the people who do the work."

—*Atlanta Journal-Constitution*

"The authors do a substantial job of presenting the research, which included more than 100 hours of interviews with Welch. Recommended for all business libraries."

—Rebecca A. Smith, Harvard Business School Library, in *Library Journal*

"*Control Your Destiny or Someone Else Will* is a harbinger of the future for managing global corporations. CEOs can use it as sort of a template against which to evaluate their own style. For the rest of us, it offers insight into one of America's most powerful corporations."

—*Toronto Star*

"Tichy and Sherman do a remarkable job conveying the mechanics of changing an organization. . . . The mix of ideology, drama, and practical examples make this book a ground breaker on how to succeed in the global economy. Its themes—empowering workers and then expecting a lot out of them, obliterating bureaucracy, continuous improvement, and more—can be adopted by any business that dares to. *Control Your Destiny or Someone Else Will* makes you want to give it a try."

"This book captures the essence of competitiveness, which is vision, leadership, and a hunger to succeed. It contains essential lessons that need to be learned by all of corporate America."

"Tichy and Sherman focus on the process that is making it possible for Welch, through GE managers and employees, to shape a flexible, responsive set of businesses out of what was once an elephantine bureaucracy. They insist that others could and should emulate this process."

"Noel M. Tichy and Stratford Sherman provide an insider's account of Welch and GE. . . . Welch quickly set down some now-famous ground rules on the businesses in which GE would participate. . . . But GE's revolution went far beyond that, the book points out. Welch's leadership energized the company's workers to accept change and challenge. . . . Welch brought GE's workforce to life."

"*Control Your Destiny or Someone Else Will* forces you to confront organizational and leadership self-evaluation. It is impossible to read this account of Welch's transformation of GE without simultaneously questioning your own organization's structure and operation. This book is filled with thought-provoking ideas."

"This is a good book for leaders, hopeful leaders-to-be, and the people who will work under their direction."

"Sherman's journalistic discipline and skepticism complement the insider knowledge of Tichy. What the pair created, in cooperation with Welch, is both history and handbook."

"GE survived a decade of revolutionary changes while earning record profits. The authors include Welch's principles of streamlining GE, which are applicable to any small or large, public or private business, or institution."

—*Mobile* (Alabama) *Register*

"Because of their personal backgrounds, Tichy and Sherman can offer a unique perspective on GE's organizational transformation—and on Welch's personal transformation. Their unusual vantage points allow them to explain Welch's management ideas and then offer their advice on how to apply them to other organizations."

—*Training and Development* magazine

"The book's great value is the insight it provides on the culture of GE—why it's managed the way it is, and why the managers act as they do. . . . The book has the look and feel of being there."

—*Across the Board* magazine

"Tichy and Sherman's work captures the essence of competing in today's rough and tough global economy. We need to emulate Welch's vision, our personal qualities, and our will to succeed so we can compete in the corporate climate of tomorrow. . . . Most people may not get as far as Welch, but the book clearly spells out the important ingredients for personal and corporate success. It makes for an inspiring read."

—*Connecticut Post*

CONTROL YOUR DESTINY OR SOMEONE ELSE WILL

Lessons in Mastering Change— from the Principles Jack Welch Is Using to Revolutionize GE

Noel M. Tichy and Stratford Sherman

HarperBusiness
A Division of HarperCollins*Publishers*

A hardcover edition of this book was originally published in 1993 by Doubleday,
a division of Bantam Doubleday Dell Publishing Group, Inc.
It is reprinted by arrangement with Doubleday.

HarperCollins books may be purchased for educational, business, or sales promotional use. For
information please write: Special Markets Department, HarperCollins Publishers, Inc.,
10 East 53rd Street, New York, NY 10022.

First HarperBusiness edition published 1994.

Designed by Richard Oriolo

Library of Congress Cataloging-in-Publication Data

Tichy, Noel M.
    Control your destiny or someone else will : lessons in mastering
change—from the principles Jack Welch is using to revolutionize GE /
Noel M. Tichy and Stratford Sherman.—
1st HarperBusiness ed.
        p.   cm.
    Originally published : New York : Doubleday, c1993.
    Includes bibliographical references and index.
    ISBN 0-88730-670-5 (paper)
    1. General Electric Company—History.   2. Electric industries—
United States—Management—Case studies.   3. Welch, Jack (John
Francis), 1935–   .   4. Industrial management—United States—Case
studies.   I. Sherman, Stratford.   II. Title.
[HD9697.A3U575   1994]
338.7′62138′0973—dc20   93-35823

99 00 01 CC/RRD 30 29 28 27 26 25 24 23 22 21

To Noel's mother, Ella Tichy,

and

to Gurumayi

Contents

Editor's Note   xiii

Authors' Note   xv

Introduction   xix

ACT ONE: THE AWAKENING   1

1. The GE Revolution   3
2. The Business Engine   14
3. The Hand He Was Dealt   32
4. The New Leader   51
5. The Power of Ideas   71
6. "Kick-Starting the Revolution"   85
7. Nothing Sacred   101
8. Facing Reality   111
9. The Mirror Test   126
10. The Turning Point   142

ACT TWO: THE VISION   153

11. Crotonville   155
12. The Politics of Speed   177
13. The New Order   188

14. Getting Excited   202
15. Globalization   219

ACT THREE: REVOLUTION AS
       A WAY OF LIFE   235

16. Work-Out   237
17. The Twenty-first-Century Organization   260
18. Head, Heart, and Guts   277
19. Jack Welch Speaks His Mind   292

GE Timeline   306
Notes   329
Sources   349

HANDBOOK FOR
REVOLUTIONARIES   365

Index   449

Editor's Note

Although written in the first person singular to reflect coauthor Noel Tichy's experiences at GE, this book is the product of a collaboration. Noel and coauthor Stratford Sherman made equal contributions to this book.

Authors' Note

For better and for worse, this is an inside story.

Our goal was not to investigate GE, but to explain it. Long before we decided to write this book, each of us had thoroughly examined the company and gotten to know Jack Welch, its CEO. Although we observed GE from very different vantage points—Noel as a deeply involved participant, Strat as a skeptical outsider—we both concluded that the ideas underlying GE's dramatic transformation merited book-length discussion.

The experience of writing *Control Your Destiny* has been a humbling reminder to us that our accomplishments are not ours alone. We are deeply indebted to more people than we can name, and offer heartfelt thanks for their kindness.

We are especially grateful to Jack Welch for permitting us to make public this very intimate view of GE. He unfailingly supported our work, even though it frequently made him uncomfortable. And he was generous with his own time: In addition to uncounted meetings with Noel over the years, Welch submitted to some fifty hours of additional interviews with us both. The CEO seemed to favor marathon sessions, two of which began before dusk and ended after 1 A.M. Such intimacy does not always foster respect, but we concluded our reporting with increased regard for Welch and GE.

Noel benefited from access no journalist could match. Even before the research process began, his file cabinets were stuffed with nonpublic GE documents. More important, he had participated in confidential meetings with GEers from Welch on down, establishing personal relationships with a much broader range of company employees than any outsider could reach. To prepare this book, Noel formally interviewed scores of GE employees, from factory workers, management trainees, and middle managers to leaders of multi-billion-dollar businesses. Although some requested that their names not be published, most appear in the list of sources beginning on page 349. The present and former GEers who gave most generously of their time to help get the story right were Toby D'Ambola, Carol Anderson, Marie Andrews, Jim Baughman, Larry Bossidy, Paolo Fresco, Reg Jones, Don Kane, John Opie, Paul Van Orden, Jack Peiffer, Jim Paynter, Phyllis Piano, Carl Schlemmer, John Trani, and Bill Woodburn.

Joyce Hergenhan, with the energetic assistance of Carla Fischer, responded cheerfully and effectively to our endless requests for information. Joyce's insights greatly enriched the text, and her company enlivened hours of difficult work. Rosanne Badowski was a constant beacon of light, reliably guiding us through Fairfield's rocky waters.

We are also indebted to Doubleday editors Harriet Rubin and Janet Coleman for the vision, perspective, and stamina they brought to this effort.

Noel wishes to thank his research team at the University of Michigan, beginning with Connie Kinnear, who created the original data base and GE Timeline and conducted many interviews. For several years Colin Raymond and John Ahlberg provided first-rate research support. Arathi Krishna made a substantial contribution during the final months. On the administrative side, Esther Sheer, Katrina Samuelson, and Nancy Tanner provided invaluable assistance.

Faculty and colleagues in the field provided insight, ideas, and constructive criticism throughout the process. Noel is especially indebted to Carole Barnett, Kim Cameron, Mary Anne Devanna, Charles Kadushin, Steve Kerr, Art Kleiner, Andy McGill, Len Schlesinger, Patricia Stacey, and Karl E. Weick.

Noel's deepest gratitude goes to his family, who offered much needed emotional support.

To all those mentioned above, Strat adds this thanks. In addition, he is grateful to the many people who helped him: Ruth McGeehee, Walter Isaacson, Mary Johnston, and Dick Armstrong, for getting him started; his colleagues at *Fortune,* especially Marshall Loeb, for offering understanding and so much rope; the creators of XyWrite and Magellan software, for the enabling technology; Sarah Bartlett and Peter Canby, for leading the way; Kurt Andersen and Geoff Colvin, for pithy criticism; David Howell and Omar Daboutie, for advice worldly and otherworldly; everyone at the Wilton Center, for keeping him centered; Laura Landro, for persevering; Jane Duce, for gracing his family; Sidney Ganis, for true friendship; and Chandler and Spencer Sherman, and Meredith Davis, for filling his heart with love. For all this and more, thank God.

NOEL TICHY AND STRAT SHERMAN
21 September 1992

Introduction

We have learned a lot since the first hardcover edition of *Control Your Destiny or Someone Else Will* appeared in January of 1993. The principles explained in this book, which seemed radical just a short time ago, are becoming widely accepted as more people understand the implications of intensifying competition. We have seen these principles applied in an expanding and very diverse group of companies, from computer maker Digital Equipment to Nedlloyd Lines, a container shipping outfit. As authors, we have benefited greatly from opportunities to discuss our ideas with several thousand knowledgeable people, including the readers we encounter in airports and the audiences at our speeches and workshops. This updated paperback edition provides a welcome opportunity to share the new insights we've gained.

We welcome the controversy that our book reliably excites. This is a call to action, not just to corporations, but to individuals; people often respond to that aggressive stance with strong emotions. As a result, many of our dialogues with readers have been characterized by what Jack Welch calls "constructive conflict"—with instructive results.

Wherever we go, the same questions arise. Some people evidently feel threatened by the book's title. They ask, "How can I control my destiny? *I'm* not a CEO." The other issues most frequently raised are these:

- I don't believe the kind of revolutionary change you describe is really necessary—at least not at *my* company, not in *my* life.

- The place where I work is totally different from GE. How can the experience of a $60 billion company possibly be relevant to me?

- General Electric still has problems. Is this example really worth emulating?

- How can you lionize a man who presided over the elimination of 170,000 jobs?

We may quibble with the way they're expressed, but these are legitimate questions. They deserve answers.

How can I control my destiny?

Life pushes us all around so much that passivity can easily masquerade as wisdom. Anybody can find someone or something to blame for unfavorable circumstances. You're in a commodity business. Your stockholders care only about quarterly earnings. Your competitors are invincible. Your boss is a jerk. Your *subordinates* are jerks. Your husband. Your wife. Your kids.

Your mortgage. No time. No money. No support. There's always an excuse.

But CEOs face constraints, too. Welch, for instance, has to satisfy GE's board of directors and its shareholders. He faces resistance from employees. He must submit to the will of the President, Congress, and the regulators and policy makers of every country where GE operates. He has to live with the up-and-down cycles of the markets his company serves as well as the unpredictable, sometimes devastating, fluctuations of the economies of great nations.

No one has absolute control over his or her destiny. The point is to control what you can.

Far from being an idea that pertains only to members of the Business Roundtable, "control your destiny or someone else will" is a philosophy of life basic enough to apply to anyone. Welch learned it as a child from his mother, Grace, a housewife who never graduated from high school.

The meaning is simple: Take responsibility. Whenever something's bothering you, whether it's a competitor stealing your customers or a bad habit you can't shake, you face a clear choice: Either solve the problem yourself or accept a fate that you may not like. Considered from this perspective, the ethic of personal responsibility gains appeal.

When change becomes inevitable, in business as in life, we believe the best policy is to embrace it and make it your own. According to James A. Taylor, CEO of Yankelovich Partners, an opinion-research firm, a growing number of Americans share this point of view. For years his pollsters have observed dwindling public trust in the guidance of institutions, including government, business, religion, the media, and even advertising. But robustly increasing numbers of people agree with the idea "I am in command of my own life."

So let's get one thing straight from the start: When we talk about controlling your destiny, we do mean you. If this feels challenging, if it makes you uncomfortable, so much the better. Challenge is the foundation of change. And for individuals and organizations alike, the ability to adapt to changed circumstances is the essence of competitive advantage.

Is revolutionary change really necessary?

Yes.

If you don't believe us, look at what has happened to so many of America's greatest corporations, from GM to IBM to Westinghouse to American Express to Sears. Even Apple Computer, regarded not long ago as the epitome of entrepreneurial vigor, has fallen from grace. The failure to adapt has unseated CEOs, destroyed hundreds of thousands of jobs, and caused billions of dollars in losses. Investors who believed their money was safe were brutally punished: During the two decades ending in 1992, the combined market value of IBM, Sears, and GM plunged $21 billion.

There's a revolution going on in the world of business. During the decades after World War II, the United States prospered as never before. Those of us who came of age during that era came to regard endless economic growth and lifetime job security almost as a birthright. But as we have learned to our chagrin, America's supremacy during those years depended on the temporary weakness of its competitors. Germany and Japan, which before the war had ranked among the world's most powerful economies, were bombed to rubble. Only when those countries finished rebuilding, sometime around 1970, did normal competition resume. The result was a shock for U.S. corporations: They discovered how easy it is to lose.

It is globalization that has revolutionized business. Suddenly every market is vulnerable to the predations of the world's most able competitors. In contrast to the days when even third-rate companies produced fortunes, now you must be as good as the best in the world—or your days are numbered.

Consumers increasingly recognize a world standard of value, which they expect every product to meet. That raises the bar for all competitors.

The phenomenon first became apparent in cars, when Toyota and other Japanese automakers began trouncing Detroit's Big Three and winning the loyalty of millions of American car owners. GM, Ford, and Chrysler complained bitterly about unfair trade practices, but ultimately Japan's success resulted from delivering value—high quality for a competitive price. To their credit, the Big Three have responded. Both Chrysler and Ford have regained market share from the Japanese, and GM has announced a strategy based on value pricing.

As the impact of globalization spreads to every industry, business people around the world learn to expect tougher competition than they have ever faced before. Back when five or ten rivals could comfortably coexist in a single market, some would offer high-quality products at premium prices while others sold lesser goods for a discount. Today, most consumers and industrial buyers won't even consider low-quality goods, and it's hard to find a company that hasn't joined the quality movement.

Quality has become a commodity. So has price. Once companies learned that they had to offer high quality, it ceased to be a differentiator. Inevitably, their battles shifted from quality to price, in markets from cars to computers. Aggressive pricing, in turn, reinforced the emphasis on productivity, as businesses sought to protect their profitability by lowering costs. But as Welch notes in Chapter Nineteen, years of hard-won improvement in productivity have enabled corporations to keep lowering their prices. The competition grows fiercer with each passing day.

First-class quality, competitive pricing, and drastic cost-cutting are still not enough. Once all the surviving contenders in a market can offer value, the battle shifts to speed and innovation. To distinguish themselves, companies must offer something unique. They all are racing to find the new ideas, the new processes, that will enable them to win customers.

These are the forces that are compelling businesses of all sizes to re-examine and ultimately to re-invent themselves. As *Control Your Destiny or Someone Else Will* demonstrates, the nineteenth-century structures and methods that still define the way most corporations work simply are not adequate to the radically intensified competition of the 1990s and beyond. Thus our passionate belief in revolutionary change of the sort General Electric has mastered.

The corporations best positioned to win in the years ahead are those that can break free of the past. At such respected enterprises as Motorola, Intel, and even AT&T, the ability to change is recognized as a crucial competitive advantage. Intel, for instance, began as a producer of commodity memory chips. It focused on microprocessors only after losing out to Japanese competitors in its original business. Since then, Intel has dominated the market for the microprocessors, such as the 486 and Pentium, that provide the brainpower for IBM and IBM-compatible personal computers. Someday market forces may require the company to transform itself again. But Andrew Grove, Intel's CEO, argues that a work force that has tasted the rewards of change can adapt again without undue trauma.

Success can deaden an organization's responses. The executives who presided over the near collapse of some of the world's greatest corporations all were leaders of proven ability. Their failures stemmed from reliance on ideas and practices that had worked splendidly in earlier times. The times changed and they didn't. Consider the challenge that the leaders of the pharmaceuticals industry face in 1993. Even some of the most widely admired companies in their field never developed the skills needed to compete in a marketplace suddenly transformed by public health care policy. For them, revolutionary change is the least threatening alternative in sight.

How can the experience of a $60 billion company possibly be relevant to me?

Sooner or later, the forces we have just described will affect everyone who holds a job. To be sure, some cozy backwaters still exist, undisturbed by world-class competition—but not for much longer. The business environment itself is changing, in what the buzzword artists call a paradigm shift. Today, affluent consumers in New Delhi expect the same products sold in Chicago. People who have discovered the values in Wal-Mart stores aren't going to settle for less anywhere else. This is a historical movement. Any business that hasn't felt it yet would be wise to heed another of Welch's rules: "Change before you have to."

The lessons we have drawn from General Electric's experience apply to almost everyone. While making an instructional video about mastering revolutionary change, we recently interviewed CEOs and other executives at AlliedSignal, Ameritech, Tenneco, and GE. Although the circumstances of these companies are very different, we observed the same principles at work in all. AlliedSignal, which makes auto parts and aerospace products, and Tenneco, a conglomerate with interests in natural gas pipelines, shipbuilding, and farm equipment, were both hemorrhaging cash when their boards brought in new leaders, each with a mandate to stage a revolution. At Ameritech, a Bell operating company based in Chicago, longtime CEO William Weiss forced change on an organization that, like GE in 1981, seemed healthy.

In all four corporations, the revolutionary process has followed patterns that are comprehensible, predictable, and controllable. Uncertainty and struggle are unavoidable, but successful corporate transformations are logical responses to reality. Despite the need for painful decisions such as layoffs, leaders can win the allegiance of employees by clearly and frankly explaining the business circumstances that provoked the decision to change. At Tenneco, that was easy: When Mike Walsh became CEO, he discovered that the company faced a financial crisis potentially serious enough to panic investors. Employees readily accepted his dramatic plan of action. Ameritech, by contrast, was earning record profits when Weiss realized that this monopoly supplier of telephone service urgently needed to prepare for a future defined by open competition. The drastic reform of Ameritech's business structure and corporate culture is likely to take years. To sustain momentum, leaders trumpet every sign of progress. Even in the early days of a corporate revolution, those signs can be impressive. Since 1991, when Lawrence Bossidy resigned as GE's vice chairman to run AlliedSignal, the company's market value has more than doubled.

The patterns that characterize the four companies we studied are equally evident at many other organizations that have experienced wrenching change. Compaq Computer, for example, defined itself as a vendor of top-quality, premium-priced PCs. But after loyal customers began defecting to value brands, the company realized it had to fundamentally redefine its mission. In less than a year it reduced its costs by more than 30% and took on the role of price leader in PCs. Since then, Compaq has gained market share. Anyone interested in corporate revolution should keep an eye on IBM, which is launching what promises to be the most dramatic business transformation of our time. If, as we believe, most companies need revolutions, then people need practical guidelines for mastering them.

The GE story shows the way. It explains why corporate revolutions are needed, reveals their governing principles, and demonstrates how successful they can be. The ideas and techniques described in this book—derived from Welch's mistakes as well as his successes—will work in a small business, a ten-person corporate department, or in a multi-billion-dollar enterprise. The "Handbook for Revolutionaries" on page 365 provides tools to help readers relate GE's lessons to their own companies.

Not all of us are leaders, of course. But every employee is affected by the transformation of business organizations. Everyone who holds a job is taking part in defining the new relationship between the individual and the corporation. The changes are both scary and liberating at once. Remember lifetime job security? The demise of corporate paternalism is forcing workers to take responsibility for their own careers. At the same time, the quest for speed and innovation often translates into teamwork and empowerment, which can make jobs richer and more interesting. Anyone challenged by these changes can benefit from a better understanding of the forces that drive them.

Doesn't General Electric still have problems?

Of course it does. This is a true story, not a fairy tale. We don't claim that Jack Welch is a saint or that GE is perfect. By Welch's own reckoning the revolution he started is far from complete. GE employees don't need much prodding to tick off the ways in which their company falls short of its ideals. By far the most common complaint is about bureaucratic, bullying bosses, who still exist in some parts of GE. Another serious concern is employee burnout.

The company's widely publicized legal and environmental problems have provoked animosity and scorn in some quarters. We discuss these issues at length in Chapter Nine.

David Letterman got laughs for years by exaggerating the failures of GE's management of NBC. The influential talk-show host, who moved his late-night show to CBS in 1993, loved to describe GE executives as "boneheads." GE's shareholders, who knew better, laughed hardest.

Every enterprise has its imperfections, and we are not reluctant to acknowledge GE's. But we believe that these blemishes are of little consequence compared to the valuable management ideas that are driving the transformation of General Electric.

Among the best of these ideas is the notion that managers should regard their decisions and actions as experiments. The personification of that attitude is John Trani, who runs GE Medical Systems. In Chapter Seventeen, we discuss a new system of organization that Trani was designing in 1992. By the time the ink was dry on the first edition of this book, Trani had tested the system, identified its weaknesses, and moved on to another. This is what happens when you write about an organization that continues to learn.

How can you lionize a man who presided over the elimination of 170,000 jobs?

Welch didn't destroy those jobs. Some of the affected people, such as the maintenance and food-service workers at GE's headquarters, simply changed employers as their jobs were transferred to outside companies. As for the many jobs that were eliminated, blame history or economics instead. Had GE's workforce remained at its bloated 1981 level, the company would be so weak that every GE worker would be imperiled. The critics who labeled Welch "Neutron Jack" during the early 1980s often pointed to IBM, with its famous no-layoffs policy, as the humane alternative. But the slow disintegration of IBM's business eventually forced Big Blue to face reality. By mid-1993, the computer maker had eliminated 100,000 jobs, and some informed observers were expecting Louis Gerstner, its new CEO, to cut 100,000 more.

It would be nice if businesses could somehow be revolutionized without human pain, but that isn't possible. Corporations are examining every aspect of their operations, and asking the question, "Would our customers willingly pay extra for this, if they knew about it?" Often, when the answer is no, bureaucracies get dismantled and jobs disappear. GE and IBM are not isolated cases: The whole Fortune 500 has been losing jobs for years. Until companies redesign themselves to meet the demands of the time, the painful layoffs will continue. Since relatively few corporations have advanced far in the process, these convulsions will likely continue for a decade or more.

The public's awakening to the need for change has transformed Welch from outcast to hero. As recently as 1992, years after we started work on *Control Your Destiny or Someone Else Will*, most people still seemed to believe that they could avoid the revolutionary process. Within a few months of the book's first publication, however, the agonies at IBM, GM, Sears, Westinghouse, and American Express had shaken popular faith in the corporate status quo. Today's workers understand the principle that the only true job security comes from satisfied customers; however reluctantly, they accept the risk of layoffs. Meanwhile, "reengineering," a new term that describes what GE has been doing for years, has become management gospel.

As for job creation—that is a problem beyond the scope of this book. Corporations certainly do have a responsibility to invest in worker training, to ensure that people who lose their jobs can qualify for good positions elsewhere. As Welch says, "Companies can't promise lifetime employment, but by constant training and education we may be able to guarantee lifetime employability." But as unskilled work moves offshore and the remaining jobs become more demanding, the United States may be forced to confront the need for better public education and training. On that issue, we must defer to the voters. We can offer only the hope that politicians will heed the lessons of the GE revolution, so that the United States can again become as strong as the best of its corporations.

Act One

THE
AWAKENING

Chapter One

The GE Revolution

One evening late in 1985, I dropped in on a classroom at General Electric's Crotonville management training center in Croton-on-Hudson, New York. Ranged around a rectangular conference table, ten young college graduates, all recently hired as GE junior managers, were ferociously debating two propositions scrawled on a flip chart at the front of the room:

Jack Welch is the greatest CEO GE has ever had.
Jack Welch is an asshole.

Rude stuff. At most major companies, including GE just a few years earlier, such irreverence might have cost these kids their careers. But as Crotonville's new director, I was delighted. In place of a traditional curriculum based on texts and lectures, we were encouraging the sort of no-holds-barred discussion that characterizes the CEO's most fruitful interactions with senior managers. The goal was to implant and nourish the values Welch cherishes: self-confidence, candor, and an unflinching willingness to face reality, even when it's painful.

By then, John F. Welch, Jr., had been GE's chief executive for nearly five years, relentlessly pursuing an agenda of change so radical, so fundamental, and so threatening that it amounts to a revolution. He has taken the established order at GE and thrown it out the window; he presided over the elimination of scores of the company's businesses and over one third of its jobs—affecting a group as large as the entire population of Salt Lake City. As for the employees who remain, Welch has challenged everything they thought they knew.

This forceful man, now fifty-seven, is creating a new organization at GE that depends as much on shared values as on hierarchy or coercion. Like most major corporations, GE previously relied on the doctrine of scientific management: the theory that any work process—including its human element—can be broken down to its component parts and then reassembled in an efficient or "scientific" manner. That sort of thinking fostered assembly lines and military-style hierarchies, which produced enormous wealth but generally alienated employees. By contrast, the values-based organization that is emerging at GE derives its efficiency from consensus: Workers who share their employer's goals don't need much supervision.

Blue-eyed and hot-blooded, Welch is a rebel who has matured into a leader. At 5'8", he is not physically imposing, but the intensity and power of his personality can overwhelm. His manner conveys urgency even when he's comparing golf scores or making friendly inquiries about your family. Relentlessly positive, he delights in his own enthusiasm; when displeased, he comes on like a battery of howitzers, flattening all opposition. "We've got a disaster here," he'll warn as he walks into a meeting, before even saying hello. Looking you straight in the eye, he'll tell you exactly what he thinks you've done wrong. But if you can withstand the barrage and talk back, Welch will listen; and if you can solve his problem, soon you will be basking in the warmth of the CEO's cheerful high spirits.

Welch's successes as a leader depend less on his personality than on the quality of his thought. Smart, intellectually disciplined, and creative, Welch has developed a management style that exploits the power of breakthrough ideas. Some of his perceptions are primarily of interest to GE's employees; others have the potential to reshape organizations around the world. In my view, the twentieth century has produced two business leaders who will be remembered for their ideas: Alfred Sloan of General Motors and Jack Welch of GE.

The company Welch inherited in 1981 was among the bluest of blue chips. Founded in 1878 by Thomas Edison, the inventor of the light bulb, General Electric was one of America's strongest competitors and one of the world's most admired corporations. Hardly anyone, inside the company or out, thought GE needed fixing. But where others saw strength, Welch saw weakness. GE's executives, disciplined but submissive, knew how to follow the company's rigid rules. But when the outside world started to change, many of GE's procedures and systems became irrelevant. The self-confidence that had characterized the company's managers began to erode. Left to pursue its course for another decade or so, this apparently healthy company might have become another Chrysler. Instead of waiting for trouble, the CEO pushed for radical change long before most people recognized it as necessary.

America's eminent corporations, from GE to General Motors to Eastman Kodak, all faced the same new challenges of lagging productivity and global competition. Welch recognized these changes for what they were: threats to his company's survival. He began by acknowledging GE's vulnerability; then he set out to rebuild its strength. Starting with a forceful attack on the company's status quo, he ultimately transformed the very nature of GE, reshaping not only its businesses but its organization and culture as well. No enterprise of comparable size had ever attempted such a task, yet Welch approached it with relish. The CEO's behavior, sometimes harsh and often misunderstood, was a response to real danger. Like a parent who forces a sick child to swallow bitter medicine, Welch was motivated by a desire to heal.

The remarkable story of GE's revitalization teaches lessons essential for the well-being of managers and lay people alike. *Control your destiny* is more than a useful business idea. For every individual, corporation, and nation, it is the essence of responsibility and the most basic requirement for success. As the world endlessly changes, so must we. The greatest power we have is the ability to envision our own fate—and to change ourselves.

The process of transformation requires personal commitment and the willingness to persevere. It begins with the recognition that change is necessary. An individual with a problem, whether excess weight or a troubled marriage, won't make much progress without admitting that the problem really needs solving. Similarly, the United States surely won't regain its economic primacy until its citizens stop whining about Japan and face the real causes of declining competitiveness, from low productivity to the ballooning national debt.

In retrospect, GE's biggest problems cannot be blamed on previous CEO's or any other employees: The world simply had changed. Now corporations around the globe, small and large alike, are beginning to recognize that the emerging business environment of the 1990s and beyond requires dramatic new responses. For anyone who has a job and wants to keep it, this is a challenge that must be faced.

In Welch's view, a strong business must consistently grow both revenues and profits: increasing revenues through a constant stream of new ideas and product innovations and increasing profits through unceasing improvements in productivity. Neither innovation nor productivity alone is enough. A winning company has to master both—in Lyndon Johnson's memorable phrase, to walk and chew gum at the same time.

When he became CEO in 1981, Welch saw major obstacles to both kinds of growth. The threat to revenue growth was the company's highly organized bureaucracy—the pitiless enforcer of scientific management—and the corporate culture that sustained it. Once-useful means of disciplining the organization had started to strangle the business. The company was choking on its nit-picking system of formal reviews and approvals, which delayed decisions, thwarted common sense, and often made GE a laggard at bringing new products to market. For executives, mastery of arduous procedures had become an art form, almost a ballet, as well as an unspoken requirement for advancement. The result: Many of GE's best managers devoted far more energy to internal matters than to their customers' needs. As GEers sometimes expressed it, theirs was a company that operated "with its face to the CEO and its ass to the customer."

The bureaucracy seemed unable to focus on GE's customers, whereas Welch wanted to serve them better. Promoting innovation at GE felt like getting a root canal. The company's elaborate controls ranged from detailed monthly budget approvals to an annual strategic planning review that required six to eight months of preparatory research and analysis. Such procedures ensured that any idea, regardless of its merit, would be treated as worthless until entombed in a lengthy formal report.

The elite bureaucrats who vetted budgets and most operating decisions were GE's strategic planners. The meetings they held to review all proposals—whether for a new way of pricing floodlamps or for a dishwasher based on a breakthrough design—were staged as inquisitions. Nay-sayers by profession, the planners liked to badger executives with "gotchas," GE lingo for tough questions designed to make people sweat. By the time an idea had run this gauntlet, if it lasted that long, its moment of opportunity often had passed.

Welch was dismayed by the results of that behavior. GE was losing share even in light bulbs, the market that had brought GE to life. In consumer electronics and small appliances, General Electric was no longer the manufacturing or technology leader. Brawny international competitors such as Toshiba and Hitachi were eroding GE's position in some key businesses.

Just as bureaucracy slowed GE's revenue growth, low productivity inhibited the growth of GE's earnings. With intensifying foreboding, Welch had been observing the productivity gains of GE's rivals in emerging global markets. While Japanese companies were boosting productivity by 8% annually, GE's gains had rarely topped 1.5%.

High productivity is essential, says Welch, because it confers flexibility. Gains in productivity drive costs down: A corporation whose costs are lower than its competitors' has the flexibility either to gain share by lowering prices or to hike profits by raising prices—at will.

The CEO wanted an organization that could systematically foster the creation of new ideas, much as the traditional GE culture had long promoted the manufacture of products. The bureaucracy had to go, and with it the inward-looking mind-set that was alienating GE from its customers. At the same time, he wanted GE to operate at least as efficiently as GE's most productive competitors. To Welch the implication was clear: Strong though it was, GE had no choice but to reinvent itself almost from scratch. Though the phrase isn't his, Welch communicated a message of *change or die,* loudly and often. Said the CEO:

> Changing the culture starts with an attitude. I hope you won't think I'm being melodramatic if I say that the insti-

tution ought to stretch itself, ought to reach, to the point where it almost comes unglued.

Many GE employees—too many—saw Welch as a tough guy who menaced not only their livelihoods but the company itself. For them, fear gradually hardened into stubborn resistance to the program of change. People who believed they would flourish in the new GE—such as workers at the fast-growing Plastics, Medical Systems, and Financial Services units that Welch had overseen earlier in his career—generally thought he was a terrific CEO. But lots of GEers, especially those in weak businesses such as electrical transformers or consumer electronics, thought their CEO was, well, an asshole.

If Welch's vision shocked GE's workers, his behavior terrified them. While he was talking about "liberating" and "empowering" GE's employees, they were worrying, with reason, about their jobs. He challenged the time-tested compact that governed GE's relationship with its employees: something approaching lifetime job security in return for loyalty, obedience, and performance. In its place he offered a new principle that struck employees as cruelly Darwinian: "Companies can't give job security," he said. "Only customers can." In other words, *Succeed in the marketplace or you're out of a job.*

To Welch, a man who passionately believes that facing reality is one of life's primary obligations, this principle seemed self-evident. Like most of his management ideas, it flowed naturally from observation of the brutal world of commerce. But as GE kept cutting its work force, many employees found it difficult to share the boss's perspective.

The numbers are staggering: Through one means or another, roughly 300,000 people left GE. When Welch began, GE had nearly 420,000 workers on its payroll. Over the years their ranks increased by 150,000 people, who were the employees of companies that GE acquired. At the same time, GE was selling businesses that employed some 135,000 people; they left General Electric, but most, presumably, kept their jobs. The painful part was the cutting of almost 170,000 positions through layoffs, attrition, and other means. The result: By the end of 1991, just under 285,000 people worked for GE; as of July 1993, there were approximately 230,000 employees, reflecting the transfer of GE Aerospace to Martin Marietta.

To enable fewer people to keep their growing corporation under control, GE designed a new organizational structure that increased managers' "spans of control"—the number of people or businesses reporting directly to each manager—from roughly six to as many as twelve, or even more. The idea was to force employees to delegate more and to eliminate unnecessary work. But GE's managers were unaccustomed to making such decisions, and some drowned in the added responsibility. Working twice as hard and half as well, these people began hating their jobs. Mixed signals added to the confusion and stress: Many GEers reported to hardened bureaucrats who scorned the new ideas.

In 1982 *Newsweek* dubbed Welch "Neutron Jack," suggesting the CEO's willingness to vaporize people while leaving the buildings standing. In fact, Welch detonated buildings too: During just his first four years GE sold 125 businesses, including the languishing line of toasters, irons, and other small appliances that many employees regarded as an essential part of the company's identity.

Before long, the opposition to Welch and all he stood for was of epic scale: roughly 200,000 people—a group larger, in all likelihood, than the entire population of Troy in the age of Homer's *Iliad*. But Welch is no Achilles. Measured against 200,000 opponents, he seems surprisingly ordinary: a middle-aged businessman with thinning hair and a Massachusetts accent, who pronounces "ever" as "evah." What distinguishes him is his self-confidence and drive. He has what one close associate calls "an absolute desire to win." Each success seems to increase his strength—and his desire to win again.

Vitality may be Welch's defining characteristic. He is a breeder reactor for energy; perhaps he uses his inner conflicts as fuel. As a younger man he nervously bit his nails, but today his tension shows in less obvious ways. To explain himself, Welch will hastily sketch chart after chart on a pad of paper, often while eating raw carrots or chewing five sticks of gum at once. His eyes sparkle, and the vivid intelligence shaping his words more than compensates for the mild stutter that has dogged Welch since childhood.

His personality integrates many seeming contradictions. Welch has firm convictions about everything from corporate management to matters of right and wrong, yet he loves to listen and readily changes his mind. He is searingly analytical and intuitive at once. In temperament, he is an enthusiast, not a bully, but whether discussing a business strategy or a recent movie, he always aims to convince. Unabashedly emotional, he can be enormously engaging in person—yet this warm and empathetic fellow has made decisions that caused enormous pain.

Change doesn't scare Welch, it excites him. Throughout his career he has benefited from his willingness to create change—not only in the organizations he has run, but in himself. During his years as CEO, Welch has evolved from a demanding boss to a helpful coach, from a man who seems hard to one who allows his softness to show. That is part of what enabled him, long after he had gotten GE's businesses into shape, to win over GE's alienated employees.

No leader can escape dependence on those he leads. Welch has wielded all the power of a CEO, but command alone could not win him the cooperation of his subordinates; without massive support, no one could succeed in a task as large as the one he undertook. This man's long crusade to remake General Electric has been defined less by such conventional managerial concerns as strategy or finance than by the ineffable difficulty of transmuting resistance into allegiance.

The CEO was never completely alone. General Electric's board solidly supported him from the start. Welch calls their endorsement "absolutely essential," arguing that no one could lead an organization through a transformation of this magnitude without strong backing. Welch also could rely on a cadre of like-minded executives and perhaps a quarter or a third of the company's employees. Even with so much backing, the task he faced was daunting.

Based on years of contact with Welch—in addition to my two-year stint at Crotonville, I've been a consultant to GE since 1982—my sense is that he never doubted his ideas were right. His convictions seem rooted in the bedrock of his personality; indeed, he says he learned many of his best ideas on his mother's knee. Much of the power of his ideas derives from the consistency with which he upholds them, regardless of what others believe. "If you have an idea *du jour,* you're dead," remarks Welch.

Reduced to its essence, his main challenge has been communication. His unconventional ideas already had proved their merit: Most of the businesses he had run were standout performers, and their workers had prospered. The trick was getting GEers to believe that they would end up among the winners. Recalls Welch:

> For a long time our actions muddied communications. We were taking out lots of people. We were taking out layers of management. We were selling off businesses. We were impacting people's lives.

Welch has plenty of ideas, but his successes as a communicator are the product of struggle. When he became CEO, many of his most powerful ideas were little more than gut instincts. His stutter is no longer an impediment, but his thinking often is more lucid than his language, and his first attempts to express ideas sometimes fail. A memorable flop was his vain attempt, in 1981, to make GEers feel and act as if they "owned" their businesses—despite the obvious fact that those businesses are owned by GE's shareholders. But he persisted, spending years refining his message. Eventually he found ways to articulate his vision for a new GE with simplicity, clarity, and vigor. Explains Welch:

> Companies need overarching themes to create change. If it's just somebody pushing a gimmick or a program, without an overarching theme, you can't get through the wall.

This is the story of how General Electric got through the wall, from one man exhorting his subordinates to a team of hundreds of thousands of people working together. A narrative of the key events of Welch's leadership of GE, from 1981 to the present, the tale is marked by dramatic conflict and by failure as well as success. Above all, though, this is a story about ideas in action. Taken together, the concepts that underlie the GE revolution add up to a comprehensive theory of change that can enable any organization—indeed, any person—to seize control of his or her destiny.

Chapter Two

The Business Engine

The GE revolution is still far from complete. Welch, after all, says he hopes to run "the most competitive enterprise on this earth." But the progress to date is astonishing. This train conductor's son, a chemical engineer who inadvertently blew up a small plant early in his career, already has done more than any other U.S. executive to bust through the limits of corporate performance. Along the way he has created and tested a set of practical management principles that are unrivaled as a guide to running a business in the twenty-first century.

To be sure, GE is unique in many respects. Its size, its strength, its business diversity, and its tradition of disciplined management presented Welch with opportunities and problems that other managers may never face. Even so, most of the ideas driving the GE revolution are so basic, so universal, that they apply not just to business management, but to ordinary human life. Consider this list of Welch's six rules, which *Fortune* published in 1989, and ask yourself whether your behavior meets his standards:

- Control your destiny, or someone else will.

- Face reality as it is, not as it was or as you wish it were.

- Be candid with everyone.

- Don't manage, lead.

- Change before you have to.

- If you don't have a competitive advantage, don't compete.

Simple ideas, perhaps, but only a fool would underestimate the difficulty of acting on them. The idea of facing reality, to consider just one, seems banal—until you try to live by it. Welch believes that "facing reality is crucial in life, not just in business. You have to see the world in the purest, clearest way possible, or you can't make decisions on a rational basis."

Facing reality means dealing with what all of us would prefer to avoid: danger, failure, our own shortcomings. One can argue, as Freud did, that in some cases we must turn away from reality in order to survive. But when such psychological defenses are deployed in attempts to avoid the unavoidable, they become symptoms of illness.

Corporations as well as individuals may suffer from this malady. When an automaker, for instance, can't admit that its products cost more, yet are worth less, than those of its prospering overseas competitors, the company's illness soon becomes apparent. Market share plunges, profits drop, employees fret, and investors flee. Welch saw symptoms of that disease at GE.

Welch has enjoyed one great advantage: His ideas work. The clearest proof is GE's financial performance since 1981.

Before Welch took office, GE, like Westinghouse and AT&T, was known as a "GNP company," because its profits consistently grew at about the same rate as the gross national product. But by the end of 1992, GE's earnings had grown at an annual rate of over 10% for the prior decade, amounting to one and a half times the GNP's. That is remarkable momentum for an enterprise of GE's mass. In 1992 General Electric earned $4.7 billion on revenues of over $62 billion. The company's return on equity, a key measure of corporate performance, topped 20%. During the first quarter of 1993, GE made $1.16 billion in profit on sales of $12.9 billion.

Another indicator of the company's strength is market share. Peter Drucker—professor, management guru, and a former consultant to GE—greatly influenced Welch by writing, "If you weren't already in the business, would you enter it today?" Welch pondered that question deeply, and acted on the answers. He insisted that every GE business be No. 1 or No. 2 in its market, vowing to "fix, close, or sell" any that didn't meet his standard. Welch sold $14 billion worth, including coal mines, semiconductors, and TV sets, while buying $21 billion of new businesses, including the investment bank Kidder Peabody, Employers Reinsurance Corp., and RCA, the owner of NBC. In 1993, GE sold the Aerospace business to Martin Marietta for $3 billion.

The Kidder acquisition was deeply troubled for years, and a few smaller deals flopped. Even so, the result of Welch's efforts is a company that boasts a leading share in almost every market it serves: from turbines for electric power plants to engines for 747 jets and B-2 Stealth bombers; from 200-ton locomotives to credit card processing services to special plastics for auto bumpers and computer housings.

The measure of performance that matters most to Welch and to GE's shareholders is the value of the company's stock, which trades on the New York exchange. At a recent $94 per share, it was worth about seven times more than when Welch started; during the same period, the value of the Standard & Poor's 500 merely doubled. According to the latest rankings in *Forbes,* GE's $75.8 billion market value in April 1993 made it the fourth most valuable enterprise in the United States—a monumental improvement from the company's showing in 1980, when it ranked No. 11. As of March 1993, among American companies, GE is surpassed in value only by Exxon, AT&T, and Wal-Mart, and abroad, only by Royal Dutch/Shell and Nippon Telegraph & Telephone. Overall, *Forbes* rates GE the world's most powerful corporation, based on a combination of revenues, profits, market value, and assets.

The need to boost both innovation and productivity is the imperative behind the GE revolution and the main challenge confronting any business that competes in world markets. Under Welch, GE has come a long way: In many of its lines, such as aircraft engines, high-risk lending, or the CAT scanners doctors use to diagnose disease, GE's products and services are among the world's most advanced.

The company's annual productivity rate has risen from less than 2% in 1981 to a peak of some 6% in 1989, roughly equal to that of GE's direct competitors in Japan and only a couple of percentage points shy of Japan's overall rate. Even during the recession of 1990–1992, GE achieved a 4% to 5% rate. For every percentage point of increased productivity, GE's annual pretax profits rise by over $300 million—year after year. In 1993, by Welch's calculation, a third of total earnings came from increased productivity.

Large American companies as a group have not accomplished as much: Consumers still look to Japan for the most exciting new products, whether in automobiles or laptop computer screens. And according to the *U.S. Statistical Abstract,* U.S. nonfarm productivity improved just 1.5% annually during the booming 1980s.

More important from the employee's point of view, GE's success is making its remaining jobs more secure. Like most

U.S. companies, GE still has spot layoffs from time to time, when businesses such as Aircraft Engines hit downdrafts. But the days of slash-and-burn management are long past. And once-troubled operations such as Power Systems, which makes turbines for electrical power plants, have been expanding and creating new jobs, along with consistent winners such as Medical Systems.

Drastic changes in the competitive environment are driving demand for new ideas about management. A decade of mergers and acquisitions forced consolidation in industry after industry, from food processing to banking, and as a result, markets are increasingly dominated by huge companies with overwhelming financial and political clout. Smaller players are getting shoved out of the game.

Moreover, globalization has changed the rules of competition, suddenly forcing companies to expand beyond their nations' borders even as they face the incursions of foreign companies at home. Efforts to improve productivity, such as "just-in-time" inventory controls, are pushing corporations into an unprecedented dependence on their suppliers. New technologies and management techniques have shortened product cycles, heightening the expectations of customers and forcing an increasing emphasis on speed.

In a paradox that Welch likes to emphasize, winning now requires all the power and resources of a world-class behemoth *and* the agility of an entrepreneurial start-up. And he insists that the game will only get tougher: "If you thought the 1980s were tough, the 1990s will make the 1980s look like a cakewalk. It will be brutally competitive."

GE's experience can provide the ideas needed to respond to these monumental changes. Almost every major corporation—like GM, IBM, and American Express—faces the same global forces of change. Many once-promising upstarts seem less promising now. Even some companies touted in Tom

Peters's *In Search of Excellence,* such as Citicorp and Kodak, have stumbled since the book was published. That leaves GE's revolution, unfinished and imperfect though it is, as the best available exemplar of the way ahead.

For the United States as for GE, failure to adapt to market changes could prove catastrophic. A 1990 study by the non-profit National Center on Education and the Economy lucidly describes the country's dilemma. To compete in world markets, American business must improve productivity in either of two ways: through lower wages or through more efficient organization. To date the country has chosen lower wages. U.S. salary increases between 1975 and 1988 averaged 6.2% per year. That's 2.1 percentage points lower than Europe's rate, and 5.4 points lower than Japan's. But low wages, like low productivity, end up hurting everyone by lowering the national standard of living. The desirable alternative is the one America has not yet chosen: better organization. Yet according to the report, 95% of U.S. corporations still organize work the way they did at the turn of the century.

The old way, exemplified by Henry Ford's production line, calls for top managers to analyze the work that needs to be done, then devise rules even an idiot can follow. Managers, divorced from the actual work, become bureaucrats, while their frustrated subordinates tighten the bolts. Brilliantly though such methods worked during most of this century, they won't help us much in the next. Even so, it is easy to understand why more companies don't change: The revolutionary process is agonizing.

The new way—GE's way—breaks the intellectual framework that defines the limits of traditional management. The goal is to transcend the concept of management itself. Instead of seeking better ways to control workers, Welch says he aims to liberate them. As he explains, that goal is based on self-interest:

The old organization was built on control, but the world has changed. The world is moving at such a pace that control has become a limitation. It slows you down. You've got to balance freedom with some control, but you've got to have more freedom than you ever dreamed of.

Welch insists that GE managers learn to master paradox. In his view, an apparent conflict between two worthy goals is no excuse for not pursuing them both: He regards the simultaneous pursuit of long- and short-term objectives as a basic responsibility of management. While pushing for organizational change, Welch has failed to boost quarterly earnings only once—and that dip, in 1991, was caused by a technical change in the accounting rules imposed on all public companies. During the quarter in question, GE's earnings from operations rose 8%.

Welch believes in teamwork, not out of idealism, but because he grew up playing hockey: He knows that teamwork wins games. When his teammates score goals, he feels good. As a manager, he knows that the most valuable innovations often come from the shop floor.

A corporation designed to meet the challenges of the twenty-first century must boost performance by stripping out layers of unnecessary management while encouraging all workers to think more, and thus to produce more. The successful organizations will be those that are "lean and agile," to use one of Welch's favorite terms. In structure they will be fluid, poised to respond rapidly to market changes. In spirit they will be relatively democratic, replacing authoritarian rigidity with openness, candor, and a willingness to reach across functional and hierarchical lines. Welch calls this "boundarylessness," his concept of integrating all the constituencies inside and outside the company.

A primary motivation for GE's transformation is the need

for speed. Until employees accept personal responsibility for their work, they need supervision, which Welch regards as a waste of time. So whenever possible, GE tries to eliminate supervisory positions, giving people more power to control their own work. Such responsibility can transform the relationship of workers to their employer: Instead of behaving like children who follow their parents' orders, employees interact with their bosses as adults and peers.

Replacing the old way with the new does not happen at the touch of a button. It requires deep convictions, enormous upheavals, a vision of what lies ahead, and perseverance even when the pain seems unbearable. But the ultimate benefits—for stockholders and employees alike—are enormous. And as GE is proving, it can be done.

I have been a student of organizational transformation since 1972, when I wrote my Ph.D. dissertation on people who had created large-scale change. The methods needed to create the degree of change I witnessed at General Electric—quantum change, Welch calls it—are fundamentally different from the managerial techniques taught at most business schools and practiced at most corporations. Understanding the new methods, no less than creating them, requires a new intellectual framework.

I see the process of corporate transformation as a three-act drama. Unlike those of the theater, these three acts usually overlap, but each depends on the one before.

In Act I, the organization awakens to the need for change. This is a time when tyrannical behavior can serve a useful purpose, since the awakening requires a frontal assault on the status quo. The goal of the attack is not to frighten employees, but to arouse the emotional energy of an entire organization. That energy, which manifests itself first as fear and later as personal commitment to a plan of action, is the only fuel that can sustain a revolution.

GE's Act I was largely complete by late 1985, five years after Welch became CEO. At first, Welch's ideas took the form of demands, such as the requirement that each GE unit be No. 1 or No. 2 in its market. Welch backed this idea—stunning at the time—with powerful actions, including massive layoffs and asset sales. During this period, those efforts seemed destructive, because he was dealing more with problems than with solutions. Act I usually leaves workers and junior managers in confusion and despair, because the process destroys what's familiar and comfortable without providing a new basis for emotional security.

In Act II the organization creates a blueprint for the future. As the old ways are swept away, even people who have resisted change begin to recognize the need for something new. The leader responds by articulating a vision. But a vision can't be acted upon until it is shared, so effective communication becomes critical. Henceforth, a leader can no longer rely mainly on his or her own power: The revolution's continued progress now depends on the support of key lieutenants throughout the organization.

At GE, winning the support of executives—especially the thousands of middle managers far removed from GE's Fairfield, Connecticut, headquarters—has proved Welch's most enduring challenge. GE's middle managers can influence tens of thousands of lower-ranking workers far more directly and powerfully than the distant CEO.

Evidence of middle managers' ability to thwart Welch's ambitions surfaced frequently at Crotonville. Students there, old hands as well as new hires, routinely write comments at the end of a course, which Welch carefully studies. It's the equivalent of market research. The most frequent complaint goes something like this:

All the words sound great—entrepreneurship, ownership, risk taking—but that's not the way it is where *I* work. At my level, making budget is all that counts.

It was during Act II that Welch found ways to get GEers to embrace his business vision. Walter Wriston, retired head of Citicorp and an influential member of GE's board of directors, once told Welch, "No one can remember more than three things at once." The young CEO began with an inchoate vision of a transformed GE, but he spent years distilling his complex ideas into a few precepts simple enough for every employee to grasp.

One of the most powerful images Welch eventually created is what he calls "the business engine," which explains how each of GE's businesses fits into the corporate whole. The idea, which did not occur to Welch until 1988, is so useful, so clear, it is a wonder that no one thought of it before. Admits Welch, "It would have been better if we had designed the engine in 1983." For the first time, one image showed GE's far-flung employees the workings of the entire enterprise from the CEO's perspective. It also enabled security analysts and investors to distinguish GE from the conglomerates to which it was often compared.

The business engine shows how different GE is from a conglomerate, a type of holding company that buys and sells large numbers of unrelated businesses without doing much to improve them. Any individual GE business, no matter how well managed, is subject to the ups and downs of the market it serves. But GE as a whole, strengthened by its participation in many different markets at once, can consistently make smooth financial progress.

The engine is driven by individual businesses working together like pistons, their performance carefully regulated by the allocation of capital. According to Welch, 40% of GE's employees work for businesses, such as Lighting, that were growing slowly during the recession of 1991–1992; they produce about 30% of corporate earnings. These less glamorous operations serve the engine by generating the cash that is its fuel. Welch describes earnings as the engine's "thrust." That comes from the hotshots like GE Financial Services, which gen-

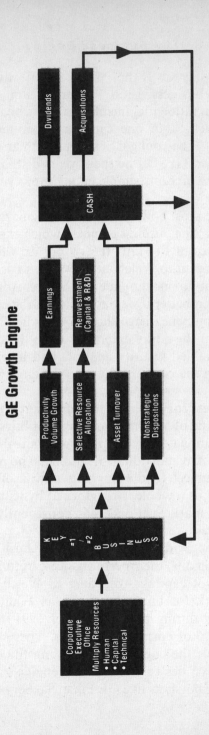

GE Growth Engine

erates 30% of GE's earnings with less than 10% of GE's employees. But the high-thrust operations are growing so fast that they need to invest more cash than they can generate themselves. While the slow-growth businesses provide the fuel, the high-growth businesses provide the thrust, and GE as a whole rockets ahead. In such an engine, every worker has a crucial role.

A recent example shows how the engine works. During the defense-spending spree of the Reagan years, prosperous Aircraft Engines provided the cash that supported Power Systems' ailing turbine business. Now it's the other way around: Cuts in defense spending are squeezing Aircraft Engines, while the revived turbine operation is throwing off the cash GE needs to develop new engine products.

The business engine also uses spare cash to fund dividends that reward shareholders, and to pay for acquisitions that, in their turn, make the engine even stronger. Thus each business, while functioning in relative isolation, lends strength to the others and derives strength from them.

By 1988, GE's Act II was complete: With the business engine and other imagery, Welch had communicated his vision to employees.

GE's Act III is still far from over. This act concerns the creation of structures to institutionalize the organization's vision. New practices are created to embody the new ideas; over time, these practices influence the way employees think.

To promote clear thinking and fast decision-making, the CEO often makes operating executives prepare a few simple slides that describe the essence of their business situations. The slides show the answers to basic questions such as these:

- What does your global competitive environment look like?

- In the last three years, what have your competitors done to you?

- In the same period, what have you done to them?

- How might they attack you in the future?

- What are your plans to leapfrog them?

A much more complex technique for pushing cultural change is an ambitious, ten-year program called Work-Out, which began in 1989. An attempt to extend the benefits of free-wheeling debates to the whole company, the program first gathers employees together, regardless of rank, for sessions at which people air their gripes and suggestions. Managers are required to take action on the issues workers raise. Later on, Work-Out organizes employees into carefully targeted teams with the authority to define solutions to business problems.

Other companies have experimented with many of the ideas behind Work-Out, but GE was the first to employ them on such a vast scale. Already, some 200,000 GE employees have participated in Work-Out. In a few more years virtually everyone in the company should have done so. The program has helped GEers learn how to walk and chew gum. It also has begun to redefine the nature of management at GE: Taking a certain amount of guff from subordinates is now part of an executive's job description.

It is still too early to judge GE's attempt to reshape itself. Plenty of time remains: Welch won't reach mandatory retirement age until the year 2000. But when the day of judgment comes, success or failure in reshaping GE's values and culture may be the truest test of his accomplishment.

Any revolution is based on ideas. In politics, some of the most potent revolutionary ideas, such as Marxist economics, have proved unrealistic. But as GE's financial performance under Welch amply demonstrates, the ideas behind this transformation are entirely practical.

What this company has done, others can do.

The GE Transformation

A Dramatic Shift in Earnings*

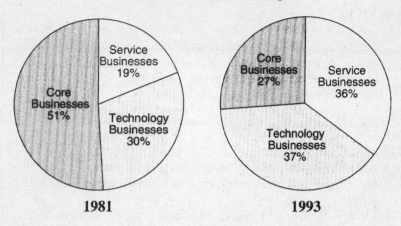

1981   **1993**

*GE no longer classifies its businesses by these three categories.

GE's 1992 Business Portfolio

SERVICES
- Capital Services: Credit cards, equipment and industrial financing, leasing, real estate loans, insurance, asset management services, investment banking
- Information Services: Electronic messaging, data network services, information storage and retrieval
- NBC: Television network, TV stations, program production, cable-programming services

TECHNOLOGY
- Aircraft Engines: Jet engines and parts for commercial and military planes and helicopters, engines for marine propulsion and industrial power
- Medical Systems: Magnetic resonance imaging, CAT scanners, X-ray systems, ultrasound equipment, nuclear imaging
- Plastics: Engineered thermoplastics, silicones, resins, laminates, manmade diamonds

CORE MANUFACTURING
- Appliances: Refrigerators, freezers, dishwashers, electric and gas ranges, washers, dryers, microwave ovens
- Electrical Distribution & Control: Circuit breakers, switchgear, controls, factory automation systems and equipment
- Industrial & Power Systems: Steam and gas turbines, generators, transformers, meters, relays, nuclear fuel and services
- Lighting: Incandescent, fluorescent, halogen, high-intensity discharge and specialty light bulbs, wiring devices, quartz products
- Motors: Electric motors for heavy industry, appliances, autos, air conditioning, heating
- Transportation Systems: Locomotives, electric wheels, transit propulsion systems

Changes in GE's Business Portfolio between 1981 and 1992

MAJOR ACQUISITIONS
($22 Billion Total)

- Calma (CAD/CAM equipment)
- Intersil (semiconductors)
- Employers Reinsurance Corp.
- Decimus (computer leasing)
- RCA (NBC television, aerospace, electronics)
- Kidder, Peabody (investment banking)
- Polaris (aircraft leasing)
- Genstar (container leasing)
- Thomson/CGR (medical equipment)
- Gelco (portable building leasing)
- Borg-Warner Chemicals (plastics)
- Montgomery Ward Credit (credit cards)
- Roper (appliances)
- Penske Leasing (truck leasing)
- Financial Guaranty Insurance Co.
- Tungsram (light bulbs)
- Burton Group Financial Services
- Travelers Mortgage (mortgage services)
- Thorn Lighting (light bulbs)
- Financial News Network (cable network)
- Chase Manhattan Leasing
- Itel Containers (container leasing)
- Harrods/House of Fraser Credit Cards
- GNA Annuities

MAJOR DIVESTITURES
($14 Billion Total)

- Central Air Conditioning
- Pathfinder Mines
- Broadcasting Properties (non-RCA TV & radio stations)
- Utah International (mining)
- Housewares (small appliances)
- Family Financial Services
- RCA Records
- Nacolah Life Insurance (RCA's)
- Coronet Carpets (RCA's)
- Consumer Electronics (TV sets)
- Carboloy (industrial cutting tools)
- NBC Radio Networks
- Roper Outdoor Lawn Equipment
- GE Solid State (semiconductors)
- Calma (CAD/CAM equipment)
- RCA Globcomm (international telex)
- Ladd Petroleum (oil exploration & refining)
- RCA Columbia Home Video
- Auto Auctions (auctions of used cars)
- Aerospace (electronics)

In 1981, only Lighting, Motors, and Power Systems were leaders in their markets. By 1992, all businesses were leaders in their markets.

The Human Story

Total Employees

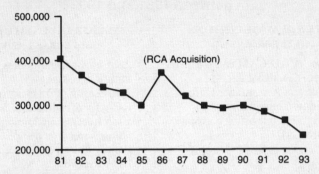

(RCA Acquisition)

Number of employees granted stock options

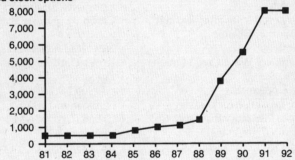

Organizational layers between CEO and shop floor

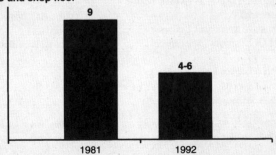

The Performance Story

Revenues
(Billions of U.S. Dollars)

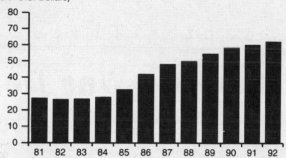

Productivity Rate
(%)

Net Income
(Billions of U.S. Dollars)

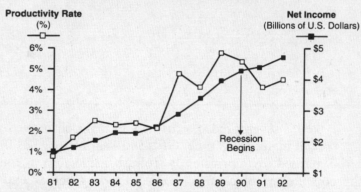

Recession
Begins

* 1991 earnings do not reflect a $1.8 billion non-cash accounting charge.

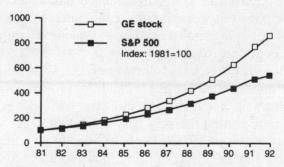

GE stock

S&P 500
Index: 1981=100

*Based on average annual return, assumes reinvestment of dividend.

Chapter Three

The Hand He Was Dealt

Like his seven predecessors as CEO, Welch proved the right man for his time. GE's 115-year history has been marked by consistently robust leadership through cyclic convulsions of change; GE's postwar chief executives have alternately tightened or loosened central controls. Welch inherited an organization and corporate culture marked by admirable discipline but weakened by a bureaucratic preoccupation with its own internal workings—a splendid company that badly needed some loosening up.

In 1980, the year Welch was chosen as CEO, General Electric was a profoundly conservative institution: proud of its history, recognized as a leader of U.S. industry, and certain that its executives were among the very best in the world. As *Management Today* wrote in 1978: "Probably no single company has made such a singular contribution to the arts and wiles, the viewpoints and the techniques of large scale corporate management as GE." The company's twenty-member board of directors comprised a *Who's Who* of business luminaries, including Lewis T. Preston, chairman of J. P. Morgan & Co., J. Paul Austin of Coca-Cola, and Ralph Lazarus of Federated Department Stores.

GE's CEO at the time, courtly, British-born Reginald H. Jones, then sixty-three, was a skilled practitioner of scientific management. He was also an accomplished bureaucrat. Long-faced and lean, with a perfect part in his slicked-back brown hair, "Reg" (rhymes with *peg*) Jones was a chain-smoking finance man who had spent his early career on GE's fearsome audit staff. He worked as a line manager for fifteen years before rising to chief financial officer. Once he became CEO, Jones remained aloof from daily operations, exercising power through his mastery of the data in the thick reports he demanded from subordinates. As he later remarked, "I found you never get all the information you'd like."

Unquestionably the most admired CEO of his day—President Jimmy Carter reportedly twice offered him cabinet posts—Jones viewed his eight-year CEO term as distinguished, yet he picked a successor prepared to completely transform much of what he had built.

One can't help wondering what drove GE to choose Welch as CEO. To a degree, members of the GE board may have underestimated Welch's determination to reshape GE, or been unable to imagine the upheavals he had in mind. Says Gertrude G. Michelson, a senior vice president at R. H. Macy & Co. and a GE director: "In a way it has been a revolution, but it did not seem like a revolution as it was happening. It was just Jack's vision of the future."

GE's stewards certainly recognized that change was necessary. Jones's letter to stockholders in the 1980 report describes a "mood of self-renewal" at GE:

> U.S. business today finds itself challenged by aggressive overseas competitors. National productivity has been declining and, in industry after industry, product leader-

ship is moving to other nations. Companies that refuse to renew themselves, that fail to cast off the old and embrace new technologies, could well find themselves in serious decline in the 1980s. We are determined that this shall not happen to General Electric.

Jones recognized three challenges grave enough to justify major changes: GE's productivity was growing slowly; it had to speed up the shift from electromechanical to electronic technology; and it needed strong responses to international competition.

He tried to improve GE's productivity mainly by investing in hardware such as factory-automation equipment. That costly approach would eventually pay off, but in 1980 it helped create GE's first negative cash flow in seven years—while productivity continued to sag.

GE's competitive position in technology had slipped dramatically. In 1977, Jones had commissioned a year-long study of the subject, which resulted in a voluminous report that consumed five feet of shelf space. The report convinced Jones that the problem was serious.

Recognizing the growing importance of global markets, Jones stated in the 1980 report that 42% of GE's earnings was earned overseas. Nearly half the foreign earnings came from Utah International, a mining company that sold Australian coal to Japan. (Jones had bought the company as an inflation hedge.) Only three GE units, Aircraft Engines, Gas Turbines, and Plastics, operated on a truly global basis. GE's strength remained in the United States.

At the time, many other U.S. corporations were struggling with the same challenges of productivity, technology, and global competition. But those were not GE's only difficulties. Many of its individual businesses were ailing, among them the troubled unit that built nuclear power plants. After the notorious 1979 accident at the Three Mile Island nuclear plant (built by

Babcock & Wilcox), Americans abruptly lost confidence in nuclear plants. Pending orders vaporized, and no new orders replaced them.

Despite Jones's modernization efforts, some GE products were antiquated. In a few areas, notably jet engines and plastics, GE was producing leading-edge products, but most of the company's sales still depended on machine-age technology. In 1970, 85% of the company's earnings came from motors, wiring, appliances, and other businesses dating back to the Edison era. By the time Jones retired, GE depended on those lines for just under half of GE's profits—a great improvement, but not good enough.

Several of these mature operations were in trouble—especially during the second U.S. economic recession in five years—and none was capable of rapid growth. Even with financial services and other high-growth businesses added in, total corporate earnings were increasing at such a sluggish rate that the effects of inflation wiped them out. That wasn't unique to GE: In constant dollars, U.S. nonfinancial corporations' net income had been declining at a 2% annual rate since 1975. At GE, that created a financial squeeze, because the company had to invest huge sums to maintain its position in aircraft engines, nuclear power and, until 1970, computers.

The company's stock was stuck. During 1980 GE's per-share price never topped $16 (adjusted for subsequent stock splits)—13% below its high in 1972, the year Jones took office. The corporation had been steadily paying out nearly half its earnings in dividends to shareholders during those years. Even so, anyone who bought GE stock when Jones became CEO, and held it until Welch was named the successor, would have lost about 25% of the investment's value net of inflation, which averaged 8% during the Jones years. During the same period, the value of the Dow Jones industrial average declined some 15%, net of inflation.

Jones probably strengthened GE as much as anyone could

without fundamentally challenging the precepts of scientific management. He funded such outstanding businesses as Plastics and Aircraft Engines, adroitly arranged GE's exit from computers, and pushed hard for growth in technology and international markets. But the business environment changed profoundly during Jones's tenure: Scientific management, which had produced enormous benefits at GE and many other companies, had outlived its usefulness and gone into decline. By the late 1970s, traditional management had reached the stage of decadence, spawning wasteful bureaucracy—not just at GE, but throughout corporate America. The only way to accomplish much more than Jones was to abandon the old paradigm and start fresh.

That was easier for Welch. He had spent most of his career at GE Plastics in Pittsfield, Massachusetts, a red-hot start-up venture that had grown to over $1 billion in sales while minimizing contact with the bureaucrats dominant elsewhere in GE. As a young man given to antiauthoritarian views in the 1960s, Welch had freely expressed his resentment of the paper-pushing company men he called "dinks"—a category that included many at GE's headquarters. Unburdened by loyalty to tradition and fiercely intolerant of inefficiency, Welch turned over more rocks than his predecessor. His philosophy of "changing before you have to" led him to attack potential problems before obvious symptoms of trouble appeared.

In temperament and business style, Welch and Jones make a striking contrast: Jones formal and relatively passive, Welch uninhibitedly aggressive. Jones had made most of his decisions in response to information that others provided. To the extent that his courtiers were blind to GE's problems, Jones himself risked blindness. In fairness, he also had spotted some important issues his subordinates didn't, such as GE's weakness in technology. Less obvious, at least to outsiders, are the similarities between the two men. Looking over GE's businesses, they saw the same issues—and reached similar conclusions often enough to enable Jones to trust the younger man.

Welch believed that GE's past successes contained the seeds of present and future difficulties, and he was willing to act on that perception. In an environment of unceasing change, few business ideas remain useful for long; after a while, even successful concepts must be abandoned. But GE's century of business experience was embodied in a rigid corporate culture and an authoritarian organizational structure.

A corporate culture is the sum of the unwritten norms, beliefs, and values that define appropriate behavior. After a while, almost every business develops its own style: Texaco, for instance, is marked by East Coast sobriety and deference to authority, while Pennzoil more frequently exhibits vestiges of cowboy exuberance.

Like human personalities, corporate cultures result from the interaction of temperament and experience. Over time, their dictates slip from consciousness into the realm of habit: People cling to once-useful beliefs and patterns of behavior as if no alternative existed.

In business as in life, sticking to outmoded ways can cause trouble. Tantrums may serve an infant's purposes, but an adult who throws fits invites rejection. Similarly, teaching employees to defer to authority may at first establish needed discipline, yet later suppress creative thought. Discriminating between useful and destructive habits requires a clearheaded objectivity that doesn't come easily, to Welch or anyone else.

The business style that every company develops early in its history is like the genetic code that determines a living creature's characteristics. From generation to generation the mix of genes will change, much as a business will evolve in response to the Darwinian force of competition. Whatever the mix, though, genetic heritage will always exert a powerful influence. In business as in science, our ability to alter underlying structures remains relatively primitive. Any action we take can have unforeseen results that may not become manifest for years.

GE's cultural heritage dates back to the late 1800s, when the "modern" business bureaucracy was just emerging. That is when the German theorist Max Weber extolled the benefits of systematic organizational controls such as clear chains of command and advancement based on merit. Corporations built on the Weberian model have relied ever since on bureaucratic schemes to reduce the inherent uncertainties of business.

The ideal was a system of such clear and enforceable rules that an organization could function with machinelike predictability. People were not expected to have ideas; the ideas were built into the system itself, as in Ford's famous assembly line. Compared to previous methods, this type of organization proved remarkably effective, and businesses around the world adopted it. The larger and more complex the company, the more obvious was the benefit of this so-called scientific management.

GEers fawned on their bosses and did what they were told, even when their orders made no sense. When criticized by superiors, they turned around and "kicked the dog"—company argot for passing on the pain to subordinates. Ambitious GE managers kept their ties knotted and their mouths shut.

The GE organization circa 1980 required business managers to report to two distinct types of authority: a military-style hierarchy of operating executives; and a group of independent, headquarters-based staffs that specialized in such functions as finance, strategic planning, and employee relations (GE organization charts appear on pages 344–346). Among the many oddities of this system was that GE's smallest businesses were subject to many more layers of review than larger and more important ones.

GE's organizational structure fostered sprawling staffs of supervisors, rulemakers, and checkers. Over time the bureaucracy established a life of its own, evolving into a self-sustaining organism with a powerful propensity for growth. According to Don Kane, one of GE's key organizational-planning experts, the mounting expense of this bureaucracy was a major reason GE became a high-cost producer, vulnerable to foreign competition.

The complex interaction of GE's culture, organization, and bureaucracy created a symphony of not-so-subtle signals that taught GEers how to behave. But as Jones realized, behavior that had been appropriate in 1878—or even 1978—might prove disastrous in the 1980s.

By then, GEers had come to regard the trappings of status as more important than real operating performance. James Baughman, a bearded sometime musician who headed executive compensation and development and was my boss at Crotonville, had come to GE from Harvard Business School in midcareer. He remembers noticing that the GE executives who entered his office for the first time would invariably tilt their heads back in an automatic, almost subconscious way. He couldn't figure out why—until someone told him that they were counting the ceiling squares in his office. In an attempt to ensure fair treatment of its workers, GE had assigned all employees to one of twenty-nine civil service style levels of rank. At headquarters, people within any given level worked in offices of almost identical size. By counting Jim's ceiling squares, visitors could calculate the square footage of his office, and thus his status in the hierarchy. That told the executives whether to grovel before Jim or boss him around.

GEers regarded this behavior as normal. Unchallenged, such destructive practices spread like cancers. Asked to describe the prevailing attitude, former executive vice president Paul Van Orden, who retired in 1990, recalls an incident that occurred shortly after he was moved to the top job at GE's audiotape operation in the early 1970s:

There were reports generated that just boggled the mind, but I saw them as the price of belonging in the club. Market share was considered very important in that business, but I had no way of calculating it. When the first call came in from headquarters, I said, "I'll call you back."

I asked my assistant what the share was last month. He said, "15.2%."

I waited a half hour, then I picked up the phone and told them our share was 15.3% this month. I marked that number down on a piece of paper and put it in my drawer. Month after month I would move the number up a tenth or down a tenth, or whatever, and it made everyone happy.

Such antics—and the system that encouraged them—horrified Welch, frustrated him, angered him so much he felt like his hair was on fire. But stopping them would not be easy.

Unlike GE's financial and operating problems, the bizarre patterns of behavior that had become common throughout GE could not be eliminated just by selling assets or making smart decisions. That is why GE's circumstances in 1980 called for a revolution: Just to get the company moving again, Welch had to attack almost everything it stood for.

Welch's situation was hardly unique: Each of GE's CEO transitions had led to considerable change. Management and a willingness to experiment always have been the company's greatest strengths. GE has always expected its leaders to foster change, and never been disappointed. During the postwar period, Ralph Cordiner dramatically restructured the organization in order to decentralize control. Next, Fred Borch set off a period of creative ferment and rapid growth. Then Jones established needed financial controls. Welch, having inherited a strong balance sheet from Jones, was free to set off in his own direction.

Almost from its inception, GE was a very large enterprise, producing such basics as wiring and even establishing a streetcar company. The rough-hewn Thomas Edison, who founded the New Jersey laboratory that grew into GE, realized early on that he couldn't sell light bulbs unless people had electricity. He envisioned the whole infrastructure of power stations, wiring grids, and electric appliances that people of our day take for granted.

Edison set out to build much of the system himself. No genius at organization, he incorporated these business units separately, allowing each to become an independent fiefdom. In 1886 he moved three of his principal manufacturing companies to an unused plant in Schenectady, New York. That operation became known as the "Works," a bit of nineteenth-century terminology that survives to this day, describing GE's traditionally autonomous manufacturing centers. To finance all his projects, Edison sought backing from a group of investors that included partners of financier J. P. Morgan.

The money helped, but ultimately cost Edison his job. The investors forced Edison out, replacing him with a former shoe salesman named Charles Coffin. In 1892, just sixteen years after Edison had founded his lab, Coffin reorganized the burgeoning portfolio of businesses under his command into the General Electric Company. The par value of its stock was $35 million—an eye-popping sum at the time and the equivalent of $500 million in 1992.

Coffin, a Quaker, had a flair for corporate organization. In an age when entrepreneurs such as the Rockefellers dominated the business scene, Coffin became known as the father of professional management. Until Alfred Sloan began reshaping General Motors in the 1920s, the management and organizational systems Coffin designed remained the world's most complex.

He created GE's rigid hierarchy, and organized each of the Works around a particular product line. Coffin also instituted extremely conservative financial controls, making GE's AAA credit rating seemingly invulnerable to economic upheaval. He moved beyond electrical products into so many new lines, such as radios and X-ray machines, that GE became the most diversified company in the world.

Far from abandoning light bulbs, Coffin, under Morgan's expert tutelage, did his best to transform that business into a cozy oligopoly. Edison already had won a patent suit that forced other light bulb manufacturers to license GE technology. That gave Coffin the leverage to negotiate cross-licensing agreements with Westinghouse, Sylvania, and many other competitors, even overseas, that effectively eliminated real competition in GE's primary business.

The federal government sued GE several times, charging price fixing and other violations of the Sherman Antitrust Act By and large, these agreements were judged legal at the time. GE defended itself so effectively that, although the resulting judgments and consent decrees somewhat reduced its clout, the company came of age in protected markets where market shares were fixed and price competition virtually unknown. Until the early 1950s, General Electric's share of the U.S. light bulb market remained around 75% to 80%. Delightful though that experience must have been, it didn't teach GEers the basics of survival.

Gerard Swope, a political liberal who succeeded Coffin in 1922, was no fonder of competition. After serving GE for a decade, he accepted Franklin Roosevelt's appointment as chairman of the Economic Advisory Board of the Department of Commerce. There he designed the so-called "Swope Plan for American Industry," which asserted that "the cause of the Great Depression was the chaos of excessive competition." Some of Swope's ideas helped underpin the New Deal.

When Swope returned to GE, he made the company a leader in enlightened labor practices. He firmly believed that a corporation should help its people avoid uncertainty. Among his innovations were generous employee benefits such as profit-sharing, bonuses, pensions, group insurance, a stock purchase plan, and home mortgage assistance. GE established one of the country's first unemployment pension plans, guaranteeing its laid-off workers $7.50 per week for ten weeks. Swope wanted workers to regard the company as a family. His paternalism paid off, as an implicit promise of lifetime employment attracted talented people to GE. That posture later caused trouble, though, by shaping a work force around a shared aversion to risk.

The pugnacious Charles Wilson became GE's fourth CEO in 1940. He grew up in New York's Hell's Kitchen and boxed as a young man; people called him "Electric Charlie," to distinguish him from Charles "Engine Charlie" Wilson, who was running GM. During Wilson's tenure, much of Swope's good work in labor relations and corporate ethics was undone. Shortly after World War II, when many labor unions were flexing their muscles, GE suffered its most serious strike to date, which alienated both GE's blue-collar workers and its top management.

Then, in 1948, for the first time in its history, GE lost a major antitrust suit. Federal prosecutors charged GE's Lighting unit with illegal patent-licensing practices that helped GE to maintain its market dominance. The company was found guilty. The judge might have broken GE Lighting into pieces, but let the company off with a slap—requiring it to provide its lighting patents to competitors free of charge—and a stern warning.

Subsequently some GE middle managers imagined themselves immune to punishment, expecting their bosses to wink at wrongdoing that helped a business grow. Partly as a result, the company was caught many times in illegal actions—and suffered for them. GE, like other companies, is still vulnerable to wrongdoing by employees, but the winking days are over.

Since Edison's day, the basic organizational scheme at GE had been that of a holding company. A relatively small group of executives at headquarters oversaw the activities of the eleven Works located in distant cities including Schenectady, New York (turbines); Louisville, Kentucky (appliances); Cleveland, Ohio (light bulbs); and Erie, Pennsylvania (locomotives). Each of the independently managed Works controlled its own research and development, marketing, and so on, creating expensive redundancies. The local chieftains who ran the Works had become powerful enough to resist repeated efforts by GE's headquarters to expand its authority over them.

Cordiner came closer to breaking this system than any other GE chairman. He did it by overlaying the structures of scientific management atop an older structure with which they were fundamentally incompatible. To exercise more power over the Works, he bolstered an existing bureaucracy of freestanding staffs. He gave the staffs, particularly finance, control over GE's most valuable resources: money and personnel. They enforced his will.

He also ordered a massive reorganization of GE, based on decentralization. Cordiner broke up the company's operations into departments, each small enough, in the CEO's phrase, "for a man to get his arms around." By 1968 the company had 190 departments, ranging in size from $1.7 million in sales to $391 million. These departments reported to forty-six divisions; the divisions reported to ten groups; and the groups reported to the CEO. Accustomed to military hierarchy from service in World War II, most GEers adapted easily to the strict new lines of authority.

But the reorganization caused some problems. It placed separate functional staffs in every department, creating enormous redundancies. It also aroused the ire of executives at the Works, who blocked Cordiner's attempt to consolidate R & D and disperse the Works' central manufacturing operations into smaller units.

Even so, Cordiner pursued his ideas with fervor. In 1951, he assembled a brainy team of GE executives, plus consultants and professors, including Peter Drucker, to recommend ways to improve GE's management. They studied fifty other firms, pored over the personnel records of 2,000 GEers, did time-motion studies of executives at work, and interviewed countless GE managers.

Two years later, they emerged with the Blue Books, a five-volume, 3,463-page management bible. Buried in endless pages of stultifyingly elaborate prescriptions are such powerful concepts as management by objective—as well as some of the most revolutionary ideas Welch would later espouse. This discussion of decentralization, for instance, sounds a lot like Welch's principle of speed: "A minimum of supervision, a minimum of time delays in decision making, a maximum of competitive agility, and thus maximum service to customers and profits to the company." To indoctrinate managers in the new principles, Cordiner founded the Crotonville school in 1956.

The unspoken purpose of the Blue Books was to reduce the messy human element in corporate decision making. Cordiner described human motivation as a "baffling area." He also regarded people as fungible: "A manager is a manager is a manager," he often said. Reassigned to a new job, and often a new city, roughly every three years, GEers gained enough confidence from the Blue Books' guidance to tackle almost any project with gusto.

When Cordiner's logical theories clashed with human nature, they sometimes produced loony results. He demanded that every general manager—the executive responsible for the profit-and-loss statement of a business unit—produce a 7% return on sales or a 20% return on investment every quarter. That goal proved almost impossible to achieve, and taught GEers to focus almost exclusively on short-term objectives. Anxious about expenses in the current quarter, GE managers often would refuse to invest in essential equipment such as new machine tools. Only after such decisions had cost them market share would they belatedly make the necessary purchases. Misguided GEers would even temporarily shut down factories despite strong demand and fierce competition, just to keep their expenses from going over budget at year-end.

GE's bureaucracy responded to Cordiner's innovations as if to a growth hormone. Decentralization added layers of supervisory management, and the rules in the Blue Books meant nothing without people to enforce them. Cordiner's formal job classifications, for instance, gave rise to a huge human resources staff that evaluated job descriptions, measured individuals' performance, and monitored salaries and promotions. Those staffers helped spread the bureaucratic mind-set throughout the entire company: They ensured that salaries and bonuses mainly rewarded seniority, not performance. Remembers Walter Wriston, former head of Citibank and a GE board member:

> It didn't make a hell of a lot of difference if the guy had just screwed up or invented LEXAN [a hugely successful GE plastic]. It was just unreal. You'd take the size of the guy's shirt collar and divide it by the Gregorian calendar and multiply it by the square root of pi, and you'd come out with a number that was totally meaningless.

Cordiner's term ended on a dismal note. Despite enormous growth in sales, GE's profits, net of inflation, hardly budged. And like Coffin and Wilson before him, he presided over a damaging scandal. A group of managers at the Schenectady Works had entered into an agreement with Westinghouse, Allis-Chalmers, and other competitors to fix prices in turbine generators. Describing Schenectady as "the center of a deep and widespread conspiracy," the government assembled such damning evidence that GE and twenty-eight other corporations had to plead guilty or no contest to the charges. Five GE executives went to jail, and though Cordiner insisted he knew nothing of the conspiracy, it ruined his career.

His successor, in 1964, was Fred Borch, former head of GE Lighting. In contrast to the buttoned-down management of the Cordiner years, Borch's tenure was a time of creative ferment. Borch had a vision of growth, and was willing to make risky investments to produce it. He presided over nine yeasty years of what some people later dubbed "profitless growth." Under Cordiner, GE had been buoyed by the pent-up consumer demand and rapid economic growth that had followed World War II. Trying to match Cordiner's record of 5.3% annual growth in earnings, Borch placed enormous bets on three new, capital-intensive lines: computers, nuclear power, and aircraft engines. He built big businesses, but made little money except in engines, which paid off handsomely. During his nine-year regime, GE's revenues grew to over $10 billion.

Among his most lasting contributions was the first large-scale implementation of strategic planning, one of the most powerful business ideas of the late twentieth century. The concept grew out of a Borch-commissioned study of GE by the consulting firm of McKinsey & Co. Upon completing their investigations, the consultants pronounced themselves "totally amazed" that GE functioned as well as it did, given its bizarre organizational structure. They proposed strategic planning as a technical solution to the problems they saw.

GE's departments were not really businesses, as McKinsey understood the term: Major Appliances alone had twenty departments, some of them created for no purpose other than to be small enough for a manager to "get his arms around." Absurdity ensued. In a company organized around what McKinsey termed "natural business units," all of Major Appliances would have been a single business. The consultants argued that GE was incapable of formulating sensible business plans, since it didn't even know what its businesses were.

McKinsey recommended drastically reorganizing GE into forty-three "natural" businesses. That would have eliminated scores of business units, and with them, scores of the coveted general-manager jobs that were the principal stepping-stones to advancement at GE—what GEers called "the Holy Grail."

Borch dodged conflict by superimposing a new layer of strategic planners on top of GE's existing structure, already creaking under the weight of layers accumulated from previous reorganizations. He defined forty-six strategic business units, or SBUs, which approximated McKinsey's natural business units. Borch then retired, leaving the task of implementing strategic planning to his successor, Reg Jones, who took office in December 1972. The resulting organizational structure was even more complicated than the one that had shocked the consultants at McKinsey. The general manager of one of GE's tiny departments would continue to report about normal operating matters to a totteringly top-heavy hierarchy of divisions and groups: By the end of Jones's term fully nine layers of increasingly isolated executives separated some managers from the CEO. They filtered the information passing up and down the chain of command and often distorted it, as in the game of telephone.

In addition, every general manager now was required to hire a full-time strategic planner and to create a formal strategic plan each year. That hefty document, the product of more man-hours than anyone dared count, went up to one of the forty-six SBUs, which would subject it to intense scrutiny. The SBUs, in turn, would send on the plan to a newly created staff at headquarters.

While it was still a fresh idea, the discipline of strategic planning proved enormously useful. But over time, the planners' success empowered them to build up a bureaucratic infrastructure, which they elaborated until finally it became dysfunctional. Jones says he sees a lesson in this: Outsiders can be invaluable allies in cultural change—but onetime change agents are as likely as anyone else to entrench themselves. The challenge for leaders is to monitor the cycle of transformation and eliminate any process or structure that has outlived its usefulness.

Planners were the most holy of GE's Inquisitors, but there

were others. To review all capital requests, planners raked executives over the coals jointly with the financial staff, examining all budget results monthly. If, having survived all these examinations, a manager tried to give somebody a raise, employee-relations staffers had to be persuaded that the action did not adversely affect the other 17,356 GE employees at that particular pay level.

Jones fulfilled his mandate to strengthen GE's finances, but the otherwise handsome legacy he bequeathed GE was diminished by the bureaucracy he empowered. The solution to one problem contained the seeds of another.

In late 1977 Jones gave Welch—then forty-two years old and a corporate vice president—his first job at corporate headquarters in Fairfield, Connecticut. *Fortune* described the scene that confronted the young maverick at this bureaucratic bastion:

> There, in a building where the office doors of top executives whoosh open and closed at the touch of a button, Welch encountered a bureaucracy that brings Imperial Russia to mind. . . . Jones's thirst for data led to ridiculous excess. Dennis Dammerman, 43, now GE's chief financial officer, says that he had to stop computers in one GE business from spitting out seven daily reports. Just one made a stack of paper 12 feet high, containing product-by-product sales information—accurate to the penny—on hundreds of thousands of items.
>
> The bureaucracy routinely emasculated top executives by overwhelming them with useless information and enslaved middle managers with the need to gather it. Old-timers say that as mastery of the facts became impossible, illusion sufficed. Briefing books had grown to such dense impenetrability that top managers simply skipped reading them. Instead, they relied on staffers to feed them "gotchas" with which to intimidate subordinates at meetings.

The cost of all this was enormous, and ultimately incalculable. Scientific management, once a great competitive advantage, had become an obstacle. As Jones himself recognized, the bureaucracy created to strengthen GE had become a weakness.

For all its financial strength and management depth, despite all Jones had achieved, General Electric was unready for the challenges it would face in the 1980s. No wonder Jones and every other member of GE's board thought the time had come for a change.

And they were to get one.

Chapter Four

The New Leader

The management-succession process that placed venerable General Electric in Welch's hands exemplifies the best and most vital aspects of the old GE culture. Jones spent nine years selecting him from a group of candidates so highly qualified that almost all of them ended up heading major corporations. Despite Jones's conservatism—and GE's—the process convincingly demonstrated that Welch's revolutionary leadership was what GE needed, and the company's board of directors gave him an explicit mandate for change.

Always thorough, Jones insisted on a long, laborious, exacting process that would carefully consider every eligible candidate, then rely on reason alone to select the best qualified man. The result ranks among the finest examples of succession planning in corporate history, and highlights Jones's considerable virtues as a manager.

Some of his personal contributions to the effort were strikingly imaginative—starting with his decision to add Welch to the list of contenders. Despite the spectacular profit increases Welch had produced wherever he went, the younger man was, if not exactly a renegade, at least a maverick by the company's straitlaced standards. Compared to the paths most GE executives had followed, Welch's career to date had been highly unconventional. Instead of taking on a wide variety of jobs around GE, for example, he stubbornly remained in Pittsfield—Plastics' headquarters—for seventeen years.

Only thirty-eight when the CEO search began, Welch was GE's youngest group executive, with a reputation for immaturity and abrasiveness. He enforced his high standards by cutting any member of his team who didn't meet them; his intolerance of the bad financial habits most GEers took for granted had turned whole businesses upside down. Many people who didn't know Welch personally assumed he was fearsome. He was known for conviviality after business hours and ferocious determination at all times: Once he spent a whole day skiing despite a dislocated knee. Some of Welch's colleagues called him a "wild man." In a 1973 appraisal form, Welch acknowledged that he needed "improvement in handling socio-political relationships." (He also stated that his goal was to become CEO.) The evaluation noted that Welch had a marked tendency to operate "outside the dots," i.e., outside bureaucratic norms.

Jones began the winnowing process by asking Theodore LeVino—the soft-spoken but intense senior vice president who ran GE's Executive Management Staff—to identify the top twelve in-house candidates for the CEO job. EMS was an elite group within the employee-relations bureaucracy; one of its main functions was to evaluate and plan the development of the company's most promising managers. Ted LeVino, one of Jones's closest confidants, pushed his staff to a central role in the CEO succession process.

When, after almost a year of careful study, LeVino gave Jones his staff's list of twelve candidates, the name of GE's future CEO was not on it. At the time LeVino didn't consider Welch qualified. That's ironic, since he later became one of Welch's strongest supporters. Indeed, once Welch got the job, LeVino and his EMS colleagues Don Kane and Ray Stumberger became part of the CEO's inner circle of trusted advisers.

When he first scanned LeVino's list in 1975, Jones remembers, "I asked the EMS staff, 'Where is Welch?' It was clear this was a guy to watch."

The GE culture had many shortcomings, but the company's earnest efforts to make a science of management paid off richly during the CEO search. Jones never had to consider looking outside GE. On the contrary, companies in need of CEOs have routinely raided GE, which has trained more chief executives than any other U.S. corporation. GE alumni are presidents or chairmen of major U.S. corporations from Allied-Signal to Owens-Corning to General Dynamics. When *Business Week* ran a story on tough bosses in 1991, three of the five men portrayed on the cover were GE alumni. One was Stanley Gault, a strong competitor to Welch who went on to a brilliant career as CEO of Rubbermaid; after retiring at sixty-five, Gault became chief executive of Goodyear, the ailing tire company.

That record is no accident. The harsh demands of GE's bureaucracy forged executives who could meet them, and the people who took shortcuts—though numerous—rarely rose very high. GEers were justly famed for their financial discipline, analytical skill, and devotion to strategic planning. The company's diversity, combined with its practice of shuttling people from one job to another, provided a breadth of business experience few companies can match. And GE's size has enabled even its second- and third-tier managers to run businesses with over $1 billion in sales.

GE's meticulous, nit-picking ways added depth to the CEO selection process. The candidates' thick files were worth reading, containing not only performance data but pungent subjective impressions as well. Employee-relations staffers had routinely interviewed the bosses, colleagues, and subordinates of key GE managers to produce reports called "accomplishment analyses," which included hard data on managers' accomplishments, strengths, and weaknesses. LeVino's EMS team supplemented those files with round after round of fresh interviews with the candidates and people who knew them. Among those interviewed were retiring executives, who could afford to be honest.

As the field narrowed—first to six men, then to three—Jones tested the contenders with challenging new jobs. He personally conducted several probing interviews with each of the finalists, asking some devilishly ingenious questions. To balance his subjective impressions, he asked EMS to rate the executives on fifteen categories ranging from toughness and intelligence to "ego management" and compassion. As a last step, Jones asked each of the remaining candidates to write a long memo assessing his strengths and weaknesses. Those memos proved fascinating—and influential.

Perhaps inevitably, the search for GE's next CEO turned into an old-fashioned horse race. The candidates, naturally, all wanted to win, and each had his backers cheering from the stands. In retrospect, Welch wonders whether Jones erred in creating such an intense, divisive competition among the aspirants for the top job. Corporate politics played its role in the process, with the EMS staff playing up its favorite candidates. But LeVino and his subordinates remained willing to change their allegiances as new information came flooding in.

Welch won for a number of good reasons. His thoroughly researched business decisions consistently paid off. The financial results he produced were superb, enabling him to outdistance his competitors. None of them matched his experience running high-technology operations. But his most important characteristic, the one that won Welch the job he coveted, was his ability to change.

By 1980, when Jones finally picked Welch, he had decided that GE needed a changemaker. During the years that Jones and LeVino were watching Welch closely, they saw the young man mature. Unflattering stories about Welch still circulated in Fairfield, but most of them concerned events long past. Welch's demonstrated ability to adapt to altered circumstances was a powerful point in his favor. Don Kane, then a senior member of the EMS staff, explains why:

> The company had a tremendous need to change, so you needed a different kind of person—a change agent—to come in. But if that change agent had not been able to change himself, how could you trust him to change the company?

> When I show videotapes of Welch speaking at Crotonville to executives from other companies, they often say, "Is there any hope for us? Because we don't have a Jack Welch."

> My response is always the same: "Bull."

> *Every* company has its Jack Welch, most likely several of them. If no forceful changemaker has made his or her way into the higher echelons of management, that can only be because corporate politics have blocked the way. Look harder, and you'll find the person your business needs to meet the challenges of the twenty-first century.

Pulling off a transformation on this scale does require a special sort of personality. Even run-of-the-mill CEOs need brains and energy. Vision, physical stamina, and a sense of urgency are essential, of course. So are respect for other people and the ability to express complex ideas in simple ways. But leading people through agonizing change draws on another, ultimately indefinable quality: the human equivalent of a planet's gravitational pull. Whatever it is, that's not something you can pick up at business school.

I respect Welch as a leader, and like him as a man. Anyone who dismisses him as simply fearsome is missing the point.

Sure, he can be witheringly forceful, and he's no fun to be around when he's mad. His willfulness can make him overbearing at times: He will "revisit" a seemingly closed issue again and again until he is satisfied with the result. He is tough, but his is the sort of toughness that brings the Jesuits to mind: He is ruthless in service of deep-rooted beliefs. For better and for worse, Welch is an honest man.

He seems to see himself as a regular guy, only smarter. Informal and unpretentious, he can be a comfortable companion. If he is charismatic—and some think he is—it's because he so obviously enjoys other people.

In 1989 Welch, having divorced, married for the second time. Jane Welch, née Beasley, now forty, is a plainspoken and fiercely intelligent former mergers and acquisitions lawyer, whom he met on a blind date arranged by Walter Wriston, the GE board member. Welch's personal life, including his relations with four adult offspring from his first marriage, seems to consume a lot of his attention.

Welch didn't expect to become one of the most successful corporate executives of his age—or a businessman of any kind. While growing up in Salem, Massachusetts, he says, "I never thought about it." Welch grew up middle class; not poor, but poorer than he wished to be. As he puts it, "I always had my nose pressed against the glass." Intensely competitive, he has spent his whole life setting tough standards for himself, and usually meeting them. Yet he insists, "My life has been very easy."

The pattern was set as soon as he was born, says Welch. "I was an only child, so I was loved, nurtured, kissed, and praised much more than most people." By 1935, when he was born, Grace and John Welch, Sr., had been trying to have a child for sixteen years; they never had another. Welch's grandparents on both sides were Irish immigrants, and neither of his parents graduated from high school. John was a train conductor for the Boston & Maine railroad, a committed union man. Welch remembers his father as kind but "passive"—a calm, quiet fellow who faded into the background. John left for work at 5:30 A.M., frequently returned after 7:30 P.M., and had relatively little influence on his son.

By contrast, Welch's mother, who died in 1966, was a monumental figure in Welch's life. Grace Welch assured her son that he could succeed at anything he tried, and he believed her. She was the one who taught him to be independent, self-confident, and resourceful; she gave him many of his best ideas. Welch still speaks of her often, and with unabashed emotion:

> She was a very important part of my life. As an only child, I hung around with her a lot. She was smart as could be. Honest as the day is long. Saw reality—no mincing words. Whenever I got out of line, she'd whack me one. But always positive. Always uplifting. Always constructive. Control your own destiny—she always had that idea.
>
> She felt I could do anything. If I was having trouble in algebra or something, she'd say, "Just go upstairs and study. You can do better than anyone." She wanted me to be independent, so I'd take the train to Boston alone when I was twelve years old. She'd take me to ball games, the Braves, the Red Sox. We'd sit in the bleachers. We also played fast games of cards, blackjack and lots of gin rummy. She loved to beat me. "Gotcha!" she'd say. And I'd try to beat her back. I was just nuts about her.

Scrappy and sure of himself, Welch grew up playing street hockey, and though his innate athletic ability was not exceptional, he became captain of the high school hockey team in a town that takes hockey seriously. He also led the varsity golf team. At the University of Massachusetts, where Welch got his B.S. in chemical engineering, he lived in a jock fraternity and played intramural sports. His delight in locker-room camaraderie continues to this day.

Hockey is a metaphor for the confrontational but free-flowing business style that Welch developed. During a game, players will smash you into the boards; when it's over, they'll cheerfully invite you out for a drink. In hockey, individuals' roles blur, as the play moves uncontrollably all over the ice at high speed. There are no time-outs. Players must adjust to new situations constantly, thinking for themselves while looking out for the team as a whole. By contrast, Welch's predecessors had run GE on a football model: Everyone had a carefully defined role in plays that the coach ordered in advance. They were accustomed to gaining ground a few yards at a time, if at all.

As a young man, Welch says, he was "an incredibly serious, believing Catholic." An altar boy through high school, he met his first wife, Carolyn, while attending Lenten masses as a graduate student. Then, with his mother's death, Catholicism suddenly lost its grip on him.

At the University of Illinois, Welch earned his M.A. and Ph.D. degrees in chemical engineering. The physicality of the subject appealed to the pragmatist in him: "It's not just a paper exercise," he remarks. Welch wrote his Ph.D. thesis on the role of condensation in nuclear steam-supply systems. Welch values the experience for teaching him to "wallow" in an intellectual problem until he finds a solution. He thinks he still does that as a manager:

> The important part [of writing the thesis] for me was going down all the blind alleys, repeating myself, feeling frustrated, until I got it to where it was simple. I'm a firm believer that simple is the most elegant thing one can be. One of the hardest things for a manager is to reach a threshold of self-confidence where being simple is comfortable.

John Sr. gave his son a brand new Volkswagen Beetle as a graduation gift. In 1960, already a husband and soon to be a father himself, Welch drove the VW to Pittsfield, Massachusetts, 160 miles from his hometown, where GE Plastics had offered him his first full-time job: an engineering post at one of GE's least important businesses, with an annual salary of $10,500.

Although Plastics was classified, Cordiner-style, as a department, it was really an R & D skunkworks with a couple of promising ideas. Its only going business was in silicones, the malleable, water-resistant sealant used in bathroom caulk and children's Silly Putty, a GE invention.

If serendipity hadn't led Welch to this isolated outpost, GE probably would have crushed Welch's entrepreneurial instincts. But Plastics was too tiny to attract much attention at headquarters, so its managers enjoyed unusual freedom. "We were all by ourselves, and we were all equal," he remembers. Casual and freewheeling, the business influenced Welch, nurtured him, and allowed him to develop the idiosyncratic business style that serves him well to this day.

His first assignment, as a junior engineer, was to help launch PPO (polyphenylene oxide), a polymer GE chemists had invented in 1956, into a commercial product. The stuff was strong and tantalizingly resistant to heat—but it was hard to mold, and it yellowed with age. No one was sure whether it would sell.

After only a year at GE, Welch suddenly quit, planning to take a post at International Minerals & Chemicals in Chicago. GE had given him the standard $1,000 raise for his job classification, and the proud young man thought he deserved more. Reuben Gutoff, the boss of Welch's boss and thenceforth Welch's mentor, sweet-talked Welch into returning. From then on, Welch got bigger raises than most of his peers. A believer in incentive compensation, he later gave similarly outsized bonuses to subordinates who performed well—and no bonus at all to those who didn't.

By 1963 GE was ready to start selling PPO, and placed Welch in charge of the new product—an important responsibility. His first important decision as a manager was to move the PPO group to a manufacturing site in Selkirk, New York. By then GE also was selling a tough, durable plastic called LEXAN, and the young manager didn't want his team to labor in LEXAN's shadow.

Just as the Selkirk plant began producing PPO, chemists back in Pittsfield made an important discovery. A blend of PPO with polystyrene, the plastic used in foam coffee cups, created a material that was somewhat less resistant to heat than pure PPO—but it didn't yellow, and was much easier to mold into products. Welch faced the choice of continuing to manufacture PPO, or investing in new processes to produce something better. After a brief debate, Welch soon recommended modifying the PPO line. With approval from Gutoff and Charles Reed, Gutoff's boss, Welch converted the line to a new plastic blend called NORYL. Remembers Michael Modan, a group member, "Now we had something we could sell."

Welch's decision-making methods have not changed much since his days at Plastics. He would corral everyone he could find who knew something relevant about the subject at hand—whether chemists, production engineers, or finance types—and thoroughly debrief them. He wanted on-the-spot answers, not formal, written reports. Then he would join his subordinates in fierce, no-holds-barred debates about which decision to make. Welch calls this "constructive conflict." His theory is that if an idea can't survive a spirited argument, the marketplace surely will kill it. Says Stephen Eickert, a product manager at GE Plastics, "He likes to be challenged. He likes to get into a pretty animated discussion."

The challenge of selling NORYL gave Welch's people the chance to distinguish themselves. There was no market for NORYL—no one wanted it—so the Plastics sales force had to create demand from thin air. As a first step, they rejected the conventional wisdom at GE that a high-grade engineering product such as NORYL should be sold to engineers on the basis of technical specifications.

Instead, they relied on "application development." Sales people would visit the manufacturers they regarded as potential customers, looking not for immediate orders but for components made of metal, glass, or rubber that could be made out of NORYL instead. If a salesman noticed, for instance, that an automaker used glass taillight housings, he would bring a sample back to the office and ask GE engineers to custom-design the same housings in NORYL—at GE's expense. When the NORYL parts proved cheaper or more useful than the original ones, as was often the case, GE usually would make the sale. NORYL went from a standing start to $50 million in sales and $5 million in earnings by 1973.

GE rewarded Welch in 1968 by making him, at thirty-three, the corporation's youngest general manager. His assignment: to oversee both LEXAN and NORYL, important enough by then to be consolidated into a department of their own.

Taking advantage of Plastics' independence and the strong support of Gutoff and Reed, Welch broke Blue Book rules by keeping the two plastic operations separate and encouraging them to compete ferociously with each other. Glen Hiner, who later became senior vice president of GE Plastics, remembers the consternation that the NORYL-versus-LEXAN free-for-all caused customers: "They'd pull out a big folder of business cards with a rubber band around them—and they were *all* from GE Plastics." The rivalry, though messy, forced everyone to fight hard for orders. Welch didn't care which plastic GE sold. He was still trying to get customers used to the idea of replacing traditional materials with GE's plastics, and he figured that every sale broadened the market.

Welch advertised LEXAN and NORYL with the same techniques used for soda pop or ladies' lingerie. Pitching LEXAN to Detroit's design engineers as a replacement for steel in auto bumpers, he aired goofy commercials featuring comedians Bob and Ray on a popular local radio station. The ploy paid off: Ford soon started installing LEXAN-based components on its cars. By the end of the 1960s, the average car made in Detroit contained 2.5 pounds of GE plastic.

He even used TV. A memorable commercial, comparing LEXAN to glass, showed a bull in a china shop breaking everything that wasn't made out of LEXAN. As *Fortune* wrote, "That image—rude havoc revealing a Darwinian truth—is Welch in a nutshell."

The shared experience of Darwinian havoc helped build a strong team spirit among Welch's subordinates. They came to see themselves as winners. One of his main goals as a manager always has been to stimulate positive emotional energy in subordinates: He says he wants "turned on" people. In the old days, according to Larry Buckley, an EMS staffer, Welch "had the best team he could assemble from the people around him, but they weren't exactly the highest quality people available in GE." Their performance shone nevertheless: Under Welch's leadership, Plastics earnings increased at an average annual rate of 34%, compounded; by the end of 1992 its revenues reached $4.85 billion.

That kind of growth, almost unknown at GE, provided Welch with what GEers call "air cover": the career-saving support of higher-ranking executives. Gutoff, for one, was delighted to protect Welch: "Jack made *my* career go faster," says he. "Jack always had the understanding that what matters in a bureaucracy is getting results. He was totally dependable." Charlie Reed and the late Herman Weiss, who was then a GE vice chairman, also consistently supported Welch. "They made my life easy," he remembers.

With their backing, Welch ran Plastics "like a family store," he recalls. "We were able to take on the big chemical companies and do very well, because we could outrun them. We had the strength of a big company and the speed of a small company." Welch never trained anyone: He'd give a person an assignment and wide latitude, and then expect results. Stealing a phrase from the flower children of that era, he told the GEers under his command to "do your own thing."

No less an information junkie than Jones, Welch lacked the patience to wait for formal reports. Instead, he just dropped in on people and grilled them. Anyone who couldn't answer a basic question wouldn't last long. Welch kept his office door open and allowed subordinates to challenge him or any other boss who seemed to be making a mistake. Delighting in the rough contest of ideas, Welch favored the feisty, hard-shouldered types who knew their stuff and challenged him often.

Perhaps the most important management idea Welch developed in those days is what I call "planful opportunism." Instead of directing a business according to a detailed, GE-style strategic plan, Welch believed in setting only a few clear, over-arching goals. Then, on an ad hoc basis, his people were free to seize any opportunities they saw to further those goals. Welch operated that way instinctively, but the notion crystallized in his mind in the late 1970s, after he read Johannes von Moltke, a nineteenth-century Prussian general influenced by the renowned military theorist Karl von Clausewitz. Von Moltke argued that detailed plans usually fail, because circumstances inevitably change. A successful strategist, he wrote, always must be willing to adapt; even broad goals must be flexible enough to respond to new events.

A typical example of planful opportunism was Welch's early decision to push into overseas markets. Pursuit of one goal—to keep overseas companies from selling LEXAN-type plastics in the United States—led him to another, far broader one: making a market of the entire world. Unlike NORYL, which was protected by patents, the polymers that made LEXAN were in the public domain, and one European outfit—Bayer of Germany—already was selling LEXAN equivalents.

Figuring, characteristically, that the best way to keep those companies out of his turf was to invade theirs, Welch built a $55 million plant in Bergen op Zoom on the coast of Holland. Explains Eickert, "If you're not a player everywhere, we felt, you're going to get clobbered." After the Dutch plant became profitable, GE Plastics negotiated manufacturing joint ventures in Japan and Australia, and created marketing centers in Germany, England, and France. By 1977, GE Plastics was the world leader in the plastics it produced, getting 26% of its revenues overseas. By the time people began talking about globalization, Welch had been living it for years.

GE Plastics grew so fast that Welch frequently had to petition his corporate masters for extra investment capital. Instead of waiting until demand was straining a factory's capacity, he would request expansion funding long before it was needed, so that shortages would not impede the business's growth. *Change before you have to* was his rule even then.

While managers elsewhere in GE aspired only to grow their business as fast as the U.S. GNP, Plastics set a higher standard. As Welch tells it:

I came from businesses with great strength. Everybody should work in a fast-growing business like Plastics or Financial Services, because if they did, their standards would be higher. If a guy's spent all his life in a business that's growing 3% a year, and he gets to 3.5%, he thinks he's got a hell of a business. A lot of managers don't know what a good business looks like.

Though he openly despised it, Welch learned to dance the bureaucratic minuet. Remembers Modan, "I think Jack's first impression was that the people in the bureaucracy were there just to criticize projects about which they had no competence." To outwit them, Welch made sure his capital requests were impeccably researched, financially conservative, and usually prefaced by a cover page that ticked off the results of his previous investments. Says Gutoff, "It showed he always delivered on his promises. Being able to deliver on your promises was the absolute magical secret."

Welch became expert at outwitting the bureaucracy. "He was the worst offender," remembers Don Kane, the EMS staffer. "He knew the game we were playing in Fairfield, and no one played the game better than Jack Welch." He became a master of chartsmanship—and of packaging. Before long he was custom-binding his strategic reports in handsome folders. Headquarters loved those reports, and smart managers throughout the company began copying their format. Says Buckley, the EMS staffer, "One of the first things Jack eliminated when he became CEO was fancy reports, because he knew how much money he had spent making them."

In 1973, at thirty-seven, Welch took charge of GE's $1.5 billion a year components and materials group, which included GE Medical Systems (GEMS) in addition to all of Plastics. Instead of moving to Fairfield like a normal group executive, he ran the whole group from Pittsfield. Herm Weiss, then vice chairman, gave Welch permission to stay there, a decision that angered Jones.

Although the products of his two main businesses were utterly different—GEMS made X-ray machines—Plastics and Medical Systems came to share the characteristics of high technology and fast growth. Welch provided the air cover for GEMS' costly decision to introduce computer-assisted tomography scanners, known as CAT scanners, which use computers to create enhanced X-ray images of internal organs. The potential market was uncertain, partly because the complex machines sold for a hefty $1 million each.

As it turned out, hospitals around the world paid the price gladly, snapping up as many CAT scanners as GE could make. Before long, Medical Systems was growing as fast as Plastics. That success made people at GEMS receptive to Welch's unusual management ideas, which were becoming ever more clearly defined:

- Practice planful opportunism.

- Wallow in information until you find the simple solution.

- Test ideas through constructive conflict.

- Treat all subordinates as equals, but reward each one strictly according to merit.

- Avoid compromise when making decisions.

- Replace hierarchical organizations with close-knit teams, using internal competition to train your varsity players.

- Give your people every chance to identify with their business. Their enthusiasm is your most valuable asset.

In 1977 Jones gave Welch a shot at the top job. By then the CEO had cut his list of potential successors to six men. Jones's initial favorite, finance chief Alva Way, disqualified himself by refusing to take an operating post despite the CEO's repeated urgings. No clear leader had emerged since. Welch, though in the running, was viewed as a dark horse.

Partly to test the contenders, Jones reorganized GE into six so-called sectors, each a multibillion-dollar portfolio of businesses. As a test, Jones tried to assign each CEO candidate to a sector containing businesses unlike any he had managed before.

Welch, GE's growth master, drew Consumer Products and Services: a collection of fusty, old-line businesses such as Lighting, Major Appliances, and Consumer Electronics, which made TV sets. The one ace in his hand was Financial Services, a hardy outgrowth of GE's longstanding practice of offering financing for consumer appliance purchases.

This was Welch's first Fairfield job, and he quickly made his presence felt. Lighting was producing plenty of cash, so he largely left it alone. But with the more than able assistance of Lawrence Bossidy—who was running heavy-equipment leasing when the CEO discovered him—Welch reshaped Financial Services on the pattern of Plastics and GEMS. Bossidy is a tall, big-boned man, the father of nine, whose intelligence and instincts closely match Welch's.

Together, Bossidy and Welch produced red-hot earnings growth by pursuing a simple, flexible goal: They would shove their way into almost any attractive financial business in which they felt they had an edge. Able to draw on GE's vast assets, the unit pushed deeper into capital-intensive lines such as equipment leasing. Before long, it owned more commercial jets, for example, than any other U.S. company, including the airlines.

Just as Plastics shaped Welch's operating style, Financial Services shaped his attitudes about managing a portfolio of businesses. Dave Orselet of the Executive Management Staff describes the Financial Services mind-set:

> The Credit Corporation [as it was then called] was completely unlike most General Electric businesses. On a Monday morning you could take ten million bucks and invest in a business that you think is going to pay off. On Friday afternoon, if it doesn't look good, you close the window and you go home. You don't lament, you don't brood. You cut your losses early and get out.

Bossidy believed that GE personnel, trained in rigorous financial analysis, should excel at a variety of high-risk lending activities such as leveraged buyouts. Because such loans are unusually chancy, and lenders willing to provide them scarce, the loans command exceptionally high rates of interest. (Despite some investor concern, as of mid-1993 the unit's writeoffs on its $80 billion-plus of assets remained acceptable: $800 million in 1990; $1.3 billion in 1991; and $1.26 billion in

1992. GE Financial Services made a killing nevertheless: its earnings have grown at a 24% average annual rate since 1978, from $77 million then to $1.5 billion in 1992. With twenty-three different financial businesses, GE is the most profitable financial-services company in the world. Bossidy rose to vice chairman; in 1991 he left to become CEO of Allied-Signal, a $12.089-billion-a-year producer of auto parts, defense electronics, and chemicals.)

The brass in Fairfield loved what Welch was doing with Financial Services, but his behavior at Appliances, which produced refrigerators, dishwashers, and ovens, raised eyebrows. When he asked deeply probing questions at Appliances, he often got unsatisfactory answers. "Why are our costs so high?" Welch particularly wanted to know. Ignoring the world beyond America's borders—where Electrolux of Sweden and Matsushita of Japan were gaining formidable strength in appliances—the GE unit had built up a cost structure high enough to invite attack from overseas.

While Welch was performing his bull-in-the-china-shop routine at Major Appliances, and expanding Financial Services, the other contenders in the CEO race took on distinctly different roles. Gault, a trim Air Force vet, got responsibility for the industrial sector, which included motors and locomotives. A terrific salesman, he was less comfortable with technical matters. He studied his portfolio of unfamiliar businesses, and moved cautiously to guide them. Thomas Vanderslice, articulate and undeniably skilled, proved too impulsive to win the support of LeVino's staff. He went on to become president of GTE, then CEO of Apollo Computer, and then CEO of M/A-Com, a producer of microwave components. Robert Frederick, a staff man who always fulfilled his assignments, never got the operating experience he needed to distinguish himself. He went on to the No. 2 job at RCA, which GE later acquired.

The two remaining contenders were Edward Hood, Jr.,

and John Burlingame. Hood, five years older than Welch, ran the sector that produced aircraft engines, and everyone agrees he did an excellent job. Deeply reserved and unwilling to play politics, Hood allowed his performance to speak for itself. Burlingame, eight years older than Hood, was a big, burly fellow who managed the sector devoted to overseas markets. He was smart, trustworthy, and a solid performer, but because of his age, he could hope to be no more than an interim CEO.

Jones subjected the CEO aspirants to the now-famous "airplane interviews." A variant of the process Jones's predecessor, Fred Borch, had used to pick him, these interviews enabled Jones to understand the whole matrix of relationships among his CEO candidates. Each person experienced the interview twice: first as a surprise, then again after plenty of time to reflect and prepare answers. Each time, Jones recalls, he would conjure up the image of an airplane ride: "You and I are riding together in the GE company jet. Suddenly, the plane crashes. Both passengers are killed. Who should be the next chairman of General Electric?"

Several of the astonished candidates wanted to climb out of the wreckage. But Jones wouldn't allow that. Instead, Jones would spend a few moments describing the challenges he saw ahead for GE. Then he would ask, "Which other top executives could rise to confront those hurdles?"

In 1979, five years after he began the search, Jones proposed Burlingame, Hood, and Welch as vice chairmen. One person who attended the board meeting says Jones's idea came as a stunning surprise to his two existing vice chairmen, Jack Parker and Walter Dance, both of whom favored other candidates. The three new vice chairmen all performed creditably for two years. Although highly qualified, Hood and Burlingame didn't have the characteristics Jones felt GE's CEO would need. Hood's experience was narrow compared to Welch's, and Burlingame's age ultimately worked against him. Moreover, Welch was the only changemaker in the group. When EMS rated the three vice chairmen according to its fifteen categories, Welch won hands down. EMS judged him the most charismatic, the toughest, the most objective, and the smartest of the lot; he got poorer grades on delegating authority and sharing credit.

Jones's final gambit was his request that each of the remaining candidates write a detailed memo assessing his own performance and aptitude for the CEO job. Having reviewed the memos and discussed them with David Orselet, Larry Buckley, and Don Kane of EMS, I can understand why they viewed Welch's memo as "the clincher" that ended the race. Burlingame's memo revealed how little his staff job had given him to brag about, while Hood simply refused to brag at all. Ted LeVino described Welch's memo to Jones as "an unabashed sales pitch on personal qualities and philosophy of managing, winding up with a strong bid for the order."

Welch stressed his virtues and found ways to minimize his flaws. Aware that some accused him of being overbearing, for instance, he wrote: "The people with whom I have been associated have worked harder, enjoyed it more, although not always initially, and in the end, gained increased self-respect from accomplishing more than they previously thought possible."

As he had done so many times before, with his requests for capital and his beautifully packaged strategic plans, Welch overcame his disadvantages and won the prize. On December 19, 1980, the board of directors unanimously named Welch CEO-elect. He took office four months later.

That is when the struggle began.

Chapter Five

The Power of Ideas

At the end of his first year as CEO, Welch addressed an audience of Wall Street security analysts at New York City's Pierre Hotel. After dutifully running through the basic performance statistics for each of GE's major businesses, he launched into his first public explanation of what he was trying to do:

> If I could, this would be the appropriate moment for me to withdraw from my pocket a sealed envelope containing the grand strategy for the General Electric Company over the next decade. But I can't, and I am not going to attempt, for the sake of intellectual neatness, to tie a bow around the many diverse initiatives of General Electric. It just doesn't make sense for neatness' sake to shoehorn these plans into an all-inclusive central strategy.
>
> What will enhance the many decentralized plans and

initiatives of this company isn't a central *strategy,* but a central *idea*—a simple core concept that will guide General Electric in the eighties and govern our diverse plans and strategies.

Welch went on to cite the teachings of von Moltke, explaining planful opportunism. To wind up the speech, Welch delivered a passionate pitch for his big idea: that GE become No. 1 or No. 2 in every market it serves. As he told the analysts, "We believe this central idea, being No. 1 or No. 2, will give us a set of businesses which will be unique in the world business equation at the end of this decade."

The analysts—practical people who made their livings crunching numbers—looked puzzled. This strategy stuff sounded awfully vague, maybe meaningless. They seemed bored.

As things turned out, of course, Welch's simple strategic idea proved powerful. By 1993, almost all of GE's businesses had become market leaders, and its competitive clout was recognized and feared around the world. But back in 1981 at the Pierre Hotel, many of those security analysts were disappointed: They wanted hard information, and the CEO was giving them theory.

When the question and answer period started, an analyst stood up to ask a question. Excited by his presentation, Welch was eager to debate his ideas with all comers. But an early question set the tone for the rest of the meeting: How would the fluctuating price of copper affect GE's earnings next year?

"What the hell difference will *that* make?" snapped the infuriated CEO. "You should be asking me where I want to take the company!"

Welch answered a series of desultory technical questions about GE's operations, and then the meeting broke up. The analysts trooped back to their offices to prepare their reports. Intrigued with the new CEO, they wrote positive comments— but largely ignored his thinking. Wall Street's best and brightest didn't understand the power of ideas.

You can't blame them. People in business generally see themselves as practical folk, hardheaded doers who sensibly restrict their attention to matters of fact. Executives are supposed to be decision makers who analyze information, make tough choices, and then enforce their wills through the judicious exercise of power.

That is what business schools and corporate experience mostly teach. And that is why many managers are ill-prepared to lead their organizations into the twenty-first century.

Most executives are neither stupid nor hostile to ideas. On the contrary, it takes brains to prosper in business. And when a hot new idea comes along—as strategic planning did in the early 1970s, or quality circles in the 1980s—managers will race to grab it and impose it on their subordinates. Often enough, the results are pleasing. But the old managerial habit of imposing ideas on employees transforms concepts into rules, stripping them of their vitality. Workers change their behavior but not their minds.

In the years ahead, corporations will sort themselves out into those that can compete on the playing field of global business, and those that either sell out or fail. Winning will require the kind of skill, speed, and dexterity that can only come from an emotionally energized work force.

Today, most large corporations are thick-skinned and ponderous beasts, responding sluggishly to environmental changes, if at all. Businesses organized on the old scientific model still build their best ideas into systems instead of encouraging employees to think for themselves. You can recognize such companies by the listlessness of their workers, who lack the conviction, spirit, and drive that characterize champions in any field of endeavor.

Managers at the top of these old-fashioned organizations issue instructions, and then wait while their orders shuttle from desk to desk down the chain of command. When underlings misunderstand, or find ways to disobey, nothing gets done. It happens all the time.

In my consulting practice, I have witnessed the attempts of many major corporations to transform the way they operate, among them AT&T, Citicorp, Chase Manhattan, General Motors, Honeywell, and IBM. The leaders of those outfits clearly understand the need for fundamental change. What they are struggling with is keeping up with the pace of change, while getting their employees to understand why change is necessary.

In 1990 I led a workshop at another company, one still imprisoned by bureaucratic traditions. Its chairman saw the problem, and assured me he knew how to solve it. "We're going to make some radical changes," he told me. "We're going to move fast. We're going to reshape senior management."

"How're you going to do that?" I asked.

"Well," he replied, "we're going to bring in some consultants, and have them study us for six months. Then we'll move on out with the new program!"

It doesn't work that way.

Ideas are the essence of the GE revolution. GEers have referred to Welch's No. 1 or No. 2 concept so often that they slur it into a single word, **number-one-or-number-two**. But that is not the company's only big idea. By the end of the 1980s, employees were talking about **integrated diversity**, the principle that GE's varied businesses can maintain their operating independence while working closely together as a team, sharing everything from financial data to people to best practices. The business engine is an application of that idea.

GEers are talking about **boundarylessness** now. This is the value that underlies GE's increasingly supple organizational style. A boundaryless organization should break down the internal barriers of hierarchy, geography, and function, while nudging the company into closer partnership with its customers and suppliers. The ability to face reality and communicate candidly are prerequisites of boundarylessness.

Above all, GE people talk about **speed, simplicity, and self-confidence**. Since his grad school days, Welch has believed that it takes self-confidence to simplify complex issues. Simple procedures, in turn, are a prerequisite for the fast action that enables GE to win in the marketplace. At bonus time, GEers' ability to manifest speed, simplicity, and self-confidence pays off in dollars and cents.

Ideas such as these serve as GE's signposts of change, but every company has ideas. What's revolutionary—and ultimately far more important than the ideas themselves—is the way GE is weaving its guiding principles into the fabric of its culture. GE's values aren't abstractions: They are becoming the basis of the corporate organization. Exclaims Welch: "We're doing it!"

Executives have substantial power over employees, but they can't tell people what to believe. Creating the pumped-up, turned-on, in-synch work force that Welch envisions requires an honest intellectual exchange between bosses and subordinates—conducted as a dialogue of equals. Welch, who enjoys paradox, calls this "leading while being led." As he declared in a 1987 speech to employees:

> We've learned a bit about what communication is *not*. It's not a speech like this, or a videotape. It's not a plant newspaper. Real communications is an attitude, an environment. It's the most interactive of all processes. It requires countless hours of eyeball-to-eyeball back and forth. It involves more listening than talking. It is a constant, interactive process aimed at [creating] consensus.

Convinced that only the best ideas can survive an open discussion, he doesn't necessarily care whose ideas ultimately win, just as he didn't care whether GE's customers bought LEXAN or NORYL. Welch's focus is on the larger mission: creating a team of like-minded people who believe in what they do and work better as a result.

American to the bone, Welch believes in the ideals of individual freedom and responsibility, and in the principle of human equality. As far back as his days in Plastics, he understood that the power of command could not get him the heartfelt allegiance that he craved. He treats subordinates as his intellectual and social peers, and rewards merit where he sees it.

The persuasive Welch usually can win over anyone he spends time with face-to-face. But as GE promoted him higher and higher, he became responsible for more people than he could possibly meet for one-on-one talks. Years passed before he discovered how to earn the allegiance of strangers. His secret? Acknowledging and respecting the considerable power that even the most junior employee commands—the power of independent thought.

Sure, Welch and every other GE executive constantly make decisions and impose them on subordinates, but they also want workers to think for themselves. Why? Because speed now translates into competitive advantage. GE cannot match the agility of small startups, but pitted against sumo-sized contenders such as Hitachi or Siemens, GE can win by being more nimble—just as Plastics rose to become a powerful competitor of Bayer and Du Pont.

The corporation can't afford to tell its employees exactly what to do—that would take too long. But like any CEO, Welch needs assurance that his workers will further the corporation's goals. He needs people who not only understand GE's objectives but sincerely believe in them. Only when managers and subordinates are on the same wavelength does turning people loose—"liberating" them, as he puts it—become a sound business decision.

The CEO often talks about the need to win "the hearts and minds" of workers. Even in a dialogue of ideas, he believes, hearts are every bit as important as minds. Bitter experience has taught him how profoundly emotions can influence human thought and behavior—and entire organizations. When GEers felt fearful, as many did during the early 1980s, they fought Welch to a standstill; when they felt successful, as at Plastics, Medical Systems, and Financial Services, their enthusiasm carried him to new heights.

Most organizations don't know how to deal with emotion, so they try to pretend it doesn't exist. By design, corporations seem emotionally barren. Feelings, one understands, are best expressed at home, where they won't gum up the machinery of scientific management. The emotional sterility of the business environment is a *cordon sanitaire* around the fear, jealousy, resentment, rage, longing, pride, ambition, and God-knows-what-else that seethe in human hearts. But the sense of sterility is largely symbolic.

Work, inevitably, is an emotional experience; healthy people can't just drop their feelings off at home like a set of golf clubs. Yet management theory long neglected this realm, and we are just beginning the search for ways to harness the vast power of workers' emotional energy.

Though Welch is a passionate person, and more than a casual student of human nature, his Darwinist creed led him to behave in ways that seemed coldhearted. Awash in the flood tide of organizational change, many GEers ignored or resisted him. Understandably enough, they were devoting much of their emotional energy to worrying about themselves: Their job security, prospects for advancement, and workday routines all seemed threatened by the changes Welch made. Says he, "I was intellectualizing the issues with a couple of hundred people at the top of the company, but clearly I wasn't reaching hundreds of thousands of other people." The employees he wasn't reaching felt that instead of throwing out lifelines to them, the CEO was shouting at them. The message they heard—*Swim better!*—wasn't much help.

Not until 1988 did Welch finally find a way to open a real dialogue with GE's whole work force. Then began the long process—still very far from complete—of winning the large mass of employees over to his way of thinking. Here is Welch's explanation:

> It's not that I changed. We just expanded the reach of our communication. We refined it, got better at it, and it began to snowball. If you have a simple, consistent message, and you keep on repeating it, eventually that's what happens. Simplicity, consistency, and repetition—that's how you get through. It's a steady continuum that finally reaches a critical mass.

> By then we had taken out the fat. Over 100,000 people were gone. For a lean organization, the only route to productivity is to build an energized, involved, participative, turned-on work force, where everyone plays a role, where every idea counts.

Like a rock thrown into a still pond, Welch's message has spread out to expanding circles of GE employees. The CEO first created a Corporate Executive Council of GE's thirty top executives—business leaders and senior staffers—who spend two intense days with the CEO each quarter discussing the biggest issues facing GE. Then he transformed Crotonville into a forum for ideas: Its training sessions, both on campus and off, gave 10,000 GEers a year extended opportunities to debate Welch's ideas. Work-Out, designed to reach the entire work force, is the most inclusive forum of all.

If Welch's ideas are powerful enough, they will survive this process and take hold throughout the company. If not, perhaps better ideas will prevail instead. Either way, the company wins.

These touchy-feely, egalitarian methods may strike people from other countries as peculiarly, perhaps even laughably, American. Without question they are rooted in American culture. But GE is no longer simply a U.S. business. Operating in over fifty countries, in partnerships with many non-U.S. corporations, GE earns over 30% of its operating profits abroad. The No. 3

U.S. exporter, GE boasts a positive balance of trade of $5.9 billion; but it is also the largest corporate exporter in France. GE's methods can work almost anywhere. Its techniques for openly airing conflicts succeed even in Japan, where reverence of authority is a way of life.

Global competition is one of many forces that are, for better or worse, rapidly diminishing the cultural differences that divide nations from one another. In another decade or two, those differences surely will seem less important than they do today. Back in 1989, Welch described GE's place in world competition:

> It's clear that the U.S. system has the most free enterprise in the world. Britain's comes next; after that, it falls off dramatically. In Japan the relationships between the government, the banks, and the companies are very intertwined. Your bank allows you to have low returns, and your government will support your R & D and finance your exports.
>
> Or take Europe. Ronald Reagan goes to Russia, and he talks about nuclear disarmament. Helmut Kohl comes one week later with all the German businessmen, and they sign contracts to do deals. That's their system.
>
> What the U.S. system has is freedom. It allows people like me to become chairman of GE in one generation. It allows the talented young engineers in our company to move up fast. If we put bureaucracy and rigidness into our system, we play into our competitors' hands in global markets. Because we don't get the benefits of the protected markets, the government support, the presidential relationships. But if we let our people flourish and grow, if we use the best ideas they come up with, then we have the chance to win.
>
> Our urge to liberate and empower the GE work force is not enlightenment—it's a competitive necessity. When

you look at the global arena, that's what our competitive advantage is. We have got to unleash it.

Before much longer, the world's biggest corporations will reach rough parity in finance and technology. To gain competitive advantage, they'll need organizations that unleash and harness the emotional energy of workers. The winners of this corporate olympiad will be flexible, constantly focused on learning. Employees will work under intense pressure; the confident ones will respond with grace.

None of this will surprise readers of management books. Peter Drucker, Rosabeth Moss Kanter, Tom Peters, and many others have described the organizations of the future. What they haven't explained is how to create them. The path GE is blazing helps show the way.

I find it useful to analyze Welch's ideas, and the actions he took to implement them, in terms of what I call **TPC.** The initials stand for the three main aspects of organizational behavior: the **Technical, Political,** and **Cultural.** By separating the main threads that define the nature of a complex institution such as GE, TPC clarifies the workings of the larger whole. It also reveals the effect of managerial actions by defining which aspect of the corporation they touch.

I envision TPC as a three-stranded rope, in which technical, political, and cultural ideas weave together. To the extent that the three strands are tightly interwoven, the rope is strong. When the rope unravels—as it inevitably does during the revolutionary process—it must be braided anew. Applied to the task of transforming an organization, this image highlights the need to deal with each strand separately in order to strengthen the corporation as a whole.

The first strand is the technical. This concerns not technology but technique: the mundane, practical strategy-setting and decision-making with which executives usually are most comfortable. In general technical acts are those, such as acquisitions, divestitures, and reorganizations, that a highly placed executive can accomplish by fiat. The tradition of scientific management, at GE and elsewhere, encouraged managers to focus primarily on the technical strand. During his first four years as CEO, Welch focused on it, too.

His most powerful technical idea is the rule of No. 1 or No. 2 market shares. Welch's predecessors already had built a massive enterprise, so the new boss made a virtue of scale, focusing on huge, capital-intensive businesses with high barriers to entry, in which GE's management expertise and deep pockets could provide competitive advantage. With a vision of market mastery in mind, Welch used GE's enormous financial resources to help lift each GE business to a position of market leadership.

His method, also technical, was the rule that GE fix, close, or sell any business that didn't meet that standard. During the early 1980s, GE bought and sold billion-dollar businesses the way kids trade baseball cards. Using No. 1 or No. 2 as a guide, GE sold cyclical businesses such as Utah International, central air conditioning, and small appliances. He bought either top-rank businesses or companies that could boost GE's existing units to leadership positions.

Welch believes managers should be "hardheaded but soft-hearted." In other words, tough-minded in competition, but considerate in dealing with people. When he and Vice Chairman Burlingame sold the Utah International mining subsidiary for $2.4 billion in 1984, Welch offset the gain by socking away over $1 billion to fund generous severance payments to the tens of thousands of people GE was dismissing. The layoffs themselves were extremely hardheaded, but Welch tried to conduct them humanely.

The second strand of the rope is the political. This concerns the more delicate matter of power relationships among people. Hiring and firing, replacing opponents with allies, forcing independent-minded people to work together—these are political acts. Welch largely exhausted the possibilities of the technical realm before taking dramatic political action. Hoping to win the voluntary support of his subordinates, he tried to avoid unnecessary conflict while consolidating his power.

GE's resisters weren't just hourly workers; they included some of GE's business leaders, ranking just below the sector chiefs who reported to the CEO. Courteous, long-suffering company men, they didn't dare to oppose the CEO directly. But they sat on their hands instead of pushing for change, and as Welch learned, passive resistance can slow you down to a crawl.

Starting in 1985, GE "delayered" and then reshuffled its top management, removing high-level resisters and placing hand-picked executives in GE's most important jobs. The Corporate Executive Council, or CEC, helped Welch consolidate these gains. The members of this group are directly accountable to the CEO.

Serving as a central information exchange, the CEC helps promote the integration aspect of integrated diversity, which is Welch's main political idea. To encourage diversity, Welch granted increased autonomy to business leaders, while cutting the central staffs in half and reversing their role: Instead of dictating to the businesses, staffers henceforth were obliged to assist them. One result: GE has replaced its single, company-wide compensation scheme with more plans than it can count, each adapted to local needs.

The third strand of the TPC rope is the cultural. This is the most nebulous area of corporate management, and by far the most challenging. It is about changing the often unspoken values and beliefs that guide any organization's conduct. Executive power can't accomplish much here; subordinates' voluntary cooperation becomes essential. The difficulty of the task is such that even revolutionary leaders usually place cultural change last on their agendas. But no transformation is complete without it. Corporate cultures continue to direct behavior long after the most dramatic technical and political acts have been forgotten.

How do you change a culture? Welch has started the process by orchestrating a corporationwide dialogue of ideas. To the degree that Welch can get employees thinking about big ideas, he can get them used to the revolutionary notion of thinking for themselves on the job. Welch is using every means at his disposal. In the technical realm, for instance, the company urged operating units to come up with compensation procedures to directly reward employee behavior that accords with GE's values. The CEO also used political means, placing committed allies in charge of businesses that were resisting change. And in the cultural realm, he promoted company-wide debates about what GE's values should be. Taken together, such methods should transform new ideas into accepted habits; as that occurs, the culture should change.

Welch's thinking has changed in response to GE's dialogue of ideas. An ardent believer in quantum change, the CEO once insisted that incremental change does not work. Since then, he has changed his mind. Welch always has seen the revolutionary process as endless, simply because the world beyond the corporation never stops changing. But he has come to appreciate the value of small changes, too. Now striving to achieve both quantum leaps and incremental change, Welch has discovered that each feeds the other. (A graphic illustration of this principle appears on page 392.) The big breakthrough opens the way for countless small improvements, and then the accumulation of small gains builds the organization's confidence to attempt another quantum leap.

The revolutionary process is agonizing for employees, and many GEers were deeply shaken by the experience. But Welch upset his employees for a reason: He could not create a new order without tearing down the old. Economist Joseph Schumpeter called that process "creative destruction." It's necessary, but it hurts.

GE's bureaucratic ways had been enormously comforting to employees. When the old ways vanished, anxiety began to eat away at GEers' self-assurance. The old job classifications had ensured predictable raises, regardless of how one performed. The many-layered hierarchy had provided plenty of general manager posts to those who sought advancement. In 1980 some 300 GE managers held jobs with P&L responsibility; by the end of 1992, fewer than 50 did. Suddenly jobs were no longer secure, and the company's requirements were less clear.

Before employees could join Welch's cause, they had to come to terms with their loss—the emotional equivalent of losing a parent. First people must disentangle their feelings of connection to what is gone; psychologists call this "disidentification." Next comes "disenchantment," the realization that disillusionment is an inevitable part of growing up. For example, the idea of lifetime job security was enchanting, but by 1981 it had no more basis in reality than Santa Claus. A mature person can understand the need to give up beliefs that don't make sense.

Adjustments like these take time. While GEers were struggling with their own emotions, many responded to the threat Welch represented by fighting his program of change. Some resisted passively, by ignoring his demands. A few battled the CEO directly. Thus the conflict between the old GE and the new became overt, making the process of transformation doubly difficult for everyone.

During Welch's early years, the three-stranded rope of GE's identity frayed. By 1993 he had twisted the technical and political strands of the organization tightly together, but his work on the cultural strand remains incomplete. "We're well beyond the halfway mark," he opines.

Chapter Six

"Kick-Starting the Revolution"

During the first two years after Welch took office in 1981, his main goal was kick-starting the revolution. In those days, relatively few people shared his vision of the new GE—many had no idea what he wanted. Trusting his instincts, the CEO relied on charm, brute force, and personal intervention to get his message across to the troops.

Jim Baughman, the fellow who later became my Crotonville boss, remembers the earful Welch gave him at the January 1981 annual meeting of GE's top 500 managers, in Bellaire, Florida. Welch had just been anointed as Jones's successor, but would not become CEO until April. Baughman, who'd left Harvard only four months earlier, was still finding his feet as a corporate executive. The two men had never met.

Welch buttonholed Baughman at a cocktail party at the

Belleview Biltmore Hotel, and hurtled straight into an explanation of his goals for GE. "I want a revolution," he said forcefully. "And I want it to start at Crotonville."

After just a minute or two of crisp elaboration—plus a cordial invitation to lunch—Welch moved on to assault the composure of another high-ranking GE executive.

Though he didn't always express himself quite so plainly, Welch's message was clear from day one: GE was going to change—and fast.

The CEO, then forty-five, began yelling "Fire!" to anyone who'd listen. In October 1981 he harangued GE's 120 corporate officers. Though he is considerate in his personal contacts with workers, Welch feels no inhibition about slamming his highest-ranking subordinates into the boards. Pacing the stage aggressively, he laid out his agenda for change: No more bureaucratic waste. No more deceptive plans and budgets. No more hiding from difficult decisions.

> Our issue is facing reality about having a troubled business situation. We [top managers] can take good news and we can take bad news. We're big people and we've been paid well, all of us. Don't sell hats to each other.
>
> You own these damn businesses. The idea of [your] coming into Fairfield, and Fairfield yells, and Big Daddy gets you—it's an insane system we've built. No, you are the owners of your businesses. For God's sake, take them and run with them. Get us out of the act.
>
> Look at where you are in 1981, where you'll be in 1985, and probably more important, where you'll be in 1990. Can you play in that arena as a No. 1 or No. 2 player?

Any business that could not become a No. 1 or No. 2 player, he warned, would not remain part of GE.

The implication should have been perfectly clear: Now

that Welch had become el supremo, many of the executives in the audience wouldn't last long at GE either.

But from the officers' perspective, Welch's speech was a big yawn. These experienced company men had seen chief executives come and go. They'd heard a zillion of these speeches. Nothing much had ever changed, nor ever would. The new boss would learn that soon enough. As far as they were concerned, GE already was a No. 1 player—*the* No. 1 player, by God! While Welch was warning that the sky was about to fall, the company was posting record financial results. Some GEers couldn't figure out why the CEO was bellyaching—after all, net income was up 9%, to nearly $1.7 billion. Only nine corporations in the Fortune 500 had earned more!

Welch had expected GEers to dislike his message. But he believed they'd see the obvious benefits of joining the revolution. He thought they'd understand. He thought they'd agree. He thought they'd help.

He was wrong. Glen Hiner, the Plastics veteran who was a close Welch comrade for decades, explained why in 1989:

> I think Jack had the vision very early, and he articulated the vision almost immediately. The trouble was, he expected to get everything done quickly. He didn't understand how big GE was. He didn't understand how deep he had to go to effect these changes. Even today, I think he continues to be amazed by the questions he gets asked at Crotonville, the ongoing lack of understanding.

Although a substantial core group of employees responded as Welch had expected, the greater mass did not. When he took office, the average employee had served GE for thirteen years; the old mind-set dominated their behavior. Some actively resisted Welch's ideas. A great many more seemed paralyzed, like deer caught in the headlights of an oncoming car.

The CEO couldn't understand their behavior. It seemed

insane—either suicidal or self-deluding. Did these people expect the onrushing future to swerve?

What Welch saw, and many others didn't, was the evanescence of GE's prosperity. The company was coasting on massive backlogs of orders for such products as locomotives, steam turbines, and nuclear power plants, which customers request years before delivery. In 1981, GE's backlogs totaled over $28 billion, and contributed one-third of annual revenues. Customers had placed most of those orders during the 1970s, long before business conditions had changed. The backlogs would continue to produce a rich stream of revenues for several years to come, but they obscured the mounting difficulties GE was experiencing in winning new orders for steam turbines and nuclear power equipment.

Welch was trying to avoid the boiled frog syndrome. If you put a frog in a pan of cool water and then gradually turn up the heat, the frog will just stay put until it dies. But if you drop a frog into boiling water, it will jump right out—and survive. It is human nature to say, "If it ain't broke, don't fix it." Left to themselves, people will ignore warnings of danger, scorning opportunities to change early and with a minimum of pain.

I see it all the time. During the mid-1980s, IBM was lulled by its unprecedented profits from mainframes. So Big Blue missed the shift from big computers to workstations and PCs—and its performance has suffered ever since. As of this writing, IBM's market value has sunk to less than one third of its 1987 level, and the company is still in the midst of restructuring its entire organization. The convulsions that have wracked several of America's great corporations are forceful arguments against delaying needed change.

The boiled frog phenomenon is not uniquely American. Philips—one of GE's major European competitors in lighting and, until 1987, consumer electronics—spent the 1980s posturing about a coming business restructuring that somehow never came. In 1990 the Dutch company abruptly ousted its CEO and laid off 55,000 workers.

Back in 1981, Welch's challenge was to remake GE before its comforting backlogs ran out. With plans that would require every dime GE could produce, he could not afford to wait. When employees ignored his warnings, conflict became inevitable.

No traditional "GNP company" could prosper in the economy of the 1980s, he thought. The U.S. was suffering a recession when Welch took office, and he expected the gross national product to grow less than 3% yearly on average during the decade. According to his calculations, GE would need to boost its profits one-and-a-half to two times faster than the GNP in order to finance the reshaping of its businesses while adequately rewarding employees and investors. As he told a reporter in 1982, "Managements that hang on to weakness for whatever reason—tradition, sentiment, or their own management weakness—won't be around in 1990."

To many, Welch's goal for growth seemed preposterous. Jones had aimed only for growth that outpaced the GNP, however slightly. But a 1980 memo by Daniel Fink, then GE's vice president for planning, predicted that even Jones's relatively modest target was beyond GE's reach. Fink argued that unless the company could miraculously fatten its profit margins—or quickly boost revenues by a seemingly impossible 25%—GE's earnings increases would not even keep pace with the GNP. In four years, Fink warned, the annual net income shortfall would approach $400 million.

By 1982 slackening demand already had caused GE's total sales to drop 3%, the first revenue decrease since 1960. Of itself that decline, to $26.5 billion, might have seemed a mere hiccup for this giant enterprise, but it worried the CEO. He surveyed GE's portfolio of businesses and pronounced it incapable of meeting his demands.

Any number of measures pointed to GE's weakness in 1981. Only a few of GE's 150-odd business units were No. 1 or No. 2 in their markets, among them Lighting, Power Systems, and Motors. Some of these market leaders were ailing, including Lighting, which was charging too much for commodity products and losing market share. Of GE's major businesses, only Plastics, Gas Turbines, and Aircraft Engines were strong overseas, and only Gas Turbines could claim worldwide market leadership. Two-thirds of GE's sales depended on aging businesses that were growing slowly or not at all. The corporation's stars—Plastics, Medical Systems, and Financial Services—were in emerging areas such as technology and services. But GE's efforts in those areas were still relatively modest, contributing under one-third of total corporate earnings in 1981. Another concern: Many of GE's operating units, particularly fast-growing or high-technology businesses such as Aircraft Engines, routinely consumed more cash than they produced.

The rule of No. 1 or No. 2 became the CEO's overarching strategy for solving all these problems. A business can be profitable without a No. 1 or No. 2 market share, of course, but Welch wanted a stable of champions. The huge revenues and fat profit margins that usually accompany leading shares would give GE the financial flexibility to dominate its markets. Welch's urge for market leadership is such that, as he later admitted, he didn't really want to allow even No. 2 businesses into the GE stable. He explains his views on competition:

> Some people say I'm afraid to compete. I think one of the jobs of a businessperson is to get away from slugfests and into niches where you can prevail. The fundamental goal is to get rid of weakness, to find a sheltered womb where no one can hurt you. There's no virtue in looking for a fight. If you're in a fight, your job is to win. But if you can't win, you've got to find a way out.

Thus Welch's vow to fix, close, or sell any business that could not achieve market leadership. This was a long-term strategy: GE would readily invest in weak units if they promised to become strong. Fixing a business, in the GE lexicon, meant solving its operating problems, or increasing market share through acquisition, or both. Selling the losers raised cash for investments to strengthen the company. Closing a business down was a drastic last resort, rarely applied to an operation much larger than a factory. Over the course of years, this approach would reshape GE's portfolio, assembling a group of winners with the muscle to meet GE targets.

In the meantime, though, the CEO was insisting on regular increases in quarterly profits. How to achieve them? GE's sales, in those early days, were sluggish at best. Welch had big plans for boosting productivity, but those efforts would not produce significant results for years; GE's productivity rate still hovered around 2%. Welch saw no alternative but to cut costs.

That meant layoffs—big ones. The linkage was inescapable. Employee compensation was GE's second largest cost, after materials and supplies, amounting to 41% of annual expenses. Here's how Welch explained his reasoning: If inflation is running at a hypothetical 5% rate and productivity at 1%, a general manager starts off four percentage points behind the previous year's performance before he starts making mistakes. As the CEO imagines the scene:

So what does the manager do? He immediately grabs the sales manager by the shirt, and says, "Get prices up." He feels he has no choice—he's got to make his budget or there won't be any earnings. But what usually happens when he raises prices? He loses share. He's strangling!

But if he could gain 6% productivity, he'd start out ahead—despite inflation. The general manager can cut prices and gain share, or he can raise prices to increase profits. He is in control of his destiny.

Layoffs alone could not produce the productivity gains GE needed; the company also was investing billions of dollars in efficient new equipment. Nevertheless, by the end of 1982 the process euphemistically called "downsizing" already had squeezed out 35,000 employees, almost 9% of the 1980 total. Not all of those jobs were lost: GE says roughly half of them moved with the ongoing businesses that it sold to other companies.

Without those job eliminations and others that followed, GE might have settled like so many other Rust Belt companies into ponderous insignificance. Simple arithmetic suggests why: In 1982 GE's net income was $1.8 billion. Imagine that GE had not already terminated 35,000 employees. Their average salary and benefits of a little over $25,000 per person would have increased GE's pretax expenses by nearly $900 million.

Of the hundreds of top GE executives who heard Welch's early speeches, only a few score initially brought much conviction and energy to the cause of reshaping GE. Among them were Larry Bossidy of Financial Services, whom Welch soon installed atop one of two new sectors devoted to high-growth businesses; Paul Van Orden, who had taken over the consumer sector when Welch became vice chairman; Glen Hiner of Plastics; Walter Robb of Medical Systems; Brian Rowe of Aircraft Engines; Frank Doyle, the senior VP in charge of human resources; Ted LeVino of EMS; and John Burlingame and Ed Hood, who stayed on as vice chairmen under Welch.

This group faced widespread, but mostly passive, resistance at first. In a corporate organization such as GE's, open rebellion isn't a viable option; besides, few potential opponents judged the new regime a serious threat. So the resisters simply ignored unwelcome orders, or delayed implementing them, or screwed them up.

Executives demonstrated their alienation most clearly in response to demands for cost cuts, and the layoffs they implied.

Ever since Swope's days as CEO, layoffs had been unthinkable at GE, except in such extraordinary circumstances as the period after the end of the Viet Nam war, when defense budgets suddenly shrank. Welch had a hard time convincing some business leaders that the cuts were necessary.

He dealt with the issue obliquely. Instead of setting numerical targets for layoffs, as so many companies have done, Welch forced executives to accept ambitious earnings goals that could only be achieved by cutting costs. He insists that he has never told a business leader to cut headcount by a certain percentage. Welch explains why not:

> If you did that, people would argue with you—and that's an easy argument to lose. The idea of having a discussion about whether you should lay off 2,000 people, or 3,000, or 4,000 is nonsense. You should be talking about how to deliver the results that a healthy business should deliver. It makes sense to talk about an earnings number. *That* number will force whatever head count or other changes the business needs.

GE gave its leaders the freedom—and responsibility—to decide for themselves how to reach the earnings targets. If they could reduce costs by means other than layoffs, such as by cutting inventories, that was fine. As a practical matter, though, the earnings goals frequently made job cuts unavoidable.

Perhaps foolishly, Welch expected his resentful subordinates to handle the downsizing with sensitivity. He wanted managers to think carefully about whom they let go, so that the resulting work force would retain the proper mix of skills. And he believed the victims of layoffs deserved compassionate treatment—not only generous financial settlements, but humane consideration of their feelings.

Most of the layoffs were handled decently, but not all. The CEO kept getting reports of mindless across-the-board cuts that shoved the wrong people out of GE, or of employees laid off just before Christmas. He personally answered letters of complaint from laid-off employees, and directly intervened in cases of injustice that came to his attention. (A sample of this correspondence appears on pages 336–337.) Executives who mismanaged the downsizing felt his wrath.

While striving to create a new organization, Welch could not allow the old one to squirm out from under his thumb. To accomplish anything at all, the CEO had to directly reach GE's employees, then totaling roughly 400,000 people. To consolidate his power, Welch immediately seized the revolutionary's three main levers of control: the police, the media, and the schools.

To a leader forced by resistance to bypass traditional chains of command, these three institutions offer the most effective means of influencing the population at large. History shows that without the support of police, media, and schools, a revolution almost certainly will fail. Consider the 1991 coup d'état in the former U.S.S.R.: The plotters foolishly left the media free to publicize the opposition movement that ultimately triumphed. Welch instinctively understood this principle, and spent his first days in office seizing the crucial levers of power. Corporations have their equivalents of police, media, and schools. At GE, the "schools" were Jim Baughman's bailiwick, and later mine: Crotonville. The "media" included executives' speeches and publications from employee magazines to the corporate annual report. Aware of the media's importance, Welch writes all his own speeches, prepares his own charts, and ad libs his Crotonville talks.

GE's "police" were the cadres of professional nit-pickers and second-guessers on the strategic planning and finance staffs, who reviewed every operating decision and supervised the allocation of capital. It was Welch's inspiration to turn the GE bureaucracy against itself: Once he got the planning and finance staffers under his thumb, every one of those reviews became an opportunity to influence the behavior of the people who actually ran GE.

Both the media and the schools submitted readily, but the police recognized the new CEO as a threat. He pinioned the high-flying strategic planning staff right away. GE first froze its budget, then eliminated 80% of its jobs. Before long, only a dozen corporate planners remained in Fairfield, as part of the business development staff; operating executives gained responsibility for their own strategic planning. Overall, Welch "downsized" the miscellaneous corporate staffs in headquarters— including finance and EMS—from 2,100 people to 900.

Once tamed, the police became powerful allies. Welch recognized that a chief executive, unlike less senior managers, has limited opportunity to run a business directly. All he or she can do is set strategy, select a team of executives, and supervise the allocation of capital. During the revolution's early days, the last of these powers was most vital. Because so many of GE's operating units were so hungry for capital, the CEO's ability to grant or deny them money proved a source of real power. Some of Welch's subordinates may not have liked his ideas, but they needed that dough.

In the organization Welch had inherited, the police on the corporate staffs played a central role in capital allocation. Every year, each of GE's forty-six strategic business units was required to submit a detailed plan for approval in Fairfield. In addition, every business unit that produced a profit-and-loss statement would undergo a formal budget review at least twice a year. Troubled units, such as Major Appliances in the early 1980s, were scrutinized as often as once a month.

The police caught business chiefs in a tight pincer grip. To win approval of plans, budgets, and capital requests, executives now had to satisfy Welch's demands: consistent increases in quarterly earnings, *and* long-term market leadership as defined by the rule of No. 1 or No. 2. These paired demands forced many GE managers to drastically slash costs while completely rethinking their businesses.

To guide the managers' thinking, GE designed a self-sustaining process—a sort of business engine—that in the short run forced layoffs, and eventually purged GE of almost all its substandard operations. The process began with the CEO's ambitious performance goals. Then it provided financial incentives potent enough to counter managers' deeply ingrained aversion to layoffs: GE set up a central corporate restructuring fund that paid severance costs including retraining, job counseling, and outplacement services, plus lump-sum payments for laid-off workers.

The set-up allowed the entire economic benefit of a payroll reduction to go straight to the individual business's bottom line. That, in turn, enabled the business to produce the improved results GE required.

Closing the loop, the company financed the restructuring fund with the proceeds from sales of its assets. The businesses it sold were those, such as Central Air Conditioning and Utah International, that weren't market leaders or otherwise failed to make the cut.

Over the years such divestitures poured billions of dollars into the restructuring fund, providing more than enough money to finance generous severance payments for terminated employees. At the same time, the divestitures demonstrated Welch's determination to enforce his rule of No. 1 or No. 2. That message, in turn, encouraged managers to focus on productivity. Once started, the cycle ran on by itself.

The formal reviews gave Welch and the vice chairmen the opportunity to meddle personally with GE's operations. Instead of delegating police work to his staff, the CEO meets several times a year with each of GE's hundred-plus managers, reviewing their strategic plans, budgets, operating results, and personnel.

Dave Orselet of EMS, who served as a consultant for the consumer products sector while Welch was running it, observed such visits. Orselet recalls how Welch pushed downsizing:

He has an incredible ability to analyze data, but he also does it by feel. Jack would press and press and press and press, until he felt that they [the managers] were screaming loud enough that the cuts probably had gone about as deep as they should go.

Responds Welch: "The starting point was always lousy financial returns. It would become obvious that cutting costs was the only solution."

Nuclear Power was one of several businesses that Welch watched particularly closely. Ranked No. 2 behind Westinghouse, it seemed on the verge of extinction. The problem was not market share, but profitability: After Three Mile Island the business began accumulating losses. In 1981 its leaders pitched a wildly optimistic strategic plan that assumed GE could win orders for three new nuclear plants every year.

When he saw the plan, Welch was incensed. "You can't believe that!" he cried to the assembled Ph.D.s from Nuclear. "You just *can't!*"

Belatedly, Nuclear Power's leaders began to rethink the whole business, returning with a revised plan that assumed no new plant sales at all: Henceforth their main business would be providing nuclear fuel and services to existing plants. Eliminating the imaginary plant sales from the budget clobbered projected earnings. To produce an acceptable level of profits, the business now proposed massive cost cuts.

This time, Welch approved. By 1991, Nuclear Power eliminated 4,400 jobs, more than half of the total before Welch became CEO. At the 1982 meeting of GE's general managers, he happily predicted a turnaround in Nuclear that would produce $700 million of earnings over the next decade; its actual profits turned out to be closer to $1 billion.

As Welch acknowledged in the mid-1980s, the experience was extremely painful:

> Our people were the best and the brightest. They'd given thirty years of their lives to nuclear power. When I said, in 1981, that there was not going to be another nuclear plant built in the U.S., they were upset, they were angry, they were writing letters.
>
> Even today, if you ran a survey of Nuclear, and asked *How do you like our strategy?* they'd say they don't like it. Not because of anything wrong with GE's strategy. They just don't like what's happened to their situation. They don't like reality. I feel for them. It's a tough deal. But the world decided nuclear power was not what it wanted.

Welch is an information junkie: When he needs a fix, nothing gets in his way. Scorning organizational charts and established procedures, Welch roamed freely throughout GE, cultivating his own sources of information among relatively low-ranking executives. As a result, he sometimes knew more about a particular business than the person who ran it. That spelled trouble, as Orselet remembers:

> With all his nosing around, Welch might be sitting there with better numbers than you had. In dealing with a fellow like Welch, if you're confident about what you're doing, and willing to stand up for what you believe, you're probably going to be okay. That doesn't mean you won't be in for some criticism from time to time.
>
> The one thing you can never do with Jack is wing it. If he ever catches you winging it, you're in trouble. Real trouble. You have to go in with in-depth information. Stand up for what you believe, but acknowledge what you don't know when you don't know it.

Paul Van Orden, who'd been one of Welch's reliable sources of information earlier in his career, remembers a chance meeting with the CEO in the early 1980s.

Van Orden was running the Consumer sector then, struggling with a portfolio of deeply troubled businesses. The sector's TV sets, clocks, and toasters were market laggards and frequently unprofitable. And at Major Appliances, known as Majors, a potentially deadly combination of high prices and declining quality was cutting into sales of refrigerators, dishwashers, and washers and dryers for clothes. In 1981, the sector's profits dropped 7%.

As the two executives were passing in a hallway at headquarters, Welch hailed Van Orden.

"How're you doing?" Welch asked. "How're things at Majors?"

"They're really struggling, Jack," replied Paul.

"Hey, is there anything I can do to help?" offered Welch.

Van Orden considered the CEO's offer for a moment, then told him, "Yeah. You can stop referring to Majors as a cesspool."

"I'll call them anything I like," snapped Welch.

"Well," Van Orden said amiably, "thanks for all the help."

By the end of 1982, GE was beginning to respond. Despite the recession, myriad operating problems, and declining revenues, the corporation reported a surprisingly healthy 10% rise in profits that year. Buoyed by a rising stock market, the price of GE's shares soared from a 1981 low of $13 (adjusted for subsequent stock splits) to $25 in 1982.

But while the corporation's performance was on the rise, the morale of its work force had begun to decline. The ideas in the CEO's crazy speeches—the ideas so many GEers wanted to ignore—were visibly changing the company. The accumulating carnage of layoffs and asset sales was causing anxiety and pain. The time of trauma had begun.

During those first two years the true nature of Welch's leadership did not become obvious even to GE's employees. Most visible was mounting evidence of drastic cost-cutting and the terrible agony of terminated employees. Beginning in 1982, when journalists started calling Welch "Neutron Jack" and describing him as ruthless, the CEO could not convincingly answer their charges. Profits were up, and so was the stock price—but productivity barely budged. The torment seemed pointless. And so what had begun as passive resistance slowly began to transform itself into active opposition.

Chapter Seven

Nothing Sacred

Welch and his allies had thrown off plenty of sparks during their first two years. But all the yelling and meddling, the agony of layoffs and the soaring rhetoric of new ideas—all this heat somehow failed to kindle an awareness within GE of how profoundly the organization still needed to change. It just made people mad.

Resistance spread from the imperiled hourly ranks all the way to top management. Some business chiefs stolidly thwarted Welch's plans to transform the company. Rather than oppose the CEO directly, they would say *yes* when they meant *no,* doing what they thought best for their businesses instead of pushing Welch's agenda of change. Shell-shocked and fearful, unwilling to change, people throughout the hierarchy stubbornly refused to let go of the old GE.

But by the end of 1984, the old GE no longer existed. Welch had cleared it away. That forced GEers to admit that change was unavoidable. And with that recognition, the GE revolution took hold.

Welch got to that point by devoting 1983 and 1984 to a nonstop deal-making spree that dismantled GE's century-old portfolio of businesses and horrified many old-timers. Making good on the vow to fix, close, or sell any operation that didn't measure up, GE divested 117 business units, from coal mines to Light 'N Easy irons, during Welch's first four years, liquidating one-fifth of GE's 1981 asset base of $21 billion.

The early acquisitions proved as shattering to the old culture as the divestitures. Some of the businesses the company bought seemed so alien to GE's proud legacy that they might have been headquartered on Mars. GE's biggest buy of that period was Employers Reinsurance Corp., acquired from Texas for $1.1 billion. It turned out among the most profitable of Welch's career, but some people wondered why the heck GE was selling insurance. Why not invest the $1.1 billion in Motors or Lighting instead? Even the people in Nuclear thought they deserved some of that loot.

The lack of consensus encouraged Welch to use force. He had a lot to accomplish, little time, and less help than he'd hoped for. Hounded by the need to win every game he played, Welch maintained his demand for steady quarterly earnings growth, even as preparations for the more distant future forced heavy investment and the turmoil of large-scale reorganizations.

Welch's critics during that period often charged that much of his activity was destructive. But there was method to the mayhem: This was the creative destruction that precedes renewal. Having faced reality early, and responded, GE prospers today while its more timid peers brace for agonies worse than any GE has faced under Welch.

In the three-act model of the revolutionary process, the first act is about awakening people to the need for change. It calls for decisive, unilateral action, and a willingness to engage in conflict. This is when a leader must eliminate whatever obstacles stand in the way.

"You're either the best at what you do or you don't do it for very long," Welch wrote in the 1983 annual report. By then, wised-up GEers understood that this was no mere expression of philosophy. The CEO meant to affirm his high hopes for GE, but anxious employees read doom in those words.

Events justified their foreboding. Having slashed the work force by 9% during Welch's first two years, GE cut 10% more—another 37,000 human beings—during 1983 and 1984.

Instead of gathering the allies he needed, the CEO often alienated people. To be sure, he won a good many converts to his cause during those early years. But the aspects of Welch's character that had most disturbed his critics—his combativeness, his ferocity, his willingness to bulldoze opponents—all came more visibly to the fore.

At the same time, Welch's public reputation came under attack. The tens of thousands of GEers whose livelihoods were in jeopardy, or whose jobs had changed under Welch in one of a thousand stressful ways, had reasons to bad-mouth the boss. And some outside observers, especially in the press, were dismayed by the spectacle—familiar today but shocking back then—of a seemingly healthy company closing plants and cutting jobs.

The severest damage accompanied the 1984 publication of a *Fortune* story ranking Welch "the undisputed premier" among America's toughest bosses. Wrote the magazine's Steven Flax:

> According to former employees, Welch conducts meetings so aggressively that people tremble. He attacks almost physically with his intellect—criticizing, demeaning, ridiculing, humiliating. "Jack comes on like a herd of elephants," says a GE employee. "If you have a contradicto-

ry idea you have to be willing to take the guff to put it forward."

The drastic, seemingly arbitrary changes in GE's business mix attracted other criticism. Michael Porter, the eminent Harvard Business School professor, later set forth the view that Welch had produced little more than a retooled version of a 1970s conglomerate. Tom Peters, author of *In Search of Excellence* and, briefly, a Crotonville professor, dubbed GE's business portfolio "a hodgepodge." (Later in the decade Peters would change his mind and call Welch, along with the late William McGowan of MCI, one of the two best managers of the 1980s.)

The defining moment of this bleak era came in 1984 with the sale of GE Housewares—the small-appliance business—to Black & Decker. The $300 million deal was modest by GE standards and based on solid logic. Nevertheless, the divestiture provoked such loud, agonized yowling from GEers and the press that you'd have thought Welch had murdered the Pope with his bare hands and then sold the Vatican to the Mob.

His crime? By selling Housewares, his accusers cried, Welch was wrenching the GE meatball from the very heart of the American home. The "meatball," in GE parlance, is the familiar corporate logo showing the letters *G-E* in antique script within a stylized circle. The terms of the sale gave Black & Decker the right to market certain products with GE's name and logo for three years; thereafter, the meatball would disappear from small appliances.

Outsiders may not easily understand the agony this prospect caused within GE. Here is another example of the surprising power of human emotion in the purportedly rational world of commerce.

Housewares had become a lousy business, but nostalgic GEers didn't care. Ever since their company had sold its first toaster in 1905, Housewares had been part of the corporate identity. The beloved GE meatball, affixed to irons, toasters, clocks, juicers, coffee makers, and hair dryers—the sort of artifacts that once defined the modern American home—was emblem of a tradition and pride that harked all the way back to Edison's lab. In the minds of some General Electric employees, it symbolized what almost amounted to a holy compact binding millions of U.S. consumers to GE.

Over time, that feeling evolved into something more dangerous: the view that Housewares was somehow essential to GE's identity. The business had become sacred, and by selling it, Welch branded himself a heretic—a threat to everything GE stood for. As the *New York Times* wrote, "It was as if GM had suddenly abandoned car making."

I observed the emotions myself. By then I was consulting for the company and spending time with GE managers at Crotonville. They shrugged off the $2.4 billion divestiture of Utah International, the mining company GE had bought in 1976. Vice Chairman John Burlingame brilliantly engineered that divestiture. Though ten times the size and importance of Housewares, Utah's commodities business had never insinuated its way into the corporate psyche. But GEers *loved* Housewares, the way they loved hamburgers and baseball. When they talked about the sale, it was in terms of betrayal, and you could see the hurt in their eyes. By attacking such a vivid symbol of the old GE, Welch had, in effect, declared war on his own employees.

Perhaps blinded by his own rationality, Welch initially had viewed the sale of Housewares as an easy, obvious decision. He knew that the most important customers, the ones whose purchases actually were making GE's earnings grow, were not householders buying electric can openers at less than $20 a pop. Already in 1984, three-quarters of the corporation's operating profit came from sales to big, impersonal enterprises such as airlines, power companies, department stores, and manufacturers.

The GE Welch foresaw would be primarily a vendor of items selling for $1 million or more: jet engines, turbines, credit card processing services, high-impact plastics sold in bulk. Indeed, by 1991 the company's remaining consumer products, such as light bulbs and refrigerators, contributed only about 10% of corporate profits.

Besides, Welch had been observing Housewares' financial weakness since his days atop the Consumer sector. In 1984, despite 50% market shares in a number of its lines, Housewares was generating no cash, and teetering frequently into the red. The advantage of the business' No. 1 status was diluted by the unusual structure of the market it served. The small-appliance market is fragmented into scores of freestanding and relatively tiny business niches: coffee makers, hair curlers, and so on. These appliances sell largely on technology and design. Companies that focused on a particular product, as Con-Air's Cuisinart did in food processors, consistently stayed ahead of generalist GE in product development. And few of the individual niches were big enough to justify GE spending big money on catch-up R & D. Like Welch, Robert Wright, the head of Housewares, couldn't see a compelling reason to keep the business. A balding, tough-minded lawyer, Wright had been a Welch protégé since his early stint as Plastics' chief counsel; he went on to run Financial Services and then became head of NBC television, which GE acquired as part of RCA in 1986.

The sale of Housewares was the first of many assaults on GEers' sentimentality that made enemies among the very people Welch meant to lead. The corporate equivalent of blasphemy became a trademark of his regime. Although the moves were financially sound, they hurt his public reputation.

Nevertheless, the conflicts this fiery Irishman sparked with such relish hastened the process of self-discovery at GE, forcing unexamined issues into the open. For the first time in memory, employees throughout the company seriously began to ponder GE's mission, questioning assumptions and discussing the unspoken.

They began, at last, to think for themselves.

During 1983 and 1984, as he focused on reshaping GE's portfolio, Welch struggled to articulate the vision guiding his actions.

While he made rapid progress in the technical realm, he had little impact on GE's politics and culture.

That dichotomy, much as it frustrated him, is typical of the early stages of the revolutionary process. Given power, a leader can easily force technical changes such as buying or selling business units; changing minds is harder. Lenin created collective enterprises throughout the Soviet Union, but power could not make those enterprises thrive.

The CEO kept trying to explain his thinking, but his early efforts often failed to convey his ideas. By far the most widely communicated expression of his grand design in those days was a sketch of three interlocking circles that he scribbled on the back of an envelope in 1982:

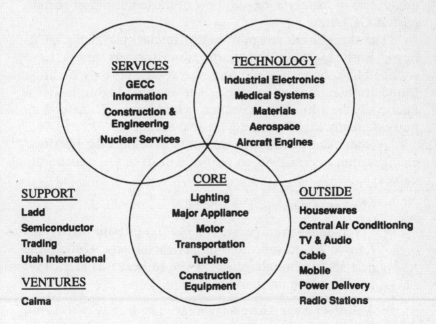

As a rebuttal to those who dismissed GE as a conglomerate, Welch's three circles defined broad categories of endeavor that promised better than average growth: Technology, Services, plus "Core," a group composed of the strongest of GE's old-line manufacturing units. Within the circles were the existing GE businesses that Welch intended to keep—fifteen in all. Each of these consolidated business units contained many previously freestanding operations. Together, they added up to most of the existing GE, producing 90% of corporate earnings in 1984.

As Welch explained, only No. 1 or No. 2 businesses were allowed inside the circles. "Anything outside the circles," he said later, "we would fix, sell, or close." What many GEers noticed first were the businesses that fell outside the circles. Of these, Semiconductors and a few other "support" operations were safe for the time being. Everything else—Housewares, TV sets, cellular communications, and more—was subject to the imperative of fix, close, or sell. Few of those businesses remain part of GE today.

The three-circles diagram began to clarify Welch's intentions. Both Lighting and Large Transformers might have sounded like core manufacturing operations, yet only Lighting found its way inside the circle. The reason: Lighting was a financially healthy market leader, while Large Transformers had essentially earned nothing for two decades.

A statement of the four main goals behind the portfolio changes appeared in 1985, as part of a draft of GE's corporate values:

- **Market leadership:** The rule of No. 1 or No. 2.

- **"Well-above-average real returns" on investments:** Welch refused to set inflexible numerical targets. During the mid-1980s, though, one measure to beat was GE's 18% to 19% return on shareholder equity.

- **A distinct competitive advantage:** The best way to avoid "slugfests" is to provide value no competitor can match.

- **Leverage from GE's particular strengths:** GE is well equipped to prevail in large-scale, complex pursuits that require technology, massive capital investment, staying power, and management expertise: jet engines, high-risk lending, industrial turbines. In fast-changing industries dominated by nimble entrepreneurs, GE might be at a disadvantage.

You may disagree with these ideas. Tom Peters, for instance, used to think the rule of No. 1 or No. 2 stifled creativity. But these principles reveal that Welch's wheeling and dealing was not arbitrary. Housewares had to go because, despite its No. 1 market position, it failed the test of above-average returns. GE was to abandon TV set manufacturing in 1987—despite the front-page lamentations of damp-eyed newswriters—because it lacked a distinct competitive advantage. On the other hand, the seemingly outlandish Employers Reinsurance deal made sense: By exploiting GE's vast capital and the analytical expertise of its managers, the operation could handily top GE's accustomed returns on investment.

The best of GE's existing businesses already met all four of its requirements. In 1984 the Cincinnati-based Aircraft Engines unit demonstrated the value of holding such a winning hand. For eight years, it had been pitted against United Technologies' Pratt & Whitney in a competition to develop new-technology engines for America's F-16 fighter planes. Reporters dubbed this "the great engine war." GE pushed the envelope of engine and manufacturing technology, and won big: U.S. and international contracts worth $7 billion over eight years.

GE also lost a few hands. Starting in 1981, Welch invested $500 million in a visionary attempt to become the preeminent supplier of factory automation systems to manufacturers. Under Reg Jones, GE had been an early user of such equipment as computer-guided robots in its factories. At plants making products as diverse as dishwashers and locomotives, the emerging automation technologies were producing impressive productivity gains. GE predicted a $30 billion market for automation equipment by 1990.

Welch believed in the vision. "We thought we could sell this directly to the CEOs," he explains. "But the people who ran the plans didn't buy the concept, and they killed us." Before Welch realized that, GE bought Calma and Intersil, relatively small companies that made, respectively, computer-aided-design equipment and semiconductors, to expand GE's automation capabilities.

The business didn't grow as expected. After accumulating losses of $120 million, GE bailed out, selling Calma and Intersil, and folding its remaining automation business into a now-profitable joint venture with Fanuc of Japan.

The lessons? One is that GE can't handle small, freestanding acquisitions. As Welch readily admits, "We don't know how to do it right. So we'll put our assets in what we do well: big, powerful, muscle-using businesses." A second lesson may be that big corporations are too thick-fingered to manage the delicate process of creating start-up businesses from scratch. A third is that Welch believes in admitting mistakes and cutting his losses: "I don't mind being wrong," he says. "The key is to win a lot more than you lose."

Welch's own behavior slowed the very process of organizational change that he was so urgently trying to accelerate. His efforts to radically change a corporation that most people still regarded as healthy caused deep emotional trauma. And as the CEO was beginning to realize, clearly communicating the reasoning behind his ideas to GE's complacent work force was enormously difficult. At the company's 1983 corporate officers meeting, held in Phoenix, Welch said:

> As people come to Crotonville I ask them: "How many of you feel that communications have improved?" We're getting 15% to 20% responses. Basically, we haven't made a hell of a lot of progress. . . . Without everybody embracing what we want to do, we haven't got a prayer.

Chapter Eight

Facing Reality

Before Carl Schlemmer became the first great hero of the GE revolution, he damn near destroyed his business. Completely misjudging the market for locomotives, he decided in 1979 to invest a budget-busting $300 million in a new model called the Dash 8—just before demand disappeared.

As Schlemmer recalls, the financial projections he used to sell the Dash 8 investment to Welch said that the locomotive market would probably double in size during the 1980s. He was as wrong as a man could be: By 1986 the global market for locomotives would shrink to a quarter of its former size. As a result, a deadly combination of plummeting sales and outsized investment soon threatened to bankrupt Transportation Systems.

What subsequently made Schlemmer's reputation was his readiness to admit how completely he'd screwed up—and then to solve the problems he'd caused. Acknowledging that his predictions were wrong, he simply changed course. He scaled back his expansion plans, focusing instead on improving productivity. By 1987 Schlemmer cut $65 million out of the Erie, Pennsylvania, operation's costs—enough to swing the business from a devastating potential loss to a $34 million profit. Working closely with a unionized labor force once known for its hostility, Schlemmer and his teammates created a stripped-down, muscular organization capable of breaking even in awful market conditions—and producing outsized profits in normal times. Overcoming his grave errors of judgment, Schlemmer reinvented the locomotive operation, transforming one of the company's most troubled units into a leading exemplar of GE's emerging business style. Lessons drawn from that experience still guide GE managers.

Thanks to methods like those Schlemmer employed, in business after business GE has been the only U.S.-owned producer to survive the 1970s in good health. General Motors' Electro-Motive Division (known as EMD) was the U.S. leader in locomotives a decade ago; now EMD is ailing and GM is trying to unload it. In lighting, power generation, and medical diagnostic imaging—all fields that used to boast several domestic producers—GE is the only entirely U.S.-owned entity to survive.

The ultimate goal of the GE revolution is for all employees to act for the good of the company without having to wait for orders. That means getting people to face facts and take responsibility—an astoundingly difficult thing to achieve, especially in large organizations.

At GE in the early 1980s, only the leaders in such upstarts as Plastics, Medical Systems, and Financial Services were showing such independence. The older businesses, which still dominated the company, crippled the incentives for individual action with their bureaucratic *yessirs* and *gotchas.* Of the men who headed those tradition-bound manufacturing units,

Schlemmer was the only one who proved capable of adapting to a rapidly deteriorating market environment.

A trim, white-haired statesman, equally at ease in a Fairfield boardroom or an auditorium packed with angry blue-collar workers, Schlemmer ran GE Transportation Systems from 1974 to 1989. He wasn't a dirt-under-the-fingernails manager. An engineer named Rick Richardson, his second in command during the 1970s, followed by Jack Dwyer, a marketing man, handled most of the operating details. Schlemmer was known for strategic thinking and salesmanship—the skills that nearly became his undoing, and then salvaged his career.

Schlemmer, Richardson, and Dwyer weren't entirely to blame for Transportation Systems' weakness. The business had long suffered from below-average financial returns. It ranked a distant second behind General Motors' EMD, which commanded well over three-quarters of the U.S. market for locomotives, and perhaps 40% overseas. With a much smaller market share, No. 2 ranked GE couldn't hope to beat its higher-volume competitor on price. And GE's locomotives were clearly second-rate—90% of them failed during their first 150,000 miles, versus a 10% failure rate during the first 250,000 miles for GM's engines.

By the late 1970s the solution seemed obvious to Schlemmer: GE needed a new product superior enough to enable the business to leapfrog GM. With the right locomotive, he believed, GE could quickly boost its market share, for a huge increase in profits. The key technological issues were reliability, fuel efficiency, and pulling power. Schlemmer set his engineers to work incorporating those attributes into a new engine design that became the Dash 8. They introduced what Schlemmer calls "space-age" computer controls to reduce breakdowns and limit energy use, along with modular construction techniques that cut manufacturing cost and improved quality.

In addition to design innovations, Schlemmer's plans called for massive productivity gains and $100 million of investment in factories. That money would buy a highly automated new diesel engine plant in Grove City, Pennsylvania, plus equipment to support a big increase in the capacity of GE's existing locomotive plant, from 500 units per year to 800.

Had the domestic demand for locomotives doubled, as Schlemmer expected, that level of investment might have paid off richly. Instead, his misguided strategy only demonstrated the futility of attempts to predict the future.

While Schlemmer was concocting his plans during the late 1970s, economists both inside and outside GE expected the U.S. economy to grow steadily through the next decade. The railroads, after losing business to truckers for years, seemed poised for recovery, in part because of deregulation. Financially strengthened by a series of mergers, GE's railroad customers were looking forward to significant growth—and that implied surging demand for locomotives. Overseas markets provided half the GE unit's sales; the forecasters spotted no problems looming there.

"There were some very optimistic expectations," remembers Schlemmer. Based on those expectations, he pitched the Dash 8 project to Welch, then a vice chairman, and to the GE board. He thought he saw an opportunity for GE to earn $280 million from locomotives in 1990, over five times more than the unit's peak annual earnings to date. Schlemmer explains: "We figured that if we had the right product and the right facilities, we could capture a major share of that rapidly expanding market. Jack heard us out, and said, 'Do it.'"

Because the improvements were scheduled in phases, Transportation Systems had completed less than one third of its $300 million planned investment before the business jumped off the rails in 1983. Here's how Schlemmer describes the hellish situation he faced:

> The U.S. got into a deep, deep recession beginning in 1981; in my industry the recession lasted until 1988. The locomotive business has always been cyclical but there was never a

cycle like this. Out of a total fleet of 27,000 locomotives in this country, the railroads junked or mothballed 6,000.

We got hit by a whole series of things. There was a major restructuring of heavy industries, which hit the railroads hard. Steel, for example, knocked out 30% to 40% of its capacity during the 1980s. Then President Carter imposed a grain embargo on the Russians, which walloped the Santa Fe Railroad. Meanwhile, the recession was forcing the railroads to work on their productivity. That helped them get their fleets down by over 4,000 locomotives—two years' worth of production. Then our Dash 8 proved so powerful and reliable that three of our new locomotives could do as much as four of the old ones in some applications—so we sold fewer units. On top of everything else, prices were falling.

Our export market went down at the same rate as the U.S. market. We had a major contract with Mexico. After we'd delivered about 450 of their 1,000 locomotives they called up and said, "Sorry about this, but we don't have any money, so we won't need any more locomotives. And by the way, we're not going to pay you for the ones you just shipped." We ultimately collected, but it was scary. Then Brazil got into the same kind of trouble. And Africa and most of our Far East customers fell apart completely.

By the early 1980s I couldn't see any light at the end of the tunnel.

The first signs of trouble had appeared in 1981. Earnings were still growing, but at a rate that suddenly began to slow. More ominous, new orders declined. No one worried much, even so. "We made a few minor adjustments," recalls Schlemmer. "We still thought this was a little dip. We expected things to get back to normal soon."

They didn't. In 1982, as Transportation Systems was starting to spend serious money on the Dash 8 program, its U.S.

unit sales plunged 50%, to 244 locomotives, and business overseas was just as bad. "We began to have a substantial amount of discussion about what was going to happen to the economy in the 1980s," Schlemmer says. "We had experienced fairly sharp declines before, and the market had always recovered relatively quickly. We were getting concerned, but not alarmed."

By 1983, though, outright panic would have been justified. The world locomotive market contracted from 2,000 units annually to 500. GE was selling roughly 300 of those. Although Transportation Systems had greatly increased its market share, the market was smaller, so the business was selling fewer locomotives than before. Its new Dash 8 was not yet producing revenues. Net income was falling through the floor, down 50% to $37 million.

Schlemmer could no longer evade the truth: Transportation Systems was in mortal jeopardy. As he recalls, "We were in a state of semipanic. We weren't sure we could resurrect the business." In 1983 he gathered his key managers for a brainstorming session at the White Inn in Dunkirk, New York. As he tells the story, they didn't waste much time denying the danger they faced:

> We asked ourselves, "What happens if this market isn't what we said it would be? How should we reprogram the expenditures?"
>
> We all agreed we had to do something dramatic, but we still didn't know what dramatic was. We decided to eliminate all the new capacity that we were planning to add. We already had expended some money on facilities, particularly in Grove City—but from then on we were going to limit ourselves to productivity programs. That decision alone took $100 million of potential expenditure out of our plans.
>
> At that point we expected the market to stabilize around 1,000 or 1,500 locomotives a year. We figured that

if we got the productivity gains we wanted, and the market went back to normal, and we offered a superior product, we'd do a hell of a lot better financially because we'd have taken so much cost out of our structure.

If I had realized what was going on, I would never have held that meeting in a place called Dunkirk. When we got back, we essentially pulled the rest of the management team in and said, "Guys, we're on the beaches and the Germans are right over there. We've got to find a way out of this." That was what started the restructuring of the business.

By then, Welch had been CEO for years, but he'd kept his eye on Transportation Systems through the regular ritual of budget and planning reviews. Time after time, Schlemmer showed up with sales projections he'd revised downward since his last visit. The numbers looked dreadful.

Why didn't Welch fire Carl Schlemmer as soon as his plans went awry? According to Jim Paynter, who was then head of Schlemmer's employee-relations staff, the reason was candor. "Welch loved Carl," explains Paynter, "because he was always very forthcoming and he always had a solution. Carl always told Welch, 'Here's the problem and here's what we're doing about it.' The only surprises came from the marketplace." His openness paid off in support from Welch.

The CEO certainly liked Schlemmer's style. As he says:

The leadership of our transportation business did a terrific job. They had a vision, and then that vision fell apart in the recession. The world had changed. They went through hell. But this team said, "Hey, we called it wrong." We didn't have to change anyone—they had the self-confidence to change by themselves.

When Schlemmer began restructuring Transportation Systems in 1983, he still had no idea how catastrophic market conditions would get. At the nadir in 1986, GE ultimately sold just 173 locomotives in the U.S.—down 85% from 1979—and roughly 130 overseas. By then GM had shut down its U.S. locomotive factory, greatly reducing its presence in the business—so GE's puny sales amounted to 80% of the world market.

Always uncertain of what was to come, Schlemmer attacked his cost problem in increments, cutting deeper and deeper as sales continued to plunge. He eliminated a quarter of the unit's 3,000 professional employees; ultimately he slashed their ranks by 60%. He took out some 40% of his 8,000 hourly workers.

Cuts as deep as these required a complete rethinking of the Transportation Systems organization and its working methods. Decisions that would have seemed impossible a few years earlier became the norm. Recalls Schlemmer:

> We knew we had to make basic changes in the way we ran this business. As the market continued to get worse, we had to change our perception of how much we could cut and still function and be economically viable. Under circumstances like those, there's no way a business can survive if it can't get its costs in line with the realities of the market.

The Schlemmer team set a pattern that has since become almost routine at GE: They eliminated whole layers of management, consolidated overlapping jobs and business units, and forced employees at every level to take far more responsibility for their own work. If something wasn't absolutely necessary—such as placing advertising in railroad magazines—they eliminated it.

Schlemmer's description of the change is memorable: "We learned to do only what's necessary, not what's nice." They stopped gathering unnecessary financial data, eliminating reports concerning minor product lines, for example. In the plant, equipment operators became responsible for the quality of their own work, reducing the need for inspectors.

The process began at the top of the organization, then worked its way down. Schlemmer called a series of meetings with all department heads, plus employee-relations staffers, including Paynter. They used storyboards—pieces of paper attached to a conference room wall—to map out roughly how the work might flow through a radically smaller organization. To fill in the details, they created multifunctional teams led by their most able executives. As Schlemmer explains:

> We told each of these team leaders, "You have responsibility for one function. You can restructure the organization any way you want to. Start at the top, start at the bottom, start at the side—nothing is sacred."
>
> We urged them to substantially reduce the top of the organization, which was sort of a unique idea at GE at that time. There aren't many people up there, but they're very expensive.
>
> We also said, "You may decide to eliminate your own job. If so, don't worry about it, because we will get you another job."
>
> And I told them they'd have access directly to me. I said, "You don't have to worry about the reaction of any other individual in this organization, not even your boss."

When Schlemmer presented the result of these deliberations to Louis Tomasetti, his sector chief, he remembers Tomasetti warning, "You've bitten off more than you can chew." By contrast, says Schlemmer, "Every time we reviewed our plans with Jack, he'd say, 'Why aren't you doing more?'"

Schlemmer needed more than approval from on high to put the new strategy into action. By their very nature, the changes he was proposing required cooperation from workers—particularly the thousands of United Electrical and Electronic Workers members on the factory floor. Were they ready to move from bolt-tightening to independent thinking?

Their assent could not be taken for granted: Transportation Systems had a history of trouble with labor. In 1976, the union staged a violent strike in which people were injured and property was damaged; the courts subsequently fined the union. Paynter, a steelworker's son, joined the Transportation Systems' employee relations staff two years later—right after a management decision to eliminate Sunday overtime, which had enabled union members to earn double their normal hourly wage. The union protested the decision with a slowdown that caused serious delays in locomotive shipments and threatened profits. Recognizing an urgent need to improve union relations, Paynter and several other executives spent months virtually living in Building 10, where final locomotive assembly took place.

Their efforts during the late 1970s made possible Schlemmer's revolutionary changes in the management-labor relationship at Transportation Systems during the 1980s. Indeed, Paynter's work clearly foreshadows GE's Work-Out program, which began a decade later. He told how it all began:

> We wanted to know what was going on in Building 10. Why were we behind schedule? We met with the supervisors. We met with union stewards. We met with the employees—salaried, hourly, everybody. We tried to find somebody who'd tell us the truth.
>
> Then this one welder came and stood in my doorway. He said, "The union would shoot me if they saw me here, but here's the problem we have in this building . . ." He told us that the flow of subassemblies coming in from other buildings was so erratic that employees often had nothing useful to do. They'd do something useless instead, and get paid for it. He said, "If you'll get the work coming in here, we are very willing to do more—so long as you don't reduce our wages."
>
> So we reorganized the flow of work coming in from the other shops and we changed the way they got paid. It was a win-win situation.

From that modest start, Richardson, Paynter, and a few other Transportation Systems executives developed a new style of employee relations that depended on candid communication. Four times a year Richardson would brief union officers in his conference room in Building 14. Paynter says that the managers held almost nothing back:

> We told them everything that you'd ever want to know—market share, income, what orders we thought we had a chance to win, and what that meant in terms of jobs. Fairfield used to get nervous, because at that time the company was not sharing income data with unions.
>
> We always tried to focus in on two things: serving the customer—the reason we were in the business—and beating the enemy, which was General Motors, not General Electric.

The executives also briefed the hourly employees, in groups of 1,000, at annual meetings held in a local high school auditorium. They got booed the first time, but by the early 1980s their disclosures inspired a measure of trust.

Paynter and his colleagues weren't above using gimmicks. Among the simplest and most successful was an offer to provide free coffee and doughnuts to workers once the plant met its monthly production quota. "It sounds like a small thing," says Paynter, "but it proved how interested employees are in being recognized for a job well done. We dug the business out of the hole it was in, and the doughnut guy got rich."

Another of Paynter's ideas was the "customer awareness trip." He'd gather a group of 150 employees—a mix of hourly workers and supervisors, plus a few managers—charter a plane, and take them on an overnight visit to one of the railroads that bought GE's locomotives.

> The idea was to talk about quality. It gave the people who maintained the locomotives out in Omaha or wherever the

chance to talk to our people. The electrical guys could ask, "Why did you wire it that way?" Once they'd talked out an issue like that, the best way to make the product usually became obvious. I can't stress enough how important it is to go to somebody else's turf. That's how you learn.

The first harsh test of the unit's improved labor relations came in 1983, after Schlemmer finally acknowledged the locomotive market's collapse. Instead of merrily handing out free doughnuts, executives suddenly began ordering major layoffs. Remembers Paynter:

> The darkest days were when we started into the layoffs. "Betrayed" is too strong a word, but employees were disappointed that we couldn't find a way to keep more locomotives coming through their shops.
>
> People did complain about the $7 million we were investing in a new, 40,000 square foot learning and communication center. They'd say, "Why are you spending all that money when we're getting laid off?" Well—that was a fair question.
>
> In the end, though, the credibility we had established paid off. They didn't like what was happening, but they accepted it. They believed that we were doing everything in our power to win all the orders we could.
>
> We demonstrated that if you talked to the people, asked them what to do about something, and then did what they said, your business normally runs better. It's a simple idea that some managers with IQs of 150 can't bring themselves to understand.

A big test came in 1984, when the business snagged the first of two contracts to sell 420 locomotives to China. With permission from Fairfield, Schlemmer agreed to sell those machines barely above cost, as a bridging strategy to keep the factory working until the market recovered. Once the deal closed, he says, Welch wrote him a letter asking how he planned to avoid losing money. Schlemmer called the Erie employees together and explained the need for more cost cuts. "You've got to do something about this," he said—pretty much the same message Welch had just given him.

The workers responded, boosting the operation's profit margin by six percentage points. In one example, workers decided, without management prompting, to redesign the locomotives' cabs, for a 45% cost savings. When a manager inquired why no one had ever mentioned the inefficiencies of the old design, the workers replied, "You never asked." Such efforts by rank-and-file employees enabled the overall business to break even, instead of losing tens of millions of dollars.

Amazingly, Transportation Systems never posted a loss during the 1980s. In 1984, its worst year, the business earned $12 million, then it rapidly improved. Without cost cuts, Schlemmer estimates, the business would have lost $100 million in 1987. Instead, it earned $34 million—about as much as it had been making before the trouble started.

By consistently lowering expenses even faster than his sales volume was dropping, Schlemmer managed the feat of posting earnings increases while revenues declined. He explains his method:

> I finally developed a philosophy: If Jack has to tell you what to do, you're way late. You have the responsibility to respond, and it seems to me that if your challenge is the size of a grapefruit, your response ought to be the size of a basketball.

Carl Schlemmer whipped the "indictment of leadership" problem. Everybody makes mistakes but no one likes to admit them. Corporate executives are no exception: Look at any number of famous CEOs who deny that they have anything to do with their companies' problems.

You can't deny reality and control your destiny at the same time. To turn his business around, Schlemmer had to admit that his own decisions were wrong. No one could blame him for what happened to the market, but Schlemmer was the one who had signed off on those optimistic projections. He was the one who pitched the $300 million Dash 8 investment. His willingness to indict himself freed him to take the actions needed to save the business.

He went nose to nose with Welch and said, "I'm responsible for those projections. I know they're wrong. Now I want to stay and clean up the mess."

I love the Schlemmer story—it inspires me. What's disappointing is that I know of no other such story at GE. Executives who make big mistakes often begin to doubt themselves; though Welch has been slow to oust such people, sooner or later many of them leave GE. "Damaged self-confidence is difficult to repair," Welch comments.

That's a problem at any company hoping to revitalize itself. The paint-by-numbers solution is to get rid of the old leaders and bring new people in—but the costs, in human pain and squandered experience, are terribly high. On the other hand, hanging on to executives who can't face facts usually turns out worse: Their mistakes can cost the jobs of thousands of lower-level employees.

Often it is easiest to face reality in a crisis situation such as Schlemmer's. It's harder to come to grips with a gradually deteriorating business situation, as at GE Lighting and Power Systems. A decline that is slow and subtle can be denied. "Hope is one of the worst things that can happen to a manager," says Welch. "Hope can overcome reality."

Managers of very successful businesses can lose touch with reality, too. According to Welch, "One of the hardest things is to get the maximum out of a rising business. The worst sins are committed in boom times, when everybody feels satisfied. That's when managers get fat and arrogant."

Facing reality, in good times and bad, is an *ethical* obligation for managers—indeed, for anyone whose actions affect other people. If that sometimes requires indicting oneself, tough. Business heads are extremely well paid these days, at least in the United States. Their employers have a right to expect responsible behavior in return.

Chapter Nine

The Mirror Test

Just as one leader can revolutionize a corporation, one crook can damage it. In a business the size of GE, with almost 300,000 employees, even the most scrupulous management can't ensure that no misguided employee will ever commit a crime. Yet the consequences of corporate wrongdoing potentially can be so severe that even a very low crime rate simply isn't good enough. One of the toughest challenges a manager can face is responsibility for the mess left behind when an employee breaks the law.

Such a mess confronted Welch in 1985, when the government charged that GE middle managers had fraudulently doctored time cards in a scheme to overcharge the federal government on defense contracts. Because it occurred on the job, the alleged wrongdoing implicated GE, which pleaded guilty to felony charges and paid a substantial fine.

The time-card scandal surprised and angered many GEers.

It also gave Welch an opportunity to clarify his message to employees: He expects them to win with their integrity intact. The CEO urged every GEer to take what he calls the "mirror test," critically examining their own actions for integrity.

That test is tougher than it sounds. Even those who honor the law can fail in other ways. Self-respecting executives commonly take home office supplies, or ask their secretaries to type their kids' résumés. Strictly speaking, that's theft. Most people who take the mirror test seriously find something in their own behavior to change.

Let's face it: People are susceptible to ethical lapses. In the real world, competitors may cheat, suppliers or customers may demand bribes, regulators may tacitly or even explicitly allow rules to be broken. Some corporate criminals may be ordinary thieves, but many are weak enough to convince themselves that they're basically honest folk doing what's necessary to get their jobs done. Instead of acknowledging the law as black and white, they convince themselves they're operating within areas of gray.

Too often, they're wrong: Studies show that well over half of all major U.S. companies have experienced corporate crime. One study of Fortune 500 firms showed that from 1975 to 1984, some 62% were involved in one or more incidents of corrupt behavior. Another study, by Clinard and Yeager, surveyed the 477 largest manufacturing and 105 largest service, retail, and wholesale companies. It found that 60% of those businesses were charged with at least one federal offense during the two-year period 1975–1976.

This is not simply a corporate problem: As a society, the United States may be failing to convince people of the value of honesty. In 1990, Donald McCabe, a Rutgers ethics professor, questioned some 6,000 university students about cheating in school. His data show that 76% of those planning business careers admitted cheating at least once, while 19% said they'd cheated at least four times, qualifying them as "regulars." Students anticipating careers in other fields, such as law, medicine, and education, cheated somewhat less—but still often enough to dismay anyone who values integrity.

At GE the challenge of keeping employees honest is tougher than at many companies. As a leading supplier to the military, and as a global company selling big-ticket items in every corner of the world, it participates in areas where abuse frequently occurs. GE's missteps are highly visible. Because the company does so much government work, the offenses of its employees are disproportionately likely to become public knowledge. Businesses serving private customers are rarely compelled to reveal their ethical lapses, and most keep them quiet. Moreover, GE is unique among leading U.S. defense contractors in selling both military and consumer products under the same brand name. Relatively few Americans think of GM as a defense contractor, even though it owns Hughes Aerospace, which produces guided missiles and has also been subject to employee crime. When something goes wrong at GE—the company that "brings good things to life," according to its TV commercials—it's front-page news.

Compared to its defense-industry peers, GE doesn't look so bad: Between 1985 and 1991, the U.S. Department of Defense took 38,731 legal "compliance actions" against the department's employees and corporate suppliers: indictments, convictions, settlements, suspensions, and debarments. Only twelve of these actions concerned GE; three resulted in convictions.

I trust Welch's integrity, and I'd argue that he has done as much as any CEO to promote high ethical standards. The substantial checks and balances GE has put into place include corporate ethics policies that are clearly articulated and enforced, and a statement that all salaried employees sign annually, stating that they either know of no wrongdoing or have reported it. Nevertheless, charges of malfeasance by GEers still grab headlines. In addition to the time-card scandal, the most serious incidents of the Welch years are these:

- The 1988 "MATSCO" case, in which employees of GE's Management and Technical Services Company, a subsidiary of GE Aerospace, overcharged the government on battlefield computer systems it was installing in military vehicles. Two GEers were sentenced to jail, and the company paid a $10 million fine.

- The so-called Dotan case, named for Israeli Air Force general Rami Dotan. He allegedly colluded with an employee of GE's Aircraft Engines business to divert over $30 million of U.S. government funds into personal accounts. Dotan was convicted in Israel and is serving a prison sentence there; the accused GEer has been fired. GE cooperated with federal investigators and signed a $69 million settlement.

In addition to these serious crimes, which GE acknowledges and regrets, the company has gotten more than its share of public-relations black eyes from matters that may have nothing to do with breaking the law. Not all of the bad press has been deserved.

In 1992, amid great publicity, the U.S. Justice Department was investigating accusations from a former GE employee that General Electric conspired with De Beers Consolidated Mines of South Africa to illegally fix prices of industrial diamonds. As of mid-1993 no charges had been filed. GE describes the matter as "unsubstantiated allegations by a disgruntled former employee who was removed for performance shortcomings." The company flatly denies his charges.

Some people object to perfectly legal behavior by GE on grounds of morality or politics. General Electric's role as a defense contractor has prompted a call for a boycott of GE products by a group called INFACT. In 1991 Hollywood gave an Academy Award to a short documentary produced by INFACT. During the Oscar telecast, which reached some 1 billion people worldwide, the producer repeated the boycott call. The film, called *Deadly Deception,* alleged among other things that GE's operation of the government-owned nuclear facility near Hanford, Washington, between 1946 and the mid-1960s, caused health problems to neighbors. GE cites government health studies that have not established such health problems. No charges have been filed concerning any of INFACT's claims.

Some environmentalists object to GE's role in nuclear power, for instance, or its production of plastics. According to the Environmental Protection Agency, GE is a "potentially responsible party" for fifty-one Superfund toxic-waste sites, more than any other listed company. Superfund rankings imply no wrongdoing, but rather the accumulation of waste permitted during times when manufacturers and ordinary citizens were not sensitive to the environment. GE says one reason for its ranking is that the company has more U.S. plants in more different industries than any other company. The other leading Superfund companies are Du Pont, Monsanto, and General Motors.

But Welch argues that there is a world of difference between debatable issues such as these and outright crime. While he is in accord with anyone who regards criminal behavior as abhorrent, he emphatically disagrees with those who criticize GE on moral or political grounds.

Almost from the beginning, the otherwise proud history of General Electric has been marred by instances of employee wrongdoing. An undeniable part of the heritage of many old-line manufacturing companies, including GE's, was a tough-guy willingness to bend and sometimes break the rules in order to win.

At GE, the attitude has its roots in the 1890s, when the company came of age. In those days, when the Harrimans and Rockefellers were forming monopolies, big business openly sought to control markets. Under CEO Charles Coffin and his successors, GE did the same. During the first half of this century, growing up in industries of its own creation—from light bulbs to electrical products—GE became accustomed to pushing the Sherman antitrust rules to their limits.

GE settled its first antitrust case in 1911, agreeing not to conceal its ownership of subsidiaries. In 1924, representatives of GE, Philips, and several other leading electrical companies met in Paris to divvy up market shares around the world; GE's CEO at the time, Gerard Swope, was the fellow who blamed the Great Depression on "excessive competition." Though the cartel, known as Phoebus, was not illegal under the laws of that era, it probably would not pass muster today. During the 1940s, GE was involved in thirteen antitrust cases; once the war ended, Electric Charlie Wilson, then CEO, negotiated a deal in which GE signed consent decrees but avoided the breakup of its lighting business.

There's no evidence that any of GE's CEOs ever committed or authorized wrongdoing. But by 1961, when the Justice Department brought GE's great antitrust scandal to an end, some GEers evidently assumed high-level managers would "wink" at crimes that benefited GE's bottom line. The result was a humiliating price-fixing scandal that finally shocked GE out of its complacency. In its 1961 story about the scandal, entitled "The Incredible Electrical Conspiracy," *Fortune* quoted a GE executive who remarked, "Sure, collusion was illegal, but it wasn't *unethical.*"

That conspiracy was the U.S. electrical industry's dimwitted response to chronic overcapacity. Companies could have addressed the underlying business issues by closing factories, improving products, or consistently competing on price. Instead, executives from many of the major outfits selling such products as industrial circuit breakers—including GE, Westinghouse, and Allis-Chalmers—tried to eliminate the risks of competition. The companies agreed on the U.S. market shares each would maintain for each product; GE's usually was the largest. The conspirators gathered two or three times monthly, often in hotel rooms, to decide which bids each company would be allowed to win. They swapped supposedly confidential pricing information, agreeing in advance on the amount of the winning bid on each particular project.

These meetings—dubbed "choir practices" by the conspirators—fundamentally corrupted the electrical business. Customers relied on the prices submitted in sealed bids to select the best supplier for each contract, and the bidding process was the market's primary means of encouraging competitive pricing. When every supplier but one intentionally submitted bids set too high to win, the ritual became meaningless.

In the end, seven GE executives went to jail and twenty-four received suspended sentences. CEO Ralph Cordiner was never formally accused of participating in the scheme, but his reputation had to be diminished by the scandal.

The Great Electrical Conspiracy taught GEers a harsh but necessary lesson: Never again could employees expect the company to wink at wrongdoing.

Welch sees high ethical standards as a business essential: "In the end," he says, "integrity is all you've got."

His approach to ethical issues suggests the lingering influence of his religious upbringing. Welch says he remained a "passionate" Catholic well into his grad school years; as a mature man he still seems to believe in unambiguous distinctions between right and wrong. Whenever an employee's actions has put GE on the wrong side of the law, he has hastened to cooperate with investigators, admit guilt, and take prompt corrective actions. Those corporate *mea culpas* have served the company well. In the time-card case and others, candor and a determination to ally GE with the forces of law have enabled GE to emerge with a minimum of agony.

The CEO seems to have trouble understanding antisocial acts. Honest himself, he's perplexed when others are not. He has no sympathy for anyone who responds to his ever-escalating demands for performance by resorting to crime. Indeed, he argues that the people who cheat are not doing it for competitive reasons. "Excellence and competitiveness are totally compatible with honesty and integrity," he asserts. "The A student, the four-minute miler, the high-jump record holder—all strong winners—can achieve those results without resorting to cheating. People who cheat are simply weak."

In many countries outside the United States, of course, the integrity issue is complicated by the prevalence of bribery. In accordance with U.S. law, GE policy prohibits the payment of bribes. In Germany, by contrast, corporations can claim tax deductions for the "facilitating" payments they pay abroad. Welch insists GE's strict rules don't make it less competitive:

> In a global business, you can win without bribes. But you better have technology. That's why we win in businesses like turbines, because we have the best gas turbine. You've got to be the low-priced supplier, but in almost all cases, if you have quality, price, and technology, you win—and nobody can sleazeball you.

During Welch's tenure, GEers' transgressions have occurred in defense businesses. In the Reagan era, as military spending surged, defense contracts became a central and fast-growing source of profits. To some individuals, the temptation to cheat must have seemed almost irresistible, as trillions of taxpayer dollars changed hands.

The 1985 time-card scandal was the first significant ethical challenge of Welch's twenty-five-year GE career. GE Re-Entry Systems was making a new nose cone for the Air Force's Minuteman missile. Federal prosecutors in Philadelphia charged it with 108 counts of criminal fraud. The indictment alleged that GE managers had altered workers' time cards, creating improper charges totaling $800,000.

Two days after the indictment was filed, Air Force Secretary Verne Orr suspended GE, then the No. 4 U.S. defense contractor, from doing business with the U.S. government. That decision might have caused big trouble for GE: Government work provided nearly one-fifth of its revenues. For mischarges that added up to less than $1 million, the company stood to lose over $5 billion of annual revenues.

The trouble occurred in a tiny corner of GE. In 1985, General Electric was producing a wide variety of military equipment, such as F-101 jet engines and Phalanx seaborne radar. Re-Entry Systems, where the crimes occurred, was a small part of GE Space Systems, based in historic Valley Forge, Pennsylvania; Space Systems produced just 3% of GE's total sales. Re-Entry Systems had won Air Force contracts to design, produce, and test the new Mark 12A nose cone, whose electronic innards steer the atomic warheads of Minuteman missiles as they plunge back into the earth's atmosphere from space. As it happened, GE's work went over budget, producing estimated losses of $3 million. According to the Philadelphia indictment, middle managers at Re-Entry Systems doctored the time cards that hourly workers submitted, misrepresenting production or testing charges as design work. The alleged falsification reduced GE's losses. Since the proceeds from the mischarges went into GE's coffers instead of the employees' pockets, the company became legally liable.

The accused managers never claimed anyone had told them to do it. Nor did they get a cent for themselves. The motivation for the mischarges, presumably, was to limit the deficits caused by the cost overruns in order to avoid career damage. Ultimately, one manager pleaded guilty; others were acquitted in court.

By then, GE had already been punished. Through the severe penalty Secretary Orr imposed, the company suddenly lost the right to sell *any* product—even light bulbs—to any government entity, from the National Weather Service to the Veterans Administration. GE's reputation and a lot of its jobs were on the line.

Two challenges faced GE: the immediate financial, legal, and public-relations crises; and, just as important, the long-term need to somehow raise employees' awareness of the need for high ethical standards.

The CEO's first goal was to quickly regain control over GE's destiny. A brief investigation convinced him that GE could be in the wrong. When the government attacked, he refused to accept the role of adversary; instead, he allied GE with its accusers, and thereby won the trust of government officials. GE cooperated with federal investigators and accepted responsibility for the acts of its misguided employees. Once Welch ascertained that GE had indeed mischarged the government, the company repaid the $800,000. And the day after one of its employees finally admitted wrongdoing, GE pleaded guilty to felony charges.

Less than three weeks after the indictment, Welch personally called on Orr, presenting a comprehensive proposal for cleaning up the mess and preventing such failures in the future. Welch promised to deliver progress reports to Secretary Orr in person every month. He created a top-level review board within GE to oversee compliance, and appointed GE's ombudsman to investigate reports of misconduct.

In private, Welch warned Orr that cleaning up the defense industry would take years. The CEO subsequently enlisted seventeen other defense company leaders to form a new organization called the Defense Industry Initiative on Business Ethics and Conduct. The group—which later expanded to over fifty companies—drew up a long-overdue code of ethics for the defense industry. It also required an annual audit of each member's compliance by an independent public accounting firm.

On the level of damage control, Welch's efforts were almost completely successful. The day after his first meeting with Orr, the U.S. government began buying GE products again. Only Space Systems remained ostracized, for a total of five months—a tolerable penalty, and one that Welch has said was well deserved. As he told shareholders that year, the suspension had "no significant financial impact."

The most enduring effect of the time-card episode is GE's more rigorous and systematic approach to ethics. Part of the deal it struck with the government was a comprehensive new policy statement that created a clear chain of responsibility for any wrongdoing at GE. Since 1985 the corporation has held its managers accountable for "inadequate leadership and lack of diligence" that enables subordinates to engage in improper activities. Compliance issues have become part of job descriptions and performance evaluations. And nearly every Crotonville course added a section on ethics as a prerequisite to success.

As the CEO recently reminded an audience of GE executives:

> On the question of integrity and company policy, the message is very clear. You are responsible for your organization's behavior. We will not shoot the Indians and let the chiefs go. There's no place in this company for any behavior by anyone that could condone or give the implication of condoning any violation.

Although his public statements remained cautiously moderate, in his internal speeches and discussions with GE managers Welch was outspoken about defense procurement. He described a system grounded for too many years in too close a relationship between the government and defense contractors.

He made it clear that GE would not tolerate anything less than "100% ethical behavior."

Welch used every available medium to transmit the message to employees. As he explains, "You can't audit integrity into a system any more than you can inspect quality into a machine. Where you *can* make a difference is by changing the culture, by tireless, forceful leadership that won't tolerate winking, rule-bending, or looking the other way." In memos and speeches, Welch explained the new attitude; for reinforcement, GE created new training procedures, distributed posters, and even made new time cards for some businesses with the words *Mischarging Is Illegal* printed in boldface.

During discussions at Crotonville shortly after the 1985 incident, managers from defense-related businesses frequently groused to Welch, "When are we going to get the government off our backs?"

His stern reply usually went like this: *You have lost your right to not have the government on your back. The system failed, there was dishonesty, and both the government and GE will stay on your back until we clean up this mess.*

The best expression of GE's new cut-the-crap approach to ethics was Welch's mirror test. He'd ask GEers, *Can you look in the mirror every day and feel proud of what you are doing?* Instead of writing down lots of rules, or debating fine points in legalese, he used that one simple question to address the conscience of every individual GE employee directly. It is characteristic of his leadership, which consistently appeals to individual responsibility, that he assumes every person not only has a conscience but cares about its dictates.

To put GE's transgressions into perspective, Welch often compared the corporation to Newark, New Jersey, and St. Paul, Minnesota, cities with populations about the same size as GE's: In a typical year, Newark's 1,000-person police force must cope with roughly 100 murders, 300 rapes, 4,300 assaults, and 12,500 thefts. Statistics from St. Paul tell a story almost as grim.

Argued the CEO, "It's utterly naive and ludicrous to believe that we have hired the only 300,000 people in the world who won't steal or cheat or take drugs or do a lot of other things."

In May 1985, a couple of days after GE pleaded guilty to the time-card fraud, Welch addressed a group of 110 senior GE managers. He explained the background of the guilty plea, and then responded to comments from his audience. When someone expressed contempt for the problems at Re-Entry Systems, Welch got angry:

> Before you point your finger, look in the mirror at yourselves. We've all got to take a much closer look at the way we behave. I'm tired of going to the gym at headquarters and finding that someone has stolen the comb from the locker room. The mirror test is a daily test for every one of us.

He believes corporate cultures will change in response to clearly articulated ideas—if the ideas are endlessly repeated, and backed by consistent action. The mirror test is a simple and lucid idea, he hasn't been shy about repeating it. Just as important, Welch has responded to each successive ethical challenge in essentially the same way.

Perhaps the clearest example is the Kidder Peabody insider trading case. In 1986, GE bought the Wall Street investment bank. Six months later, a former Kidder banker named Martin Siegel confessed that he had engaged in criminal insider trading with arbitrageur Ivan Boesky, in return for suitcases stuffed with cash. Siegel's revelations, melodramatic and pitiful by turns, bolstered the government investigations that resulted in the jailing of Ivan Boesky and Michael Milken, then Drexel Burnham Lambert's overlord of junk bonds.

Along the way, Siegel's actions implicated Kidder Peabody; GE, having acquired the Wall Street firm, was stuck with legal responsibility for Kidder's crimes.

Enter Larry Bossidy, then GE's vice chairman. Beefy, brilliant, and blunt-talking, he so closely matched his boss in attitudes and skills that one GE director described him as "Jack Welch, Jr." Bossidy launched an investigation of Kidder's potential vulnerability to civil and criminal charges.

Quickly concluding that the firm "had no choice" but to settle, he helped negotiate agreements with both the SEC and U.S. Attorney Rudolph Giuliani. Kidder did not admit or deny guilt, but agreed to pay fines of more than $25 million. In addition, GE made management changes at Kidder that ravaged morale at the investment bank, but saved it from destruction. Several years later, the firm was enjoying unprecedented profitability.

As in the time-card case, the crisis quickly passed. The government was satisfied, the press portrayed GE as unwise but honorable—and the company reinforced its unyielding insistence on ethical behavior.

Since GE is an organization of human beings—fallible by nature, and eternally subject to temptation—a certain amount of lawbreaking is almost inevitable. But that does not make any wrongdoing acceptable.

David Calhoun, the corporate vice president in charge of GE's audit staff, regularly reports on wrongdoing by GEers to the audit committee of the board of directors. His data cover all allegations from all sources, and range from trivial personal grievances to potentially significant ethical violations. The number of reports has been rising since 1985, as GE's ethics education programs have taken hold; the company regards them as a healthy demonstration that the reporting system is working. Roughly a quarter of the 1992 reports concerned violations of GE's ethics policy. GE's internal investigations determined that only two of those violations were "both significant and intentional." The government defines "significant" violations with specific criteria such as impact of at least $25,000.

GE policy requires the disclosure of its violations, including all significant ones, to the government.

To the degree that it is rooted in human nature, employee misbehavior lies beyond the reach of any corporate ethics program. The example of General Electric illustrates the difficulties such programs face. Some people simply can't cope with our society's schizophrenic system of rewards and punishments. On the one hand, we tell people they've got to win; on the other we insist they play fair.

GEers are as subject as any to that double bind: Their CEO creates fierce profit pressure, but also insists, "It is better that profits be lost than corners cut or rules bent." No GEer has any reason to believe that the company will "wink" at transgressions. Promptly repaying overcharges, admitting guilt, and siding with the forces of law at every opportunity serve as visible demonstrations that GE's commitment to ethics is real. But the insistence on performance is real, too.

This is the "no-wink paradox." Some people are just incapable of working it out for themselves—and not only at GE. The paradox explains why some corporate employees break the law, why some Olympic athletes take drugs, why some politicians accept illegal campaign contributions. Losers who feel compelled to win can convince themselves that wrong is right. Dealing with such people remains one of the great challenges of management.

Welch's mirror test shows a path through the morass of corporate ethics that has the virtues of simplicity, honesty, and common sense. But that approach depends on his own strong personal convictions—values and beliefs that other executives may not share. The challenge for all corporations is to find management systems to ensure that employees live up to high standards of integrity.

As Welch concedes, he is still searching. GE continues to experiment with new methods, such as interactive videos, to get the integrity message through to employees. And Welch personally spends a half day per year with each of GE's thirteen businesses reviewing their compliance with GE's ethics policy. On international trips, he conducts compliance reviews with local GE managers in every country he visits. Obviously, he'll never get 275,000 people to behave impeccably at all times— but it won't be for lack of trying.

Chapter Ten

The Turning Point

Sometime in 1985, GE's progress seemed to stall. When I started consulting there, after a turbulent half decade of Welch's leadership, many GEers seemed exhausted, emotionally drained. I observed what I saw as a spreading malaise that, unchecked, might have destroyed the very spirit of the GE revolution.

The danger stemmed more from such human imponderables as fatigue, anxiety, and hurt feelings than from any tangible difficulty in operations or finance. Welch was demanding much more of employees than dutiful compliance with his ideas: He needed people as zestfully committed as he was.

Many of them still weren't. Far from it. This was the era, remember, when some of the GEers attending Crotonville were calling their CEO an "asshole."

So relentlessly upbeat is Welch that he now denies GE

stopped making headway in 1985. "I never felt that," he recently told me.

> I think you're dead wrong. You came out into Crotonville, a place where ferment is constant, where complaints and concerns and objections are not only encouraged, but expected, and you concluded the company's morale was a disaster. It simply wasn't.
>
> Of course there was some anger and resistance and fatigue in 1985. It was there in 1982 and it will always be there. Massive change in a company of hundreds of thousands of people does not come without it. But we never lost momentum, even in a year when the economy was in the tank.
>
> If your actions get results, you keep getting satisfaction, and so your self-confidence builds. As your self-confidence builds, you try more—and the feedback generally gets better and better. That's been the experience of all my years here.

Welch and I will always disagree on the depth of resistance in 1985. We had different vantage points. At Crotonville and in workshops for managers, I was close to the pain, exhaustion, and frustration that were inevitable in times of radical change. Welch saw the bigger picture: The flow of change since 1981, and GE's long-term momentum. Besides, he is an optimist who characteristically describes the glass as half-full, never half-empty.

There's no denying that the pace of GE's financial gains slowed dramatically around 1985. The U.S. economy turned sluggish that year, slowing sales companywide. As a result, corporate net income increased just 2% that year, versus an average annual gain of nearly 11% since Welch had become CEO. He points out, correctly, that GE's small earnings gain in 1985 outpaced the S & P 500, whose earnings dropped 12% that year.

Productivity also slowed: By 1983 GE had nudged its rate roughly from 2% to 2.5%—but then it plateaued. GE was still far below the 6% productivity rate that Welch regarded as necessary for effective competition against its global competitors.

Some GEers were demoralized by the company's recently acknowledged flop in factory automation—the "$30 billion industry" that never was. Symbolically, automation had become GE's best hope of building an important new business from scratch. Creating a new venture big enough to budge GE, whose revenues topped $29 billion in 1985, now began to seem almost impossible. Even Welch became resigned to adding new lines primarily by acquisition.

But GE wasn't buying much, either—which reinforced the impression that GE's sails were luffing. Welch had been making good on his promise to fix, close, or sell any businesses that didn't fit GE's strategy: By the end of 1985, the company had unloaded operations worth $5.4 billion. So far so good, but GE hadn't reinvested all that money in productive assets. Indeed, despite a few large acquisitions such as Employers Reinsurance the corporate balance sheet still showed $2.5 billion of cash.

The takeover market was white-hot in those days, with acquired companies routinely fetching 50% more than their stock was worth before a bidder approached. GE was reluctant to fork over premiums of that size. So even though GE staffers considered some 6,000 potential acquisition candidates, and then winnowed their list to the best 100 or so, Welch couldn't find many companies he was willing to buy.

Among the manic dealmakers of the mid-1980s, General Electric seemed awkward, even frumpy. It was as if GE insisted on dancing an old-fashioned fox-trot when everybody else was rocking out. In the era of down-and-dirty junk bonds, Welch clung to GE's impeccable AAA debt rating; while hostile takeovers were becoming commonplace, he insisted on friendly deals. And when other CEOs were throwing shareholder money around as if it were worthless—practically lighting their cigars with the stuff—Welch fretted about overpaying for assets. Today he seems wise, but at the time, some thought him a wimp.

To any GEer inclined to resist Welch, the bloodletting of the early 1980s—the nonstop layoffs, factory closings, and asset sales—had become a call to arms. At Crotonville, I talked to many GE managers who seriously believed their CEO was ruining the company. The 1984 "toughest bosses" story only bolstered their case; Welch says it marked one of the worst moments in his career.

GE's naysayers regarded the defense industry scandal of 1985 as the final proof that their company was falling apart. In their view, GE's famous control systems hadn't worked, and Welch had betrayed loyal employees by failing to stand up to the government. The result was that their proud corporation had suffered its worst public humiliation since the electrical-conspiracy trials of the early 1960s.

The defense scandal became what management theorists March and Cohen call a "garbage event"—an incident that causes people to focus on their bad feelings. In emotional terms, it seemed to give any depressive on the GE payroll ample reason to conclude that the company was going to hell. So instead of experiencing snowballing enthusiasm, many employees felt miserable about working for GE.

At Crotonville, I noticed a marked increase in signs of unrest. Managers were spending more time complaining, particularly about the CEO. GEers increasingly characterized Welch as "heartless," a man with "brass balls." Frightening, unfounded rumors spread wildly. I can't tell you how often I heard that the GE board was demanding Welch's resignation. People told baseless stories about Welch's ruthlessness as a hockey player, alleging that he spent more time in the penalty box than anyone else on his high school team.

Thus my view that 1985 was a hard year for GE. As if aware that defeat was inevitable, the forces of resistance came out of hiding to make their last, futile efforts to block the GE revolution. Welch's job was never at risk, though: The price of GE's stock had been increasing at a 25% annual rate since Welch took office.

In 1984, Welch commissioned a survey of GE's top several hundred officers, asking them how they viewed the company. I recall that when the results came back the following year, they conveyed the mixed feelings and frustration felt by many of these managers. Characteristically, Welch used the negative data to help refine his message, but interpreted the survey as a demonstration that GE was making progress.

GEers needed something powerful enough to cause a complete shift in mood; if GE had been a person, you'd have been tempted to throw a bucket of cold water in its face.

The CEO did the only thing he could: He persevered. And before too much longer, he found a way to bring GE back to life.

Welch wasn't exactly gloomy in 1985—he's not the type—but as the months dragged on and the problems piled up, he struck me as shorter-tempered, more obsessive, noticeably less exuberant than usual. Then, a couple of weeks before Christmas, I found myself walking past his office at headquarters. The shirt-sleeved CEO was visible from the corridor, cracking jokes with his two secretaries at the time, Helga and Sue. I immediately noticed the change of mood: Welch's irrepressible glee was back. He turned to greet me as I passed, and his blue eyes sparkled as he grinned.

I didn't know it, but GE had just agreed to buy RCA for $6.3 billion in cash. A big, bold, attention-grabbing deal, this transaction became the biggest nonoil acquisition to date—and the emotional inspiration that GEers desperately needed. Suddenly, their company was back in the game, playing to win.

Welch, of course, had been playing to win all along, but his efforts had been concealed from public view. When Ted Turner briefly threatened a hostile takeover of CBS in the spring of 1985, GE privately offered to protect CBS through a friendly "white knight" deal. Nothing came of that: Turner ended up buying the MGM-UA film company, and CBS eventually fell into the tight grasp of Laurence Tisch, the tough-minded billionaire who also controls Loews Corp.

But the CEO had discovered broadcasting, which in 1985 was still one of the richest businesses in the world. Largely thanks to NBC, the top-rated TV network and the owner of a money-minting string of television and radio stations, RCA was producing $300 million of cash annually. Much of that came from the hugely popular "Cosby Show." Hungry for a deal substantial enough to affect GE's financial performance, Welch began breakfasting regularly with Felix Rohatyn of Lazard Freres, one of New York's most respected investment bankers. According to the *New York Times,* Welch kept pressing Rohatyn to set up a meeting with RCA Chairman Thornton Bradshaw.

On November 6, Rohatyn invited Bradshaw and Welch to cocktails at his Park Avenue apartment. According to Welch, they discussed U.S. competitiveness, the Japanese—everything but the GE-RCA deal that was on their minds. "We both thought we knew what we were talking about," he says.

One month later, he called the RCA chairman. Bradshaw invited him to a tête-à-tête in Bradshaw's apartment at the Dorset Hotel, a few blocks from RCA's Rockefeller Center headquarters. There Welch informed his fellow chairman that GE was offering to buy RCA for $61 per share in cash, a substantial premium over RCA's $47 market price. In less than a week, they had a deal.

The press loved the transaction. Front-page stories nationwide certainly didn't portray Welch as frumpy. He had moved quickly many times before—negotiating the Employers Reinsurance deal in a single day, for instance—but this time he got public credit. GE presented the business combination as a patriotic victory, arguing that the GE-RCA merger would "help improve America's competitiveness in world markets"— i.e., against the Japanese. Raved a *Washington Post* headline: "MERGER TO CREATE GLOBAL POWERHOUSE."

Time magazine described the deal as a "reunion of technological titans." In 1919, a few years after buying the U.S. rights to Guglielmo Marconi's radio technology, GE created the Radio Corporation of America. RCA did not become an independent company until 1933, when GE sold it under threat of antitrust litigation.

Fifty-two years later, RCA and GE still seemed to belong together. RCA, with 85,000 employees and 1985 revenues of $10.1 billion, increased its new parent's size by one-third, bumping it from No. 10 to No. 6 on the Fortune 500. Though ranked only No. 23 among U.S. military contractors, RCA got some 15% of its sales from defense work. To a remarkable degree, RCA's products complemented GE's: In radar, for example, RCA produced seaborne equipment, whereas GE's was used on land. GE made military satellites; RCA's were civilian. Its TV-set business, though weak, bolstered GE's. The broadcasting operation strengthened GE's position in services. And, as Wall Street investment analysts immediately recognized, the NBC network's cash flow was prodigious enough all by itself to justify the entire acquisition financially.

The parts that didn't fit soon would be sold, quickly reducing the cost of buying RCA by $1.4 billion, or one-fifth of the purchase price. Among the RCA businesses GE unloaded were RCA Records, Coronet Carpets, and the Nacolah Life Insurance business.

Financially, the RCA deal was a home run, to use one of Welch's favorite expressions. He says GE's discounted rate of return from RCA has averaged 14% annually. NBC alone produced $1.9 billion of cash during its first six years under GE ownership. More recently, NBC has dropped to third place in the ratings, behind CBS and ABC; though still profitable, it's no longer a gusher.

Over the years, RCA has created its share of minor headaches for GE, as well. As the new head of NBC, Bob Wright alienated broadcasters. He couldn't help noticing that the inexplicably complacent network TV industry had been losing viewers for years to cable, videocassettes, and other competition. David Letterman, the irreverent host of NBC's "Late Night" talk show, routinely described his new corporate masters as "knuckleheads." And GE horrified sentimentalists in the U.S. press once again when it swapped the consumer electronics business to Thomson S.A. for the French company's medical-imaging unit in 1987.

The greater difficulty was dealing with RCA's bureaucratic traditions and its many employees. The CEO worked hard to ensure that RCA people got equitable treatment, and its top executives initially did well at GE. In every business where GE and RCA combined their separate operations into a single unit—such as consumer electronics, semiconductors, radar, and communication services—an RCA executive won the leadership job. But GE subsequently sold semiconductors and consumer electronics. By 1993, one member of the Corporate Executive Council hailed from RCA: Eugene Murphy, the head of Aircraft Engines.

Thousands of lower-ranking people from RCA soon left GE. By 1988 GE had fewer people on its payroll than it had the year before it bought RCA. Many of those who left ended up working for other companies, when GE sold the businesses for which they worked. Some of the remainder stayed on as GE employees; many others lost their jobs.

The closing of the RCA deal in 1986 marked the end of Act I of the GE revolution. By 1986 the fusty, bureaucratic company Welch had inherited no longer existed. The weak businesses, the huge staffs, the padded budgets—all were gone.

Exercising his power as CEO to the fullest, Welch had cleared away most of the obstacles in GE's path.

As yet, though, he hadn't clearly defined the new GE he hoped to build. Welch's vision still seemed too amorphous to win the gung-ho allegiance of employees. Clarifying the vision, and winning converts, would be the work of Act II.

The RCA deal reenergized Welch and marked a turning point in the GE revolution. But despite the CEO's enthusiasm, GE still had a long way to go. Evidence of how much the corporate culture still needed to change was a video that David Letterman showed on "Late Night." It captures the pathos of a transformation that led so many thousands of people to fear that they might soon lose their jobs.

Shortly after General Electric announced that it would buy RCA, Letterman visited the old GE building in New York City with a camera crew. The resulting videotape, broadcast to a national audience, is among the funniest send-ups of uptight corporations I've seen.

Letterman introduced the segment from his desk:

> You never know what you're in for when you get a brand-new boss. So when General Electric bought this company, RCA and NBC, I thought I would drop by the GE building here in midtown Manhattan, meet my new employers, kind of, you know, get things off on the right foot.

Then he cut to the videotape: Wearing a baseball jacket and carrying a large, cellophane-wrapped basket of fruit in both hands, Letterman addressed the camera, in his patented folksy deadpan, as he walked down Lexington Avenue:

> Sometime in August, I guess, the takeover will be complete, and we're all now getting a little curious as to what kind of effect it's going to have on NBC as we know it today—the programming and, I guess, specifically, how is

it going to influence me? And what I'm really trying to get at here is, am I going to have a job? So this is the General Electric building, and I have a little gift, and we thought: What the heck? Let's just drop in and say hello, just see how it's going. They can't object to that, can they?

At the doorway of GE's former headquarters, Letterman was greeted not by a person but by a disembodied voice from a loudspeaker: "This is not a building to film in," said the unseen security guard. "Clear the front of the GE building, please."

"Yes, sir," said Letterman. "We just wanted to drop off a little fruit basket and say hello to the folks on the board of directors."

A woman stepped through the revolving doors, flanked by a male security guard. "I'm not sure you're able to do this," she warned. "We haven't gotten any authorization."

"You mean we need authorization to drop off a fruit basket?" Letterman asked. He faced the camera. "Oh, this is going to be fun to work with these people, isn't it? To drop off a fruit basket you need paperwork."

After some more chat, Letterman faced the camera again. "I'll just go on in and see what happens." He and the crew jostled their way through the revolving door.

Inside, a scowling security officer in a suit accosted them. "I'm going to ask you to turn the cameras off, please," he said.

Letterman gave the man a big, toothy grin and stuck out his hand. "Okay," he said. Letterman presented the classic mask of corporate passive resistance: a tone of cheerful acquiescence unaccompanied by any effort to comply with requests. The cameras kept rolling. "We just wanted to drop off this basket of fruit—"

The officer started to shake hands, but abruptly pulled his hand away, jabbing his thumb up in the air instead. "Shut off the camera, please," he insisted.

The impasse ended when the security officer blocked the

lens with his hand and (as far as the viewers could tell) threw them out of the building.

That night the GE videotape became the highlight of Letterman's show. "Maybe you didn't realize that we got to see a glimpse of the official General Electric handshake," he chortled. Then Letterman presented, in slow motion, the image of the "security gentleman," as he called him, almost shaking the talk show host's hand but then evading contact. Letterman showed the "GE handshake" again and again, while crowing in voiceover.

GE's reaction to the spectacle demonstrated how far the company had progressed since Welch became CEO. Instead of ignoring or condemning it, Welch brought a copy of the videotape to the GE boardroom, where he showed it to the assembled directors. He says they found it hilarious. "It was fun," he remembers. "We'd tease the guard when we went in the building—give him the 'GE handshake.' "

Since the directors had all seen it, I figured it was okay to show the tape at Crotonville. I've used it ever since, to demonstrate the disastrous effects of the bureaucratic mind-set. Whether he likes it or not, David Letterman has become a regular part of the Crotonville curriculum.

Act Two

THE VISION

Chapter Eleven

Crotonville

W elch's vision for GE hasn't changed much since his days at Plastics, but by the mid-1980s he still hadn't expressed it powerfully or clearly enough to win over GEers. Before the CEO could hope to change the corporate culture, he had to refine his message and implant it in people's minds. Crotonville, which provided advanced training to 10,000 GE executives per year, was the logical place to start.

In 1985, I signed on for a two-year stint as manager of GE's Management Development Institute, overlooking the Hudson River. The new job put me in charge of GE's management education worldwide. My assignment: to accelerate the transformation of Crotonville, so Crotonville could help transform GE. I reported to Jim Baughman; after running Crotonville for five years, and beginning the process of change there, he'd been promoted to head of organizational planning, management development, and executive compensation.

Baughman challenged me to work with him and the Crotonville team to lead an even more radical transformation.

By the time I accepted the job, I'd been consulting for GE long enough to know that I had to establish my credibility fast, particularly since I was an academic who was parachuting in for just two years. GE's performance-driven culture is so powerful that when you start a new job as a manager, you want to demonstrate your self-confidence and leadership right away, to establish your credibility with your fellow workers. I felt I had just one turn at bat—and I'd better hit a home run. If I missed, I feared, GEers would lose respect for me, maybe forever. My boss might not give me the "air cover" I'd need to get budgets approved and keep the corporate office off my back. My subordinates might ignore my orders and find ways to make me look bad.

The pressure was exhilarating and scary—and not only for me. Baughman, who knew better than anyone what the job entailed, understood that he was taking a big risk by hiring an outsider to lead an institution as crucial as Crotonville. He tells me that Welch and Jack Peiffer, the head of the Executive Management Staff, were worried, too. We all decided to take the risk.

The CEO himself had interviewed me for the job—twice—and his expectations were extremely high. He was relying heavily on the police, the media, and the schools, and counted Crotonville among his principal instruments of change.

Hiring me was one of many expressions of the CEO's intense interest in Crotonville. While cutting costs almost everywhere else, GE was spending $45 million on new buildings and improvements there—a decision that, in the context of so much cost-cutting, outraged some GEers. Welch stuck to his decision despite the protests: He insists that investing in sources of future productivity, such as management training, is entirely consistent with running a lean organization. GE regularly approved the institution's hefty annual budget, even though the return on that investment was impossible to calculate.

The CEO was confident the payoff would come. A devotee of creative ferment, he saw Crotonville as a laboratory to create a new kind of management, and a place to produce new ideas. He wanted "action learning" based on solving real, pending business problems. He wanted participants to learn teamwork skills, while developing companywide networks of contacts to aid them throughout their GE careers.

Above all, he wanted Crotonville to provide a wide-open channel of communication between GE's top management and the more junior employees taking courses. Welch didn't simply want to lecture—he also wanted to listen. "That's how we get the pulse of the organization," he says.

His needs inspired unprecedented candor. To promote the no-holds-barred debating style that Welch sees as the best way to "fertilize ideas," the Crotonville team had to build on what Baughman had done, eliminating any remaining constraints of rank and hierarchy from an institution whose cultural heritage traditionally had reinforced them.

Welch also expected Crotonville to indoctrinate managers in GE's new values, from constructive conflict to integrity to "ownership." So Crotonville had to become deliberately evangelical, its every graduate a missionary capable of spreading the word to the larger organization. As Welch had told Baughman, "I want Crotonville to be part of the glue that holds GE together."

In addition to the pressure from Fairfield and from the heads of GE businesses, I faced a challenge below. Knowing I couldn't accomplish anything substantial by myself, I set out to build a team, but some on my staff were ready to resist. Baughman had assured me that the folks at Crotonville were delighted I'd been hired. No doubt they'd told him that, but it simply wasn't true.

The support staff, administrators, trainers, and other members of the Crotonville organization were a microcosm of the GE work force. Proud of their accomplishments, they saw themselves as contributors to a very successful operation that didn't need fixing. Many viewed me with skepticism, and some saw me as an interloper and a threat. Some of the highest-ranking Crotonville staffers had to struggle hard to follow my leadership despite harboring deeply ambivalent feelings about me.

Even though Baughman had brought in many new staffers while running Crotonville, some people there struck me as more focused on Crotonville's glorious history than its future. Crotonville had been the corporate world's first major in-house business school, and it remains the most prestigious. Its success spawned imitators around the globe, from IBM's Sands Point School to Hitachi's Management Development Institute in Japan.

By defining, codifying, and teaching GE's most effective techniques, Crotonville had greatly enhanced the company's reputation as a leader in management science. It popularized any number of breakthrough ideas, including strategic planning and management by objective. The very idea of training executives as general managers, which today seems as basic as brushing your teeth, began there in the 1950s.

At first, Crotonville was an effective instrument of change. By the late 1970s, however, Crotonville's mission was no longer clear. The institution began to lose touch with some of its customers, the GE businesses that were sending participants to courses. Unlike a profit and loss center, Crotonville was not clearly accountable to anyone, and its performance seemed impossible to measure. The staff drifted into the habit of comparing Crotonville's other schools. As a result, the courses— which were mostly taught by leading academics from major universities—gradually became more generic and less relevant to GE.

My modest legacy to GE is the set of developmental processes I helped introduce at Crotonville. I teach people how to change large organizations radically. One of my inspirations was political historian James MacGregor Burns, who defined the term "transformational leadership." This is leadership that transcends the mcrc management of what already exists, to create something fundamentally new. The field itself is new, a study not of heroes, but of the ways ordinary people can bring institutions through the convulsions of dramatic change. A goal is to foster leaders who can address human emotions and values—the "soft" issues, in B-school parlance—as well as the traditional "hard" issues of market share and financial performance.

Over the years, with substantial borrowings from others, I've developed an instructional stagecraft designed to transform students or workshop participants into effective agents of change. The key is to put people at risk—intellectually, emotionally, and at times even physically—so they can experience the personal breakthroughs that enable them to change.

The challenge of the new Crotonville team was to clear away the last remnants of the old methods while developing programs that exemplified GE's new ideas. Instead of helping people become leaders, conventional programs usually teach them how to execute orders. The emphasis is on skills training and cognitive development—learning new ways to think about problems. That's fine as far as it goes, but it's superficial.

Change can be terrifying. Anyone who hopes to revolutionize an entire organization had better know how to cope with change on the personal level. You can't teach that with case studies or books; it comes from experience. To provide participants with that experience in a way that's safe, reliable, and cost-efficient, we drew on a wide variety of disciplines and techniques, from academic social psychology to the "compressed action learning" of Outward Bound training.

Adults learn best in conditions of moderate stress, so conflict and discomfort are essential parts of the process. Outward Bound brilliantly shows the way: They'll take deskbound executives, give them forty-five minutes of training in rock-climbing techniques, and then order them to rappel down a sheer, hundred-foot granite cliff—and climb right back up. To the executives, the assignment seems life-threatening. It isn't—safety measures include alert instructors and stout ropes to halt any slip—but the illusion of great risk spurs performance and transforms learning into a life experience.

Action workshops can achieve similar effects even in conventional corporate surroundings. The trick is putting participants to work on real business issues, with measurable results. The managers who take these programs arrive in teams, each sent by its employer with an assignment to solve an actual, pending problem. For instance one team had to figure out how to patch up the relationship with a major Japanese supplier infuriated by their business's frequently changing product specifications.

The stakes are clearly defined. By the end of a workshop, each team must present its proposals to its boss, for rejection or implementation. If the ideas are good, they can be put to use at once. To add rigor to the process, GE surveys the boss, colleagues, and subordinates of each workshop participant, once before the session begins, and again a couple of months after it ends. The feedback from these assessments also helps participants learn about themselves and develop as leaders.

The teamwork aspect of this training is not just fun and games: Participants feel that if their team's proposals stink, the career of every member might be hurt. So people learn to work together—some for the first time in their lives. And when the participants return to normal work, they remain part of the team they formed in class. Working together as a group, the team members are far likelier to change their organization than any individual would be.

Properly run, such workshops can serve usefully as miniature corporate think tanks. By generating plans and ideas that actually get used, the learning center vastly increases its ability to influence organizational change directly.

That's the ultimate goal. Though I've spent most of my

career in academe, I see myself not as a professor, but as a professional agent of change. I suppose I formed my world view during the activist 1960s, when everybody wanted to change the world. I earned a Ph.D. in social psychology at Columbia, writing my thesis on different types of change agents. Among them were community organizer Saul Alinsky, consultants with McKinsey & Co., activists working with Ralph Nader, members of the Black Panther party, and radical anarchists. The result was a typology of change agents, based on their values, how they conceptualized organization, and their methods—which ranged from linear programming to investigative studies to setting bombs.

After teaching at Columbia, I moved on to the University of Michigan's business school, where I remain a professor of organizational behavior and director of the Global Leadership Program. That is a five-week, action-learning experience for high-level executives that includes country-assessment trips to Russia, China, India, or Brazil. I've maintained a sideline as a corporate consultant, staying directly involved in the process of transforming organizations. During my years at Crotonville, I took a leave of absence from my university post.

Crotonville was a full-time job.

Right after I arrived at Crotonville in September 1985, I met with my new team to discuss goals. The marching orders I'd gotten from Baughman were to continue the process of dramatic change at Crotonville, by introducing new methods, new courses, and new goals. Our job was to make Crotonville a leading influence over the change process at GE. If that made the participants in our programs nervous, fine. If it meant exposing Welch or any other corporate officer to face-to-face criticism, so much the better: Crotonville should be a learning opportunity for them, too.

The staff members at the meeting were all terribly polite, but some of them obviously thought I was nuts. Some thought

I could be stopped, or at least ignored. In the decorously passive-aggressive manner common to corporate types everywhere in the world, they began saying *yes* to me when they really meant *no*. They were making the best of something that didn't suit them at all.

My first turn at bat came with the Corporate Entry Leadership Conference, or CELC, held soon after I arrived. This brand new, three-day course was Welch's idea, a way to reach, in groups of 100, all of the 2,000 engineers and other professionals GE hired straight out of college each year. The sessions would orient the new recruits to global competition and GE's changing values, while helping them figure out how they fit into the company.

Designing a suitable course was challenging. As a consultant to GE, I had interviewed middle managers by the score, so I knew the company was in turmoil in 1985. Many employees were scared, or angry, or both. Resistance to Welch and all he stood for seemed to be reaching an emotional peak. Although the opposition was not organized or even very visible, it included business heads as well as thousands of middle managers and hourly workers. At the same time support for Welch was growing rapidly. The result, increasingly, was polarization.

Baughman encouraged me to redesign the course myself. "Give it your best shot," he said. "That's why we hired you."

Our goal was to give new hires an honest orientation to GE. We couldn't expect anyone to commit to GE's emerging values unless they understood the ideas and reasoning behind them. And let's face it: If they didn't like the values, we couldn't expect them to stay at GE. That's why we required that each CELC participant interview four seasoned GE managers before arriving at Crotonville, as described in chapter 1.

When the first group of 100 recruits arrived on campus one Sunday afternoon in October, they brought the results of their 400 interviews. You can imagine how the most disaffected of GE's old-timers responded to those questions: That's where the kids got the "Jack Welch is an asshole" statement. But the interviews captured the whole range of feeling among GE managers, from hostility to ignorance to interest to enthusiasm.

We had plenty to talk about. And since openness, candor, and constructive conflict were prominent among GE's emerging values, we had a *way* to talk about it—uncensored debate.

After an introductory session and dinner, we divided the participants into small discussion groups, with more experienced GE managers as facilitators.

By 11 P.M. they had boiled down the concerns of GE's middle managers to three big questions:

- How can GE motivate its work force without offering job security?

- How can GE help reindustrialize America when it is moving jobs offshore?

- Does Jack Welch really have a strategy or is he just reshuffling the portfolio?

The next morning, at eight o'clock sharp, the whole group gathered in the intimate, 110-seat Crotonville amphitheater that GEers call "the Pit." The time had come to get answers to the young managers' three questions—but not from me. Facing the participants was Larry Bossidy, then the second most powerful person at GE.

The prospect of this morning's dialogue had horrified the traditionalists on Crotonville's staff. Rather than exposing the vice chairman to such uncertainty, they'd urged me to send Bossidy a complete list of questions ahead of time. Otherwise, they warned, the session would only alienate him—and the rest of GE's top management—from Crotonville and this reckless new training approach.

Remembering their qualms, and feeling some of my own, I asked the vice chairman at the last minute whether he wanted a briefing before going into the Pit.

Bossidy is not as polished as Welch, but he's one of the smartest people I've ever met. "Nah," he said. "I'll just go in and interact."

The mood in the Pit was electric. The young people piling into the room were visibly pumped up from their Sunday debates, more than ready to take on the No. 2 man at GE. As for me, I felt this would make or break my GE career. A few of my Crotonville colleagues in the Pit seemed to be gleefully awaiting my comeuppance.

Soon after Bossidy came on stage, a young professional bluntly raised the job-security question. The room hushed. Everyone had known this moment was coming—but still, the kid had just delivered the corporate equivalent of a sock in the jaw. How would the big guy react?

Bossidy took the blow with grace:

You're right to raise this. It's an extremely tough issue, and very relevant. We think the only honest way to handle this is to tell people that there is no job security in GE— other than what the customer can provide. Therefore, if you're making turbines that cost 40% more than Korean or Japanese turbines, and they make a better turbine with more quality, then you will face downturns. That's the reality of the marketplace. . . .

This is very painful, and I think you need to empathize with the middle managers who have worked for GE for twenty-five years and face terrible downsizing. We must deal with this with compassion, and with fairness— but we must deal with it.

Asked about the effects of moving U.S. jobs to other countries, Bossidy responded with candor: "Maybe we're paying the price for being sloppy and poorly managed for so many years after World War II. But what alternative do we have now? All we can do is try to make our businesses stronger."

After a spirited discussion of GE's values, from integrity to constructive conflict, here's how Bossidy wrapped up the meeting:

I passionately believe in these shared values. But I'm not naive enough to think that everyone in GE believes in them. Some people don't know about them; some managers think the values are a crock. But I believe in them, and my challenge to each of you is that you need to decide. Get clear on what your values are and whether they fit with GE. If they don't fit, make the decision to get out. If they do fit, terrific—but make that decision based on a clear understanding of what GE is, what we are attempting to accomplish, and what you want to do.

By the time I took Bossidy back to the car, I was feeling terrific. The vice chairman evidently had relished the give and take, and so had the new managers. Even so, it was great to hear Bossidy say he was glad that difficult questions were raised.

I wasn't the only one who gained confidence that day: As they met with other GE officers during the remainder of the course, the new recruits demonstrated a healthy willingness to challenge any idea, regardless of who presented it. One corporate officer tried to dodge a criticism about job security by saying, "We don't have that problem in my particular business, so I really can't answer you."

A newcomer shot back, "Now wait a minute—that's a cop-out. As an officer of the General Electric Company, don't you have to take some responsibility for what's going on?"

Roger Schipke, then head of Major Appliances, addressed the group late Monday afternoon:

This has been one of the toughest days of my career. I did not realize how bad it was in GE. That's not a reflection on you; the data you've collected from the middle of the organization is profound and troublesome. I leave here very troubled, but committed to want to do something about it.

Listening to Schipke, I knew we'd hit a home run.

We couldn't have accomplished much without solid support not only from Baughman, but from Welch. Every time we needed backup he gave it, and he demonstrated his commitment to Crotonville in the most visible way: Once every few weeks a GE helicopter would thunder down from the sky. As soon as it landed the CEO would burst out, ready for another Crotonville debate.

Welch loved being in the Pit, bashing big ideas back and forth with GEers. After all, he hadn't promoted constructive conflict for theoretical reasons—it was his natural way of communicating. In face-to-face discussions he's hard to resist, and he knows it. Welch relishes every opportunity he can get to win others to his point of view, and the Crotonville Pit allowed him to do it to 100 people at a time.

Candor is his secret weapon. It wins him trust, and affection, too. Whatever is on his mind, the CEO usually says. According to a joke that circulated around Plastics when he worked there, the worst way to hurt Welch is to tell him a secret and then lock him in a closet before he can tell anyone else. Welch protects himself as much as he can, by strictly barring journalists, security analysts, and even consultants from the Pit. (I wasn't allowed in until I became Crotonville's manager.) But inside that safe room, with fellow initiates of the GE fraternity, Welch will say almost anything.

In 1986, after the RCA deal had closed, a manager from RCA's Coronet Carpets unit raised his hand at Crotonville. Coronet was a tiny business by GE standards, and everyone knew it didn't fit into the three-circles strategy. Obviously worried, the executive asked Welch what would become of Coronet.

The CEO didn't hesitate. "I'd better tell you this," he said. "You know that we've been thinking about selling your business? Well, we arranged a deal this morning."

A similar thing happened during another session. A manager from the robotics group in Orlando—a component of GE's unsuccessful factory-automation business—asked about its future.

Welch replied, "If I were you I'd get my résumé ready. I know you don't want to hear that. But we're not making it in that business. To be fair to you, you've got to face that." At the cocktail party after the session, he made a point of spending a few minutes with the man from Robotics, making sure the fellow was okay. That's what Welch means by the phrase "tough-minded but softhearted."

The CEO spends so much time talking that some people don't realize how carefully he listens. At Crotonville, he installed a systematic new approach to gathering feedback, requiring every participant to fill in a one-page appraisal sheet that asks three questions:

- What did you find about the presentation that was constructive and clarifying?

- What did you find confusing or troublesome?

- What do you regard as your most important takeaway from this session?

In practice, those comment sheets are report cards on his stewardship of GE. Welch reads them by the hundred, with the eagerness of a brand manager absorbing test market data.

Not all the comments are pats on the back:

- "Somewhere between the corporate office and the department workers, the information flow ceases. I believe there would be less fear of the changes to come if the reasons for change were presented."

- "It sounds like GE is becoming a conglomerate."

- "Welch's shots at middle management bothered me. I'm middle management and I work very hard to stay current and guide my business into tomorrow. Maybe we should come at this problem with middle management from a positive side rather than the negative."

- "Perhaps the upper management is not up to the challenge. I have my résumé ready in case my group gets killed."

Welch hears the same complaints over and over and comes back for more. Even today, when griping is becoming less common, the complaint most frequently aired comes from managers who say they share Welch's values but their bosses don't.

That problem frustrates Welch, too. Once, in 1986, while we were driving from Crotonville's helipad to the Pit, the CEO grimaced as we discussed the comments he'd been reading. "This is unbelievable!" he exclaimed. "I'm getting the same questions I've gotten for five years! Doesn't anyone understand anything? I'm just not getting through to them."

"What's the alternative?" I asked. "They obviously haven't gotten the message yet. Don't you have to keep saying it over and over again?"

"You're right," he said. "I've got no alternative." He pulled himself back into his usual upbeat mood, and strode into the Pit for another energetic session. The perseverance to repeat the same message day after day, year after year, with no end in sight, may be Welch's greatest strength.

The CEO's personal participation greatly adds to Crotonville vibrancy, but the programs must create excitement without him—indeed, roughly half take place on GE business sites far from the campus. Our team redesigned every one of Crotonville's programs and assembled many new ones. Typical of the new workshops was a five-day Team Experienced Manager Course that took place in Gotemba, Japan, in March 1987.

Bossidy, an instinctive populist, used to keep asking us what Crotonville was doing for the tens of thousands of GE middle managers who weren't invited to the prestigious courses held on Crotonville's campus. Workshops like this one, held at the base of Mount Fuji, were my answer to his question.

The Gotemba course gathered about thirty mid-level managers, five each from the local operations of six different GE businesses. As in most Crotonville workshops, the goal was to develop leaders as change agents while solving real business problems. Each five-person team came with an assignment, such as these:

- Plastics needed to coordinate its research and development activities in Japan more closely with those in GE's U.S. labs.

- Power Systems, facing declining turbine sales in the U.S., needed a strategy for attracting new customers in Asia.

The session opened with a half-day, stage-setting presentation on transformational leadership. This was more than a lecture: For instance, after explaining TPC—the analysis of business issues in technical, political, and cultural terms—the participants would examine their own work projects in those terms.

These middle managers were too far down in the organization to see how they fit in to the larger picture, so in the afternoon Don Kane, GE's organizational-planning expert, explained how the corporation itself was being transformed.

After dinner that evening and every other, the teams separated to work on their own assignments.

On day two Harvard Professor Mike Yoshino talked about global strategy. His function was to give the participants some necessary conceptual tools.

We spent that afternoon outdoors, working Outward-Bound-style on building team skills.

On day three, Hiro Takeuchi, a marketing professor from Hitotsubashi University in Tokyo, taught global marketing for half a day.

In the afternoon we conducted "visioning" exercises. To explain how forcefully a clear vision can influence events, we showed Martin Luther King's "I Have a Dream" speech. We discussed the essential components of King's vision, then abstracted them into terse points written on flip charts. Then the managers had to craft a vision for their projects by each writing a magazine-style article, set two years in the future, describing the project and its effect. Afterward, their colleagues interviewed them and wrote down the main themes on flip charts. Each team member's themes filled one page.

Although the overlap was substantial, the visioning exercise didn't create a consensus. To achieve that, each of the teams gathered to define its goals formally. The debates, often highly emotional, lasted until midnight. But by the time the managers went to bed, each team had its own clear vision.

The next morning, the teams met separately to translate their visions into specific plans. The Power Systems group had set a goal of opening three new Asian markets, for example. Now the question was, how? How much would it cost? How would they get the money?

After lunch on day four, we staged a dress rehearsal of the presentations to business leaders that were scheduled for the next day. Members of all the other teams listened to each presentation, then offered critiques—hardball criticism as well as ideas for improvements.

The business leaders arrived in time for dinner. While the teams of middle managers feverishly polished their presentations, we explained the rules to their bosses: After listening to his team's presentation, and discussing it with the team, the executives were required to announce what action they'd take on each recommendation. Any business leader who failed to take the process seriously risked alienating the managers who'd been working eighteen hours a day to put these proposals together. And once the business leader made the public announcement, he'd have to live with his decision. So tomorrow would test the bosses as well as the students.

On the final day, the teams made their presentations, and then everyone gathered to hear each of the six business leaders declare whether or not he would implement his team's ideas. Another home run for the Crotonville team. At Gotemba, the bosses accepted almost all of the proposals.

Again and again Welch has said, "There are no textbook answers to the problems we face. We have to write our own textbooks every day." His commitment to that approach was most evident in the drafting of the GE values statement, a Crotonville preoccupation for years.

The work was well underway before I began consulting at GE in 1982. I joined Jim Baughman, Don Kane, and Jack Peiffer in the creation of a document intended to define the new GE culture: a simple sounding list of the corporation's core beliefs. Our group met endlessly and created countless drafts, consulting often with Welch and Vice Chairmen Larry Bossidy and Ed Hood.

At some companies, a group like ours might just have typed up a list of its values—or, more likely, the CEO's—and considered the job done. That's not the GE way. Welch wanted the final statement to be something all GEers could "own." He insisted we keep exposing our draft values to debate at Crotonville, until thousands of managers had considered them and given us their responses.

The process was exhausting, but it gave me a visceral

understanding of why top managers must constantly engage workers in dialogue. The feedback is very useful, but that's not the most important thing. By listening to people, you encourage them to think; and by encouraging them to think, you can win their involvement and commitment. The years we spent interminably discussing and revising the GE values statement at Crotonville resulted in more than a piece of paper listing our ideals. Those who criticized Welch for his inability to nail down a final values statement missed the point: A statement of values never should be considered done. We forced a large percentage of GE's most influential managers to consider what the company's values should be. Continuous reexamination and discussion is what makes values come alive.

In 1985 our group wrote a discussion document that was, admittedly, an expression of our own beliefs. This five-page manifesto (similar to the one Larry Bossidy referred to in the Pit) contained simple statements without much explanation. Each was controversial enough, new enough, or bold enough to spark an emotional reaction. Here are a few samples:

- Only satisfied customers can provide job security.

- Change is continual, thus nothing is sacred. Change is accepted as the rule rather than the exception.

- Leaders share knowledge rather than withholding it as an element of power. Everyone benefits when they know what the leader knows—nothing is "secret."

- Paradox is a way of life. You must function collectively as one company and individually as many businesses at the same time. For us, leadership means leading while being led, producing more output with less input.

- We encourage the sharing of these values because we believe they are both fair and effective, but we realize they are not for everyone. . . . Individuals whose values do not coincide with these expressed preferences will more likely flourish better outside the General Electric Company.

When GEers read the document, their reactions were almost always the same. They'd get to that final paragraph and their jaws would drop. "You've got to be kidding," they'd say, often with anger. That final statement—the "flourish off," as it came to be known—affronted some. They said it felt like being asked to take a loyalty oath. Remembers Welch, "The feedback shocked us."

A typical comment:

The paper should end on a positive note. The tone of the last paragraph appears to contradict much of the discussion under openness and constructive conflict. The same intent could be accomplished by a positive statement such as "We believe that these values are both fair and effective. We are firmly committed to instilling them throughout the General Electric Company."

Every idea in the statement found both allies and opponents. Some said the document was too long; others, that it was too short. It was pabulum; or too tough. It sounded like "shape up or ship out"; or like "motherhood and apple pie." Some wondered: "Why even bother to write it down?" Others, often younger managers, were glad to see some stakes firmly planted in the ground. "At last!" They'd say.

To many GEers, the values document was profoundly challenging. As one executive wrote on a comment sheet:

In my view, no one is comfortable with the notion of change. Some would argue that there are things in this world that are sacred: family, identity, one's self-determination, and it would seem that constant change can cause confusion. Do we value change or even the process of questioning and looking for change?

At first, few participants in these debates believed we really cared about their comments. Those doubts were reinforced when Welch included parts of the values statement in the 1985 annual report. Suddenly the ideas seemed set in stone: "Jack Welch's commandments," one manager called them.

Instead of giving up, we continued to hold debates on values; indeed, similar discussions are still taking place today, as part of Work-Out. Welch's personal presence at Crotonville, his obvious willingness to listen, convinced participants that the discussions were worthwhile. We released a new draft of the values document in 1987; anyone who compared it with older versions could see how the statements had changed.

Welch described the long process in a speech at the Harvard Business School:

> We went to the organization. We took two or three years to develop this thing on values . . . reality, candor, integrity, etc. We worked out every word. It was brutal. We talked to five thousand people at Crotonville. Now we have the words . . . We're measuring our people against these values and now we're in the process of transforming.

I never wanted to be a manager; that's one reason why I accepted the Crotonville job only for a two-year term. Nevertheless, by taking on the assignment I accepted the responsibilities of a transformational leader, with none of the cop-outs and escape hatches usually available to academics and consultants. The experience of helping reshape Crotonville, though admittedly small in scale, helped me better understand the larger revolution Welch was leading at GE.

Like Welch, Baughman, and so many others, I faced stiff resistance. My way of dealing with it doesn't deserve the highest marks. To begin with, I shot myself in the foot by letting everyone know I'd be gone in two years: That encouraged resisters to try to wait me out. For true bureaucrats and company men, there exists a corporate equivalent of geologic time—and from that perspective, my Crotonville stint would be over in the blink of an eye. So they stalled.

During the early months at Crotonville I struggled in particular with one person who reported directly to me. He seemed unimaginative, and incapable of providing leadership for new initiatives. I observed and worked with him for several months to make sure my judgment was sound, and gathered the views of others. Then I made a very tough decision. I went to Jim Baughman and made the case for removing that manager. Baughman considered the evidence and supported the decision. Then came the hard part: I had to talk the decision through with the manager, take care of his outplacement counseling and financial needs, and help him find another, better job. The process took months, but ended well for all concerned.

By giving me permission to replace that manager, Baughman signaled GE's commitment to the work I was doing. Everyone on the Crotonville team understood that ignoring me wouldn't enable them to avoid change. Unfortunately, such demonstrations of power seem to be an essential part of the transformation process.

But you can't replace everyone. In the end, leaders have to work with the people they've got. To define Crotonville's goals and shared values, we held a series of off-site meetings with Crotonville's top five managers, trying hard to promote open debate. We'd argue and compromise until we at least approached consensus.

It was at one of those meetings that I finally confronted my biggest mistake as a leader. My colleagues were complaining about me with unprecedented bitterness. They seemed uniformly upset—allies and resisters alike. I was pushing too hard, they said, *much* too hard. I was bulldozing them even when they agreed with me, alienating my own supporters. The clear message: *Back off, Noel!*

It became obvious that they were right. Much of the

behavior I'd been interpreting as resistance actually was exhaustion. We were changing or adding so many courses so fast that Crotonville's administrators simply felt overloaded. Every now and then someone would blow a fuse. Instead of understanding, I'd brand any sluggish response as resistance, and push doubly hard for whatever I wanted. Well, it didn't work. Belatedly, I realized that I was the person who needed to change.

Baughman and Welch took big risks and every time we needed backup they gave it without hesitation. Ultimately, Welch deserves the credit for Crotonville's success. The operation has become a vital, central part of his ongoing effort to reshape the GE culture; indeed, its effectiveness in that role is what inspired Work-Out.

The achievement of Crotonville is that it gave thousands of GE managers the benefit of hands-on learning. The combination of powerful stagecraft and an environment that deliberately encouraged risk-taking provided 10,000 people per year with experiences profound enough to change them. Today, those people are changing GE.

Chapter Twelve

The Politics of Speed

Only after five years of pushing technical change and consolidating his power did Welch dare to address the political problems he faced within General Electric. Then, in December 1985, GE eliminated the sectors—the layer of executive vice presidents who intervened between the CEO and the heads of the company's thirteen main businesses. That delayering enabled Welch to seize direct political control of GE at last.

Inevitably, a shakeout soon followed. Eight months after eliminating the sectors, and one month after closing the RCA purchase, GE parted company with the heads of three businesses. These events helped trigger a broader reshuffling of top management: By the end of 1986, GE had placed new leaders in roughly two-thirds of its main businesses. For the first time since Welch took office, the CEO had the luxury of deciding which person belonged in which job.

The sector chiefs had stood in Welch's way even though they largely shared his values. That's because the very existence of sectors slowed communication and reduced the integration of GE's businesses, allowing bureaucratic ways to continue. When you try to move information through layer after layer in an organization, it's like playing the children's game of telephone: The data get corrupted.

GE's new structure eliminated the twilight zone that had separated the office of the CEO from the operating units. So long as the sectors had insulated GE's business heads from one another, they could comfortably maintain values and goals that differed from the CEO's. But once in direct contact with the CEO, they could only agree or clash.

What's remarkable is that the CEO had waited so long, both to get rid of the sectors and to pick his own executive team. The RCA deal, by introducing more new executives to GE's top ranks than the company needed, had made some sort of rationalization inevitable. And it had seemed odd that a company that could eliminate so many tens of thousands of jobs should be reluctant to act against a few top managers.

Welch admits that he hesitated to move against the sectors:

> I delayed fixing the structure for two reasons: First, I felt I hadn't been in the job long enough, and I didn't want to disrupt the place. And second, I liked the people. They were my friends—I'd put some of them into those jobs.
>
> The problem with the sectors was the structure, not the people. They were some of our best people, but they were stuck in impossible jobs.

The sectors, in turn, prevented the CEO from directly observing the underlying businesses closely enough to be sure of his own judgments about their leaders. Says Welch: "The biggest challenge is to be fair. No one trains you to be a judge." But once the sectors were removed, the need for new leadership in certain businesses became glaringly obvious.

Welch saw no need for the sectors. Jones had created them, in 1977, partly to protect the CEO from a deluge of undigested information from the newly formed strategic business units. Sectors also provided a handy testing ground for Jones's potential successors; Welch himself had run the Consumer Products and Services sector.

The organizational structure Welch inherited was complicated. At the bottom were departments, which produced and marketed particular products such as refrigerators or circuit breakers. These departments were collected into divisions, the divisions were collected into groups, the groups reported to the sectors, and the sectors reported to the CEO. Within that operating structure, GE had superimposed the forty-odd strategic business units, which regrouped those same departments a different way for planning purposes.

Welch viewed all this complication as unnecessary. He already had shifted responsibility for strategic planning back to GE's operating managers. With years to go before his own retirement, he certainly had no interest in running another CEO horse race. And he gathered far less information than Jones, enabling him to oversee more businesses.

From the CEO's point of view, the sector organization wasted time and got in the way. As Welch explains:

> The people running the sectors had no power. Their role was transmitting information, so they acted as filters. They were in-betweeners, with no way of actually knowing anything firsthand. They would waste three days getting ready to come to talk to us. Then we would talk to them for one day. And none of us would know any facts! We would ask a question and we wouldn't get the answer. When I'd ask a question, they had to go check with somebody who knew—someone who was running a business.
>
> People think of delayering as a cost reduction, but it's really a way of enhancing management. We did a study

that showed we saved $40 million by removing the sectors, but that's just a fraction of the real value. That doesn't account for the improved quality of our leadership, or how fast we can get to market now. Delayering speeds communications. It returns control and accountability to the businesses, which is where it belongs.

We got two other great benefits from the sector delayering. First, by taking out the biggest layer of top management, we set a role model for the whole company about becoming lean and agile.

Second, we identified the business leaders who didn't share the values we were talking about—candor, facing reality, lean-and-agile. We exposed the passive resisters, the ones who were right for another time but didn't have the energy to energize others for the global challenges ahead.

The first act of the GE revolution had come to an end. "Sometime in 1985," remembers Dave Orselet of the Executive Management Staff, "Jack began to feel that all the years he'd spent relentlessly driving, pushing, screaming, and kicking were beginning to pay off. I don't mean he was satisfied, because he never is. But he could see that this monstrous ship he was steering was finally beginning to turn."

Like it or not, employees were becoming accustomed to change. Gone were the comforting orderliness and certainty that once had defined their professional lives. Now hazard and risk, like a low-lying fog, obscured the path ahead. Once-complacent GEers were energized—but also frightened and confused. They could no longer deny their need for leadership.

For Welch, this was the great opportunity that defined the second act of the revolutionary process. To seize it, he had to help his organization define a new guiding purpose, a new set of rules—a new vision. This is not something a leader can impose by fiat. And Welch had nearly reached the limit of his ability to influence the organization through unilateral, mostly technical, actions. The time had come to deal with the political strand of the rope. Before the CEO could lead GE much farther, he had to win GEers' allegiance. Together, somehow, the leader and the led had to define a vision that everyone could share.

The sectors had borne such a heavy load in the architecture of GE's organization that eliminating them forced a radical redesign of the whole corporate structure. To use Jim Baughman's imagery, GE had been organized vertically like a many-tiered wedding cake; henceforth it would look like a cartwheel lying on its side, with a hub in the middle and spokes radiating out.

The hub was the so-called "office of the CEO": Welch and Vice Chairmen Larry Bossidy and Ed Hood, plus Executive Vice President Paul Van Orden. The spokes were GE's thirteen main business units, which would now report directly to Welch or one of the vice chairmen.*

The main effect of this new order was to empower the autonomous business leaders, the class of managers that included Roger Schipke of Appliances, Glen Hiner of Plastics, and Brian Rowe of Aircraft Engines. For instance, GE greatly increased their authority over capital allocation, one of the most important functions of management. In the old days, no executive below sector level could approve a major capital investment without going to the CEO. Now business chiefs have the same authority to approve investment as the CEO. When they need to spend more than they can approve themselves, they present their cases directly to GE's board.

The hub-and-spoke structure obliterated much of GE's lingering bureaucratic uniformity. Suddenly it seemed natural to custom-tailor compensation schemes and other policies to

---

*Several months after Larry Bossidy took the CEO job at Allied-Signal, Welch added two men to the office of the CEO; Paolo Fresco, now vice chairman, and Frank Doyle, now executive vice president.

the needs of each of GE's wildly dissimilar businesses. Before long, variation became the rule. The effect, as Baughman notes, was to create organizational structures driven by the needs of the market rather than the bureaucracy.

Welch didn't want to entrust GE's operations to people who thought only of pleasing their bosses and meeting their budgets. Marketplace performance and leadership were the qualities he valued most. As he told a group of managers at Crotonville in 1987:

> The world of the 1990s and beyond will not belong to "managers" or those who can make the numbers dance. The world will belong to passionate, driven leaders—people who not only have enormous amounts of energy but who can energize those whom they lead.

Unhappy with the sector structure from the first, Welch had urged Don Kane of the Executive Management Staff to study GE's organization. In typically methodical GE style, Kane analyzed the effect of the company's management structure on the entire business, from Fairfield to the factory floor. He recommended eliminating the sectors on the basis of the data he collected, and in the context of a whole program of delicately interrelated structural changes. The basic theme of his argument applies to almost any company: Eliminating layers increases an organization's responsiveness to leadership.

Welch had been cautiously and very publicly testing the notion of eliminating sectors for years. When he took office, the company had six sectors. Carefully, delicately—probably too delicately—the CEO cut the number of sectors to four without attacking the structure itself. One sector vanished in 1984 with the sale of Utah International, the mining outfit; another, Services and Materials, was abolished when its chief, Larry Bossidy, became a vice chairman.

Kane was impressed by the experience of businesses that

once had reported to sectors but now dealt directly with the CEO. Among them, Kane observed:

- Far fewer time-consuming requests for information

- Less time spent in the formal review process

- Much faster decisions

- Quicker, clearer communication

He proposed what he called a "next step in the evolution of our GE management system," defining a new collegial style of interaction to replace the old hierarchical ways. Kane cautioned that CEO edicts would only impede the process of change; and Welch eagerly accepted the point. He was already trying to build consensus through Crotonville debates and other means, but progress was slow. As he remembers, "We knew we wanted GE to move faster. We knew we needed people who represented the shared values. And we wanted to communicate faster and better with people."

Gradually, Welch recognized the structure of the GE organization as one of the major obstacles remaining in his way. When he became CEO, the most powerful resistance had emanated from some of the planners and business heads. By the end of 1982, GE had virtually abolished the central strategic-planning staff. The logical next step was clearing the sectors out of the way, to permit direct interactions with the business heads.

Under the old system, the CEO met with his sector chiefs every month. Spending all their time in the netherworld between the CEO and GE's businesses, these men were out of touch by definition. When they were unable to answer questions about the operations under their command, Welch expressed his frustration to them in a manner that made those meetings uncomfortable. Then, in time-honored GE fashion, the sector heads would turn around and "kick the dog," sharing their discomfort with the business leaders who reported to them. And then those executives would kick their direct reports, and so on down through the hierarchy.

Distanced from operations, the sector chiefs had no alternative but to focus on numbers and budgets. Every month, before their meeting with the CEO, the sector chiefs scheduled full-day performance reviews with each of their main businesses. Despite Welch's efforts to stem the collection of useless data, the sectors had routinely scrutinized business results in excruciating—and unnecessary—detail. The required reports compared a business's projections against its actual sales, with data segmented by market and by channel of distribution—the equivalent of an internal planning audit every month. Preparing reports for just one business's monthly sector review could occupy twenty people full-time for a week.

Line executives didn't go to these meetings expecting to learn anything. Their goal was to emerge from the ritual unscathed. After studying the sector structure, Don Kane concluded that it fostered a tendency to minimize person risks, to volunteer nothing, and to restrict channels of communication. In such an atmosphere, Kane wrote, a CEO had few tools to influence the organization.

A high-ranking GE executive described another pernicious effect of sectors on the business heads:

> I think we would have accomplished more if [our sector chief] had just run the business himself. It's like a lot of things in life: You get used to the role you have. You begin to rely on the sector chief's involvement. You want to have him involved in your decisions. So frequently you would elevate the tough decisions to that level, one step farther away from your business. You'd gotten used to the mothering.

When he finally announced the decision to "delayer the sectors," Welch presented it as a necessary refinement of GE's organizational structure. He had no need to fire the sector chiefs, nor even to criticize them. One of the sector chiefs retired; the other three stayed on in big jobs. Paul Van Orden of the Consumer Products sector joined the office of the CEO as executive vice president. John Urquhart of International became head of the Power Systems business. Louis Tomasetti of Industrial Products took charge of Aerospace.

As executive coups go, this one was remarkably genteel.

Welch didn't understand until later the enormous cost of having tolerated the resisters hidden beneath the sectors. The business leaders who opposed the GE revolution were all fiercely loyal to the company. Their ultimate goals were identical to Welch's; they just disagreed about how to get there.

The resisters didn't need to take on the CEO directly: Their passive-aggressive behavior did at least as much damage as open opposition could have. They presented new ideas without enthusiasm, damned them with faint praise, and embodied the old way while feigning allegiance to the new. Like the Crotonville administrators who kept giving me empty assurances that they agreed with my ideas, some business leaders pretended to push the new program while behaving in ways that blocked it.

Feelings of vulnerability provoked many resisters. All three of the business leaders who lost their jobs in 1986 had been running once-prominent businesses that suffered marketplace reversals and deteriorating financial results. But unlike Carl Schlemmer, whose locomotives unit faced even graver difficulties, these managers never fully faced reality. Well-intentioned but reluctant to change, they were right for another time, but unready for the intensely competitive late 1980s. Despite the CEO's efforts to help them transform their businesses, they had left many of their operating problems unsolved.

Taking away the sectors shone a spotlight on the attitudes

as well as the performance of the business heads. It wasn't always flattering.

Some couldn't stomach constructive conflict. The *Wall Street Journal* called it Welch's "hazing-as-shouting-match approach, that requires managers to argue strenuously with [Welch] even if they agree." One of the three top executives GE replaced in 1986 later complained to the *Journal*: "You can't even say hello to Jack without it being confrontational. If you don't want to step up to Jack toe-to-toe, belly-to-belly, and argue your point, he doesn't have any use for you."

Others had trouble—to use Welch's phrase—"facing where we're going to be." One major GE business, which produced heavy machinery, was coasting on profits from its five-year backlog. It lost its technological lead to Japanese competitors, yet continued to price its products up to 40% higher than theirs. The unit's huge backlogs acted as a narcotic: During the early 1980s, as its orders began to drop, the business enjoyed the highest net income of its history.

By 1982 the CEO had seen that a major downturn was inevitable in that business. Bypassing the sector chief, Welch says he and Bossidy spent years "jawboning" the business's leader. They asked for cuts in investment and staff, with the goal of lowering both costs and prices. The executive appeared to agree intellectually, and did seek local tax breaks. But he ignored suggestions about downsizing and fundamentally repositioning his business. He made excuses for the "temporary slowdown" his unit was experiencing, and talked about the comeback ahead.

His backlog had begun to run out by 1985. As a "bridging strategy" to slow the loss of market share to more efficient competitors, the unit began to bid on projects at prices at or below their cost. The worst of these deals produced millions of dollars in losses, but the business announced the order with great fanfare, as if it were a major financial coup. The local city government and the unions saw nothing to celebrate: If GE was doing so well, they wondered, why the hell did the company need so many concessions? Larry Bossidy, to whom this particular business reported, saw nothing to celebrate either.

Before long, GE removed the business's leader, who had presided over the loss of several points of market share, leaving his successor no choice but to downsize the operation by thousands of jobs. Had GE moved sooner, many of those jobs might have been saved.

Once the restructuring was complete, Welch had allies, or at least like-minded people, in all of GE's biggest jobs. Bob Wright, who made a name for himself at Plastics, Housewares, and Financial Services, became head of NBC. John Opie, a star as general manager of GE's $1 billion-a-year construction equipment unit, moved up to a bigger job running Lighting. David Genever-Watling gave up a corporate vice presidency assisting Bossidy to head Motors. In all, the CEO picked new people for sixteen of GE's biggest jobs.

Eliminating the sectors and putting the new team in place drastically reduced the political friction that had been slowing GE. No high-level resisters remained. For the first time since Welch took office, the people who controlled the company—not just the CEO, but the executives who actually ran businesses—largely agreed about what they were doing, and why. It's amazing how much easier it is to run a company that way.

Chapter Thirteen

The New Order

I t sounds so easy: Zap the sectors, pop the right people into the right jobs, and presto, your company runs like a charm. The reality isn't so simple. Don Kane, the thirty-year EMS veteran whose thinking helped guide GE's mid-1980s reorganizations, points to some of the subtleties:

> We were changing the entire fabric of the business—the management system by which the enterprise is orchestrated—not just some boxes and lines on the organization chart. Not only did the process change radically, but nearly everyone changed jobs concurrently. I'm not simply referring to those who switched to brand new positions, but also the myriad folks whose titles and offices were unchanged, but whose roles were very significantly changed.

> The purpose of any organization is control. GE's old wedding cake structure achieved control by brute force. At every

level of the organization, managers spent professional lifetimes issuing and enforcing orders: from the CEO to the sectors, from the sectors to the business chiefs, from them to the heads of smaller and smaller operating units—and all the way down to the hourly workers who weld pipes or answer phones and don't get to boss anyone around until they get home.

When you think about it, this sort of hierarchy isn't much more complicated than "me Tarzan, you Jane"; simplicity is one of its main virtues. At GE, as at most American companies, the formal structure created an unambiguous chain of command that reliably kept the enterprise under control.

But as a side effect, it also shaped the attitudes and behavior of employees, often in destructive ways. People learned to do what they were told and not much more. They avoided conflict with their supervisors. They evaded responsibility, forcing their bosses to sign off on decisions they could have made themselves. Emotionally, the structure fostered a schoolyard sullenness, with bosses acting as disciplinarians and subordinates as kids. Open communication was almost unthinkable.

Once Welch decided that the old hierarchy was slowing the company down and limiting its competitiveness, he could not avoid fundamental organizational change. And no matter what new method of organization he chose, the CEO knew he'd be toppling dominoes by the thousands. That made the task of designing a better system dauntingly complex.

Getting rid of the sectors was not enough; the CEO needed something to replace them. Though troublesome, the sectors had helped bind GE together, encouraging a measure of unity among the corporation's otherwise independent operating units: Everyone was saluting the same flag (or, in this case, meatball). But what would unite GE's collection of largely autonomous businesses from then on? And what would induce GEers to start thinking for themselves?

The new hub and spoke structure didn't resolve those issues. Though it shortened the lines of authority, it was every bit as hierarchical as the old sector organization. Indeed, by making the business chiefs directly answerable to the CEO, the new order increased Welch's ability to dominate the corporation.

Far from uniting GE, the new organization seemed by its very design—a hub with thirteen spokes but no encompassing wheel or rim—to abet the centrifugal forces that have always threatened to pull GE apart. Relations among GE's business chiefs traditionally were cordial, but distant. They rarely saw one another. And these men were competitors, struggling against one another to win more capital, to win the CEO's favor—and perhaps one day to win his job. Now, without the sectors to impose a crude communality upon them, the heads of businesses such as Aircraft Engines might have even less reason to care about, say, a problem in Appliances.

Welch's solution, in 1986, was to create the Corporate Executive Council, or CEC. A group of GE's thirty highest-ranking business chiefs and senior staffers, it meets quarterly to discuss the most important issues facing GE, whatever those might happen to be at the time. The embodiment of Welch's ideas about leadership, this executive council has little overt authority and no clear role in decision making, yet has come to function effectively as GE's political center.

Two of the CEC's members are women. Joyce Hergenhan, vice president for public relations, works directly with Welch and is respected in her field. Hellene Runtagh, president of the $650-million-a-year Information Services unit, joined GE straight out of college in 1970 and worked her way to the top of one of GE's thirteen main businesses. She is one of six women who run GE operations with combined annual earnings of $220 million.

The CEC provides a structural context for the more collegial style of management Welch is trying to promote. It is also a device for indoctrinating GE's leaders in the corporation's shared values. The council's formal mandate is to share information, swap ideas, and help guide GE toward its goals. In practice, the CEC is a high-level think tank, where the company's best informed (and presumably most talented) people work together on issues of common concern. If the definition sounds fuzzy, that's partly intentional: A main purpose of the CEC is to build trust and kinship among executives who might otherwise be slitting each other's throats.

GE's executives are free to lead their own businesses, each according to its own culture and rules; but CEC members are always expected to subordinate their interests to those of GE as a whole. When Welch talks about his "team" it's more than a smiley-face metaphor: He damn well expects these people to work together. I once asked the CEO how he could possibly expect teamwork from CEC members. After all, GE's compensation schemes are designed to reward good financial results in any given business, without regard for behavior toward the rest of GE.

Without hesitation Welch shot back, "Yes, we reward them for performance. But they won't last long if they're not team players."

The CEC's gatherings take place at Crotonville, in a cozy little amphitheater called the Cave. Coats and ties are taboo, as are formal reports. When he isn't addressing the group, Welch sits amid the other executives, to reinforce his view of the CEC as an assembly of peers.

Fascinated by the architecture of social relationships, he thinks deeply about the design of the CEC's gatherings. Much as Walt Disney insisted on orchestrating every aspect of the Disneyland experience, Welch thinks it's essential to create a seamless environment to help the CEC fulfill its potential. He never stops tinkering, and no detail is too small to attract his notice, from the suitability of the council's agendas to the length of its coffee breaks. One early change was the addition of dinner speeches by outsiders he admires, such as Donald Soderquist, vice chairman of Wal-Mart, Wayne Calloway, CEO of PepsiCo, and management consultant Peter Drucker.

In the Cave, as in Crotonville's larger Pit, openness and candor are the rule. Says Welch:

> We strive for the antithesis of blind obedience. We want people to have the self-confidence to express opposing views, get all the facts on the table, and respect differing opinions. It is our preferred mode of learning; it's how we form balanced judgments. We value the participation, involvement, and conviction this approach breeds.
>
> It works partly because people feel comfortable in a "pit." Everyone's close together. The people asking questions are looking down at the speaker. Somehow that opens up the questioning.

The wide-open debating style that Welch calls constructive conflict illuminates more than ideas: It reveals the participants themselves. If someone lacks confidence or interpersonal skills, it shows. There's no place to hide, and snow jobs don't work. Unlike budget reviews, CEC meetings are not meant to be combative, but nervous executives and newcomers sometimes have found them so, particularly during the CEC's early years. As one described his first days on the council: "Boy, those are tough meetings. Really uncomfortable at times. Not a lot of fun. If you come there with a bullshit synergy idea, Welch will nail you."

Welch insists the atmosphere isn't so tough:

> If you were a first-timer there, you might feel a little intimidated. But there's a lot more sensitivity. If someone comes the first time and doesn't have a good presentation, everyone there feels it, senses it. But he gets a call after the meeting, not at the meeting.

During the earliest CEC meetings, some executives were reluctant even to speak. As Kane remembers, "It was too much a dialogue between Jack and other individuals." But over time, as members got used to the process, the level of trust increased. "We tee up a subject and then they take each other on," says Welch. "We end up with a consensus." His relative youth encourages easy communication: With the CEO succession so many years away, CEC members have little incentive as yet to play politics.

A typical session begins with a scene-setting talk from the CEO: an overview of GE's current status and prospects, and a sounding of the big themes Welch wants to cover. Each member presents a very brief oral report—rarely longer than ten minutes—on his or her business situation. From then on, loosely guided by a prepared agenda, the meeting is given over to wideranging discussions marked by profanity, jokes, and frequent interruptions.

The main agenda items usually concern either problem solving or the sharing of good ideas. Or sometimes both: In the late 1980s, for instance, Welch and a few CEC members became worried about signs of volatility in the U.S. inflation rate. In an enterprise the size of GE, the difference between setting prices that do or do not reflect the actual inflation rate can amount to a substantial swing in operating profit. Professional economists can't help much: Dependent on price data gathered on a quarterly basis, they are chronically behind the times. What to do?

Deciding that early information about price rises could be a valuable competitive advantage, CEC members agreed to start faxing data to one another about changes in the prices their businesses were paying for supplies. Precisely because those businesses are so diverse, that information provided a reasonably accurate, up-to-the-minute gauge of inflation, which individual managers used to adjust their prices. The CEC's informal fax network lasted six months. Then, once it became clear that inflation was no longer a serious threat, the faxes abruptly stopped—there was no need to institutionalize the practice. But the informal fax network has been revived several times since to pool information on other breaking issues.

One of the CEC's functions is to serve as GE's main nerve center, ensuring that good ideas—what GEers call "best practices"—get communicated throughout the company at lightning speed. If Plastics has come up with a great way to cut its insurance costs, or if Aircraft Engines has developed an effective employee-involvement program, the CEC is where they spread the word.

Welch wants a company characterized by "integrated diversity." GE's varied portfolio of businesses makes the diversity part easy. Finding ways to link all those operations, to integrate them into a whole with a distinct identity of its own, is infinitely harder. Without the CEC, I don't know how GE could have done it.

Sociologist Amitai Etzioni described three methods of organizational control: coercive, utilitarian, and normative.

Coercive control, the least effective type, is what you get when you point a gun at someone and tell him or her to do what you want. The method is alienating, and works only as long as you keep aiming the gun.

Utilitarian control—paying people to do what you want—works much better; it's the method on which most organizations still rely. The weakness of the utilitarian system is that your money buys labor but not goodwill.

Far more powerful is normative control, which relies on a system of shared values to direct behavior. Normative control is what induces people to devote themselves to a cause: An example is the religious missionary who might voluntarily work for years in a hostile environment for poverty wages.

No business can expect to be inspiring enough to rely exclusively on normative methods of control. Corporations exist to make money, after all, and smart employees will always want to share in the loot. Incentive compensation is here to stay.

Nevertheless, I'm convinced that the most effective competitors in the twenty-first century will be the organizations that learn how to use shared values to harness the emotional energy of employees. As speed, quality, and productivity become ever more important, corporations need people who can instinctively act the right way, without instructions, and who feel inspired to share their best ideas with their employers.

That calls for emotional commitment. You can't get it by pointing a gun. You can't buy it, no matter how much you pay. You've got to earn it, by standing for values that other people want to believe in, and by consistently acting on those values, day in and day out.

GE's CEO is no sap: He pushes values because that's the way to get results. Delegating more of the control function to individuals—in effect, to their superegos—reduces the need for reports, reviews, and other external mechanisms. A boundaryless organization can achieve the same level of control as a hierarchical one—but at less cost, with less friction, and faster. As Welch told a group of senior GE managers:

> You have to break down the walls that bind us and slow us down. You have to walk the talk. Never compromise. Go back and look at everybody you've got. Be sure they have the values.

Welch remains very much the boss, controlling the CEC's membership and agenda, not to mention the salary and career prospects of every participant. But as the CEC has gradually transformed GE's most senior managers into emissaries of the corporate values, he has allowed their collective authority to increase—and spent less of his own energy giving orders.

Managing doesn't interest Welch much. Leadership is what he values, because that's what enhances his control over the organization. He devotes his considerable talents to orchestrating CEC meetings that inspire high levels of emotional energy in participants. To the degree that the meetings are exciting, challenging, fun, and useful, CEC members will emerge pumped up and ready to inspire the people in their businesses to new levels of achievement.

There may be no more efficient way to influence a large organization. Although the public attention that has been focused on Welch might suggest the contrary, his unique personality traits are not what make the system work. Any sizable company employs plenty of people capable of running meetings and interacting with other people with just as much brio. The trouble is that few companies have yet recognized the value of their executives' interpersonal skills, and so have not made them a primary basis for promotion.

GE cherishes those skills, and creates many opportunities for its employees to hone them. Each of GE's operating businesses now has its own version of the CEC, enabling every business leader to play the Welch role. Lower-ranking executives get other opportunities, such as serving as facilitators at Work-Out sessions.

The ability to relate effectively to other people in such settings has become a major factor in performance reviews. GE has begun to breed a new generation of leaders distinguished by the ability to elicit cooperation from others. When, years from now, they rise in large numbers to the company's top jobs, their example may redefine the art of management.

This much is certain: Although the CEC lacks much formal power, it has become a potent instrument of change at GE.

By design, the CEC is a workshop in GE's core values. As at Crotonville, ideas and stagecraft combine to create dramatic effects. Consider the impact of just a modicum of candor:

At CEC meetings, every member gets the details of every

other member's quarterly financial results—and discusses them. If one business leader has a problem, the others will propose solutions. This is a startling change from normal corporate practice, in which open discourse about peers' operations is considered a grave breach of etiquette.

Sharing information of all kinds is an important aspect of boundarylessness. As the CEO argues, "Managers traditionally haven't shared information. Information was power, so they held it back. They saw their job as control. I see that as unproductive, a waste of energy." Giving everyone the same data at once speeds decision making and makes for better decisions. The information itself has changed the way CEC members think. Instead of focusing only on their parochial concerns, the line executives now observe the whole of GE from the same lofty perspective as Welch. They can't help but make better judgments.

Welch argues that shared information also helps create consensus:

> If you put a group of bright people together, and you give them the same facts, they'll come up with the same answers. This may not be true in religion and philosophy and a lot of other things, but in business you're dealing with a fairly quantitative process. It's concrete. It's simple. This is not rocket scientist work. If we all have the same information, we'll all come to roughly the same conclusions.

Finally, sharing information creates peer pressure that goads people to ever higher standards of performance. In the old days, GE executives were masters of obfuscation, using splendidly packaged reports and 35-mm slides to avoid the tough issues and snow their masters in Fairfield. But when you're stuck in a room where everyone knows everything, with no props at your disposal, you have to face reality. If your performance stinks, if you're avoiding a major strategic challenge, you won't be able to hide it. The result is openness, candor, and an incentive to produce real results.

The teamwork that the CEC fosters among GE's top executives has been tested by disasters. Among the most memorable was Appliances' $500 million compressor fiasco.

Back in 1981, Appliances had a problem. Borrowing an idea previously used in small air conditioners, GE engineers had designed an advanced rotary compressor to cool its refrigerators. Compared to GE's existing compressors, it would require one-third the parts, half the manufacturing cost, and far less energy to operate. On the other hand, the technology required parts manufactured to tolerances of as little as one one-hundredth the width of a human hair, creating considerable production risks. And the cost included a $120 million investment in a new automated factory. After much agonizing with executives from Appliances, Welch approved the plan to make the new compressors instead of buying them. In retrospect, it was the wrong decision.

According to a middle manager at Appliances, one problem was that frustrated managers there kept bucking decisions up to their bosses: "They were feeling kicked, and pushed, and shoved, and not appreciated. So they just said, 'What do you want me to do, boss?'—and it ended up going all the way to Jack." Says Welch, "With all the layers of approval we had then, no one had ownership of the decision. Ownership is essential."

When the new refrigerators appeared in 1986, people bought so many that GE's market share rose two percentage points. Employees at Appliances were proud of their technical achievements, too: The rotary compressors represented breakthrough engineering. And their new automated factory worked splendidly, turning out one compressor every six seconds.

Then, in July 1987, a rotary-compressor refrigerator broke

down in Philadelphia. Soon, others failed, in Puerto Rico and elsewhere. Since these appliances were all covered by GE's five-year warranty, the failures soon came to the attention of GE engineers. Their preliminary investigation suggested that certain critical parts might be far less durable than expected—and very difficult to repair. The conclusion: Many of the new compressors might fail. Eventually, GE decided to replace them all, with conventional compressors purchased from other manufac turers.

In 1988, Roger Schipke, then head of Appliances, had to present this mess to Welch and the whole CEC. A few months earlier, he and GE's other business leaders had submitted operating plans that together would have increased GE's 1988 net income by some $500 million. Although Schipke didn't know it at that time, the pretax cost of dealing with the bum compressors would amount to considerably more than half of GE's projected earnings rise.

Here's how the situation would have played out in the old days, according to Welch:

> Let's say we have a disaster in one business where they were minus $30 million. The chief financial officer would call the heads of the other businesses and ask them to make up the $30 million.
>
> The heads of the businesses would say, "Why?"
>
> The financial officer would say, "Because this unit over here blew up."
>
> Then the head of the business would say, "Well, those guys are jerks. They don't know how to run the business anyway. Why are they causing me trouble? I hate them!"
>
> Everybody starts blaming the person who has the problem, and the organization gets very destructive.

But when the refrigerator compressors went bad, CEC members knew they would have to help make up the shortfall. So Schipke's problem automatically became their problem, too. Moreover, Welch has rigged the incentives to force team-work. CEC members know he is always judging them on that basis, obliging even the most heartless CEC member to come to the aid of a suffering colleague.

So Bob Wright volunteered at one early meeting, "Ad sales are going well at NBC. Our earnings might be up an extra $30 million this year."

Offered Brian Rowe of Aircraft Engines, "Look, I think we may be able to help you by getting a dozen compressor engineers to take a look at that compressor problem." Implicitly, everyone knew that Rowe would pay their costs.

There was no need for Welch to get directly involved. He didn't have to prompt Wright, Rowe, or anyone else to offer help. The CEC members knew what to do.

After replacing more than 1 million defective compressors, Appliances survived, with its market share in refrigerators intact. Schipke kept his job (years later, he left GE to become CEO of Ryland Corp., a builder of single-family homes).

And GE's 1988 net income rose $471 million to $3.4 billion, not far off from plan.

The process has taken years, but by the early 1990s the CEC had become the power center of GE, influencing the company's direction more than any other institution. Though it lacks an explicitly managerial role, the council provides checks and balances to the CEO's authority that certainly exceed any that existed before at GE.

The real power of the CEC is subtle, stemming from its ability to educate. Welch explains:

> The enormous benefit we get from our meetings is that we end up being smarter than anybody else. It's not that we have a higher I.Q. But after two days with the CEC, having to talk about everything from TV networks to the Indonesian economy just to understand our own busi-

nesses, we can walk out and talk to anybody at a cocktail party, and be the smartest guys in town. And we may not be as smart as most of the other people there—it's just that we're exposed to so much more information.

During the 1980s there was a trend to break up any multibusiness company. Get rid of the diversity. Focus on a single thing. I think that if we didn't have the CEC, we probably would be unfocused. Diversity was part of the hand we were dealt. In the CEC we've found a mechanism to turn that diversity into our strength.

Chapter Fourteen

Getting Excited

"When a business becomes productive," says Welch, "it gains control of its destiny." He continues:

In restructuring, you go through trauma, you bottom out—and then you start to see results. Once you get back to being productive, the jobs come back, you succeed in the marketplace, your profit margins rise. You were hurting for a while, but now you feel great.

Lighting is a classic example: It was a high-margin business that was drifting downward. It needed help. In 1986 we put a new man in there, John Opie, and he put in a new team, and they looked at everything, from manufacturing to packaging to distribution to incentive compensation. Three years later, Lighting had the highest productivity rate in GE, around 9%.

That was the breakthrough that showed everyone in GE how productive wc can be. By accomplishing so much with one of our slowest growing businesses, Opie and his team broke the dam for the whole company. We put them up on pedestals, we talked about them at every company meeting.

High productivity was supposed to be limited to the exciting, high-growth businesses with new product lines. When the 114-year-old Lighting business got 8% and then 9% productivity, the myth was shattered. No one in the company had an excuse for not becoming productive. Everybody had to go to Cleveland to find out how they did it. And before you knew it, other businesses were getting 5% and 6% productivity rates.

We proved that productivity is not a matter of cut and burn. It has nothing to do with whips and chains. It's a never-ending process that's based on empowerment. It's what happens when you get people excited about finding solutions to their problems.

By 1986 the second act of the GE revolution was well under way. The era of large-scale cost-cutting, of mass layoffs and factory closings, had largely passed. The company had been awakened to the need for change, and Welch was beginning to shape his vision into words employees could understand. Throughout GE the emphasis shifted to the wellsprings of profitability: revenue growth and productivity. Revenue growth, perhaps the clearest demonstration of customer satisfaction, is essential to maximizing profits over the long term. Productivity is the best measure of efficient operation, as well as a potentially rich source of earnings.

Despite all the cutting and burning of the early 1980s, many GE businesses still performed poorly by both measures. Partly because the need to trim RCA's bloated 85,000-person organization had slowed GE's progress, the corporate productivity rate hovered stubbornly around 2%, the prevailing level in 1981. More disturbing, several key businesses, Lighting included, weren't growing their revenues at all.

GE remained a long way from Welch's goal of becoming "the most competitive enterprise on this earth." As the corporation's lingering weaknesses proved, cost-cutting and CEO edicts—what Welch calls "whips and chains"—were not, by themselves, the solution to GE's problems. What the company needed to progress further was positive leadership, based on vision and backed by real-world results.

Lighting, GE's oldest and traditionally most powerful business, was struggling in 1986, when Opie became its leader. Opie's predecessors had eliminated ten factories and 3,000 jobs, but the Cleveland-based operation's costs still were out of line, and some of its light bulb products were technologically out of date. Though still very profitable, GE Lighting was flabby and unready for battle. Yet it faced unprecedented attack from overseas, as Philips of Holland, Siemens of Germany, and myriad Far Eastern importers raided GE's traditional customer base with low prices and new products.

Though GE Lighting remained No. 1 in North America, its awesome market share was eroding from its accustomed postwar level of roughly 50%. The trouble began in 1983, when Philips bought Westinghouse, traditionally GE's main competitor in light bulbs. In that one stroke, the ambitious European outfit displaced GE as the world's leader in lighting. Philips lifted its North American market share from 5% to 21%—and then used that new clout to introduce fiercer competition to a marketplace that had been shaped by the easy give and take of oligopoly during the first half of the century. In 1986 Lighting's sales and profits dropped for the second year in a row. GE's market share continued to slide while Philips's increased. Unless GE Lighting radically altered the way it operated, further decline seemed inevitable.

Lighting needed a revolution of its own, and Opie, then

forty-eight, was the right person to lead it. I've always seen him as a Boy Scout: clean-cut, clear-headed, well intentioned, and utterly self-controlled. Though his emotional range is much narrower than Welch's, and his need for control commensurately greater, Opie has proved he can be an inspiring leader.

His great advantage is the self-confidence that comes with success. An engineer by training, Opie spent part of his early GE career at Plastics, where he witnessed the effectiveness of Welch's methods firsthand. A member of the Welch team from the first, Opie rose fast to division VP in Plastics. Later, as head of the business that makes circuit breakers and other electrical controls, he launched a large-scale transformation effort. Then he got the Lighting job.

Once Opie moved to Cleveland, his confidence showed: Certain he knew how to put together a better business, he didn't hesitate to disassemble it first. When his employees screamed and howled, Opie remained firm, holding the organization together by sheer force of will until Lighting's improved performance in the marketplace finally gave people the reassurance they needed to carry on. According to Bill Woodburn, who then ran Lighting's business development and planning department, "John does not have trouble sticking to his guns. He doesn't have opinions, he has convictions."

Looking back on his tenure at Lighting, Opie defines three distinct periods:

During the first two years, he gained control and pushed change—restructuring management along functional lines, pushing for the productivity gains needed to lower prices, and trying to convince anxious workers that he wasn't going to sell or destroy their business.

Then in 1988 and 1989, as financial results improved, he worked on reshaping Lighting's corporate culture—building a team, indoctrinating managers in new ideas, pushing authority down the hierarchy, and establishing the tenet that productivity and product improvement are never-ending processes.

The third phase is still in progress. Having started to regain share in the United States, Lighting is pushing for global reach, attacking Philips and other competitors where they live.

The essence of Opie's accomplishment, the quality of leadership that has made him a standout on Welch's team, is his ability to make believers of Lighting's disgruntled employees. He defined a vision of what they could accomplish becoming first the low-cost light bulb producer, and then the leading global producer. Then he helped them make that vision a reality.

GE's overwhelming strength in lighting ultimately became its greatest weakness. From the day in 1879 when Thomas Edison invented the light bulb until a few years before Opie arrived, GE Lighting's stature as the leading lamp producer in North America, where one-third of all light bulbs are sold, remained unchallenged. Comfortable at home, Lighting haughtily ignored the rest of the world until the middle of this century.

For most of that period, GE remained the world's most profitable bulb producer. But by ignoring opportunities for growth abroad, GE ultimately weakened itself and gave Philips its leadership opportunity.

North America used to be GE's safe fortress. Starting with Charles Coffin, General Electric's early CEOs were men who plainly preferred to avoid competition whenever they could. Taking advantage of GE's patents—which amounted to ownership of essential light bulb technologies—the company used cross-licensing agreements to form partnerships with competitors both at home and abroad that enabled GE to remain unchallenged in the U.S. market.

GE negotiated cross-licensing agreements with its major U.S. opponents, Sylvania and Westinghouse. In return for an exchange of technology, the smaller companies agreed to follow GE's lead. General Electric signed similar cross-licensing agreements with almost all the world's major light bulb producers. The effect of these agreements was to keep all signatory companies within the borders of their home markets.

Before long, GE controlled 75% or more of North American lighting sales, with Sylvania, Westinghouse, and a few small outfits squabbling over the rest. In his unpublished history, *Problems and Performance of the Role of Chief Executive in GE,* Jim Baughman explains that Lighting's strategy was to protect the domestic market rather than to grow worldwide.

To ensure that its influence persisted even after its patents expired, GE bought equity stakes in light bulb manufacturers around the world. By 1935, according to *Anatomy of a Merger* by Robert Jones and Oliver Marriott, GE owned 10% of Philips, 40% of Tokyo Electric, 29% of Germany's Osram, 44% of France's Compagnie des Lampes, 34% of Britain's General Electric Company, 100% of China's Edison Electric, and more. In the ensuing decades, GE gradually sold off those stakes—a pity, since they'd probably be worth billions of dollars today.

The Justice Department tried several times to break up the cross-licensing agreements on the basis of antitrust law. But prior to two cases brought in the early 1940s, U.S. courts ruled in GE's favor. In a 1926 case, for example, the court reasoned that the agreements were legal so long as the profits derived from them were "reasonably within the rewards" to which a patent holder would be entitled. The 1940s cases ended with consent decrees that terminated the restrictive cross-licensing agreements and prohibited such agreements in the future. However, GE, Sylvania, and Westinghouse still benefited from the huge market shares that were the legacy of the prewar era, and all continued to prosper.

After World War II, GE's share of the North American market gradually drifted down to roughly 50%, and then stabilized at that still-handsome level. Meanwhile, the overseas markets Lighting was ignoring had developed characteristics as distinct as those of Galápagos fauna: European electrical power flowed at 230 volts, versus 100 volts in Japan and 120 in the

United States; in Southern Europe, consumers picked light bulbs from bins, like onions.

In North America, sheltered from all-out competition, Lighting developed a distinctly complacent corporate culture, relaxed about costs and remarkably willing to pamper employees. In 1913 GE spent $1 million—an extraordinary sum at the time—building the world's first industrial park on a ninety-two-acre site outside Cleveland. In addition to a light bulb factory and a research center, the park offered a swimming pool, bowling alley, gym, tennis and handball courts, rifle range, and fields for baseball, football, and field hockey. The facility kept doctors and dentists on staff, and the park maintained its own bank for employees' convenience. GE even encouraged its people to linger at night, organizing activities from tap dancing and language courses to bridge tournaments and an instrumental band. Few could work there without developing a strong feeling of loyalty.

Bill Woodburn says that Lighting's culture of comfort endured:

> The culture was clublike—fraternal to the point that relationships counted more than performance. If you were a part of the right group, you were pretty much protected. Your future was secure.

Protected by its rich stream of profits, Cleveland became the most autonomous of the Works. As a 1987 article in a GE employee magazine recalled, "Lighting's independence drove Headquarters crazy, and GE managers sent to change things were swallowed by the culture and went native, like, some said, the Jesuits in China." In this insular environment, Lighting's leaders saw little reason to change their ways. Nor did Welch push for change when he ran the sector that included Lighting. "The business was very profitable then," he recalls. "Short-term performance can hide many flaws."

But GE Lighting needed to change. Despite enormous unit

volumes, it was on the way to becoming the high-cost producer of light bulbs. By 1982, the tentative incursions of overseas competitors had become an invasion, with companies from Hungary, Poland, Japan, Taiwan, Korea, and elsewhere pushing deeper into the North American lighting market. The quality of their bulbs had improved, the market was enticingly vast, and American consumers had amply demonstrated their willingness to buy imported products, from automobiles to TVs to cheese. The newcomers arrived with an unbeatable business proposition: good-quality bulbs priced well below GE's.

This price advantage was based in part on labor costs that GE couldn't match. While GE's workers in Cleveland earned $14 per hour, their counterparts abroad made much less: $7.00 in Japan, for instance, and $1.00 in Korea.

Once Philips bought Westinghouse, it fought hard for North American market share, and often won. The Dutch firm slashed prices, invested heavily in consumer advertising, and offered distributors cash or free goods as incentives to handle its products instead of GE's. Philips, which earned most of its light bulb profits elsewhere, suffered little from its expensive price war in the United States.

The cozy environment that had nurtured GE Lighting no longer existed.

Opie's well-meaning predecessors struggled mightily to cope with these unexpected threats. When Lighting's sales finally began to drop in 1985, they maintained profitability by raising prices. GE's opponents didn't match the increase. That left GE stranded with retail prices up to 40% higher than competing brands. The downward spiral began.

Realizing that their costs were too high, Lighting's leaders seized on automation to reduce them. The business spent millions installing three new Pro80 production machines, designed and built by GE itself. Each of these machines could manufacture 6,000 incandescent lamps per hour—roughly twice as many as existing equipment could produce. Within two years, Lighting's team avowed, the Pro80s would lower unit production costs 17%.

Realizing the need to trim costs further, they cut Lighting's R & D budget. That decision cost GE its leadership in new products, an important spur to sales growth. With higher prices and increasingly outdated technology, GE Lighting now had little to offer customers but a familiar brand name. That was no longer enough.

Lighting's weakness was revealed in 1986. Its sales declined again; this time earnings fell, too. The Pro80 machines went into operation, but they were plagued with design problems and operating bugs: It cost GE nine cents *more* to make a bulb with a Pro80 than with the older equipment. Lighting's productivity, which had dropped to zero in 1985, hovered around 3% in 1986.

Lighting decided to raise consumer light bulb prices yet again. Now some of its products were priced up to 50% higher than competitors', and Lighting's market share deteriorated faster than ever.

Then Opie got his turn.

Athletic and intense, relentlessly methodical and focused in pursuit of his goals, Opie is a manager in the Welch mold—analytical, decisive, candid, sometimes abrasive.

Here's how he assessed the situation:

> I knew it was going to be a tough job. The business was much worse than it looked. It was on the skids and the numbers were only beginning to show it. The return on investment had dropped from 30% down to 20%, and was headed lower—but right then that 20% return on investment still looked very good. So I knew the reaction of the organization was going to be, "Why are you doing this to me when we're still doing pretty well?"

Though new to Lighting, he quickly defined his vision for the business. Abandoning his predecessors' insular approach, he articulated business goals in the context of a world market for lighting products. As Welch might have done, he boiled his thinking down to a few big ideas, which he called "drives":

- A drive to achieve the industry's lowest costs.

- A drive to increase sales by creating new markets, much as GE Plastics had done.

- A drive to lead the world in customer service, with sophisticated fulfillment and distribution systems.

- A drive to regain leadership in product quality.

Opie's push for productivity had the weight of inevitability. Achieving cost leadership had to come first, he knew. Progress toward the other goals would require substantial investment, and since Welch wasn't in the habit of funding losers, the only way to raise the necessary funds was by boosting sales. Later on, new products and new markets would help, but in the short term, the only way to increase sales was to cut prices. And that, in turn, forced cost-cutting, to avoid a sickening slide into unprofitability.

In effect, Opie was designing a scale model of the GE business engine. By lowering prices, he would goose Lighting's sales. Productivity gains would clear the way for higher profits. And the combination would create the cash flow the business needed to invest in its future.

He began by stamping out fires. He canceled all outstanding orders for new Pro80s, and set out to recoup the costs of the machines Lighting already owned. As he later explained, Opie discovered that what had appeared to be technical problems with the equipment were actually cultural problems with the people running it:

We put foremen and manufacturing engineers on the machines instead of design people. Their orders were to stop running the machines for innovation and new ideas; run them for productivity and lower cost per unit instead. In 1987, they got the cost per unit down about 30%.

At first, almost everything Opie did aroused ferocious resistance. He abandoned the investment-intensive business of designing and manufacturing Lighting's own production equipment. In the past, Lighting made better machinery than outside vendors could supply, and the designs of its factory equipment became trade secrets that Lighting people guarded with fanatical care. But the Pro80 fiasco inspired Opie to probe for facts, and he concluded that GE's machinery was no longer the best available. By implication, the proprietary methods that GEers still treated with mystical reverence actually weren't worth much. Shutting down the production machinery operation saved millions of dollars, but caused an uproar.

Much of the opposition to Opie was rooted in misunderstanding. Employees viewed him as Welch's hatchet man, a characterization that even Opie accepts as fair. But many misjudged his intentions: Remembering the Housewares sale, they wrongly presumed he was preparing to sell Lighting, another treasured emblem of GE's heritage. Some old hands thought Opie lacked the necessary experience to change Lighting's established practices; they viewed him as ill-informed and clumsy, likelier to destroy the business than to fix it. Having observed Welch's exposure to similar criticism, Opie decided the only way to change people's minds was with results. Their complaints did not deter him.

In Opie's opinion, the resisters simply didn't realize how essential it was to lower GE's costs below competitors'. As he explains:

It's one thing to establish objectives. It's another to get people to believe they just *have* to reach them to be successful. Our prices were eroding, and they weren't accustomed to that. We weren't the cost leaders and yet everybody thought we were. So it took a couple of years for people to realize that we didn't have cost leadership, and that we weren't going to win if we didn't get it.

Instead of waiting for employees to catch on, Opie raced ahead with an ambitious, top-to-bottom restructuring of the whole organization. Like Welch, he's comfortable with complexity, playing the managerial equivalent of three-dimensional chess. His team devised a new structure that would not only cut costs, but also simplify and speed decision making and bring the business closer to its customers.

First, he merged Lighting's three P & L centers into one. Stephen Rabinowitz, who was Lighting's technology vice president, explains the principle:

We have a plant that makes wire, a plant that wraps the wire into coils, and a plant that assembles the coils into lamps. If I organize those as three separate businesses and optimize each one, I may not optimize the total.

But if I organize those three plants as a single unit, they can seek the optimum balance of opportunities. It may make sense to make a costlier wire—if it helps us produce a cheaper lamp.

Within the one large operation, Opie created a lean matrix structure of the sort popularized by Procter & Gamble. This flexible type of organization groups employees according to functions, such as manufacturing, human resources, and finance. Each functional group, such as the component manufacturing operation at Lighting, gains responsibility for serving an entire business. Linking the functions together are product managers, each of whom is responsible for a particular product, such as incandescent lamps. To get things done, people from different functions work together in teams; and to force those people into a customer service mentality, product managers are the team leaders. What's confusing about the matrix organization is that most people report to two bosses: a product manager and a functional chief.

The efficiency of the new matrix organization more than compensated for the disruptions it caused. The structure enabled Lighting to reduce seven layers of management to four. In all, the reorganization eliminated 700 white-collar positions. Sales per salaried employee increased 35% in two years, versus 25% for the hourly work force.

Almost everywhere the Lighting team looked, it found opportunities to simultaneously cut costs and increase effectiveness. When Opie arrived, Lighting's distribution depended on a system of thirty-four regional warehouses. At a cost of $35 million, Lighting closed them all, replacing them with nine modern facilities. Similarly, the team shuttered Lighting's twenty-six customer service centers, and invested $25 million in a single, state-of-the-art operation in Richmond, Virginia. "When you're at the other end of a telephone," Opie argues, "nobody cares where you're located as long as you provide the service."

Large measures like these generated more than half of the savings the team achieved. But Lighting's leaders paid as much attention to incremental changes as to quantum leaps. Much of the remaining productivity gain came from small-scale programs designed to get employees involved and reward them for success. Rabinowitz explains:

> Big programs are great if you win. But none of us wins all the time and when we don't it's painful. We began with a mix of two-thirds big programs—ones that required investments of many millions of dollars, big project teams, and years to pay off. We very deliberately shifted to two-thirds small programs—each costing a million dollars or less, accomplished by one or two people, and completed in a couple of years at most.

That permitted us to build up a momentum of success. Instead of having ten big programs, you'd have 200 small ones. Ten of them could miss and you wouldn't even notice. But the ones that work give you a very quick infusion of benefits. That helps you fund still more projects—and more important, it builds your confidence.

The Lighting team linked those productivity programs directly to employee compensation. Salaried workers became eligible for bonuses based on their individual performance, and/or the performance of the business as a whole. And every Lighting employee could claim a share of the benefit from suggestions he or she made to increase productivity. A program called Impact, for instance, passed on 10% of the savings from small-scale changes that cost an average of just $14,000 each to implement. A collection of seemingly inconsequential ideas—such as cutting a site's garbage pickups from twice weekly to once—quickly reduced Lighting's costs by millions of dollars per year and helped turn more employees into productivity devotees.

Not all the programs were trivial. Lighting saved big money by selectively purchasing more materials from outside vendors, some overseas. It substantially lowered manufacturing costs by reducing the number of components in its products. Standardizing product packaging created another big savings.

The final element of the productivity drive was Opie's call for "continual change productivity"—in other words, revolution as a way of life. Says Rabinowitz:

The good things that I do today, I fall in love with. So if you come tomorrow and say, "There's a better way," I'll resist you.

I'll say, "Hey, I just thought of that. They gave me a management award. They told me it was good."

So now I've become an obstacle. Somehow you've got to get me to say, "You're right, that's a great idea."

You've got to constantly keep adjusting the organization, so you don't allow those habits and assumptions to become entrenched.

The new methods worked. Within a couple of years Lighting was producing solid results as sales, profits, and market share all rose. Most impressive were the productivity gains: by 1987 Lighting's rate reached nearly 9%.

In a paradox familiar to students of revolution, Lighting's employees resented the changes that had made their business so successful. No one denied the financial success of Opie's strategy; but they had trouble accepting its cost. Between 1986 and 1990 Lighting trimmed more than 6,000 full-time jobs.

When the big cuts began in 1988, employees reacted with disbelief. GE Lighting was generating a handsome amount of cash flow. It was twice as profitable as Philips. No other Lighting business could match its return on sales. Bill Woodburn describes how people felt: "This wasn't an obvious problem like Chrysler in the early 1980s. Why ruin families and destroy lives when we are that profitable, and we are exceeding the industry average by multiples of three and four?"

Now that they'd achieved some success, many employees figured they deserved to relax. Opie remembers:

Questions continued to come up about when we would be through reducing cost. And I kept saying, "Never." Because if we stand still, the competition will go right on by us. Just to maintain our position, we have to keep pushing.

Few employees understood how much more their business still needed to improve. Everyone likes to pause after an early victory. Lighting's managers tried to explain, but the resisters felt too stressed out to listen. The cutbacks had reduced their staffs and resources, while the pressure to perform increased.

Nevertheless, as Lighting's results continued to improve, more employees became believers. Welch's very public enthusiasm about their achievements, the accumulating effects of all the productivity programs, and noticeably fatter paychecks all contributed to improved morale. After years of pushing and shoving, the Lighting team was finding more people who were willing to cooperate. Then came the biggest lift of all, and the biggest challenge: a pair of acquisitions that made GE Lighting a global player for the first time in its history.

In 1989 GE ranked No. 2 in the $9 billion world market for light bulbs, its global share trailing Philips's by only a few percentage points. Yet GE did hardly any business outside North America. In a competition with global players, matching and even beating their prices is not enough. You need access to their markets, for two reasons: first, to maximize your revenue opportunities; second, to weaken your competitors by attacking them in their home markets, just as Philips had hit GE.

After years of transatlantic meetings that led nowhere, Lighting's leaders finally snagged their first big overseas prize in 1989: a majority stake in Tungsram. This Hungarian lighting company suddenly went on the block as communism began to collapse in Eastern Europe. Bill Woodburn, then head of Lighting in Europe, and Paolo Fresco negotiated the deal. Although inefficient, Tungsram produced good quality bulbs and had 7% of the European market—a nice addition to GE's scrawny 2%, and enough to push GE Lighting back to No. 1 status worldwide. Soon after, the same negotiating team enabled Lighting to buy the light bulb business of Britain's Thorn, which had 9% of the European market. Having accumulated an 18% share in Europe, GE has become a credible opponent to Philips on its own turf. In addition, Lighting has established many smaller ventures in India and elsewhere in Asia.

Going global is a long-term game, and GE Lighting is still learning how to play. With more employees outside the United

States than any other GE unit, Lighting faces enormous challenges as it tries to integrate its far-flung operations. Opie admits that Lighting's European operations "are not exactly world-class income generators." Tungsram, in particular, presents a tremendous challenge for GE's revolutionary management ideas. Hungary's inflation rate has soared since GE bought Tungsram, nearly offsetting the benefit of a one-third reduction of the work force. Besides, this business had been run on socialist lines. Individual performance reviews were unknown. Management pushed for production volume, but didn't even track consolidated profits. In 1989, Tungsram's 18,000 workers produced sales of $300 million, while in the United States, 19,000 Lighting employees—a group only slightly larger—produced sales of more than $2 billion. Improving Tungsram's performance—despite the barrier of an unusually obscure language and in a country plagued by all the lingering ills of a Communist regime—surely will take years. By mid-1993, Tungsram's work force had been reduced to about 10,000 people.

Even with these continuing struggles, Lighting has become a demonstrably healthy business. Profits are rising at a respectable rate; sales reached $2.7 billion in 1992, have grown at a 7% annual rate under Opie, versus some 13% for GE as a whole. Lighting's culture is changing, and morale, at least in the United States, is back to normal. But the competitive environment doesn't allow for complacency, and globalization still presents a challenge substantial enough to preoccupy Lighting for years.

Chapter Fifteen

Globalization

While in France to attend the French Open tennis tournament in June 1987, Welch met with Alain Gomez, chairman of Thomson S.A., the largest French electronics company. During a half-hour conversation, the like-minded CEOs conceived a transaction based on a major evolution in Welch's strategic thinking. Although smaller in financial terms than the RCA purchase, this deal evidenced a much more important strategic change.

GE agreed to swap its $3-billion-per-year Consumer Electronics business, America's leading maker of TV sets and VCRs, for the Thomson-CGR medical-imaging unit, which was selling about $750 million of X-ray and other diagnostic machines annually in Europe. In addition, since the businesses were of unequal size, Thomson agreed to pay GE $800 million in cash.

This was one of the best deals of Welch's career—"a masterstroke," according to Paolo Fresco, fifty-nine, the debonair, silver-haired Italian who rose from GE's senior vice president for international operations to a vice chairman in 1992. The TV-set business, which GE sold at book value, was in trouble: Despite a 25% U.S. share, it ranked only No. 4 in terms of the world market, and was subject to frequent fits of unprofitability. "There's no room for third-tier players," Welch argues. "In TVs we were at the end of the whip: We'd have a good year, then all of a sudden TV would cost us $40 million."

Thomson-CGR was losing money, but it had over 10% of the European market for medical imaging equipment—an entrée that the leaders of GE's Medical Systems business believed they needed to ensure long-term prosperity. Siemens and Toshiba had begun chipping away at GE's leading share of U.S. medical-imaging equipment sales.

While roughly half of all CAT scanners, X-ray machines, and other such diagnostic equipment were sold outside the United States, GE Medical Systems—known as GEMS—made less than 15% of its sales overseas. The Milwaukee-based business's only major international outpost was a 75%-owned manufacturing joint venture with Yokogawa Electric Works, its former distributor in Japan. The venture company, Yokogawa Medical Systems, or YMS, combines GEMS' technology with Japanese miniaturization to make mid-priced CAT scanners. Even with YMS, remembers John Trani, the head of GEMS, "We had a significant imbalance. It was clear that we had to become global."

So the Thomson deal solved two problems at once, greatly fortifying GEMS while eliminating a business that had never measured up to Welch's standards. And it increased GE's cash hoard to nearly $2.7 billion.

To GE's astonishment and dismay, the Thomson deal also provoked furious howls from the U.S. press. The financial and strategic aspects of the transaction attracted scant attention. But the passing of the venerable GE and RCA electronics businesses into foreign hands outraged many newswriters and editorialists. The earlier sale of GE Housewares to Black & Decker also had aroused protest, but at least the buyer was a U.S. company. This was a case of wounded national pride.

The *New York Times* ran a page-one story under the headline "G.E., A PIONEER IN RADIO AND TV, IS ABANDONING PRODUCTION OF SETS":

> The General Electric Company, bowing to unrelenting Japanese competition, said yesterday that it was selling its $3-billion-a-year consumer electronics business to Thomson S.A., France's Government-owned electronics giant.
>
> The announcement that G.E. would abandon production of radios, which it had pioneered with the Radio Corporation of America in the 1920s, and television, where it had been one of the industry pioneers in the 30s, sent a shock through the nation's dwindling consumer electronics industry. Only the Zenith Corporation will remain as a major United States manufacturer of television sets and other video equipment.

The *Los Angeles Times* showed less restraint. It asked querulously, "Has GE's controversial Chairman John F. Welch Jr. sold an American birthright for the proverbial mess of pottage?" In a companion piece, the paper quoted an unnamed consultant who complained: "Here is a fabulously wealthy company with so much cash. So why isn't he pouring it into businesses this country can still compete in instead of throwing in the towel to the Japanese?"

The journalists seemed to believe that GE was radically out of sync with American public opinion; Welch thought the press was out of touch with reality. He believes the best way to project jobs is by beating the competition. That was the point of the rule of No. 1 or No. 2.

During the mid-1980s, GE abandoned the domestic context of this most basic strategic tenet. Previously, it had measured the competitive strength of its businesses by their position in the U.S. market. In 1987, Welch announced that "number one or number two, for us, refers to *world* market position." The predations of corporations that drew their strength from international reach had convinced the CEO that leadership in the domestic market no longer ensured success. "Somebody rewrote the script," as he later put it.

In the environment of the 1990s, globalization must be taken for granted. There will only be one standard for corporate success: international market share. Success within a particular country will not even guarantee corporate survival. The winning corporations—those which can dictate their destiny—will win by finding markets all over the world.

Fortress America had become a trap. For nearly a century, GE's main opponent had been Westinghouse; now Matsushita, Philips, Siemens, Toshiba, and perhaps a dozen more emerging global giants were challenging GE's preeminence in markets from light bulbs to CAT scanners to industrial turbines. As a GE employee magazine wrote, the huge size of the domestic market, the government protection of certain industries, and the lack of meaningful foreign competition had "delayed the onset of the need as well as the development of the skills needed to hunt in the global wild." What Opie said of Lighting became true for many GE businesses: "We felt that North America was a sitting duck."

Hordes of overseas companies were using mergers and acquisitions to bulk up. In 1986 Sweden's Electrolux bought White Consolidated of Cleveland, a leading U.S. major-appliance company whose products sell under the Frigidaire, Kelvinator, and Westinghouse brands. GE Power Systems faced tougher competition after two of its European competitors joined to form ASEA Brown Boveri, and then bought Combustion Engineering, a major American producer of boilers for power plants. The list goes on and on.

Meanwhile, new technology and increased trade were causing structural change. Computers, fax machines, and improved telephone service were reducing the difficulties of doing business on an international scale. The growth of intercountry and intercontinental trade was stitching together an increasingly integrated world economy. Companies that took advantage of these changes benefited from the savings of purchasing components and labor in low-cost countries, as well as increased sales volumes from entering additional markets. Over time, these global enterprises created their own international networks for distribution, communication, and so on, an infrastructure that further strengthened them vis-à-vis GE.

Once again, Welch was hearing the fearsome call of *change or die*. He responded none too soon—yet long before most Americans saw the need for a global perspective. Inevitably, Welch faced resistance, not only from GEers this time, but also from plenty of his fellow citizens.

In 1987, the year of the Thomson deal, GE was still almost completely preoccupied with its domestic market. Just 23% of its revenues came from outside the United States—one-third less than in 1981, when the Australian mining outfit Utah International had been a big contributor.

Most of the individual businesses suffered from the same made-in-America mind-set that had victimized GE Lighting. To be sure, Lighting's use of patent-licensing agreements to protect its home market during the early twentieth century was unusual; but nearly all of GE's operations had prospered without much consideration of the world beyond their country's borders. Few had experienced much direct competition from sophisticated corporations of global reach. Only three of GE's thirteen businesses, Plastics, Aircraft Engines, and Turbines, functioned on a global basis.

Until the mid-1980s, GE was under no great pressure to

build its strength overseas. For most of its early history, the company's main strategy had been to protect and dominate the domestic market. As a result, what it called "foreign business" had averaged less than 8% of GE's net sales from 1892 to 1952. Jones clearly perceived the global opportunity and greatly increased the amount of business GE did overseas. He also chose a successor who had been doing business on a global basis since the 1960s.

As CEO, Welch did not immediately impose globalization on the rest of GE. Until as late as 1984 ot 1985, the corporate revolution and GE's domestic problems preoccupied him, so he gave second priority to international efforts. Besides, he was convinced that the only way to make the strategy work was for each business to take responsibility for its own globalization, creating and implementing a plan appropriate to its particular needs. Having witnessed the failure of many corporate-wide policies, he believed that any cookie-cutter approach would be doomed.

One such failure was International General Electric, which GE disbanded not long after Welch took office. For sixty-three years this headquarters-based group had operated overseas businesses structured as mini-GEs. Fresco believes that many people misunderstood the decision to shut it down: "The organization decided that everything which was international was not interesting to the chairman," he says.

Giving autonomy to the individual businesses further slowed the process. In 1983, the CEO introduced the concept of "ownership"—the idea that managers should run their businesses as if they owned them. The idea was to replace bureaucratic, buck-passing habits with a willingness to accept responsibility. To give ownership a chance to work, Welch had to grant the operating businesses a large measure of freedom. And during his first years in office, before he established the CEC, most of GE's autonomous business heads had scant interest in globalization. Recalls Fresco:

I think the real obstacle was the parochial mentality of many businesses. They were thinking domestic. And Jack had to abide by that.

Moreover, Welch had a few reservations of his own, especially about Europe. Socialistic labor policies in Germany, France, Italy, and elsewhere drastically limited companies' freedom to improve productivity by laying off employees or changing their work rules. Such stricture are anathema to him. Even as Europe warmed to free-market capitalism and began to liberalize its regulations, Welch's concerns lingered.

The main incentive to delay, though, was the inherent difficulty of globalization. Achieving it, particularly at U.S. companies, requires a revolution. And the United States, for all its progress, ranks among the least cosmopolitan of the world's major economic powers, with a citizenry still largely ignorant of foreign languages and susceptible to isolationist urges.

Paolo Fresco urged his boss to act soon. The twelve nations in the European Community, known as the EC or Common Market, had agreed to eliminate most intro-European tariffs and other obstacles to trade with one another by the end of 1992. That would create the world's largest single market, with 337 million consumers. (By making Eastern Europe available, the collapse of the Iron Curtain has since greatly expanded the EC's potential size.) The agreement also promised to make European trade far more profitable, since EC nations had promised to cut back on wasteful regulations.

The opportunity seemed enormous, but no business could benefit from it without access to the European market. While the EC planned to lower internal trade barriers, it would maintain or even raise the barriers around its perimeter. That made 1992 a deadline for non-European companies: To join the club, outsiders had to transform themselves into Europeans—fast. For most of GE's businesses, that meant merging or joint-venturing with local firms, or buying them outright. But that was no longer easy, since everyone else in the world suddenly got the same idea.

Welch might not agree with me, but I think the urgency of the need to globalize struck him during a twelve-day world tour in May 1985. Accompanied by Fresco, he met with CEOs in Japan, Korea, and Europe. Many, such as Thomson's Gomez, were representatives of a younger generation of leaders whose attitudes matched Welch's surprisingly often. During a meeting in Europe, Olivetti chairman Carlo Benedetti told Welch, "Give me the best CEOs in the United States, and I'll line up the six best CEOs in Europe, and they'll eat your lunch globally."

Welch wasn't exactly intimidated, but he returned with a deepened conviction that the world had changed and the time to globalize was now. Here's Fresco's analysis:

> He was exposed to a number of changes which had occurred in Europe. But more important, I think, he was touching hands with a new generation of business leaders in Europe who thought the same way as he was thinking.

Adds Fresco, "A couple of years later would have been too late."

In 1986, the CEO began pushing hard for globalization. In CEC meetings, the corporation's vulnerability became a frequent topic of discussion, as Welch pitched the idea that GE had to become global to survive. To him, the idea seemed the obvious response to competitive reality; but certain businesses, such as Appliances, initially resisted. Sincerely believing their markets were not global, they figured that remaining best-of-class in the United States was good enough. Building a consensus took time.

The real resistance came from much further down in the hierarchy. As Welch admits, "The lower you are in the organization, the less clear it is that globalization is a great idea." Fresco describes the plight of a typical Medical Systems employee after the merger with Thomson-CGR:

Globalization is to certain people a threat without rewards. You look at the engineer for X-ray in Milwaukee and there is no up side on this one for him. He runs the risk of losing his job, he runs the risk of losing authority—he might find his boss is a guy that does not even know how to speak his language.

Moreover, for any organization accustomed to domestic success, the introduction of global standards of performance can be deeply threatening. It's a classic example of what Welch calls "raising the bar": demanding a higher level of performance than was ever expected before.

In addition to the complex issues of language and culture, going global requires massive transformations in the way a company does business and measures success. As in domestic competition, only a few top-ranked players can expect to prevail in a global marketplace. Winners must achieve best-of-class status in four areas:

- **Products and services:** Offering the world's best design and technology at the world's best prices.

- **Organization:** Integrating worldwide purchasing, manufacturing, distribution, and marketing networks. Balancing economies of scale with responsiveness to the particular needs of local markets. Institutionalizing learning and communication processes to enable the organization to adopt new techniques quickly.

- **Human resources:** Developing a cadre of cosmopolitan executives marked by what GE calls "global brains": the ability to understand and respect the national and ethnic biases of others, and to feel comfortable anywhere in the world.

- **Alliances:** Finding ways to cooperate with other companies—sometimes even competitors—who can help you quickly surmount trade barriers and other obstacles.

Facing challenges such as these—and having paused to win the agreement of CEC members—the CEO couldn't wait for everyone else in GE to catch on to the need for globalization. The 1992 deadline loomed.

The remaining opportunities to expand overseas were few, and often hotly contested. Welch pushed every business leader to identify potential partners and propose deals, in the Orient as well as in Europe. As he likes to say, business is simple. In each of GE's major lines, only a few companies—rarely more than five—rank as serious global contenders. And within any given country, the important producers of a particular product, whether appliances or gas turbines, are easy to identify. So in a very short time, GE's business leaders defined their main globalization opportunities and set their number-crunchers to work pricing potential deals. They soon knew exactly what they wanted and how much they were willing to pay.

The Thomson-CGR deal is a perfect example of planful opportunism in action. As the Prussian strategist von Moltke had advised, Welch established a clear general goal—globalizing every GE business—while remaining flexible and open to serendipity about how to reach it. When the opportunity appeared, GE was ready to move fast. Welch explains:

> We didn't need to go back to headquarters for a strategic analysis and a bunch of reports. Conceptually, it took us [Welch and Gomez] about thirty minutes to decide that the deal made sense, and then a meeting of maybe two hours with the Thomson people to work out the basic terms. We signed a letter of intent in five days.

The easiest part was the decision to sell Consumer Electronics, known within GE as Consumers. Welch had never liked selling TV sets, a low-margin commodity business in which GE remained a global also-ran even after the RCA acquisition. GE sold VCRs (putting its meatball on machines made in Japan), but had seen margins erode in that line, too. Welch bitched and moaned about Consumer Electronics' frequent losses but was powerless to prevent them.

The situation demonstrates why the CEO decided that GE must be No. 1 or No. 2 on a global basis. Even though Indianapolis-based Consumer Electronics was the U.S. market leader, it couldn't control its destiny. The world's biggest producer, Matsushita, boasted the industry's lowest costs and unit volumes much larger than GE's. Taking advantage of its edge, Matsushita kept pushing prices down. That left GE with the nightmarish choice of having to give up either market share or profitability.

GE probably could have lifted itself to a No. 1 or No. 2 market position through acquisitions. But since even the top manufacturers were losing money on TV sets, Welch saw no sense in increasing GE's commitment. He preferred to put GE's money into profitable businesses such as medical equipment, in which the company had the advantages of technological and financial strength. Selling Consumer Electronics was the obvious solution. The trick was finding a buyer.

Medical Systems, meanwhile, was facing many of the same problems as many old-line GE businesses. Despite its high-tech image, the GE unit had been making X-ray machines since 1920. For years after it introduced CAT scanners in the mid-1970s, GEMS kept the rich U.S. market largely to itself, and prospered. In 1981 GE negotiated the Yokogawa joint venture. YMS could produce some scanners for considerably less than GE's Milwaukee plant, while providing an entrée into the Japanese market.

GEMS faced its first real challenge in the mid-1980s, when hospitals and other health-care providers introduced new measures to control costs. The rules cut the market for CAT scanners in half almost overnight. At the same time, Siemens and Toshiba introduced good-quality scanners at competitive prices. One GEMS marketing manager remembers encountering Toshiba at a trade show:

> I came back and made a report that said in five years Toshiba would be a major competitor. To the product representative I said, "If the Japanese are half as good in medical as they are in automobiles, we're in big trouble."

When Trani arrived at GEMS in 1986, the business was losing ground globally. Impressed by the productivity of the joint-venture plant in Japan, GE boosted its ownership share of YMS from 51% to 75%. He realized that GEMS also needed to expand in Europe, where its presence was very small. Remembers Trani:

> We started to ask, "Where is the market?" We told Jack that our position in Europe was not terrific, especially in X-ray. Outside the United States, we had just a 3% share of X-ray. We knew there were certain medium-sized players who might be viable, and Thomson-CGR was one of them. So when the opportunity presented itself, we were ready.

Welch and Fresco spent several months trying to buy Thomson-CGR. But Gomez didn't want to sell—until he came up with the idea of swapping it for Consumer Electronics. The deal left both parties with stronger businesses. Thomson moved from the back of the pack to No. 2 among the world's TV-set producers, while GEMS moved from No. 2 in diagnostic imaging equipment to No. 1.

Corporations rarely achieve globalization in a single, dramatic stroke like the one that transformed GEMS. Some of GE's thirteen businesses are among the most global enterprises in the world; others still retain a mainly domestic orientation. GE doesn't release much data on this subject, but here's the scorecard so far for the twelve businesses other than GEMS:

- **Aerospace,** maker of radars and other military products, grew up a captive of the U.S. government. Worldwide defense spending has declined sharply in recent years, limiting opportunities for overseas expansion, but the unit is finding overseas buyers for communication satellites and radar equipment. A fifth of its 1991 orders came from outside the United States.

- **Aircraft Engines** has always had customers around the world for both its commercial and military jet engines. Its joint venture with France's SNECMA, a model of successful alliance, is expanding its share in Europe. A growing percentage of sales come from outside the United States.

- **Appliances:** This unit tried to buy Philips' European appliance business, but lost the deal to Whirlpool. In 1989 Appliances established several Asian joint ventures, and merged its small European operation with the household appliance business of Britain's General Electric Co. (Despite the name, GEC is no relation to GE). As of now, though, Appliances' business remains predominantly in the United States.

- **Electrical Distribution and Control** gets about one-third of its revenues overseas. It has formed ventures with Fuji of Japan and other partners, and has made acquisitions in Spain and elsewhere.

- **Financial Services** is still one of GE's less global businesses, with only a small fraction of its assets overseas. Among its recent acquisitions was Avis's European automotive fleet operation.

- **Information Services** is by definition a global business, offering data networks and information processing on a worldwide basis. Recent ventures include an inventory control system for Benetton, the Italian clothing manufacturer, and a data-exchange system for New Zealand's customs service.

- **Lighting:** Since the acquisition of Hungary's Tungsram and Britain's Thorn—plus joint ventures with Toshiba and others in Asia—a major portion of sales comes from overseas. Lighting's profits are still mainly domestic.

- **Motors:** Traditionally a U.S. operation, Motors expanded its international reach through a 1988 alliance with Robert Bosch of Germany, and has established production facilities in Singapore and Malaysia.

- **NBC:** Despite a couple of small overseas ventures, this remains an almost entirely domestic business.

- **Plastics:** Global since the early 1970s, this remains one of GE's most international units, with manufacturing operations in both Europe and Asia.

- **Power Systems,** long accustomed to substantial international sales, faces increased competition from ASEA Brown Boveri. Its overseas business has been booming again, thanks in part to a network of some sixty partners and licensees outside the United States. Joint ventures in Germany and Austria enabled the business to log some $1 billion in European orders in 1991.

- **Transportation Systems** is shooting for 15% annual growth in overseas revenues. By the end of 1992, about one-fourth of its unit sales were from outside the United States.

In 1993, GE is still struggling, business by business, to grow stronger overseas while improving the organization of what it has already got. It is no longer simply a domestic company, but not yet completely a global one either. GE lost a good part of its non-U.S. sales when it sold Utah International; since then, non-U.S. revenues have more than doubled, to $16 billion.

As the pieces fall into place, the importance of the soft issues becomes more obvious. Ninety percent of GE managers are U.S. citizens. Some are extremely sophisticated; others are middle-American engineering types. As Welch acknowledges, building a cadre of managers with "global brains" ranks among his most substantial challenges.

Inducing GE's most talented executives to move overseas isn't always easy. While international stints are a requirement for advancement at Plastics and, increasingly, Medical Systems, executives at some other businesses see them as a waste of time. If the real action is happening in the United States, that's where managers will want to be. To fight that tendency, Welch has encouraged CEC members to give more big jobs to GEers who have completed overseas stints, in order to create success stories of "people who went overseas and came back and did well."

Crotonville courses are also playing a role in creating a new breed of global managers at GE. Crotonville routinely sends GE executives on learning assignments overseas, and builds teams of managers from around the world.

As with Work-Out or any other ambitious project of cultural change, globalizing GE probably will take a decade or more. There's still a very long way to go, but as overseas revenues grow and more GEers become accustomed to the new way of thinking, the rate of progress is likely to accelerate.

Act Three

REVOLUTION AS
A WAY OF LIFE

Chapter Sixteen

Work-Out

One warm September afternoon in 1988, Welch emerged again from the Crotonville Pit in a state of intense frustration. For the zillionth time, a bunch of middle managers had bombarded him with complaints about the way things worked at their local GE outposts. Stripped of particulars, the grievance was always the same: The speaker believed in GE's shared values, but his or her boss didn't.

The CEO kept hearing comments like these over and over:

"The goal of downsizing and delayering is correct. The execution stinks. The concept is to drop a lot of less-important work. But this just didn't happen. We still have to know all the details, we still have to follow all the old policies and systems. We have no time, and more demands than ever."

Or:

"If this is the best business in the world, why do I go home feeling so miserable?"

Nearly eight years after Welch had become CEO, he knew that far too many GE managers still weren't "walking the talk." By almost any other measure the GE revolution had made enormous progress: The corporate productivity rate, for instance, finally had broken into the 4% to 5% range, roughly twice its previous level. Welch was basically satisfied with GE's portfolio of businesses, and the worst of the layoffs had ended long ago. Progress was visible almost anywhere you looked, resistance had become rare—and yet they still lingered, these unimaginative, frightened, bureaucratic bosses-from-hell, the ones who demanded that fewer people do everything that once had been done by many more. These were the managers or supervisors who snored through the videos of Welch's speeches, then pushed their subordinates to work weekends and nights under intolerable pressure, with no end in sight, often to accomplish tasks that seemed irrelevant, senseless, or worse. When anyone complained, they blamed Fairfield.

Welch had to find a way to get past those people, to directly touch the great mass of GE employees. The boundaryless organization he envisioned couldn't work without the active participation of the whole work force—but he couldn't expect people to participate in something they didn't understand. How to reach them?

On that particular day in 1988, the GE revolution reached its turning point. Welch suddenly experienced an epiphany that enabled him to embody his whole understanding of business in a single, very practical idea. It was a big idea, the sort of transforming thought that comes along only once or twice in a lifetime.

Walking with Jim Baughman to the helicopter that would fly them from Crotonville back to Fairfield, the CEO was angry enough to pound nails with his fist. He'd been hearing the same complaints from GEers for years; unless something changed,

Welch feared, he'd still be listening to the same broken record when he reached retirement age. Remembers Welch:

> I got in the helicopter, and I said to Jim, "I must have had to say, 'I don't know' about twenty times today, or 'That's not my job, that's your job,' or 'I'm sorry, I don't know why you do that stupid thing, and why you don't fix this.' It wasn't much of a learning experience."
>
> And so finally I said, "Jim, we've got to change this. We've got to get these issues dealt with. We've got to put the person who knows the answer to these frustrations in the front of the room. We've got to force leaders who aren't walking the talk to face up to their people."
>
> That was the start of Work-Out. The idea was nothing more than trying to re-create Crotonville in a thousand different places.

Baughman designed Work-Out to Welch's specifications: an ambitious, ten-year program that Harvard Business School professor and GE consultant Len Schlesinger has called "one of the biggest planned efforts to alter people's behavior since Mao's Cultural Revolution."

Welch's desire to make believers of GE's middle managers was based on pragmatism as well as passion. By 1988, as he often said, GE had done about all the slashing and burning it could do. Although in certain areas GE still lagged behind such productivity champions as Toyota, Honda, and Canon, it had largely matched or exceeded the achievements of its direct competitors. At that level of accomplishment, just maintaining GE's productivity rate required enormous effort.

And Welch still believed GE had to improve. As he later wrote, "Without productivity growth, it is possible to lose in twenty-four months businesses that took a half-century, or a century, to build. Productivity growth is essential to industrial survival."

By 1988 GE's top-level executives understood Welch's

ideas, and embraced them. The Corporate Executive Council had become an effective mechanism for pushing shared values; CEC members were accustomed to mining good ideas in one part of GE, and moving them quickly to the rest of the company. The CEC, in turn, had spawned similar councils at all of GE's thirteen major businesses, engaging another layer of executives in the new style of management.

But as the complaints at Crotonville indicated, managers further down in the organization were far less likely to share the new GE values. Middle- and lower-level managers still did not see any urgent need to change. Despite delayering, GE still had a substantial hierarchy; a few levels down in most GE businesses, junior managers were still filling out unneeded reports, taking superfluous measurements, and coping with draconian goals.

Although Welch's ideas were clear, his communication methods still weren't effective enough to change people's minds. In one way or another, the police, media, and schools all failed him. The police (financial controls) could deal only with such technical matters as budgets and plans; the schools (Crotonville) lacked the capacity to affect enough people. As for the media, Welch told me:

> I learned pretty early on that videotapes and speech reprints alone are of little value. Because people don't use them. They're not alive or dynamic. The idea is to convene a group, use the videotape [of a Welch speech] as a catalyst, and then have a discussion. Well, what managers would do is just show the tape. There would be no communication with the people. Nobody talked to them.
>
> Worse than that, with their body language some would communicate their own reaction to the tape—that it was bullshit.

Welch identified the problem in a tersely worded memorandum he wrote to CEC members a few months before his fateful helicopter ride with Baughman. The memo started off with a statement of the problem: "Disconnect between CEO and middle management on what CEO says and what middle managers feel." Among the possible causes he suggested was this: "Business leaders like the hierarchical system. . . . They don't want to buy in." In other words, resistance.

The memo lists and rejects two possible solutions: changing the corporate message, or eliminating it. In both cases Welch's response begins with a telegraphic "Don't want to." Finally, on page five, Welch arrives at the solution he recommends:

1. Buy into Corporate message. If cannot: Come and talk to any of us [Welch or the vice chairmen] about what bothers you and what you would like to change/modify. We can/will react to what is troublesome.

2. After buying in, sit with all direct reports and dialogue about Corporate message. Invite us to participate, as you see fit, in sharing the Corporate message with your direct reports.

3. Ask your direct reports what they can buy into—and what they can't. Dialogue to achieve consensus on Corporate message. Use examples and illustrations pertinent to your business.

4. Have each of them meet with their direct reports—and you participate. Then bring it to the next level until every manager in the Company has met with his/her leader—and if they are troubled, see you.

5. Devote some time—at each staff meeting, at each level—to discussing progress in support of the Corporate message. One-time announcement/discussion will not achieve intended result.

THE OBJECTIVE IS TO HAVE EVERY PERSON IN THIS COMPANY BE EXPOSED TO AND HAVE A DIALOGUE ON THIS CORPORATE OPERATING OBJECTIVE AND ITS SUPPORTING MESSAGES BY JULY 1, 1988.

The idea excited Welch, but his July deadline came and went without much action. A few CEC members took his memo to heart, but most dawdled or simply forgot about it. The hoped-for transformation never happened.

The CEO was fed up, both with the issue and his inability to resolve it. "One of the things we can't do as top management is solve local problems," he admits. That's why Welch had been preaching liberation and empowerment and responsibility for years: He wanted local people to find their own solutions.

To illustrate what he was up against, Welch tells the story of a typical question-and-answer session that took place at GE Plastics' factory in Holland:

> This engineer says to me, "The plant is nothing like it used to be. It's nowhere near as much fun as it was ten years ago. What the hell are you going to do about it?"
>
> I looked at him and said, "Let me tell you what I'm going to do. I'm leaving for Paris in about thirty minutes and I won't be back within a year, maybe two years. So, personally, I'm going to do very little about it.
>
> "Why don't you get fifty people who were here ten years ago, and why don't you, for the next two and half days, go and write down, in the left-hand column, why it was fun before? And in the right-hand column, put down why it isn't fun now. And then why don't you fifty people change it and move everything back to the left side, so you're having fun again. Because you're the only people who can do it."

As Welch will cheerfully concede, the intellectual underpinnings of Work-Out, from worker involvement to continuous improvement, are concepts familiar to the point of being shopworn. The uniqueness of the program is its vast scale, evidence of GE's commitment: By mid-1993, over 200,000 GEers—85% of the work force—had experienced Work-Out. On any given day, perhaps 20,000 are participating in a related program. Within another few years Work-Out will have touched every single person at GE. By contrast, Crotonville programs annually can reach just 10,000 people, an elite 4% of the corporate population.

A mechanism to change minds, Work-Out is designed to deliver the Crotonville experience to the great mass of GE employees. Crotonville can powerfully affect those who go there, but it can't touch those who hear about it second-, third-, or fourth-hand, because the experience depends on personal participation. You've got to be there. In the Pit, employees directly confront the CEO. In workshops, they learn by doing. People get emotionally involved. They grow.

Trying to replicate that rich experience for 300,000 people was like trying to design a mass-market Rolls Royce, but GE found a way. Work-Out began with four major goals:

- **Building trust:** GEers at all levels had to discover that they could speak out as candidly as CEC members do, without jeopardizing their careers. Only then would GE get the benefit of its employees' best ideas. Welch regarded this goal as so important that he allowed the program to proceed for years without proof that it was working.

- **Empowering employees:** The people closest to any given task usually know more about it than their so-called superiors. To tap workers' knowledge and emotional energy, the CEO wanted to grant them much more power. In return, he expected them to take on more responsibility. "There's both permission and obligation," he says.

- **Elimination of unnecessary work:** The quest for higher productivity was only one reason for pushing this goal. Another was the need to provide some relief for GE's overstressed workers. And Welch hoped to show employees some direct, tangible benefits from Work-Out, to generate enthusiasm for the program.

- **A new paradigm for GE:** Ultimately, the CEO wanted Work-Out to define and nurture a new boundaryless organization. The process was analogous to the way Crotonville participants defined GE's shared values, but the scale was much larger. In effect, Welch wanted the whole organization to participate in defining itself.

Once Baughman designed Work-Out, he formed a small GE team at Crotonville to implement it. He retained two dozen outside consultants, all world-class experts on organizational change. Each was assigned to work with the top management team of a GE business to implement the generic design and tailor it to specific needs. Baughman and his Crotonville team, responsible to Welch, led the company-wide effort. Their role was to integrate the Work-Out activities of the GE units and their consultants, and to facilitate the sharing of best practices throughout GE. I was one of the outside consultants Baughman retained. He assigned me to Medical Systems because I was already involved in a program there called the New Way Workshop.

Work-Out began in October 1988. The first stage was a series of local gatherings patterned after New England town meetings. In groups of 30 to 100, the hourly and salaried employees of a particular business would spend three days at an off-site conference center discussing their common problems. No coats. No ties. The setting and behavior was so different from business as usual that Work-Out consultant Steve Kerr called these meetings "unnatural acts in unnatural places."

To ensure that people could speak candidly without fearing retribution, bosses were locked out during discussion times. And Welch made it clear to managers that he would treat any obstruction of Work-Out as "a career-limiting move." Facilitators, all outside consultants at first, ran the workshops.

Meeting in small groups, the employees would define problems and develop concrete proposals. On the final day, the bosses would return. According to Work-Out's rules, they had to make instant, on-the-spot decisions about each proposal, right in front of everyone. Some 80% of proposals got immediate yes-or-no decisions; the remainder that needed study had to get decisions within a month. As Welch had hoped, the process quickly exposed those GE managers who didn't "walk the talk."

At first, people spent much of their time griping. In his 1991 story on Work-Out, *Fortune*'s Thomas A. Stewart quoted an electrician from Aircraft Engines' Lynn, Massachusetts, plant, who explained, "When you've been told to shut up for twenty years, and someone tells you to speak up—you're going to let them have it."

But in the course of complaining, GEers also would identify lots of problems that could be fixed without too much effort. As Opie and Rabinowitz had demonstrated in their productivity drive at Lighting, picking such "low-hanging fruit," as GEers call it, is a way to build momentum and trust in a hurry. A middle manager at Appliances tells how the Work-Out process worked at one plant there:

> We were getting screws from one supplier that was not so good. The bits would break off the screw heads, and scratch the product, and cut people's hands—we had one guy get eighteen stitches. Tempers flared, but management never went and fixed it. They said, "Okay, we'll go get you some screws from the good supplier." But then the bad screws would always reappear.
>
> So a shop steward named Jimmy stood up at Work-Out and told the story. This guy was a maverick, a rock thrower, a nay-sayer. He wanted to test us, to see whether we really wanted to change.
>
> He knew what he was talking about. And he

explained the solution, which had to do with how deep the bit could be inserted into the screw head, and also the point contour on the screw.

We listened, and then said, "Okay, what do you suggest?"

And he replied, "We need to go tell the supplier what the problems are."

Well, I was nervous about it, but I decided to charter a plane to fly Jimmy and a couple other guys to the plant in Virginia where they made the bad screws. They left that very night.

Jimmy got the problem fixed, and it sent a powerful signal to everyone here. He became a leader instead of a maverick, simply because we gave them the forum and allowed him to have some ownership. Now we don't even have supervision in his part of the plant. He carries a two-way radio, and if he needs help he asks for it.

As the GE revolution progressed, the pace of change continued to accelerate. Act I lasted until 1985; just three years later Act III began. By 1988 Welch had clearly defined his vision. Through trial and error, he had reduced it to a few simple ideas: integrated diversity, boundarylessness, global leadership, the business engine. In technical and political terms, GE already was largely transformed; the time had come to change its corporate culture.

Preeminent among Welch's ideas is boundarylessness. Here's how the CEO described it in an annual report:

Our dream for the 1990s is a boundaryless Company, a Company where we knock down the walls that separate us from each other on the inside, and from our key constituencies on the outside. The boundaryless Company we envision will remove the barriers among engineering, manufacturing, marketing, sales, and customer service; it will recognize no distinctions between "domestic" and "foreign" operations—we'll be as comfortable doing business in Budapest and Seoul as we are in Louisville and Schenectady. A boundaryless organization will ignore or erase group labels such as "management," "salaried," or "hourly," which get in the way of people working together. A boundaryless Company will level its external walls as well, reaching out to key suppliers to make them part of a single process in which they and we join hands and intellects in a common purpose—satisfying customers.

This is an admittedly grand vision, requiring unprecedented cultural change, and we are nowhere near achieving it. But we have an idea of how to get there—an idea that is rapidly becoming reality across the Company. It's called Work-Out.

Only through boundarylessness, Welch argued, could the corporation reach its productivity goals. But even for a much-changed GE, boundarylessness remained a challenging proposition. It implied much more than just eliminating bureaucracy: "Ultimately," Welch said, "we're talking about redefining the relationship between boss and subordinate." He envisioned the replacement of hierarchy with cross-functional teams, the transformation of managers into leaders, and a radical empowerment of all the workers who were still getting bossed around. As he explained:

My view of the 1990s is based on the liberation of the workplace. If you want to get the benefit of everything employees have, you've got to free them, make everybody a participant. Everybody has to know everything, so they can make the right decisions by themselves.

In the old culture, managers got their power from secret knowledge: profit margins, market share, all that. But once you share that information with everyone, it often turns out that the emperor has no clothes.

In the new culture, the role of the leader is to express a vision, get buy-in, and implement it. That calls for open, caring relations with every employee, and face-to-face communication. People who can't convincingly articulate a vision won't be successful. But those who can will become even more open—because success breeds self-confidence.

Work-Outs took place all over GE, hundreds of them. As Stewart wrote: "Like kernels of corn in a hot pan, they began popping one at a time—in GE Plastics' silicones unit in Waterford, New York; at NBC; in the lighting business—then in a great, noisy rush."

By 1989 the pent-up demand for change was enormous. Work-Out's carefully designed stagecraft made employees feel safe, freeing them to voice their complaints. Managers added to the momentum by sharing once-secret data. In those early Work-Out sessions we picked a lot of low-hanging fruit.

The key was our insistence on emerging from every session with a list of "actionable items"—things people were committed to start working on right away. At the Schenectady turbine plant, for instance, hourly employees bitched about the milling machines they used. They won authorization to write the specifications for $20 million worth of replacement machines, which they tested and approved themselves.

The result: cycle time—the time needed to mill steel—dropped 80%, lowering inventory cost while increasing responsiveness to customers. Wrote Welch, "It is embarrassing to reflect that for probably eighty or ninety years, we've been dictating equipment needs and managing people who knew how to do things much better and faster than we did."

While Work-Out was getting started, a related movement called Best Practices got under way. One of GE's great weaknesses always was its susceptibility to the "not invented here" syndrome. The corporation had been so accustomed to producing good ideas for so long—ever since Edison, really—that GEers rarely bothered to find out what other folks were thinking. Figuring that no company could corner the market for good ideas, Welch forced the organization to look outside.

His systematic approach was characteristic of GE management tradition. While Welch railed against bureaucracy, he never lost his reverence for the thoroughness and diligence with which GEers think through business issues. During the summer of 1988, Welch assigned Michael Frazier of GE's Business Development staff to develop a list of companies worth emulating, and then to study their achievements. Frazier and his team selected nine companies to study, including Ford, Hewlett Packard, Chapperell Steel, and two of Japan's best-known multinationals, both of which participated on condition their names be kept confidential. The team's ten members fanned out around the world, and spent a full year collecting on-site data at these companies. Although they absorbed lots of minutia, they retained an Olympian perspective: They were seeking answers to the question, "What is the secret of your success?" Their report argued that the accomplishments of the world's productivity champs depended on common traits:

- They managed processes rather than people. Instead of tracking how *much* they produced, they focused on *how* they produced.

- They used process mapping and benchmarking to spot opportunities for improvement. Process mapping is a matter of writing down every single step, no matter how tiny, in a particular task. Benchmarking means comparing oneself to an objective standard, such as a competitor's performance.

- They emphasized continuous improvement, and lauded incremental gains.

- They relied on customer satisfaction as the main gauge of performance. That overcame the tendency to focus on internal goals at customers' expense.

- They stimulated productivity by introducing a constant stream of high-quality new products designed for efficient manufacturing.

- They treated their suppliers as partners.

No less valuable to GE than these overarching ideas were the mind-blowing stories of these companies' achievements. A typical one came from the laundry products business of one of the Japanese participants, a leading producer of washing machines in Japan. According to GE's case study, this company had realized by 1984 that demographic changes would soon fragment its market into niches. That implied a need to switch from producing a few washing machine models in high volumes to making a broad selection of models, which would sell at lower volumes. The challenge was to accomplish that without creating profit-threatening assembly line snafus.

The company created a flexible production system designed to respond directly to the ebb and flow of sales. In five years it tripled the number of new washer models it introduced. The washer factory became accustomed to eleven model changes per day, versus two and a half daily in 1985. Spending only $2 million to $3 million per year to make all these changes, the business doubled both its manufacturing capacity and the dollar amount of sales per employee. At the same time, quality dramatically improved.

After hearing the Frazier team's presentation, Welch became an instant convert. He ordered up a major new Crotonville course on Best Practices, and assigned to Work-Out teams the task of spreading Best Practices throughout GE. He frequently quoted a favorite Baughman line: "Best Practices has legitimized plagiarism."

In phase two of Work-Out, which gathered steam through 1990, GE shifted to unnatural acts in *natural* settings. Now the sessions began to involve groups of people who would ordinarily work together, such as the cross-functional teams of finance, manufacturing, purchasing, and marketing experts collectively responsible for a particular product. Their sessions would begin with a clearly defined problem and a mandate to solve it. With that shift, Work-Out began to become a regular part of the GE way of life. And self-sufficiency became a key goal: GE trained its own people as facilitators, to replace the outsiders.

Work-Out now depended heavily on tools acquired from the Best Practices study, process mapping in particular. In business after business, GEers would gain control over processes by identifying every step in them. Some process maps were so complex that they covered whole walls and resembled diagrams of the wiring in computer chips. The maps noted even such seemingly minor matters as the signatures required to approve purchases or shipments. Since a document tends to sit on a desk for a day before it's signed, cutting out a few unnecessary approvals can significantly speed up a process. (When process mapping failed to help, it usually was because the attention to detail got out of hand.)

To forge a shared commitment to speed and customer satisfaction, GE invited customers and suppliers such as 3M and Sears to join in these sessions. These gatherings were very effective at building trust, but not always pleasant: At a similar session, I remember feeling deeply embarrassed to hear the complaints aired by three companies that worked with GE Aerospace—a Union Carbide division, a major shipbuilder, and a large construction consulting firm. Point by point, executives from the other companies demonstrated how arrogant behavior by GEers was costing them business. I saw for myself that this part of the company still had its "ass to the customer and its face to the CEO."

An early example of GEers vaulting over the high bar was the Quick Response program at Louisville-based Appliances. Process mapping there showed that while a fifth of the parts in any given appliance model were unique, only 5% were expensive enough to substantially affect inventory costs. GE found that it could speed manufacturing and cut costs by keeping ample stocks of the cheap components, while working out just-in-time programs with suppliers to quickly deliver the others as needed. The biggest gains of all came from controlling the sequence in which parts were delivered from a plant's loading dock to its assembly line.

Measures such as these enabled Appliances to reduce its inventory by $200 million—and to increase the business's return on investment by 8.5 percentage points. Appliances cut the eighty-day cycle time from receipt of an order to delivery of a finished product by over 75%. As he had done earlier with Lighting's winning team, Welch put the Appliances group up on a pedestal, touting it as a leading in-house example of best practices.

Louisville became a regular stop for executives from all over the company. But this was more than a corporate tourist attraction: To create a corps of Quick Response experts, each GE business sent a few managers for a full year of action learning in Louisville. By the time these people returned to their own units, they had mastered the intricacies of Quick Response and could serve as effective advocates of the method.

More recently, Aircraft Engines used Work-Out to help it figure out how to meet a heroically ambitious 1992 income target. A big winner during the defense-spending spree of the Reagan years, the unit had produced stellar results through the 1980s and thereby avoided the need to do too much hard thinking about productivity. But demand for military engines is slowing down. "Where's the enemy?" Welch asks with a shrug.

In 1992, Aircraft Engines' sales declined slightly from 1991 levels of about $7.9 billion and are expected to decline further in 1993. Yet the CEO challenged the business to reduce its inventories by $1 billion, to help reach a net income goal of $750 million— as much as it had made in its very best year.

To achieve that, logically, Engines must match its revenue cuts with cost cuts. For months, Aircraft Engines' managers searched for ways to achieve the massive productivity gains they needed to meet their earnings target. During Work-Out, they decided that the business could increase its efficiency enough to halve the time between customers' orders and the delivery of finished engines. That would boost cash flow and enable Aircraft Engines to cut its inventories by up to 40%, reaching Welch's goal.

Is the CEO crazy to set goals so high? He doesn't think so:

What right do I have to do that? It always works. And it's rational. This is not a business that's going to recover any time soon, so it's reasonable to squeeze. And there were lots of inefficiencies built in during the boom times.

One of the hardest things is to get the maximum out of a rising business. You're satisfied, so you don't try as hard. Why did America become noncompetitive in the 1970s? Because it was living off the fat of the 1960s. When are the most sins created in business? In boom times, when managements get arrogant.

In a growing business, it's hard to know whether you've picked the right goal. You pick one based on the peak returns of other global businesses—but maybe that's too low.

During a slump you have to find out what you can do. Our Aircraft Engines business is going to get to four inventory turns a year—then five, seven, who knows? We've been trying to get them there for three years, but they've been stuck at 2.5, 2.7, 2.8 turns. Now they're going to do it, because it will reduce the number of employees they would otherwise have to let go.

GE spent nearly a decade getting in shape; then, in just a couple of years, Work-Out enabled GE to bust through the wall. I was a facilitator at the Aircraft Engines Work-Out in 1992. As I observed the managers debating ways to cut their inventories, I noticed that no one was arguing that the cuts were unnecessary. I've been seeing the same phenomenon all over the company during the past couple of years: GEers aren't resisting much anymore. They understand the imperatives of global competition, and they're determined to win. So instead of bitching when the bar is raised, they focus on how to surmount it.

Phase three of Work-Out began in 1992. Called the Change Acceleration Program, or CAP, it is a systematic attempt to use Work-Out to breed a new type of GE manager. Welch wants all GE's leaders to be professional change agents rather than mere managers. The idea behind CAP is to disseminate to top management all GE's accumulated knowledge and wisdom about the change process itself: how to initiate change, how to accelerate it, and how to make it stick.

Work-Out is a forum for teaching the skills that Welch expects to prove most valuable in the years ahead. Here is where GEers explore the implications of boundarylessness, where competence becomes more important than position, where nobody can hide behind a title or a desk. If the CAP training works, outside facilitators won't be needed. Program graduates will fan out throughout GE to spread the revolutionary message. "In seven years," says Welch, "people who are comfortable as coaches and facilitators will be the norm at GE. And the other people won't get promoted. We can't afford to promote people who don't have the right values."

The epiphany that Welch experienced in the helicopter with Baughman was emblematic of his own transformation as a leader. The cranked-up ferocity of the CEO's interactions with subordinates was giving way to a more wholesome attitude— an urge to respect and empower people that began to seem convincing and genuine. Having started out as the man with the bullhorn, in effect yelling at subordinates who couldn't keep pace, he evolved into a coach, willing to pause (for a nanosecond or two) to help others along.

To some observers, the change was astonishing. As a GE manager told me:

> You know, I've watched the rebirth of Welch, or the renaissance of Welch, or whatever has happened to him. I don't know all the elements that went into his being born again, and I don't even care what they are. But I'm sure glad it's happened. He's a different man than he was in 1981.

When I suggested to Welch that he seemed to have remade himself by around 1988, he challenged me with every bit of his old aggressiveness:

> I haven't changed a thing! I try to adapt to the environment I'm in. In the seventies, when I was helping grow new businesses—at Plastics, at Medical—I was a wild-eyed growth guy. And then I got into the bureaucracy and I had to clean it out, so I was different in 1981. And now I'm in another environment. But that's not being "born again."
>
> The ideas were always the same. We've been talking about reality, agility, ownership, and candor since the beginning. We just got it simpler and more carefully articulated over time: Work-Out, eight years later, is a more meaningful way of communicating the idea of ownership—but it's the same idea.
>
> You don't get anywhere if you keep changing your

ideas. The only way to change people's minds is with consistency. Once you get the ideas, you keep refining and improving them; the more simply your idea is defined, the better it is. You communicate, you communicate, and then you communicate some more. Consistency, simplicity, and repetition is what it's all about.

I think it's been a steady continuum that finally reached a critical mass. We were always consistent in how we talked. We went from videotapes to more meetings, to talking to groups, to round tables, and then to Work-Out. We never changed, we just got better at it. And after a while it started to snowball.

Unquestionably Welch's thinking has remained consistent from the first. But I still think that the man himself has changed. Some smart people share my point of view. Says Gertrude G. Michelson, a senior vice president of R. H. Macy & Co. and a GE director since 1976, "He's changed from competitive to cooperative, in the broadest sense—he understands that's the real top leadership role." Adds Larry Bossidy:

I do think there was a change, vividly, from yelling and screaming for performance, to a much more motivational kind of approach. He became a lot more understanding, much more tolerant: *Hey, if you get the job done even though your style is different from mine, that's fine.* He wasn't that way in the beginning.

The nice thing about Jack is that he keeps growing. The Jack Welch who took over GE is not the Jack Welch you see today.

I view Work-Out as evidence of a major change in Welch's thinking. The CEO used to argue against incremental change, on the theory that only quantum leaps made enough of a difference. Work-Out represented Welch's personal commitment to the Japanese idea of *kaizen,* or "continuous improvement."

This is really a cultural attitude guiding people to constantly seek ways to get better; small improvements are as important to the process as big ones. By 1988, *kaizen*-style methods had produced impressive results at Lighting and Transportation Systems, and he became a convert.

Another major shift, made possible by GE's progress during the previous eight years, was "from hardware to software," in his phrase. Once the organization's survival was no longer at risk, Welch had the luxury of working on the soft issues of corporate culture and employee behavior, freeing Welch to devote more energy to boosting self-confidence. That, in turn, required different behavior from the CEO: You can't boost people's self-confidence by yelling at them.

Welch had always been interested in the soft side of management; now he was beginning to appreciate its power.

Work-Out has not been perfectly successful. Cynical GEers have described it as "Work-In." I know many stressed-out GEers who still regard liberation as little more than a distant dream. And there remain some fascinating issues that Work-Out has yet to address. An important one is compensation. Work-Out parcels out authority, but not money, according to individual merit. Eventually, GE probably will have to devise more equitable gain-sharing systems, to share the rewards of improved productivity with those most responsible for it—regardless of rank.

As occurred earlier with strategic planning, the change-makers GE brought in to spread new ideas are becoming part of the corporation's establishment. There's always the danger that former revolutionaries, having achieved their goals, will entrench themselves and remain on the scene long after they are needed. It would be dismaying if the members of GE's brilliant Work-Out team made that mistake.

By now, so much low-hanging fruit has already been picked that it's reasonable to wonder how much longer GE can sustain the momentum of the last few years. But as the Work-Out process becomes more muscular and people gain trust, more opportunities for improvement come into view. The supply of low-hanging fruit may be inexhaustible. A Work-Out session led GEMS, for instance, to patch a major supplier into its internal electronic-mail network. The two companies also decided to build new-product prototypes jointly. As they work more closely together, they keep stumbling over additional opportunities to improve designs, lower costs, and speed processes. As in human relationships, intimacy can become its own reward.

Work-Out's success is hard to measure. As Welch explains, that's intentional:

> It's best to present big ideas without time frames or rigidly defined goals, because there is resistance to every idea that's different from the current norm. If you allow the nay-sayers to measure and quantify your idea, they can come back and blow it away before it has a chance to work.
>
> For the first year of Work-Out, some people would have loved to measure it. Then they'd have been able to say, "I held twenty-one meetings and 591 people attended, so now it's over."
>
> How will we know if Work-Out is successful? We'll know because over time we'll become more productive. Our attitudes will be better, people will be happier, better ideas will flow.

Work-Out has made believers of GE's top 1,000 or 2,000 executives. I've been inside scores of the world's best and biggest companies, and I can't think of another where intellectual freedom and like-mindedness coexist to an equal degree.

As a formal mechanism for sustaining a revolutionary process—and for transferring real power to employees—Work-Out is unsurpassed so far. But for those tempted to try the program themselves, I offer this caution: GE's already successful transformation is what enabled Work-Out to succeed. Without that foundation, without all the pain and difficulty of Welch's early years, I doubt Work-Out's techniques would have much effect. As Welch says, "You better be lean before you play these games."

The Twenty-first-Century Organization

Welch defines an effective corporate executive as "someone who can change the tires while the car's still rolling." John Trani, forty-seven, fits the description.

His challenge has been to create a boundaryless organization in a high-tech, rapidly globalizing business—while engaged in an all-out slugfest with first-rate competitors. Trani has made Milwaukee-based GEMS the equivalent of an R & D lab for organization, testing new ways of applying the lessons of the GE revolution, from the abstract idea of boundarylessness to the pragmatic focus on processes learned in Work-Out. His experiments haven't all worked, and the newest ones can't yet be judged. But his ideas seem promising.

In GE-speak, keeping the car rolling means producing terrific financial results. Under Trani's leadership, GEMS' income has grown at double-digit rates for the last six years, while sales tripled. But the numbers tell only part of the story. One legacy of his years may be the global organization that has been evolving at GEMS since Trani took over in 1986. The latest of their organizational innovations began in mid-1991, when GEMS launched an effort to create a process-based management system. New systems usually prove difficult to implement, and this one will likely go through many permutations before reaching its final form. But if GEMS succeeds, it may represent an important advance in the quest for the twenty-first-century organization.

GEMS' transformation occurred in three phases. In the first, which I call the "hardware" phase, the business focused on technical issues such as cost structure and acquisitions. The second, "software" phase emphasized the transmission of new values and a global mind-set. The third phase, still under way in 1993, is the attempt to design a new social architecture through which global processes and operating mechanisms become a way of life.

Medical Systems has been operating in uncharted territory because of globalization. GEMS had to go global to seize opportunities in markets abroad, and to defend itself from aggressive competitors from overseas; thus the Yokogawa venture in Japan and the Thomson-CGR deal in France. GEMS' non-U.S. sales rocketed from less than 15% of the total in 1985 to well over 40% three years later.

Warp-speed overseas expansion compounded the already considerable difficulties of managing Medical Systems. As local interests ceased to be paramount, many employees felt anxious—regardless of whether they were located in Milwaukee, Tokyo, or Paris. In addition to the normal conflicts between GEMS' various product lines (ultrasound versus CAT scan, say), and between management functions (such as marketing versus manufacturing), managers began to have differences based on geography.

Trani, a brainy, warmhearted, self-styled "win-aholic"

from a blue-collar neighborhood in Brooklyn, established himself as a grow-or-die manager before taking charge of GEMS. He is one of the most intense, focused, and determined business leaders I have ever met. He has a forceful personality, a booming voice, and a propensity for laughter. Uncompromising about holding people to their commitments, he also has great personal warmth, and goes out of his way to offer emotional support when his managers need it.

Since I left Crotonville in 1987, I've worked for him as a consultant; his willingness to experiment with social architecture makes GEMS an interesting place to work. Trani devotes tremendous amounts of time and energy trying to understand the business he runs. That involves much more than mastering the numbers: He's also fascinated with organizational design and the many levers that influence organizational behavior and performance.

The son of a longshoreman, Trani joined GE in 1978 at thirty-two, after stints in engineering, financial management, and strategic planning at other companies. During those early years he also attended night school, earning three master's degrees, in industrial management, operations research, and business. In every GE business he has led, sales, earnings, and market share have grown, and new-product development has accelerated. Placed atop GE's Audio unit—which Welch had placed outside his three circles—Trani achieved No. 1 market share in radios and No. 2 share in tape recorders. He also pushed Audio into the emerging business of selling telephones, a very profitable, $130-million-a-year operation by 1987, when Thomson bought the business from GE. Trani's next posting was at Mobile Communication, a troubled unit that made commercial radio-communication equipment. He quickly turned it around; Ericsson of Sweden eventually bought the business from GE for a handsome price.

Appreciating Trani's skills and the results he produced, Welch put him in charge of GEMS. With sales of over $1 billion in 1986, Medical Systems already was the world's biggest maker of diagnostic-imaging equipment. Its product line ranged from ultrasound and X-ray equipment at the low end, through several types of CAT scanners, to the high end of magnetic resonance machines.

Under Walt Robb, Trani's able predecessor, GEMS had developed its technology leadership. Until the mid-1980s, the ability to produce the clearest possible images of internal organs was what customers wanted most, and GEMS' images were the best. Although the machines cost as much as $1 million apiece, they enabled doctors to save money—and lives. The images facilitated early diagnosis of medical problems, often on an outpatient basis; diagnostic imaging provided a very attractive alternative to cutting people open with scalpels and visually inspecting their innards. GEMS led the U.S. market with shares as high as 50% for certain products. It consistently ranked among GE's fastest-growing businesses, along with Plastics and Financial Services.

Even so, Trani's arrival followed a startling wake-up call for GEMS. By 1986 technology was no longer Medical Systems' most critical need. Its cost structure had been premised on continual growth—but the market had changed, and the growth of the business had nearly stopped. In order to grow, GEMS had to globalize, and in order to globalize, it had to reshape its organization. To use Larry Bossidy's word, the operation was showing early signs of becoming "disheveled." People in GEMS' various functions and product lines were accustomed to focusing on their own little boxes, paying scant attention to the business as a whole. To many of them, globalization seemed more threat than opportunity.

GEMS already had a foothold in Japan, through Yokogawa Medical Systems, and was increasing its ownership share in the venture from 51% to 75%. When GE swapped its TV set operation for Thomson-CGR, GEMS suddenly became General Electric's most complex global enterprise.

That forced a radical change in Medical Systems' identity. Nothing in the lives of GEMS' employees had prepared them for the changes they now faced. Globalization would require unprecedented levels of teamwork among people who didn't know each other, felt they had little in common, and in some cases distrusted each other. Some executives in Milwaukee were barely on speaking terms with their colleagues in Europe and Japan. Before moving Trani to Medical Systems, Welch had installed a new head of GEMS' European operation, instructing him to "ignore the Milwaukee bunch" and do whatever was necessary to build business in Europe. The European chief did just that; he was not the most popular man in Milwaukee.

The Thomson-CGR deal introduced thousands of unhappy Frenchmen to an organization that already had many anxious Americans and Japanese. The French felt betrayed by their former masters at Thomson, and fearful of GE. The joint venture with Yokogawa also caused rancor. The Japanese company aroused scorn from some of the technologists in Milwaukee. For their part, the Japanese at YMS criticized GEMS for its quality and cost problems. And they resented any interference from GE, even though GE owned a majority of their company. The Japanese believed their destiny was to fight Toshiba within Japan, and only secondarily to help the American owners.

The conflicts annoyed Welch. I remember hearing a Milwaukee manufacturing manager confront him: "Sell machines made by Yokogawa Medical Systems? Why should we give them the business over our own people?"

Replied Welch, who had overseen Medical Systems earlier in his career, "Them is us. We *own* YMS. Now figure out what to do."

Like so many of the markets GE served, the diagnostic-imaging business began to change dramatically during the mid-1980s. Pressured by the U.S. government and their own patients, health care providers became cost-conscious buyers.

And CAT scanners, once the pinnacle of rarified technology, had become a product that several competent manufacturers could supply. Siemens and Toshiba saw an opportunity to penetrate the U.S. market with lower-priced machines.

In 1985 profits fell, and GEMS had to lay off hundreds of employees. That compounded the difficulty of building a global enterprise. Deeply concerned, Welch commissioned a Boston Consulting Group study of Medical Systems' costs; it concluded that GEMS's cost structure was higher than Siemens'.

Once Trani arrived, change came in cascades. The hardware phase began with a program called Focus 80 to wring out the excess cost and make the business leaner and faster. As you'd expect, Trani delayered, consolidated manufacturing sites, laid people off, reduced inventories, redesigned products, and so on. He created countless task forces to involve as many people as possible in these efforts, delegating to them the power to decide what to cut.

The Trani team also had to shepherd GEMS through a painful cultural transition—from a single-minded focus on leading-edge technology to simultaneous concentration on technology *and* marketing, manufacturing, and cost. In organizational terms, the goal was to retain the best qualities of GEMS' independent, free-spirited frontiersmen and teach them the disciplines necessary to achieve sustainable cost-competitiveness. He insisted that productivity and R & D investment were directly related: The higher the productivity, the more GEMS could spend on research. Medical Systems' productivity rose from less than 2% in 1985 to over 7% in 1992, while R & D investment quadrupled.

Inevitably, Trani aroused resistance. Says he:

What we have to avoid is breaking people's spirits. I would argue that the most sensitive approach is to err on the side of action. Decide what you're going to do, and then do it quickly. There is nothing worse than change by a thousand cuts. As for organizations—they are much more malleable than people think, and their fragility is, sometimes, only in people's minds.

Globalization added exponentially to the difficulty of running a business that was already entangled in the intricacies of running five high-tech product lines. Trani regrouped GEMS into three geographic "poles"—based in Milwaukee, Paris, and Tokyo—each with worldwide responsibility for a particular group of imaging products.

That new organization scrambled existing power structures throughout the business. For starters, Trani insisted that "no kings were allowed," meaning that he would not permit Milwaukee to dominate. The poles would share responsibility for developing and manufacturing products to be sold worldwide, but each pole would independently market those products within its geographic sphere of influence. In addition, each pole would take primary responsibility for certain products. The United States got top-of-the-line CAT scanners, ultrasound systems, and nuclear-imaging equipment. The Japanese took charge of mid-priced CAT scanners and ultrasound machines. The French got most X-ray systems.

Suddenly, getting ordinary jobs done required crossing more boundaries than ever before—not just the familiar boundaries defined by function or product line, but time differences of up to fourteen hours, language barriers that sometimes forced GEMS to hire simultaneous translators for meetings, and the deep-rooted prejudices of three of the world's most arrogant national cultures.

The Americans, French, and Japanese each see themselves as superior, an attitude that injects conflict into any endeavor involving all three. This isn't unique to GEMS; I've seen it at many global companies. As employees were quick to notice, each culture had its down side. In workshops, I heard them complain that the Americans too often acted like cowboys, impulsive and careless. They said the French, enraptured with Cartesian logic, sometimes carried on annoyingly pointless arguments for hours. And the Japanese, unwilling to offend, could smile and nod in apparent agreement with an idea—and then resist it with all their might.

Everything became more complicated. Even a global electronic mail system, which has become an important means of binding this business together, was difficult to launch. Creating a single, integrated network was technologically challenging. Many Japanese and some of the French weren't fluent in English. Another obstacle was that many of them didn't know how to type. The pieces came together only gradually.

By the time I arrived in 1987, GEMS' software phase had begun. Trani asked me to help him manage the transition to a global organization, so I formed an international team that also included Ram Charan, originally from India, Michael Brimm, a professor from INSEAD in France, and Hiro Takeuchi from Tokyo. Our mandate was to create a program using Crotonville-style compressed action learning to indoctrinate GEMS managers in new ways of working—while they were developing solutions to pressing business needs.

The essential skills we wanted to teach included the ability to communicate effectively with others despite the barriers of language and geographic distance, and the capacity to motivate and work comfortably with teams. Inventiveness and flexibility were important, too: There's no paint-by-numbers approach to globalization.

Under what we called the Global Leadership Program, seven small teams, each with executives from the United States, Europe, and Japan, were assigned major projects that took nine months to complete. Sample assignments: devising a system to quickly transfer new technologies across the business; globalizing new-product planning; and creating a strategy to compete with Siemens, the world's No. 2 producer of diagnostic-imaging equipment, in its home market of Germany.

Trani regarded the program's goals of long-term executive development and short-term problem-solving as equally important. In the early years, the Global Leadership Program also served to build the human network that helped tie GEMS together, while Trani's team experimented with more formal mechanisms.

The first event of the Global Leadership Program took place in June 1988, not long after Trani's three-pole reorganization. We yanked fifty-five high-ranking GEMS managers out of their normal lives, and flew them to Faro, Portugal, for an introductory workshop. There, colleagues from America, Japan, and France met for the first time.

Early on, they debated whether GEMS really needed worldwide teamwork to win. The topic was plenty controversial, but the emotional energy of the discussion was deflated by the simultaneous translation, which slowed the pace of conversation. Even so, the participants managed to display all their native prejudices and resentments.

The ice broke—or at least cracked—during the Outward Bound-style activities of the second day. We set up two challenges designed to force people to communicate despite the barriers of language. In the first, multinational teams of people had to grope their way across wobbling rope bridges while wearing blindfolds; that forced them to communicate by touch and tone of voice. Each safe crossing inspired another small increment of confidence.

Then we put the group in front of a sheer, fourteen-foot wall and ordered them to surmount it using nothing but their bodies. That called for trust, thoughtful teamwork, and lots of sweaty exertion. By the end of the day, exhausted participants were beginning to like each other more than they liked the people running the program—the sort of healthy, us-against-them camaraderie that Marine boot camp inspires.

Then, between lengthy classroom teaching sessions, the hard work began. After dividing the group into seven teams, we handed out the assignments. Each team also got a senior GEMS manager as its coach. One of our rules is that the coaches all work outside their areas of expertise: The head of the technology staff, for instance, coached the team working on a marketing project. That helped the coaches leave the hard business issues to the teams, which were qualified to handle them, while helping out with subtler human problems.

These so-called soft concerns often proved hard to deal with: How, for example, were people accustomed to hierarchy supposed to act in a team that had no designated leader? The idea perplexed many participants.

At the end of the five-day Faro event we assigned the groups one last physical challenge. In just a few hours, each team had to design, build, and race a raft in a nearby inlet of the Atlantic Ocean. Each raft had to carry an entire seven-member team plus the coach. Using the barrels, wood, and rope we provided, the teams lashed together rough crafts and tried to paddle them around some buoys several hundred yards offshore.

Besides being a lot of fun, this event tested the teams' ability to handle conflict and cultural differences. Under intense time pressure, and without a shipwright's skills or the aid of simultaneous translators, they had to reach consensus on a raft design, then build and race the craft. The contest produced clear winners and losers. One team got around all the race buoys, while another team's raft capsized almost immediately in the shallows. That provided a vivid demonstration of the benefits of teamwork—and the penalty for lacking it.

At the end, every workshop member got feedback from the group on his or her behavior. We wrote these comments down on flip charts, a practice that proved especially useful with the French and Japanese, whose comprehension of written English often far exceeds their understanding of conversation. The process forced the shy, silent types out of the shadows.

The teams' work on their projects continued long after the Faro workshop ended. Knowing they would have to report real results to a real boss, participants had to teach themselves how to communicate with their teammates across two oceans via fax, electronic mail, two-way video systems, and in-person meetings. People who'd never left the United States became accustomed to flying to Tokyo one week, and Paris the next. As team members quickly discovered, globalization is a pain in the ass. The discomforts range from lost sleep to the resentment of the stay-at-home managers stuck with the work that globetrotters leave behind.

The only reason to put up with so much complication and disruption is that globalization so clearly seems to be the winning strategy. Market forces are compelling businesses to transfer technology and expertise throughout their organizations regardless of geography. And the economies of scale that come with globalization are impressive; if you can't figure out how to exploit them, your competitors will.

Halfway through the first year of the Global Leadership Program, our seven teams reconvened at the Hotel Seiyo in Tokyo's Ginza District. This meeting, soon dubbed the "Ginza event," proved awkward and painful for all of us. Everyone was suffering from the stress of coping with so much novelty and extra work. We couldn't reach a consensus about what was important; one divisive question was whether to focus on soft issues such as values, or hard business matters. The meeting lasted three days and resolved nothing. We returned home feeling serious reservations about the whole process. But GEers are disciplined folks, so everyone kept pursuing the assignments even so.

We held the Global Leadership Program's final event in March 1989 in Chicago. At this meeting, the seven teams presented their functional plans; after spending a half-day evaluating each project, Trani and the leaders from the three geographic poles announced which proposals they would adopt. By the end of the day Trani had allocated millions of dollars.

When we asked the participants to tell us what they'd learned, several key themes emerged.

- When the Americans dominate team discussions, as they are prone to do, people of other nationalities quickly lose interest and nothing gets done. It helps to speak slowly and write things down—and sometimes to restrain the impulse to speak.

- The French love of argument can make emotionally neutral remarks seem combative and hurtful.

- The Japanese too often keep their good ideas to themselves.

- Almost everyone was astounded at the amount of time and effort necessary to accomplish meaningful work across global boundaries. The consensus was that true globalization would require years of effort.

- The program's most obvious payoff was the grid of interlacing global networks formed by participants. Forcing people to get to know one another during the workshops, and then obliging them to work together, encouraged people to form lasting personal bonds. Those networks of personal relationships provide the best way to steer work projects through the maze of a global organization.

One of the participants summarized it well when he wrote:

If there's anything we've learned, it's to give equal time to both the project and the globalization experience. If you walk away from this with an excellent project completion, but don't know how a Frenchman lives, don't know why a

Japanese businessman gets promoted, haven't tasted sushi, haven't ridden in the British subway, etc., you've blown it.

To be global, you must know how the other poles think, what their customers want, and, basically, what makes them tick.

This isn't as complex as it sounds. Just talk to them as colleagues, not aliens.

In the distant future, no doubt, the skills required for international communication will become more widespread. For now, though, it makes no sense to waste resources teaching language and other complex skills to the adults who are already established in business organizations. Welch, one of the best global managers around, speaks no language but English. Trani, though widely traveled, is not the sort of guy who visits temples while in Japan. You don't need to know how to bow correctly, or enjoy eating brains, to succeed as a global manager.

If you're good at what you do, and know how to get along with people, you're 90% of the way there.

By 1991 GEMS' software phase ended. The Global Leadership Program had produced some 250 graduates, a group of change agents large enough to influence the entire organization. Trani felt GEMS was ready for the next big step: an evolution of the organizational structure designed to address the complexities of global business.

As he tells the story, Trani began to see a process-based organization as the way to get beyond GEMS' limitations:

We decided to try to get five times better in both quality and speed by 1995. Before we even got to the question of how to get there, we had to figure out how to measure our progress. We got a group together and started talking about it, and everybody had a different measurement.

Well, everyone was sitting around the table, thirty people. And it was impossible to get them to agree.

It became clear that this wasn't going to work. It wasn't really until after that meeting, when I thought about the complexity of it, that I realized processes were the way to go.

Trani believes that the way to cope with complexity is with a stripped-down, extremely flexible organization that trusts employees to find their own paths through the maze. In simpler, more leisurely times, leaders could achieve greatness by telling people exactly what to do; today the most advanced organizations are forced to rely on individuals who can make decisions by themselves.

The formal networks laid out in organization charts rarely work as well as the informal ones that people create ad hoc. Anyone who has served in the military knows that the best way to get supplies is not through the cumbersome official requisition process, but through back channels, as Milo Minderbinder did so memorably in the book *Catch-22*. Individuals' ability to outsmart the organization becomes more crucial as corporate structures become more complex. At GEMS, one person may simultaneously be working on several project teams, reporting to several different people in widely scattered parts of the business, and working closely with multiple sets of colleagues, some of whom may be located thousands of miles away. A few months later, the same person may be working on entirely different projects and dealing with a new cast of characters. Organizations simply aren't smart enough to cope with so much complexity; only people are.

Trani moved to the third phase of the organization's development: the creation of a new social architecture. His team designed an organization built on six basic processes:

- **Advanced Technology:** The equivalent of research and development, this is the process of developing the basic technologies on which future products will rely.

- **Offerings Development:** The design of products and services based on those technologies.

- **Go-to-Market:** The identification of market needs—including the particular demands of individual national markets—and the fine-tuning of product designs to meet them.

- **Order-to-Remittance:** This sprawling process encompasses everything that gets done from the placing of a customer's order to the delivery of the equipment, including sales, purchasing of supplies, manufacturing, distribution, on-site installation and testing, and billing and collection. Here's where GEMS can leverage its global position and integrate its operations to achieve important economies of scale.

- **Service Delivery:** Providing repairs and upgrades to the installed base of GEMS machines—a business that produces a very substantial portion of GEMS' profits.

- **Support:** This includes all the staff functions, from finance to human resources to government relations.

If it occurs to you that these processes should all work together, Trani would heartily agree. In particular the first two processes, concerning product development and production, need extremely careful synchronization. One of Trani's goals is to force employees into an awareness that, no matter how it is divided, GEMS remains a single organization with the shared goal of serving customers. That idea got lost in the tangle of functional, product, and national rivalries.

The most important links between processes will be informal. Trani is counting on help from the Group Operating Council, the GEMS equivalent of GE's Corporate Executive Council. Trani also expects the growing ranks of global execulives under his command to develop their own person-to-person lines of communication across the various process-based organizations.

Trani didn't try to define the links himself. Instead, he assigned teams of GEMS executives the task of inventing systems to suit their needs. The result will be a plan that they can "own." With their commitment bolstering Trani's— and their detailed knowledge of the businesses refining his more general ideas—the new vision should be easier to implement.

In 1991, Trani named an eight-person team for each process, consisting of a chief, two senior executives from each of the three geographical poles, and one staffer. Even though the Milwaukee-based "Americas" pole accounts for more than half of GEMS' sales, Trani gave it no more representation than the other poles; he was determined to foster teamwork. He gave the teams enough authority to commandeer whatever people and resources they would need, and instructed them to return in a year with detailed plans.

Creating the new process-based organization has proved more complicated than Trani expected. Instead of trying to establish all the global processes at once, he now plans to start with just the two that promise the biggest payoff: Order-to-Remittance, and Service Delivery. Trani is candid about the difficulty of creating a global organization:

> An organization is a learning laboratory. The more we get into this, the more we realize we have to scale back and simplify. It was just too complex to try to do the whole thing at once. We're discovering that to get global is even more difficult than what you might think.

If the process structure succeeds, Medical Systems will better balance three competing goals: maximizing economies of scale, to lower costs; maximizing responsiveness to local markets, to increase sales; and maximizing the whole organization's ability to learn from the experiences of each of its parts, to push both productivity and revenue growth. No business as large and complex as GEMS—its 1992 revenues reached just over $3.5 billion—has ever done that. Being the first would give GEMS a boost likely to keep it ahead of the competition for years.

Chapter Eighteen

Head, Heart, and Guts

Management is fine as far as it goes, but leadership is the way to win. GE has created an organization designed to demand leadership from every one of its members. As an employee at Appliances wryly notes, "We hired the arms and backs and legs of people for years, and we never knew the brains came free."

Delayering and drastic staff cuts eliminated the bureaucratic infrastructure that used to prop people up. That has forced GEers to better understand their businesses, instead of delegating the responsibility to strategic planners or subordinates. And GE executives can't avoid tough decisions about what's important enough to spend time on: They once directly supervised an average of seven people each; now they typically oversee fifteen to twenty and sometimes more.

The only way to cope with so much responsibility is to lead—management would take too much time. GEers have no choice but to find their own resources, design their own organizations, and invent their own ways of getting jobs done. Leaders' success depends on the ability to assemble and motivate teams of people who can accomplish tasks by themselves. Measured in terms of human stress, the cost of GE's leadership system is still extremely high—but it remains unmatched as a method to deliver new ideas to the marketplace fast.

The real substance of the GE revolution is the new relationship it created between employer and employee. The traditional corporate hierarchy, premised on the mutual mistrust of workers and bosses, was too plodding and cumbersome to suit Welch. In its place, the CEO envisioned an enterprise that relied more on ideas and shared values to win the commitment of employees. "The glue is an affinity among people who want to grapple with the outside world and win," he says. Based on emotional energy rather than coercion, the new organization had to be flexible enough to allow many workers to manage themselves, and nimble enough to beat competitors still bound by bureaucratic controls. Today, that vision is becoming a reality.

The notion of an organization based on shared values evolved from the CEO's perception that control had become a competitive liability. His thoughts on the subject bear repeating:

> The old organization was built on control, but the world has changed. The world is moving at such a pace that control has become a limitation. It slows you down. You've got to balance freedom with some control, but you've got to have more freedom than you ever dreamt of. To measure value, we're trying to look at what you contribute instead of what you control.

Looking back over the Welch years at GE, it is clear that he always intended to create values-based organization. Those who dismissed him as "Neutron Jack" in the early years completely missed the point. The urge to unlock the latent power of ideas explains almost everything Welch has done since he became GE's chief executive in 1981. From the first, his goal has been to get GE's employees to see the world as it really is, and then to act on that understanding. That's what he means by "facing reality." The idea sounds simple, but the turbulent history of the GE revolution demonstrates the difficulty of putting it into practice. It also shows that the payoff can be enormous.

When Welch started out, the values that counted at GE admittedly were mostly his own, as the CEO acted on strong personal convictions about matters ranging from personal ethics to fine points of corporate management. In 1993, the values that count at GE are shared by thousands of employees. With roughly 230,000 people on its payroll, the company surely harbors some dissidents, but anyone who spends much time at GE can feel the energy that results when allegiance once compelled by force is given freely.

Increased unanimity may be the greatest achievement of the eleven years Welch has spent refining and repeating the same handful of big ideas. Much as he cherishes diversity, in people as well as businesses, he knows that teams of people need common goals to win. The emerging consensus about GE's goals is the ultimate result of everything the CEO has done, from the painful early decisions to sell off weak businesses and lay off unneeded employees, to the soft-and-fuzzy concerns of the late 1980s and early 1990s: the Crotonville debates about values, Work-Out, and the ongoing effort to create a boundaryless organization.

The outside world finally began to understand GE's long obsession with values when the company released its 1991 annual report. In his chairman's letter, Welch repackaged one of his oldest ideas in a way that suddenly riveted the attention of business people around the world. He defined four types of executives:

The first is one who delivers on commitments—financial or otherwise—and shares the values of our Company. His or her future is an easy call. Onward and upward.

The second type of leader is one who does not meet commitments and does not share our values. Not as pleasant a call, but equally easy.

The third is one who misses commitments but shares the values. He or she usually gets a second chance, preferably in a different environment.

Then there's the fourth type—the most difficult for many of us to deal with. That leader delivers on commitments, makes all the numbers, but doesn't share the values we must have. This is the individual who typically forces performance out of people rather than inspires it: the autocrat, the big shot, the tyrant. Too often all of us have looked the other way—tolerated these "type 4" managers because "they always deliver"—at least in the short term.

And perhaps this type was more acceptable in easier times, but in an environment where we must have every good idea from every man and woman in the organization, we cannot afford management styles that suppress and intimidate. Whether we can convince and help these managers to change—recognizing how difficult that can be—or part company with them if they cannot, will be the ultimate test of our commitment to the transformation of this Company and will determine the future of the mutual respect and trust we are building. . . . We know now that without leaders who "walk the talk," all of our plans, promises, and dreams for the future are just that—talk.

Such talk draws credibility from the consistent record of action. Since 1989, GE has rated its top 200 or so managers on shared values such as candor, speed, and self-confidence—and relied on those ratings in decisions about pay raises and bonuses. The CEO claims that when GE executives fall short of the company's standards these days, the problem in the vast majority of cases is not financial performance but a failure to live up to the shared values. "If *you* wouldn't want to work for somebody, why would anyone else?" he asks.

Welch has applied this test to his own executive team. The CEO recently said that for the first time since he took office, he is satisfied with every member of the CEC. The council's lineup has continued to change as other companies lured away such prized executives as Larry Bossidy and former Plastics chief Glen Hiner, who became chief executive of Owens-Corning Fiberglas. But Welch also quietly removed a few people who didn't belong.

The manifesto about the four types of managers may become one of Welch's most broadly influential ideas, but those who would apply it won't succeed by taking shortcuts. Though other companies have long been accustomed to picking up hot management ideas from GE, from strategic planning to management by objective, such borrowings more often consist of the husks of ideas than their substance. When stripped of context and commitment, concepts lose meaning; divorced from the revolutionary gestalt, the idea of rating executives on values doesn't mean a thing.

At GE, the integration of shared values into the management process represents the culmination of a long, arduous, and highly disciplined effort. The focus on soft values was always accompanied by the demand for financial performance. Transforming the GE of 1981 into today's revved-up business engine required all the layoffs, asset sales, and reorganizations that made the early 1980s so agonizing at General Electric.

Those hardheaded decisions, in turn, forced a redefinition of the psychological contract between the company and its employees. As Welch explained in an interview I conducted with my colleague Ram Charan for the *Harvard Business Review:*

Like many other large companies in the United States, Europe, and Japan, GE has had an implicit psychological contract based on perceived lifetime employment. This produced a paternal, feudal, fuzzy kind of loyalty. You put in your time, worked hard, and the company took care of you for life.

That kind of loyalty tends to focus people inward. But given today's environment, people's emotional energy must be focused outward on a competitive world where no business is a safe haven for employment unless it is winning in the marketplace. The psychological contract has to change.

The new psychological contract, if there is such a thing, is that jobs at GE are the best in the world for people who are willing to compete. We have the best training and development resources and an environment committed to providing opportunities for personal and professional growth.

The new compact gives employees more freedom than ever before, and potentially, greater rewards for performance. But their jobs remain at risk every day. Over time, the idea of exposing every member of the organization to the common risk has become one of GE's most fundamental values and an essential part of the corporate culture.

This is not for the weak or the squeamish. As a GE deal-maker puts it: "The company gives me all the resources and independence I need. If I perform well, I can make more money here than anyplace else. If I don't, I'm out. That's the way it works at GE, and I knew it when I came. We all know it." About 45% of the corporation's current employees arrived after Welch became CEO: They knew what they were getting into when they signed on. The old-timers who can't stand the risk have mostly bailed out.

GE's toughness and its emphasis on shared values are not

contradictory. Both spring from the same source: The insistence that the company control its own destiny. They are different manifestations of a single idea, that the competitive realities of the late twentieth century and beyond require a new relationship between employer and employee. In the years ahead, even a well-tuned business engine won't be enough. The winning corporations will be those that can create *human* engines, powered by turned-on, committed, responsible employees. Companies with old-fashioned, control-based organizations will disappear in the dust.

By revolutionizing the way GE was organized, Welch inadvertently robbed many GEers of the sense of how to get ahead. Shared values helped employees adjust.

The decentralized GE organization Welch inherited in 1981 was based on some 150 business units. Each was devoted to a single product or product line and equipped with all the necessary support functions, from finance to manufacturing. Each had its own profit-and-loss statement. Though not always meaningful as a token of managerial independence, P & L responsibility became the "Holy Grail" to ambitious GE managers, who generally started their careers in functional posts. Since general managers got all the big jobs, promotion, not increased pay, became the most prized reward for performance.

The CEO likened GE's proliferating business units to "popcorn stands," and railed at their inefficiency. The old organization called for redundant functional staffs and encouraged battles over turf that thwarted teamwork. He toppled the whole edifice, consolidating related businesses and minimizing the number of P & Ls. Appliances, for instance, went from a collection of six P & Ls to just one. By 1992, GE had fewer than fifty jobs with P & L responsibility—roughly one per 5,500 employees. Businesses also consolidated their staffs, increasing the responsibility of functional jobs but reducing their number, too.

Given the scarcity of senior management positions, the tradition of frequent promotions had to go. As the image of climbing the ladder became an anachronism, it hasn't always been easy to convince people that the available management jobs were good ones. Functional posts, long scorned as mere stepping-stones, are about the only ones left. To replace the "Holy Grail," GE now emphasizes challenge, increased responsibility, opportunities to learn—and handsome financial rewards, such as stock options and bonuses. In 1981, only 500 GEers received stock options; by 1992, the number had soared to nearly 8,000.

Having changed the way it operates, GE began looking for a new kind of manager, with different skills than the old general-manager jobs required. Most GE units have turned to product-management matrix organizations of the sort used in Lighting and Medical Systems. Such organizations are cost-efficient, customer-focused, and wonderfully adaptable, but complex: Staffers from different functions work together in teams led by product managers. The ability to collaborate, and to find one's own way through the maze become essential. Also vital is the ability to cope with constant change: People usually work on several teams at once, and as they complete their tasks, they get new assignments and teammates. Globalization adds additional layers of complexity, as managers join teams of people scattered around the world, intensifying the need for independence and interpersonal skills.

The company's expectations have changed in other ways. GEers once feared getting "entrenched" in any job or business: A much-cited study by Don Kane of the Executive Management Staff showed that the company's 248 top managers had changed jobs every 2.2 years, on average, during their careers. But Welch, who values commitment and experience, wants people to stick around—often for four years or more in a single job.

Forced to give up their expectations, many GE managers

initially felt screwed. During my time at Crotonville, I joined
Don Kane and Eugene Andrews, also of EMS, in a task force
assigned to chart a new career path for GE managers. As our
1987 report noted, we found "malaise, confusion, and disorien-
tation increasingly evident across our professional and managerial population insofar as their own careers are concerned."

The new organization couldn't work unless GEers came to
see their own roles in it as meaningful and rewarding. Incentive
compensation alone can't buy the depth of employee commitment Welch is after. That's why values become a central element of Welch's reorganization plans.

The CEO's vision of a boundaryless organization is as much an
expression of values as a description of corporate structure.
Boundarylessness is such an all-encompassing idea that many
people have trouble understanding it. Welch uses the term to
express the quintessence of everything GE stands for: A boundaryless manager should embody speed, simplicity, and self-
confidence; serve customers with devotion; act with integrity;
serve as an active agent of unceasing change; and more, much
more.

At the most basic level, boundarylessness is a matter of
cooperation across all the artificial barriers that can separate
people with common interest. To explain his thinking, Welch
uses the image of a house, which presents barriers in three
dimensions:

- The **horizontal** barriers are the walls—such as function,
  product line, or geographic location—that divide groups
  of peers into isolated compartments. Why shouldn't
  marketing talk to Design, or Tokyo to Milwaukee?

- The **vertical** barriers are the layers—the floors and ceil-
  ings—that come with hierarchy. Even a boundaryless
  organization needs a few layers; at GE an average of
  four or five now separate business leaders from factory

workers. But when differences in rank obstruct open communication, hierarchy becomes self-defeating.

- The **external** barriers are the outside walls of the company itself. Beyond them are found many groups with whom close relationships are essential, such as customers, suppliers, and venture partners.

The idea of boundarylessness is particularly useful at GE, which specializes in complicated businesses that involve processes too complex for individuals or even small groups to manage alone. Indeed, the company's ability to handle complexity ranks among its chief competitive advantages in many lines, from Aircraft Engines to Locomotives to Financial Services. Succeeding at such businesses requires teamwork on a grand scale, making cooperation an essential characteristic of organizational success. Given the right kind of people and clearly understood goals, intricate webs of informal networks among employees can accomplish much more than any rigid, traditional organization, producing tangible competitive advantages.

Not everyone is suited for this style of work. Welch makes the cut on the basis of what he calls "head, heart, and guts." By **"head,"** he means intelligence and technical expertise. **"Guts"** is just another word for self-confidence, one of the qualities he values most in people. As for the elusive quality of **"heart,"** it is a mixture of human understanding, consideration, willingness to share—and the ability to keep one's ego in check. Not many executives embody all three attributes. People with "head" aren't hard to find, but the business world attracts fewer capable people with "heart" than it needs. As for "guts"—many of those who appear to have it actually don't; genuinely self-confident people are surprisingly rare.

Accustomed to producing many more talented managers than it needs, GE almost never recruited outsiders for senior positions until Welch became CEO. In order to change the culture, the company occasionally hires brainy outsiders. They serve two purposes: introducing new perspectives, and providing an objective standard against which to benchmark GE's homegrown managers. Many of these transplanted executives start out in GE's corporate Business Development staff, which evaluates potential mergers and acquisitions. Graduates include Michael Carpenter, a Boston Consulting Group alumnus who handled the RCA deal and now runs GE's Kidder Peabody investment bank; Chuck Peiper, also from B.C.G., who heads Lighting's European businesses; and Nigel Andrew from Booz Allen, who runs Plastic's multi-billion-dollar-a-year North and South American operation.

GE's main focus, though, is on developing in-house talent. Welch is convinced that people with "head" are easy to find, and those who don't have "guts" can acquire it by surmounting failure and experiencing success. As for "heart"—Welch has always insisted that sensitivity can be developed, too. I wonder if he is still so sure. Without question, GE can help shape a more humane new generation of leaders, with a recruiting program that values heart, and the sort of relationship-based leadership training that the company offers in its Work-Out Change Acceleration Program and elsewhere. But inspiring teamwork is a lot harder than bossing people around; some GEers once regarded as terrific managers turn out to be type fours. The only way to deal with inveterate bullies may be to part company with them.

Long before Welch came to power, GE's human resources system was among the most disciplined and sophisticated in the world. By combining the best of the old GE procedures with the new emphasis on values, Welch fostered an effective apparatus for corporate transformation.

The CEO's personal commitment is what made those methods work. I've never heard of a chief executive who devotes as much time to people issues as Welch does. Take a look at his calendar: At least twice every month, he spends a half day or more talking with rank-and-file employees, either at Crotonville or local Work-Out programs. Every January, he devotes several days to reviewing and adjusting the incentive compensation for each of GE's top 400 executives. And he spends a full month every year on the rigorous management-appraisal and succession-planning reviews called "Session C."

The CEO's Session C is the pinnacle of a painstaking system for appraising executives and helping them improve their skills and plan their careers. GE's 3,500 or so most senior managers have traditionally been regarded as corporate property, although nearly all of them work in operating businesses. Out of this group, the CEO figuratively "owns" the top several hundred. During the yearly Session C reviews, the CEO spends a day visiting each of GE's thirteen business leaders and their staffs, discussing the qualifications, achievements, and developmental needs of every single member of that top echelon of managers. These are substantive discussions based on hard information. Rated on their ability to develop subordinates, business leaders take that responsibility seriously.

GE's elite, six-person Executive Management Staff amasses information to bolster those judgments. As you might expect, a GE personnel file is no random collection of scribbled notes. It includes comparisons of the GE manager's work goals to actual results, and the appraisals prepared for compensation reviews and for annual succession and development evaluations.

Perhaps the most fascinating such report is the Accomplishment Analysis, a ten-to-fifteen-page document that two-person teams of HR professionals spend a full week preparing. Each contains a detailed, thoughtfully argued appraisal of a manager's strengths and weaknesses, covering anything that seems relevant, from financial performance to psychological quirks to physical fitness. The reports suggest ways to develop further: recommending an overseas posting, or a graduate course—or things as basic as showing up at meetings on time, or treating underlings with respect.

Accomplishment Analysis was designed in the 1970s as a tool to evaluate executives. Under Welch it has become a device to help them grow, part of the extensive feedback and coaching process GE uses to develop its executives.

An HR team begins the process by conducting a very lengthy interview with the target executive: These sessions often last five or six hours. Next they interview the subject's bosses, former bosses, colleagues, subordinates—sometimes even customers and suppliers. The development process begins when the subject of the report reads it and discusses it with the HR staffers. These meetings are often textbook examples of constructive conflict at work. Trained to be truth-tellers, HR people are very polite but don't pull their punches; their candor forces managers to confront themselves. The feedback can cause considerable pain, but GE's HR professionals are trained to help people through the emotionally turbulent process of self-discovery: shock, anger, rejection, and acceptance. Repeated exposure to this challenging process has helped GE's managers earn their reputation for excellence.

Accomplishment analysis is one piece in the complex system that culminates in Session C. Others include:

- **Recruiting:** Welch has urged business leaders to visit campuses personally, instead of delegating the job. New recruits learn about GE's values during their initial interviews.

- **Compensation:** To increase flexibility, most GE businesses have reduced the twenty-nine pay levels that existed in 1981 to a few broad bands. Incentive pay such as bonuses now comprises an average of 25% of total compensation for GE's 3,500 most senior employees; in addition, most of them also get stock options. For the top 450, incentive pay amounts to 35–40% of compensation. Type-one employees—those who produce good financial results and share the values—do best.

- **Appraisals:** GE asks employees to rate themselves—and their peers, subordinates, and bosses—by any number of criteria, including the shared values. The person being rated always sees the data and discusses it with a capable person.

- **Training:** Crotonville exists only to further the development of GE leaders. Since 1986 every single program the school offers has included explicit discussion of GE's shared values, and most programs are designed to further them.

- **Reward and Punishment:** A system of values is meaningless unless enforced. GEers who can't live up to the shared values are less likely to rise—and major shortfalls are punished with dismissal. People who embody the values can advance very fast: Most of GE's thirteen business leaders are in their forties.

By 1989 the CEO had begun systematically using shared values to run the company. Welch recalls the howls of protest that greeted his suggestion that GE numerically rate executives on their adherence to GE's shared values:

We must have discussed this for two hours in the CEC. People kept saying "You can't put a number on how open somebody is." Or, "How can you put a number on how directly people face reality?"

I said, "You're going to have to. Come up with the best numbers you can, and then we'll argue about them."

And that became one of the tools for our Session C review. Are they power oriented? Fair? Are they open, are they self-confident? Do they believe in boundarylessness or are they protecting their turf? Are they mean-spirited?

We're forcing an evaluation of all our people against these values.

The particular values that GEers share aren't for everyone. Reflections of a distinct corporate identity, they shouldn't be imposed willy-nilly on anyone else. But the broader idea of using shared values as the guiding principle of corporate organization may be Jack Welch's greatest contribution to the art of management.

Chapter Nineteen

Jack Welch Speaks His Mind

As GE's managerial focus has shifted from cost-cutting to the murky realm of human values, you may wonder whether the man once dubbed as America's toughest boss has gone soft after twelve years on the job.

Not bloody likely.

"Our standards are tougher than ever," says Welch. "They have to be. The Value Decade has already begun, with global price competition like you've never seen. It's going to be brutal. When I said the 1980s was going to be a white-knuckle decade and the 1990s would be even tougher, I may have understated how hard it's going to get."

He is pushing soft values because he sees them as the only way to maintain the pace of GE's productivity drive. To prevail in the coming years, he argues, GE must keep improving its productivity. But most of the company's fat is long gone. Since

1981 General Electric has more than doubled its revenues, to more than $62 billion, while greatly reducing total employment. The only way such a lean, disciplined organization can continue to better its performance may be by inspiring the remaining workers to produce more.

Welch has been pushing soft values all along, but GE became receptive to them only recently. It took the CEO years to get his ideas across, first to GE's top-management elite, then to wider circles of executives. At the same time, he was relentlessly pushing hard values, such as global market leadership. Through a gradual, cumulative process, those efforts profoundly altered GE—and then, rather suddenly, the organization ripened, ready for a different kind of change. So now, for the first time, Welch has the opportunity to put his soft ideas into practice on a mass scale.

The revolutionary process, once begun, can never end; each achievement reveals a new challenge. With its portfolio of efficient businesses and willing work force, GE is well into Act III of its transformation. But the dream of a boundaryless organization is not fully realized, and the urgent need for cultural change is undiminished. So long as the world keeps spinning, change will remain a constant, and self-renewal the mark of success.

In mid-1992, we went to GE's headquarters for one final interview. We met in a small, by now familiar conference room with a round table and an expansive view of Fairfield's wooded hills. As Welch struggled for nine hours to summarize his years at GE and his sense of what lies ahead, his energy and stamina were striking—indeed, almost dismaying. The CEO, fifty-seven, had just returned from a fifteen-day, seven-country world tour that had taken him from Saudi Arabia to Indonesia, India, and much of Europe. After a workday crowded with meetings he met us in mid-afternoon—and the conversation continued till 1 A.M., interrupted only for the few minutes we spent serving ourselves a cold buffet dinner.

Here's the gist of what he said:

My main takeaway from all that running around the world is that the capacity-demand equation in most industries is out of whack, and could remain that way for several more years. That's why the Value Decade is upon us.

Everywhere you go, people are saying, "Don't tell me about your technology, tell me your price." To get a lower price, customers are willing to sacrifice the extras they used to demand. The fact is, many governments are broke, and people are hurting, so there's an enormous drive to get value, value, value.

During the global expansion of the 1980s, companies responded to rising demand by building new factories and facilities in computers, airplanes, medical equipment— almost every industry you can think of. Then, when the world economy stopped growing, everybody ended up with too much capacity.

Globalization compounds the problem: It doesn't matter where you are anymore, because distribution systems now give everybody access to everything. Capacity can come from anywhere on the planet, and there's too much in just about every industry in every developed country. No matter where you go, it's the same story.

This worldwide capacity overhang, coming at a time when everybody feels poor, is forcing ferocious price competition. As it intensifies, the margin pressure on all corporations is going to be enormous.

Only the most productive companies are going to win. If you can't sell a top-quality product at the world's lowest price, you're going to be out of the game. In that environment, 6% annual improvement in productivity may not be good enough anymore; you may need 8%, or 9%. And while that bar keeps getting raised higher, higher, higher, we're all going to be experiencing slow revenue growth. It's brutal!

We're focusing our efforts on value-driven products because in business after business, wherever you look, value is what people are buying. With a few exceptions such as pharmaceuticals, the demand for the newest, most expensive, fanciest products is not booming. Look at the sales of European luxury cars—or supercomputers, for that matter. That's not what people want anymore.

In Aircraft Engines, our customers aren't asking about the latest advances, the last 2% of fuel burn. They want to know, *How much will it cost? Can we provide financing? Can they walk away from the lease?* Boeing and ourselves just lost a $1 billion-plus bid at United Airlines to Airbus. Simply put, we couldn't afford to sell them the planes.

Technology is still absolutely critical, but in industry after industry it will be value-driven. Who can make the most energy-efficient light bulb or refrigerator? Whose medical-imaging system is the most cost-effective? The medical diagnostic-imaging business is a perfect example of what's happening everywhere. The market is shifting away from the "technology leader" in the high-end niche to the guy with the basic, proven, low-priced systems that produce acceptable images. Governments have decided they don't want to pay more for health care, so if you're trying to pitch some new hot technology, the customer's going to say, "See you later."

Environmental soundness is another form of value. For instance, we recently won an order from Swissair for jet engines because ours produced the lowest emissions. Multinational companies have to maintain world-class environmental standards wherever they go—even where local laws are lax—in their plants as well as their products. In the end, there's going to be a global standard for the environment, and anyone who cuts corners today will wind up with enormous liabilities down the road. If we're going to be global citizens, we can't have one set of standards in some countries and different standards in others.

Some of the biggest dangers I see ahead come from governments. You can do everything right as a manager and then government deficits, or interest rates, or whatever, can cause a currency to change value by 30% or 40% and knock your business completely out of whack. About 65% of GE's manufacturing base is still located in the U.S. I have to worry about whether government policies here will allow us to deliver the productivity we need to win on a global basis.

But it's not just the United States: Wherever you travel these days, you encounter increasing fear of government. Constituents want more. And to get more, they seem willing to accept enormous increases in government power. I worry about a return to overregulation and protectionism. I don't want to see governments meddling in industrial policy—bureaucrats picking winners and losers. Governments set out to create Silicon Valley and wind up building the Motor Vehicle Department.

In terms of jobs, government may become the world's main growth industry. When the European Community was formed, it created thousands of jobs for bureaucrats. Now they are telling the French which cheese is good and which isn't. It's frightening!

I think the U.S. is in a great position, competitively. We're looking better compared to Germany and Japan than we did five or ten years ago, and many of our companies are in a position to win. We've restructured our industries. Our businesses have better leaders than ever before.

Our people have learned the value of their jobs, and the principle that job security comes from winning. Some of the most passionate pleas for worker productivity I've ever read have been made by tough union leaders. They lecture our managers on the subject at Crotonville. That change in attitude is one of the most positive developments I've seen.

The U.S. did have a gap in product quality before, but during the 1980s we made great strides in closing it. Our cars are better, and so are our computers and semiconductors. We thought they'd all be Japanese by now, but they're not. And if you look at the J. D. Power surveys of customer satisfaction—U.S. versus foreign auto companies—we're pretty close. A few years ago, not many would have believed that could happen.

The United States faces some serious issues—but our country isn't being torn apart to the extent of Czechoslovakia, say. What we have to do now is educate our people. Companies have to get involved in the school systems, with dollars and volunteers. Within GE, we've got to upgrade workers' skills, through intense and continuous training. Companies can't promise lifetime employment, but by constant training and education we may be able to guarantee lifetime employability. We've got to invest totally in our people.

For U.S. companies, at least, globalization is getting increasingly difficult. The expansion into Europe was comparatively easy from a cultural standpoint. As Japan developed, the cultural differences were larger, and U.S. business has had more difficulties there. Looking ahead, the cultural challenges will be larger still in the rest of Asia—from China to Indonesia to Thailand to India—where more than half the world lives. U.S. companies will have to adapt to those cultures if they are to succeed in the twenty-first century.

Trying to define what will happen three to five years out, in specific quantitative terms, is a futile exercise. The world is moving too fast for that. What should a company do instead? First of all, define its vision and its destiny in broad but clear terms. Second, maximize its own productivity. Finally, be organizationally and culturally flexible enough to meet massive change.

The way to control your destiny in a global environment of change and uncertainty is simple: Be the highest value supplier in your marketplace.

When I try to summarize what I've learned since 1981, one of the big lessons is that change has no constituency. People like the status quo. They like the way it was. When you start changing things, the good old days look better and better.

You've got to be prepared for massive resistance.

Incremental change doesn't work very well in the type of transformation GE has gone through. If your change isn't big enough, revolutionary enough, the bureaucracy can beat you. Look at Winston Churchill and Franklin Roosevelt: They said, *This is what it's going to be.* And then they did it. Big, bold changes, forcefully articulated. When you get leaders who confuse popularity with leadership, who just nibble away at things, nothing changes. I think that's true in countries and in companies.

Another big lesson: You've got to be hard to be soft. You have to demonstrate the ability to make the hard, tough decisions—closing plants, divesting, delayering—if you want to have any credibility when you try to promote soft values. We reduced employment and cut the bureaucracy and picked up some unpleasant nicknames, but when we spoke of soft values—things like candor, fairness, facing reality—people listened.

If you've got a fat organization, soft values won't get

you very far. Pushing speed and simplicity, or a program like Work-Out, is just plain not doable in a big bureaucracy. Before you can get into stuff like that, you've first got to do the hard structural work. Take out the layers. Pull up the weeds. Scrape off the rust.

Every organization needs values, but a lean organization needs them even more. When you strip away the support systems of staffs and layers, people need to change their habits and expectations, or else the stress will just overwhelm them. We're all working harder and faster. But unless we're also having more fun, the transformation doesn't work. Values are what enable people to guide themselves through that kind of change.

To create change, I believe in the Crotonville/Work-Out concept: Direct, personal, two-way communication is what seems to make the difference. Exposing people—without the protection of title or position—to ideas from everywhere. Judging ideas on their merits. You've got to be out in front of crowds, repeating yourself over and over again, never changing your message no matter how much it bores you.

You need an overarching message, something big but simple and understandable. Whatever it is—*we're going to be No. 1 or No. 2, or fix/close/sell, or boundarylessness*—every idea you present must be something you could get across easily at a cocktail party with strangers. If only aficionados of your industry can understand what you're saying, you've blown it.

Another takeaway for me: Simplicity applies to measurements, too. Too often we measure everything and understand nothing. The three most important things you need to measure in a business are customer satisfaction, employee satisfaction, and cash flow. If you're growing customer satisfaction, your global market share is sure to grow, too. Employee satisfaction gets you productivity, quality, pride, and creativity. And cash flow is the pulse—the key vital sign of a company.

One thing I've learned is the value of stretching the organization, by setting the bar higher than people think they can go. The standard of performance we use is: *be as good as the best in the world.* Invariably people find the way to get there, or most of the way. They dream and reach and search. The trick is not to punish those who fall short. If they improve, you reward them—even if they haven't reached the goal. But unless you set the bar high enough, you'll never find out what people can do.

I've made my share of mistakes—plenty of them—but my biggest mistake by far was not moving faster. Pulling off a Band-Aid one hair at a time hurts a lot more than a sudden yank. Of course you want to avoid breaking things or stretching the organization too far—but generally, human nature holds you back. You want to be liked, to be thought of as reasonable. So you don't move as fast as you should. Besides hurting more, it costs you competitiveness.

Everything should have been done in half the time. When you're running an institution like this you're always scared at first. You're afraid you'll break it. People don't think about leaders this way, but it's true. Everyone who's running something goes home at night and wrestles with the same fear: *Am I going to be the one who blows this place up?* In retrospect, I was too cautious and too timid. I wanted too many constituencies on board.

Timidity causes mistakes. We didn't buy a food company in the early 1980s because I didn't have the courage of my conviction. We thought about it, we discussed it at Crotonville, and it was the right idea. I was afraid GE wasn't ready for a move like that. Another thing we should have done is eliminate the sectors right away. Then we could have given the sector heads—who were our best people—big jobs running businesses. We should have invented Work-Out five years earlier. I wish we'd understood boundarylessness better, sooner. I wish we'd understood all along how much leverage you can get from the flow of ideas among all the business units.

Now that we've got that leverage, I wonder how we ever lived without it. The enormous advantage we have today is that we can run GE as a laboratory for ideas. We've found mechanisms to share best practices in a way that's trusting and open. When our people go to a Xerox, say, or their people come here, the exchange is good—but in these "fly-bys" the takeaways are largely conceptual, and we both have difficulty getting too far below the surface. But when every GE business sends two people to Louisville for a year to study the Quick Response program in our own appliance business, the ideas take on intensity and depth. The people who go to Louisville aren't tourists. When they go back to their businesses to talk about Quick Response they're zealots, because they're owners of that idea. They've been on the team that made it work.

All those opportunities were out there, but we didn't see them until we got rid of the staffs, the layers, and the hierarchies. Then they became obvious. If I'd moved more quickly in the beginning, we'd have noticed those opportunities sooner, and we'd be farther ahead than we are today.

The only way I see to get more productivity is by getting people involved and excited about their jobs. You can't afford to have anyone walk through a gate of a factory, or into an office, who's not giving 120%. I don't mean running and sweating, but working smarter. It's a matter of understanding the customer's needs instead of just making something and putting it into a box. It's a matter of seeing the importance of your role in the total process.

The point of Work-Out is to give people better jobs. When people see that their ideas count, their dignity is raised. Instead of feeling numb, like robots, they feel important. They *are* important.

I would argue that a satisfied work force is a productive work force. Back when jobs were plentiful and there was no foreign competition, people were satisfied just to hang around. Now people come to work with a different agenda: They want to win against the competition, because they know that the competition is the enemy and that customers are their only source of job security. They don't like weak managers, because they know that the weak managers of the 1970s and 1980s cost millions of people their jobs.

With Work-Out and boundarylessness, we're trying to differentiate GE competitively by raising as much intellectual and creative capital from our work force as we possibly can. That's a lot tougher than raising financial capital, which a strong company can find in any market in the world.

Trust is enormously powerful in a corporation. People won't do their best unless they believe they'll be treated fairly—that there's no cronyism and everybody has a real shot.

The only way I know to create that kind of trust is by laying out your values and then walking the talk. You've got to do what you say you'll do, consistently, over time.

It doesn't mean everybody has to agree. I have a great relationship with Bill Bywater, president of the International Union of Electronic Workers. I would trust him with my wallet, but he knows I'll fight him to the death in certain areas, and vice versa.

He wants to have a neutrality agreement in GE's nonunion plants. He wants to recruit more members for the union.

I'll say, "No way! We can give people everything you can, and more."

He knows where I stand. I know where he stands. We don't always agree—but we trust each other.

That's what boundarylessness is: An open, trusting sharing of ideas. A willingness to listen, debate, and then take the best ideas and get on with it.

If this company is to achieve its goals, we've all got to become boundaryless. Boundaries are crazy. The union is just another boundary, and you have to reach across, the same way you want to reach across the boundaries separating you from your customers and your suppliers and your colleagues overseas.

We're not that far along with boundarylessness yet. It's a big, big idea, but I don't think it has enough fur on it yet. We've got to keep repeating it, reinforcing it, rewarding it, living it, letting everybody know all the time that when they're doing things right, it's because their behavior is boundaryless. It's going to take a couple of more years to get people to the point where the idea of boundarylessness just becomes natural.

Who knows exactly when I'll retire? You go when it's the right time to go. You pray to God you don't stay too long.

I keep asking myself, *Are you regenerating? Are you dealing with new things? When you find yourself in a new environment, do you come up with a fundamentally new approach?* That's the test. When you flunk, you leave.

Three or four times a year, I hop on a plane and visit something like seven countries in fifteen days. People say to me, *Are you nutty?* No, I'm not nutty. I'm trying to regenerate.

The CEO succession here is still a long way off, but I think about it every day. Obviously, anybody who gets this job must have a vision for the company and be capable of rallying people behind it. He or she has got to be very comfortable in a global environment, dealing with world leaders. Be comfortable dealing with people at all levels of the company. Have a boundaryless attitude toward every constituency—race, gender, everything. Have the very highest standards of integrity. Believe in the gut that people are the key to everything, and that change is not something you fear—it's something you relish. Anyone who is too inwardly focused, who doesn't relish customers, who isn't open to change, isn't going to make it.

Finally, whoever gets the job will have to have what I call an "edge"—an insatiable passion for winning and growing. In the end, I think it will be a combination of that edge and those values that will determine who gets this job.

Well after midnight, Welch finally began to show signs of fatigue. The forest beyond the conference room window had disappeared into blackness. The round table at which we sat was littered with financial charts, dirty dinner plates, candy wrappers, and scribbled-on pads of paper. Time to leave.

Looking at Welch across that table, searching for a final question, we reflected on some lingering concerns about the GE revolution. Can any company maintain such momentum indefinitely? Won't employees eventually burn out?

Over the years, GE's financial and stock-market performance seemed to legitimize Welch's controversial decisions. But what if the numbers betray him? Although GE is outperforming most industrial corporations of comparable size, its growth has slowed during the recession of the early 1990s. Meanwhile, the fast-growing Financial Services business is producing ever larger percentages of corporate earnings. In 1993, over 30% of GE's earnings are expected to come from financial services, versus less than 9% in 1981. The trend could become awkward: Since the 1987 stock market crash and the savings-and-loan crisis, wary investors have generally traded the stocks of financial services companies at a steep discount to the S & P 500. What if Wall Street cools on GE?

Ultimately, the question is whether Welch's sometimes fuzzy-sounding ideas about empowering employees can produce the concrete results—in terms of cash flow, and customer and employee satisfaction—that GE will need to prevail in the Value Decade ahead. In 1992 *Time* magazine wrote up the former Neutron Jack in an article titled, "Is Mr. Nice Guy Back?" That sounds like progress—but does Mr. Nice Guy have what it takes to win?

So we asked our last question: What's your response to those who dismiss your talk about values and empowerment as bunk?

For an instant, Welch seemed dumbfounded by the idea that anyone could seriously entertain such a thought. Then, reaching his hands toward us, he made one final effort to explain:

> I think any company that's trying to play in the 1990s has got to find a way to engage the mind of every single employee. Whether we make our way successfully down this road is something only time will tell—but I'm as sure as I've ever been about anything that this is the right road.
>
> If you're not thinking all the time about making every person more valuable, you don't have a chance. What's the alternative? Wasted minds? Uninvolved people? A labor force that's angry or bored? That doesn't make sense!
>
> If you've got a better way, show me. I'd love to know what it is.

GE Timeline

WORLD EVENTS   **CORE IDEAS**

1879

1882 Pearl Street Station lighted one square mile of New York City.

THOMAS ALVA EDISON 1879–1889 Edison's vision was of a company that would light a nation, producing all the components of electrical power stations and electric lamps to accomplish this feat. He believed that politics should not constrain business, that businesses should receive the rewards derived from patents and that management and not unions should make business decisions.

1885

1886 American Federation of Labor (AFL) founded.

890

1891 The manufacture of incandescent lamps in Europe begun by the Philips Holland Company.

1893 Financial "Panic."

CHARLES A. COFFIN, PRESIDENT 1892–1895; CHAIRMAN 1913–1922 Coffin broadened Edison's vision to include any and all applications of electricity in GE's domain. He set in place GE's domestic policies of business governed by the principles of market control through patents and alliances with competitors to enforce licensing agreements. The liquidity of the company was of primary concern to Coffin after a cash shortage threatened GE's existence during the economic recession known as "The Panic of 1893."

1895

1895 Roentgen announced the discovery of x-rays.

1900

1903 Wright Brothers flight.

905

1907 Niagara Falls illuminated by arc searchlights with 1.15 billion candlepower.

COMPANY EVENTS	PRODUCT INTROS	FINANCIAL RESULTS (in millions)
ORGANIZATION Began as a loose federation of independent manufacturers, but the need for control brought Edison to establish the Schenectady Works where all manufacturing was consolidated. **1879** Edison Electric Light Company founded.	**1880** First incandescant light bulbs sold commercially.	
1886 Manufacturing facilities moved to Schenectady "Works."		
LABOR RELATIONS Edison sought to reduce the influence of the growing labor union movement on his company by moving all facilities out of New York City to Schenectady, N.Y. **1891** Edison received patent on thin-filament, high-vacuum incandescent bulb. **1892** Merger with Thomson-Houston formed the General Electric Company.		**1892** Revenues $11.7 Net Income $2.9 Employees 4,000
1896 Working agreement with Westinghouse to share patents. **1898** The assets of the Fort Wayne Electric Corp. were purchased, becoming the Fort Wayne Electric Works of GE.	**1895** GE built the world's largest electric locomotives (90 tons) and transformers (800 kw).	
ORGANIZATION Coffin created a hierarchical, vertical organizational structure for GE. Reporting to him directly were the functional vice-presidents of Sales, Accounting, Manufacturing & Engineering, Law & Patents, and Treasury. Sales forces were deployed along product lines. The managers of GE "Works" facilities reported to the vice-president of Manufacturing & Engineering. R&D was located at each "Works," with Research & Engineering Labs at Schenectady. Functional disputes were settled by CEO. **1900** Steinmetz established the General Electric Research Laboratory, first industrial research laboratory in the U.S. **1900** Registration of the GE trademark (the monogram). **1901** Formation of National Electric Light Assoc., with 40% GE backing centered in Cleveland, Ohio.	**1902** James J. Wood, consulting engineer at the Fort Wayne Works, received patents for stationary and revolving electric fans. **1903** First large Curtis Steam Turbine introduced.	**1900** Revenues $28.8 Net Income $6.9 Employees 12,000
1905 GE controlled 97% of U.S. lamp business and organized Electric Bond & Share to aid small utilities. **1907** The Stanley Electric Manufacturing Co. of Pittsfield, Mass., became the Pittsfield Works of GE.	**1905** GE's first electric toaster, the model X2, placed on the market. **1905** Commercial electric refrigerators with compressor motors and controls manufactured by GE were sold by Federal Automated Refrigeration Co.	

GE Timeline

WORLD EVENTS	CORE IDEAS

1910

1914 World War I began

1914 The Panama Canal opened with controls by GE's Switchboard Engineering Department and using GE's towing locomotives.

1915

1917 Bolshevik Revolution in USSR.

1918 World War I ended.

1920

1923 Transcontinental airmail service began using GE radio transmitters and receivers.

OWEN D. YOUNG, CHAIRMAN 1922–1939, 1942–1945; GERARD SWOPE, PRESIDENT 1922–1939, 1942–1945
Under Swope and Young, there was a broad diversification of the number of products manufactured by GE for the electrification of the American home. The growing demand for these products also resulted in increasing sales of the generating and distribution equipment needed to provide electricity. Swope and Young also initiated an extensive enlargement of GE's advertising, marketing, distribution and service organizations. Swope's plan calling for industry associations to establish and enforce codes of fair competition influenced FDR's New Deal. Swope also espoused the idea that the company was the steward of the balanced best interests of shareholders, workers and customers called Corporatism. Swope expanded GE's domestic market control policies by entering into non-aggression pacts and by investing in foreign competitive manufacturers.

1925

1927 The first home television reception took place at the residence of GE scientist E.F.W. Alexanderson.

1927 Lindbergh's Cross Atlantic Solo Flight

1929 Stock Market Crash

COMPANY EVENTS	PRODUCT INTROS	FINANCIAL RESULTS (in millions)
1911 Dept. of Justice required GE to purchase remaining interest in NELA and it became the National Quality Lamp Works of GE; NELA Park became GE's lighting center.	**1910** George Hughes, founder of Hotpoint, manufactured his first electric range.	**1910** Revenues $71.5 Net Income $10.9 Employees 36,200
1912 The General Electric Pension Plan began.	**1912** GE began the molding of plastic parts using phenolic resins	
1913 GE applied for a patent on an inert gas-filled lamp, improving lamp efficiency.		
1913 E. W. Rice, Jr. became the second president of GE; Charles A. Coffin was elected Chairman of the Board.		
1919 International General Electric Company formed.	**1917** Limited production of the first household refrigerator began at GE's Fort Wayne Works.	
1919 Under the encouragement of the U.S. government, GE organized the Radio Corporation of America (RCA).		
ORGANIZATION Swope and Young believed that each of GE's six "Works" should produce all product lines to encourage competition in all areas of development, engineering and manufacturing. Under Swope, R&D began reporting directly to the CEO. The CEO was involved throughout GE in all financial issues.	**1920** William D. Coolidge developed an x-ray tube and transformer assembly weighing only 20 pounds and suitable for dental and portable x-ray use.	**1920** Revenues $318.5 Net Income $35.4 Employees 82,000
1922 General Electric radio station WGY, Schenectady, began regularly scheduled broadcasting using its 1500-watt transmitter.		
1924 Phoebus Contract with foreign lighting manufacturers entered into.		
1925 Formation of Plastics Department.	**1927** The GE Electric Refrigeration Department was established and began production of the "Monitor Top" hermetically sealed refrigerator.	
1928 GE's station WGY initiated broadcasting of TV programs twice weekly.		

GE Timeline

WORLD EVENTS	CORE IDEAS

1930

1930–1940 The Great Depression.

1933 Roosevelt began the New Deal.

1935

1935 The first major league night baseball game played under GE Novalux lamps.

1937 Howard Hughes set a transcontinental air record employing the GE supercharger

PHILIP D. REED, CHAIRMAN 1939–1942, 1945–1958; CHARLES E. WILSON, PRESIDENT 1939–1942, 1945–1950 Under Wilson and Reed, GE greatly expanded its defense related business and moved into several new markets under the slogan "Progress is Our Most Important Product."

1940

1940 GE's television station WRGB became the first to relay television broadcasts from NYC, marking the formation of the first TV network.

1941 U.S. entered World War II.

1945

1945 World War II ended.

1949 NATO founded.

COMPANY EVENTS	PRODUCT INTROS	FINANCIAL RESULTS (in millions)

LABOR RELATIONS Corporatism had a large impact on labor relations. It espoused the importance of communication and personal contact between management and labor. Compensation was based on piecework, profit bonuses and pension plans to keep employees happy and away from union influence.

1930 The General Electric X-Ray Corporation name given to GE affiliate the Victor X-Ray Corporation.

1931 The Swope Plan proposed.

1932 Swope became Chairman, Economic Advisory Board of the Dept. of Commerce.

1932 GE Contracts Corporation began to finance purchases of refrigerators (ancestor of GE Financial Services).

1932 The GE Air Conditioning Department was established to develop electric devices for home heating, humidifying and temperature control.

1932 RCA became an independent company when the U.S. government decreed that it should be separated from GE. The memory of GE lingered on in the notes of the famous NBC chimes—GEC— which stand for the General Electric Company.

1939 The GE Radio and Television Department was formed; the first lines of TV and FM receivers were announced.

1931 The one millionth GE electric refrigerator, a product introduced only four years earlier, was presented to the Henry Ford Museum.

1932 The three-way lamp was developed for multi-level illumination.

1932 The first GE dishwashers were marketed.

1934 The first fluorescent lamp was constructed at NELA Park.

1930
Revenues $376.2
Net Income $60.5
Employees 78,400

LABOR RELATIONS Policy of "Management Knows Best." Influenced work force directly to avoid union conflict. Expanded number of facilities from 35 to 60 to disperse union influence.

1942 To meet wartime needs, GE plants manufactured 400 plastic parts for aircraft, demonstrating important engineering plastics applications.

1942 Wilson resigned to become a member of the War Production Board; Swope came out of retirement to serve as GE President. Reed resigned to help administer the Lend-Lease Program and later became Chief of the U.S. Mission for Economic Affairs in London; Young returned as GE Chairman of the Board.

1942 GE built and tested first U.S. jet engine.

1940
Revenues $411.9
Net Income $56.2
Employees 76,300

1945 International GE had 5,000 employees selling and manufacturing products abroad.

1946 GE began study of power generation by nuclear energy.

1946 Nine-week labor strike against GE.

1947 GE found guilty in carboloy suit.

1947 The first completely automatic clothes washer was introduced.

1947 The Erie Plant produced the first two-door refrigerator-freezer combination.

GE Timeline

	WORLD EVENTS	**CORE IDEAS**

1950

1950 U.S. entered the Korean War.

1951 Start of the European Economic Community (EEC).

1953 The Korean War ended.

RALPH J. CORDINER, PRESIDENT 1950–1958; CEO, CHAIRMAN 1958–1963 Cordiner sent GE on a path to take advantage of the new markets and technologies that opened after WWII. Following his slogan of "Go for it," GE saw a 20-fold increase in the number of market segments it competed in during Cordiner's tenure. GE's organizational structure changed to a market and product focus under Cordiner's Decentralization. Management Science became the main tenet of Cordiner's career philosophy; Crotonville was established to teach how to manage.

1955

1957 USSR launched Sputnik I.

1960

1961 Alan Shepard first U.S. astronaut in space.

FRED J. BORCH, PRESIDENT 1963–1968; CHAIRMAN, CEO 1968–1972 Borch called the GE Growth Council which identified nine growth sectors in the U.S. economy and GE decided to "Beat the GNP" by entering them all. During his tenure, Borch essentially added another GE to the one whose direction he assumed. GE's sales and earnings doubled between 1963 and 1972. Borch commissioned the McKinsey Study, which called for greater corporate strategic planning to manage the increasingly decentralized structure and prioritize investment decisions.

COMPANY EVENTS	PRODUCT INTROS	FINANCIAL RESULTS (in millions)

ORGANIZATION Cordiner's decentralization of GE changed its 15 centralized components to more than 46 Executive Office and 100 Operating Departments, including those in such new markets as aircraft engines, computers, nuclear energy and aerospace. Each operating department had P & L responsibilities and managers were appraised primarily on profit goals. Teaching managers how to manage any business with standardized procedures was the purpose of the Crotonville Management Institute. Great expansion of Corporate staff occurred in the areas of management consulting, research, employee and public relations, and all functional coordination.

1950 Ralph Cordiner became GE President.

1951 Cordiner cut the dividend rate for GE stock for only the 8th time in GE's history; it has not been reduced since.

1951 Construction began on Appliance Park, Louisville, Ky.

1952 Cordiner's decentralization reorganization began with the company's 15 centralized components converted into more than 100 operating departments.

1953 GE's foreign sales 10% of its total sales.

1953 Dr. Daniel W. Fox combined heated bisphenol A and diphenyl carbonate and discovered a tough, unbreakable, impact resistant, transparent, polycarbonate thermoplastic. This discovery led to the development of LEXAN® thermoplastic.

1954 First industrial installations of numerical controls for machine tools.

1954 GE designed J79, world's first jet engine to move aircraft twice the speed of sound.

1950
Revenues $2,233.8
Net Income $179.7
Employees 206,000

LABOR RELATIONS GE's number of production facilities grew greatly due to the need to specialize production in each facility for its own product line. The training given managers at Crotonville served to create a growing division between management and labor.

1956 Management Development Institute opened in Croton-on-Hudson, N.Y.

1959 GE's International Business was organized as one of the Company's major Groups.

1955 GE announced creation of industrial-grade diamonds.

1955 America's first commercial nuclear power is distributed over the Niagara Mohawk Power Company system; a GE turbine-generator and the Seawolf submarine nuclear reactor prototype were used to produce electric power from a plant in West Milton, N.Y.

1956 PPO discovered by Alan S. Hay. It represented a fundamentally new way to make polymers and became GE's biggest scientific breakthrough in polymers.

1957 The U.S. government's first nuclear reactor license for the five megawatt Vallecitos atomic power plant near Pleasanton, Calif., was granted.

1957 GE Housewares Division introduced the first commercially marketed spray steam and dry iron.

1955
Revenues $3,463.7
Net Income $208.9
Employees 250,300

1960 Federal grand jury indictments were handed down against 17 GE executives for participation in a conspiracy to set prices in turbines and electrical machinery.

1963 Fred Borch succeeded Cordiner as President of GE.

1964 GE Plastics globalization began with a joint venture with Algemene Kunstzijde Unie NV in the Netherlands to market the PPO polymer in Europe.

1960 GE entered the plastics market with the commercial introduction of LEXAN® resin

1961 The GE Space Division developed NIMBUS, an earth-oriented meteorological satellite, the first of a series of seven that supplied scientific data on atmospheric and environmental conditions.

1960
Revenues $4,197.5
Net Income $200.1
Employees 250,600

	WORLD EVENTS	CORE IDEAS

1965

1965 American troops entered combat in Vietnam.

1969 Neil Armstrong stepped on the moon with boots of GE silicone rubber and a helmet visor of LEXAN polycarbonate.

1970

1970 Invention of the Computed Tomography (CT) technology in England.

1973 Last U.S. ground troops left Vietnam.

1973–1974 Energy Crisis.

REGINALD H. JONES, CHAIRMAN, CEO 1972–1981
Jones, a man whose background was in finance and who believed in running GE with a rein of strong financial control, increased the role of corporate review of business strategy and investment prioritization. Jones believed in the importance of R & D in providing growth and instituted Sector Executives as the positions within GE charged with looking for long-term opportunities for growth. Jones felt that it was important to build a constructive dialogue between business and government. To this end, he accepted positions as the Chairman of The Business Council and Co-Chairman of The Business Roundtable.

1975

1979 Three Mile Island nuclear facility accident.

1979–1980 U.S. Energy Crisis.

Hostage Crisis ended January 1979.

COMPANY EVENTS	PRODUCT INTROS	FINANCIAL RESULTS (in millions)

ORGANIZATION During Borch's tenure, the number of departments within GE grew to over 350. These were divided into 43 strategic business units (SBUs) considered to be truly viable businesses. Planning staffs in each of these SBUs were added to GE's already large layers of management. Strategic business plans were reviewed annually by a new corporate planning staff and a newly established Corporate Executive Office of the CEO and three Vice Chairmen.

1968 At age 33, Jack Welch was named general manager of the entire Plastics Department; he had been promoted through four management levels in only eight years.

1968 The McKinsey study led to the establishment of GE's SBU organization and the instituting of strategic planning for GE's component business.

1969 GE sales were at an all-time high while profitability was at an all-time low.

1966 NORYL production began in Selkirk, N.Y.

1968 In the first commercial order for GE engines, GE CF6 engines with 40,000-pound thrust were chosen to power the McDonnell Douglas DC-10 trijet wide-bodied airliner.

1969 GE Appliance Division announced the first side-by-side refrigerator-freezer with an automatic dispenser for ice cubes and chilled water through the door.

1965
Revenues $6,213.6
Net Income $355.1
Employees 333,000

ORGANIZATION Jones ended the dual organization structure of Departments and SBUs, having only the SBUs be planning units within GE and allowing each of the now 49 SBUs to internally organize along product (department) lines or functionally. A new corporate management layer consisting of six Sector Executives was created as the position to which SBU managers reported and were reviewed. The recommendations of the Sector Executives for each business were reviewed by the Corporate Executive Office.

1970 GE bought land in Bergen op Zoom, the Netherlands, for a production facility for LEXAN and NORYL in Europe.

1970 International sales accounted for 16% of GE's total sales.

1971 New $30 million Medical Systems complex built in Waukesha, Wis.

1974 The General Electric Company officially transferred its corporate headquarters from New York City to a new facility in Fairfield, Conn.

1970
Revenues $8,762.7
Net Income $328.5
Employees 396,600

1976 GE Medical systems first CT prototype installed at Univ. of California San Francisco School of Medicine.

1978 GE's international system employed over 100,000 people outside the U.S.; it included 129 affiliated companies manufacturing products in 23 countries and using more than 350 distributors serving markets in 150 countries.

1975 The Aerospace Electronic Systems Department built the GEOS-3 Radar Altimeter; GEOS, the Geodynamics Experimental Ocean Satellite, studies, measures and maps the oceans from orbit.

1976 A computed tomography (CT) scanner developed by the Medical Systems Division took detailed cross-section x-ray pictures of the human body in less than five seconds, four to 60 times faster than other total-body scanners in use.

1977 GE Medical Systems introduced the CT8800, the world's most successful CT scanner.

1978 The largest nuclear plant in the world is completed in Japan, jointly built by GE and three of its licensees in Japan.

1978 The largest rated turbine-generator in the world, Palo Verde I, was shipped to the Arizona Nuclear Power Project; the unit was capable of producing 1,559,100 kva.

1975
Revenues
$14,105.0
Net Income $688.0
Employees 380,000

WORLD EVENTS	CORE IDEAS

1980

1980–1982 U.S. Recession with highest rate of unemployment since the Depression.

JOHN F. WELCH, JR. 1981 A chemical engineer by training, Welch rose through the ranks while building the GE Plastics business. Upon becoming CEO, he realized that, with key markets growing more slowly, technology moving faster, and world competition intensifying, only businesses on top of their markets would survive in the 1990s and beyond. He articulated a strategy whereby businesses that were not #1 or #2 in markets in which GE wanted to participate would have to be fixed, closed or sold.

THE #1 OR #2 STRATEGY AND FIX/CLOSE/SELL With key world markets growing more slowly, technology moving faster, and world competition intensifying, only businesses on top of their markets would survive in the 1990s and beyond. With this in mind, Jack Welch divided the GE businesses which met the requirements of being #1 or #2 globally into three strategic circles: Core Manufacturing, Technology-intensive and Services. Any businesses outside these circles would have to be made more competitive or be closed or sold.

1981

1982

JACK WELCH'S ORIGINAL KEY ISSUES As he sought to define his vision of GE's new culture, Jack Welch spoke of key attitudes and policies which were to be reshaped and reworked over the decade of the 1980s. No longer would there be formal, inwardly focused *budgets*. Managers were to take *ownership* of their businesses, working with a spirit of *entrepreneurship* and *stewardship* and in an environment in which *reality* and *candor* and *open communications* were the mode of operations. Managers were to demand *excellence* from themselves and others. GE's businesses were to be *lean* so that they could be *agile* and fast moving with *quality* in everything produced. Lastly, *investment* as each business required would be made to make each business its very best.

QUANTUM CHANGE As Jack Welch gained experience with trying to change GE, he came to believe that quantum, or bold, large, structural change was required. Incremental change was easily circumvented by established bureaucracy and gave outside competitors time to thwart the strategy. As Welch said, "Understand today fast. Shape tomorrow in your mind, and then leap to tomorrow."

COMPANY EVENTS	PRODUCT INTROS	FINANCIAL RESULTS (in millions)
PRODUCTIVITY Factory automation investments were designed to make GE businesses more cost competitive with their global competition. Programs designed at eliminating waste, down-time, excess inventory, and distribution problems were instituted in plants. The result was an increase in productivity from 2% for the period from 1981 to 1986 to greater than 4% in 1987 and 1988. Each 1% of productivity improvement equaled nearly $300 million in pre-tax profit contribution. **1980** GE Medical Systems (GEMS) acquired portions of Thorn-EMI medical equipment sales and service operation and entered the Ultrasound modality. GE Corporate R&D in Schenectady, N.Y. began Magnetic Resonance (MR) development project for medical diagnostics.		**1980** Revenues $24,959.0 Net Income $1,514.0 Employees 402,000
DOWNSIZING/DELAYERING LEAN AND AGILE Between 1981 and 1988, approximately 100,000 positions at GE were eliminated through restructuring, attrition, and dispositions. Jobs aimed at producing information, "nice to know" but not "necessary to know," were cut. Many layers of management were removed. With less bureaucracy, less second-guessing and reviewing of decisions, GE businesses could be faster-acting and more competitive.	**1981** Introduced CT 9800 scanner for medical diagnostic imaging. Introduced Quick-Fix system for do-it-yourself appliance repair. The USS Ohio, first of the TRIDENT class ballistic missile submarines was commissioned, powered by nuclear reactors designed at GE's Knolls Atomic Power Laboratory and GE Power Systems.	**1981** Revenues $27,240.0 Net Income $1,652.0 Employees 404,000
DIVESTITURES GE businesses which were not #1 or #2 in their markets or which did not provide GE with any unique comparative advantage were divestiture candidates. Among those sold were: Utah International, Consumer Electronics, Housewares and Central Air Conditioning. In total, $8.5 billion in cash was generated. **1982** Opened the GE Answer Center, award winning 24-hour toll-free customer service answering center. Dedicated $130 million expansion of R&D Center in Schenectady, N.Y. Invested $130 million into automating locomotive business in Erie, Pa. Sold central air conditioning business. Joint venture with Yokogawa Electrical Works of Japan established Yokogawa Medical Systems (YMS); GE had 51% ownership. **OWNERSHIP/ENTREPRENEURSHIP/STEWARDSHIP/EXCELLENCE** The goal of ownership within GE was to delegate more decisions and drive the ability to act down several layers. Entrepreneurship meant the creation of an atmosphere in which ideas from all levels could surface. Stewardship was an obligation to take the assets of the business and make them grow. All this required excellence, managers demanding and reaching for the very best from within themselves and from each coworker.	**1982** Introduced GE Medical Systems' first Magnetic Resonance (MR) machine. GE Plastics introduced XENOY thermoplastics for use in automotive exterior body parts GE Lighting introduced the Miser Maxi Light, a 55-watt bulb that delivered as much light as brightest setting of the 150-watt three-way-bulb and has 4–6 times the life of ordinary light bulbs.	**1982** Revenues $26,500.0 Net Income $1,817.0 Employees 367,000

GE Timeline

WORLD EVENTS	CORE IDEAS

1983

1983 The Reagan Era.

1984

COMPANY EVENTS	PRODUCT INTROS	FINANCIAL RESULTS (in millions)

EXTERNAL FOCUS The only results that counted were those in comparison to external competition: Do sales show increasing market share? Do margin figures show that GE had a cost advantage versus its competition? The numbers that now counted at GE were outward-looking and competitively focused.

1983
GE sold Family Financial Services, a second mortgage subsidiary, for $600 million.
Opened new dishwasher plant in Louisville, Ky., as first phase of $1 billion investment in Major Appliances.
Refocused nuclear energy business on fuels and service.
Received major locomotive order from the People's Republic of China.
Expanded mortgage insurance business by acquiring AMIC Corporation.
Common stock split two-for-one.
GE-sponsored Horizons Pavilion opened at Epcot Center in Orlando, Fla.
GEM Polymers (Japan) established as joint venture between GE Plastics and Mitsui Toatsu Chemical and Mitsui Petrochemical Industries to build $50 million thermoplastic resins plant in Japan to serve automotive, electrical and electronics industries.
GE Plastics also began a joint venture with Nagase to build a polyphenol oxide resin plant in Japan.
Philips purchased Westinghouse Lighting, giving this global competitor a 21% share of the U.S. market.

REALITY & CANDOR/OPEN COMMUNICATIONS Reality & Candor in GE: seeing the world as it is rather than as one might wish it to be. With this outlook, a change in the marketplace became an opportunity for action and not something to be feared or ignored. Reaching these opportunities required teamwork with two-way, open communication.

1983
Introduced Signa magnetic resonance (MR) technology for medical diagnostic imaging.
XENOY used in bumber of Ford Sierra manufactured in Europe.

1983
Revenues
$26,797.0
Net Income
$2,024.0
Employees 340,000

1984
GE sold Utah International, its natural resource subsidiary, for $2.4 billion.
GE sold its housewares business to Black & Decker for $300 million.
GE acquired Employers Reinsurance Corp. from Texaco for $1.1 billion; grouped with GECC to form General Electric Financial Services, Inc.
Began $250 million investment to modernize GE Lighting.
Received 75% of U.S. Air Force contract for new fighter engines in the Great Engine War.
GE Medical Systems began joint venture with Samsung in South Korea, forming SMS.

INVESTMENT/QUALITY To accomplish #1 or #2 businesses today and ten years into the future, money would be allocated to that future, by investing in acquisitions, joint ventures, Property Equipment, and R&D to ensure the longterm. The goal of this investment was to have the best products and services for each market served—the quality of offerings needed to stay on top.

1984
GE made first flight-test of the CF6-80C2 commercial aircraft engine.

1984
Revenues
$27,947.0
Net Income
$2,280.0
Employees 330,000

WORLD EVENTS	CORE IDEAS

1985

INTEGRATED DIVERSITY GE was not a conglomerate of 13 unconnected businesses. GE made long-term commitments to winning on a global basis in each of the businesses. In GE, financial, technological and human resources were moved across and among businesses, best practices were shared, and the success of the entire company was the responsibility of each of its parts. Diversity at GE also meant being both a "big" and "small" company at the same time. To its competition, GE was "big": a well-resourced, highly talented, technology-leading, fast-moving, self-confident and very formidable competitor. To its customers, GE was to be "small": serving each on a "first name basis" with real customer satisfaction and retention. GE wanted to be "small" to its employees: making each one's voice and ideas heard and acted upon. Lastly, GE wanted to be "small" in its dealings with the community: taking its place as a responsible part of the environment and a solver of social problems.

THE BUSINESS ENGINE Building on the #1 or #2 strategy, Jack Welch used The Business Engine analogy to show how GE would continue to grow in the future. The office of the CEO allocates GE's human, capital and technical resources among the businesses for productivity or volume growth, selective resource allocation, asset turnover or non-strategic disposition opportunities. The outcomes of these opportunities produce earnings and, with earnings, cash for dividends, acquisitions or to provide the resources for the next round of strategic allocations. Each GE business has a critical role in the Engine and should be rewarded for earnings growth and/or cash flow.

1986

1986 Chernobyl nuclear facility accident.

THE HUMAN ENGINE From the human side of the corporation, growth can only be achieved when emotional energy is released at all levels of the organization, when creativity and feelings of ownership and self-worth exist at every level. The key characteristics of The Human Engine are self-confidence, simplicity and speed. Self-confident people are able to be simple, not clutter the organization with bureaucracy, and hence create speed.

SHARED VALUES For change to succeed, all players at GE must accept and sign on to common values. The values determined to make GE the best company to work for were openness, ability to face reality, self-confidence, fast action, candor, honest communication, and integrity. At GE such values were not just platitudes, but they were actual measurement issues in personnel review.

COMPANY EVENTS	PRODUCT INTROS	FINANCIAL RESULTS (in millions)

ACQUISITIONS GE acquisition strategy was to add businesses which would either enhance the market position of its #1 businesses or purchase businesses which were already #1 or #2 in their markets. In the 1980s, some businesses acquired by GE were: CGR, Borg-Warner Chemicals, Roper, RCA, ERC, Kidder, Peabody, GELCO, and Montgomery Ward Credit Corp.

ALLIANCES GE has entered into joint ventures with foreign firms to achieve technical or marketing advantages. Every GE business has taken steps to join into such alliances. Potential strategic partnerships are limited in number; speed in achieving them is very important.

1985
GE Plastics opened facility to produce NORYL resin in Brazil to serve Latin American and African markets.
GE acquired Decimus Computer Leasing.

SECTOR REMOVAL In order to improve speed and communication, Welch removed the Sector Executive positions in 1985. Each of the businesses now reported directly to one of the members of the CEO. As a result, more decision making power was placed in the hands of the business leaders

1985
NORYL GTX resin introduced in automotive class "A" surface body panels in U.S.
GE shipped the first Dash 8 computer-controlled locomotives.

1985
Revenues
$32,624.0
Net Income
$2,277.0
Employees 299,000

GLOBALIZATION Globalization, becoming a true producer and seller in each of the major markets of the world, became a requirement for GE in the 1980s if it was to maintain its #1 or #2 competitor position in each of its businesses.

1986
GE acquired RCA, including the National Broadcasting Company (NBC), for $6.4 billion in cash.
The Statue of Liberty relighted for 100th aniversary by GE.
GE acquired 80% of Kidder, Peabody & Company.
GE formed factory automation joint venture with FANUC Ltd. of Japan.
GE increased ownership of Yokogawa Medical Systems (YMS) joint venture in Japan from 51% to 75%.
GE Lighting prices for light bulbs began dropping 2–3% per year, instead of rising 2–3% per year as they had in the past.

THE CORPORATE EXECUTIVE COUNCIL (CEC) Two days each quarter, the Corporate Executive Officers, the 13 heads of GE businesses and the senior corporate staff meet in what is more like a business laboratory. All see and discuss the numbers, the goals and the problems at the same time and work until consensus is reached. The CEC creates a sense of trust, personal familiarity and mutual obligation at the top of the company. At each meeting, new programs are discussed so that best practices can be transferred from one business to the next. At the end of each CEC meeting, each leader has the same playbook and knows the plays for each individual business and for GE as a whole.

HUB & SPOKE STRUCTURE GE's Hub was its Corporate Executive Office. Here, resource allocations would be made among all GE businesses. The Spokes in GE, the businesses, were to be highly differentiated. For example, each had its goal for the GE Engine, its own structural variation, and its own reward and compensation system.

WELCH'S VARSITY TEAM In August 1986, due to the acquisition of RCA, Jack Welch moved many of the business heads to different businesses. Now, he had at the helm people who had bought into his management philosophies and strategies.

1986
GE's Unducted Fan (UDF) engine successfully completed its first flight. The UDF offered expected fuel savings of 40% to 70% over conventional turbofans.
The 1986 Ford Taurus and Mercury Sable represented a landmark of GE Plastics; each contained some 70 pounds of GE resins.

1986
Revenues
$42,013.0
Net Income
$2,492.0
Employees 373,000

WORLD EVENTS	CORE IDEAS

1987

1987 October 19th stock market crash.

LEADERSHIP CHARACTERISTICS Good business leaders create and own a vision, articulate the vision, and relentlessly drive it to completion. They are open, use all channels of communication, and are accessible to all. They are truthful with co-workers. Their job is to create and add value, not control or focus on personal power. A leader's task is to make others more effective.

1988

THE BOUNDARYLESS ORGANIZATION This is a call to break down all barriers to communication and action. All employees should go wherever necessary to get needed information or to give input on decisions they can impact. The goal is to increase the level of mutual respect for the parts played by people in each function, each level, each business across all of GE. Furthermore, communication channels should extend to outside stakeholders in GE to suppliers, customers, shareholders, and communities.

COMMUNICATION Communication is *not* achieved through pronouncements on videotapes or in newspapers. Communication comes from give and take constant personal interaction aimed at achieving consensus. Everyone must know, understand and buy into goals or achieving those ends cannot come with speed and decisiveness.

1989

1989 Berlin Wall tumbled.

NEW PSYCHOLOGICAL CONTRACT In the modern, highly competitive world, no business is a safe haven for employment unless it is winning in the marketplace. GE is striving to be the best place in the world to work for people willing to compete and take risks. It is not the place for those seeking an implicit lifetime employment contract.

COMPANY EVENTS	PRODUCT INTROS	FINANCIAL RESULTS (in millions)
REVIEW PROCESS In addition to being evaluated on business results, GE managers are also judged on the leadership principles included in the GE values statement: openness, ability to face reality, self-confidence, speed of decision making, honesty of communication, candor and integrity.		**1987** Revenues $48,158.0 Net Income $2,915.0 Employees 322,000
1987 GE swapped the GE/RCA consumer electronics business to Thomson, S.A. of France for CGR, a medical diagnostic imaging business, and $800 million in cash. GEFS expanded worldwide financial services business by acquisition of Navistar Financial Corporation Canada, Gelco Corporation and D&K Financial Corp. GE selected by NASA to produce major portions of its planned space station. Common stock split two-for-one. GE acquired WTVJ in Miami; merged with NBC.		
REWARD SYSTEMS Each GE business can design its own management compensation and bonus plans to best meet its markets and goals. Furthermore, $30 million has been set aside for management awards to individuals each year.		**1988** Revenues $50,089.0 Net Income $3,386.0 Employees 298,000
1988 GE bought Borg-Warner Chemicals, the worldwide leader in ABS resins with sales of $1.25 billion in 1987, for $2.3 billion. GE expanded its appliance business by buying Roper Corporation for $507 million, outbidding Whirlpool. GEFS acquired Montgomery Ward Credit Corporation. GE sold semiconductor business to Harris Corporation. Formed a joint venture in motors with Robert Bosch of West Germany. Signed an alliance in lighting with Toshiba of Japan to manufacture fluorescent lamps in the U.S. with 50% of production to be shipped to Japan. Employers Reinsurance Corporation purchased Baltica-Nordisk Reassurance of Denmark. GE rated first in quality by U.S. consumers in Gallup Poll. 50% of GE Medical Systems business came from outside the U.S.		
REAL-TIME PLANNING This idea deals with the removal of any bureaucracy that slows down the decision making process—reviews, filling out of forms or preparation of lengthy reports. GE must know clearly what the strategic needs of each business are and be ready whenever an opportunity arises to move fast to grasp the moment.	**1989** Introduced new line of RCA major appliances. Announced new arc-discharge lighting for automobiles. GTX fenders introduced on Cadillac DeVille and Buick Reatta. CNBC cable-TV network launched by NBC.	**1989** Revenues $54,574.0 Net Income $3,939.0 Employees 292,000
WORK-OUT Work-Out is a company-wide drive to improve the work process by identifying and eliminating unproductive tasks—unnecessary reports, reviews, forecasts, budgets—so as to energize employees. Removing these tasks will allow more stimulating and creative work environments to emerge. Employees at all levels are asked to give their input on better ways to do their jobs and service customers.		
1989 GE authorized $10 billion share repurchase. Broadcasting record set by NBC with 68 consecutive weeks as top-rated U.S. TV network. Formed mobile communications joint venture with Ericsson of Sweden. Opened Living Environments concept house for showcasing the use of plastics in the building construction markets. Awarded contract from Tokyo Electric Power Company for world's largest combined-cycle power cycle. "Work-Out" began.		

| | WORLD EVENTS | CORE IDEAS |

1990

1990 Iraq invaded Kuwait.

WORK-OUT (The Process)
SELF-CONFIDENCE (The Driver)
SPEED Speed is the indispensable ingredient of success in this decade. It is accomplished by implementing the Work-Out processes which create employee self-confidence in pursuit of a Boundaryless Corporation. With fewer boundaries speed is picked up—or the competitive advantage.

1991

1991 The Gulf War—Operation Desert Storm.

1991 Disintegration of U.S.S.R.

BOUNDARYLESSNESS (The Vision)
SPEED (The Result)
ONLY LEADERS WHO "WALK THE TALK" The ultimate test of the commitment to company transformation will be how it deals with those leaders who deliver on commitments but do not share GE's values. These autocrats and tyrants force performance out of people rather than inspire it. GE has to convince these managers to change or depart. Because without leaders who "walk the talk," all corporate plans, promises and dreams for the future are just that—talk.

COMPANY EVENTS	PRODUCT INTROS	FINANCIAL RESULTS (in millions)

BEST PRACTICES One effort of boundary-busting has been the wringing of not-invented-here—NIH—from GE's culture. GE teams are now searching within their own entity, within other GE businesses and in corporations around the world, for better ways of doing things. One example: a truly innovative method of compressing product cycle time was found in New Zealand, tested in a GE company in Canada, transferred to the largest appliance complex in Kentucky and is now studied by other GE teams.

1990
GE acquired majority interest in Tungsram Company Ltd. for $150 million.
GE presented with Harvard University's Dively Award for Corporate Public Initiative.
GEFS acquired certain leasing operations of MNC Financial Inc. for $341 million; service operations of the Burton Group, U.K., for $316 million; Travelers Mortgage Services Inc. for $210 million; ELLCO Leasing Corporation for $160 million.
GE sold Ladd Petroleum Corporation to Amax Oil and Gas Inc. for $515 million.
GE Appliances launched Quick Response, reducing cycle time by 70%.

1990
Unveiled the new fuel efficient, super thrust GE90 aircraft engine.
Introduced the F-technology gas turbine, the world's most powerful and efficient.
Introduced Heavy VALOX resin, which can have the feel and aesthetic qualities of glass, ceramic, porcelain, metal, and ivory.
British Airways became launch customer for GE90

1990
Revenues
$58,414.0
Net Income
$4,303.0
Employees 298,000

COMMUNITY BOUNDARYLESS In the spirit of boundarylessness, employees volunteer in the communities that the company's hundreds of plants and installations call home. Efforts range from mentoring in schools, working on homeless shelters to environmental clean-ups. Some GE efforts involve the 35,000-member Elfun Society. Volunteerism has become a winning experience for GE's communities, employees and company.

TRUST Leaders in the 1990s must trust and be trusted. Successful leaders are those who have the self-confidence to trust and empower others. Empowered, highly involved work forces trust their leaders. Trust is gained over time by walking the talk, creating an environment where trust can flourish—Work-Out, Open Communication, Facing Reality, Candor, Compassion, Integrity.

1991
GE established joint ventures with: MABE, Mexico; Godrej & Boyce Mfg. Co. Ltd., India; GE Hangwei Medical Systems Co., the People's Republic of China; India Petrochemicals Corporation Ltd., India.
GE Industrial and Power Systems cut cycle time in parts of the power generation business by over 80%.
GE Plastics honored with Business Enterprise Trust for community service.
GE ranks #1 on Forbes "Most Powerful" companies list.
NBC acquired FNN
GE Lightning acquired light source from Thorn EMI.

1991
Introduced "Energy Choice" energy efficient fluorescent lamp.
Introduced CT HiSpeed Advantage system, which permits one-second scan with only a one-second delay between scans.
NBC launches around-the-clock News Channel.

1991
Revenues
$60,236.0
Net Income
$4,435.0*
Employees 284,000
(*Does not include $1.8 billion non-cash accounting charge.)

GE Timeline

WORLD EVENTS	CORE IDEAS
1992 Civil wars in the former Yugoslavia, Somalia, and Cambodia	Manage to three core measures: customer satisfaction, employee satisfaction, and cash flow.
1993 Economic contractions around the globe.	

1992

1993

COMPANY EVENTS	PRODUCT INTROS	FINANCIAL RESULTS (in millions)
QUICK MARKET INTELLIGENCE (QMI) QMI is a process that gives every salesperson direct access, every Friday, to the key managers and the CEO of the business to lay out customer problems and needs. The product of the meeting is not deep or strategic in nature, but action—a response to the customer right away.	**1992** GE Capital launches GE Rewards credit card. GE Motors introduces high efficiency ECM™ programmable motor. GE Appliances introduces Profile™ line.	**1992** Revenues $62,202 Net Income $4,725 Employees 268,000
QUICK RESPONSE (QR) QR is a cycle-time reduction technique. It erases most of the barriers between the functions of GE businesses and the customers—it took GE Appliances from an 18-week order-to-delivery cycle to a 3/12-week cycle, on the way to 3 days.		
CO-LOCATION This is the ultimate boundaryless behavior. Teams from all functions are put together in one room to bring new products to life.		
1992 GE Aerospace merger with Martin Marietta announced. GE lighting completes APAR Ltd. joint venture in India. GE Capital acquires Avis Lease in Europe. ED&C's Eurolec joint venture acquires Lemag of Spain. GE Lighting announces joint venture with Hitachi in Japan.		
QUICK MARKET INTELLIGENCE, QUICK RESPONSE, AND CO-LOCATION CONTINUE. **1993** GE Aerospace merger with Martin Marietta completed. GE Capital acquires Weyerhauser's GNA Corp. GE announces $70 million investment for home laundry upgrade at Appliance Park. GE Capital buys 45 aircraft from Irish Guiness Peat Aviation.	**1993** GE Transportation Systems unveils new AMD-103 passenger locomotive for Amtrak.	**1993** First quarter Revenues $12,900 First quarter Net Income $1,160 First quarter Employees 230,000 (reflects the transfer of GE Aerospace to Martin Marietta)

Notes

Chapter One: The GE Revolution

Page 7 ". . . with its face to the CEO and its ass to the customer . . ."

This is one of the core elements in what I call the "Old Way" mechanistic organizations. Other attributes include:

- Large Physical Locations

- Many layers from top to bottom

- Strong functional and staff groups

- Suppliers regarded as adversaries

- "Doing it by the book" instead of doing it right for the customer, employee, or business

- Business as Islands unto Themselves

From *Creating the Competitive Organization of the 21st Century: The Boundaryless Corporation* by Mary Anne Devanna and Noel Tichy, *Human Resource Management,* Winter 1990, vol. 29, number 4, pp. 455–71.

Page 8 . . . While Japanese companies were boosting productivity by 8% annually, GE's gains had rarely topped 1.5% . . .

GE's measure of productivity is a four-step calculation designed to create a realistic picture of the company's overall performance.

- The first calculation deducts from GE's annual *revenues* the total dollar effect of that year's price increases.

- Step two is the subtraction of inflation's effects from GE's total *costs* for the year.

- In step three, GE divides the revised revenue figure by the revised cost figure, to calculate the ratio of output to input.

- The final step is to calculate the percentage change in that ratio versus that of the previous year. The resulting percentage is the number that defines productivity at GE.

Page 10 . . . "Neutron Jack," suggesting the CEO's willingness to vaporize people . . .

Remarkably, despite all the cuts, GE ranked as the world's twelfth-largest employer in *Fortune*'s 1991 Global 500 list.

Chapter Three: The Hand He Was Dealt

Page 41 . . . Coffin . . . had a flair for corporate organization . . .

Charles Coffin set the stage for the GE culture through his eleven interdependent and complementary strategic preferences:

1. Internal growth
   —growth from within preferable to acquisition or merger
   —GE should generate its own capital, technology, and management
   —debt unthinkable

2. Constrained diversity
   GE prior to World War II was a generalist with a specialty—design, manufacture and sale of goods related to the generation and utilization of electricity

3. Oligopolistic competition
   —minimizing the number of competitors through control of entry and industry concentration
   —allocation of markets by region, product, and function
   —minimization of price competition
   —nonrelative growth among competitors
   —neutralization of government intervention

4. Domestic saturation
   The goal was to dominate the industry in the domestic market:
   —dominate electrical science and technology
   —maintain fixed ratios of market share and price with competition
   —prevent entry of new competitors
   —do the above legally enough to avoid antitrust prosecution

5. International defense
   Protect its domestic market position through:
   —domestic cross licenses with Westinghouse and other American electrical manufacturers
   —a set of nonaggression pacts with foreign electrical manufacturers
   —portfolio of foreign securities
   —the International General Electric Company

6. Vertical centricism
   The GE organizational structure resembled a wedding cake.

7. Definite chain of command

8. Functional specialization
   Interfunctional problems and opportunities were almost exclusively handled by the president, thus all levels below him were primarily defined in functional terms.

9. Structural uniformity
   Each organizational layer had defined authority and responsibility; all operating components at any given level of the company were to be of equal size; ratio type of performance measures; structural uniformity bred a complex and bureaucratic system of procedures, standards, and controls.

10. Liquidity
    Pay-as-you-go policy.

11. Anticipatory relations
    The pursuit of anticipatory and nonadversary relationships with government, labor, and the public.

From James Baughman's unpublished manuscript *Problems and Performance of the Role of Chief Executive in the General Electric Company, 1892–1974.*

Page 44 . . . In 1951, he [Cordiner] assembled a brainy team of GE executives, plus consultants and professors . . .

The task force Ralph Cordiner put together was led by Harold Smiddy, VP of GE Management Consultation Services Division, a former consultant and partner at Booz, Allen and Hamilton, and president of the Academy of Management. Many of the ideas presented in the Blue Books and by Cordiner bear Smiddy's trademark.

From *Harold F. Smiddy: Manager by Inspiration and Persuasion* by Ronald G. Greenwood, University of Wisconsin.

Chapter Four: The New Leader

Page 51 . . . among the finest examples of succession planning in corporate history . . .

Reg Jones's thoroughness and thoughtfulness in selecting the next CEO is reflected in the carefully planned activities for the last months before he was due to present his evaluation of the vice chairman to the GE board.

Page 58 . . . By contrast, Welch's predecessors . . .

Welch's predecessors and most of his competitors for the CEO job were caught in the old scientific management mold, reflected in their style and mode of operation. For an in-depth discussion of these concepts see Peter Drucker, *Concept of the Corporation*, New York: John Day, 1946.

MANAGEMENT ATTRIBUTE/ STYLE	WELCH	ALFRED SLOAN SCIENTIFIC MGMT.
Style of Communication	Speaking	Writing
Behavior	Aggressive Confrontational	Cautious Harmony
Tends to assign responsibility to	Individuals	System
Approach to decentralization	Large units "Business"	Small units Defined as "P & L centers"
Method of integration	Processes	Committees
Relies on	Key data "Employee feedback"	Reports Committees
Belief in planning	Limited In tune with market	Unlimited forecasting
Attitude to uncertainty	Accept	Avoid
Attitude to change	Accept	Control

Page 69 . . . When EMS rated the three vice chairmen according to its fifteen categories . . .

The contenders were rated on a five-point scale ranging from "very weak" to "very strong" on the following items: leadership—even-handed, objective, consistent, charismatic; decisive; savvy; fun; intelligence; balance of delegation/involvement; people judgment; ego—ego management, share the credit; long-term view; toughness.

Page 70 . . . each of the remaining candidates write a detailed memo assessing his own performance . . .

Below is an excerpt from Welch's seven-page letter to Reg Jones followed by Ted LeVino's assessment:

> Obviously, looking at any of these issues, there is great distance today between where you are and all three of us [vice chairmen]. However, I feel I have the intellectual capacity, breadth, discipline, and most of all the leadership to get there. General Electric has been my business life and its importance to me has grown with each succeeding year. Whether I can properly assemble and discharge the multiple responsibility is for others to judge—but obviously I would like the chance . . .

Ted LeVino:

> . . . an unabashed sales pitch on personal qualities and philosophy of managing winding up with a strong bid for the order. He had seized this opportunity to state his case with just enough vice chairman accomplishment content to make it appear responsive to the request. It is an extremely well-written amalgam of performance, concepts and achievements, examples, etc. He covers the short-comings you may see in him extremely cleverly.

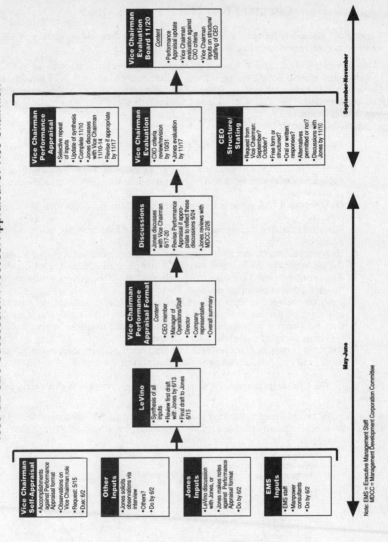

1980 GE CEO Succession Process: Appraisal of Vice Chairmen

Vice Chairman Self-Appraisal
- Accomplishments against Performance Appraisal format
- Observations on Vice Chairman role
- Request: 5/15
- Due: 6/2

Other Inputs
- Jones solicits observations via interview
- Others?
- Do by 6/2

Jones Inputs
- LeVino discussion with Jones, or
- Jones makes notes against Performance Appraisal format
- Do by 6/2

EMS Inputs
- EMS staff
- Manpower consultants
- Do by 6/2

LeVino
- Synthesis of all inputs
- Review first draft with Jones by 6/13
- Final draft to Jones 6/15

Vice Chairman Performance Appraisal Format
Content
- CEO member
- Manager of Operations/Staff
- Director
- Company representative
- Overall summary

Discussions
- Jones discusses with Vice Chairman 6/17-20
- Revise Performance Appraisal if appropriate to reflect these discussions 6/24
- Jones reviews with MDCC 2/26

Vice Chairman Performance Appraisal
- Selective repeat of inputs
- Update of synthesis
- Complete 11/10
- Jones discusses with Vice Chairman 11/10-14
- Revise if appropriate by 11/17

Vice Chairman Evaluation
- CXO criteria review/revision by 10/31
- Jones evaluation by 11/17

CEO Structure/Staffing
- Request from Vice Chairman: September? October?
- Free form or structured?
- Oral or written responses?
- Alternatives permitted or not?
- Discussions with Jones by 11/10

Vice Chairman Evaluation Board 1/1/20
Content
- Performance Appraisal update
- Vice Chairman evaluation against CXO criteria
- Vice Chairman inputs on structural/staffing of CEO

May-June

September-November

Note: EMS = Executive Management Staff
MDCC = Management Development Corporation Committee

Chapter Five: The Power of Ideas

Page 75 . . . ultimately far more important than the ideas themselves—is the way GE is weaving its guiding principles into the fabric of its culture . . .

Many of Welch's ideas in the 1980s are, on the surface, not dissimilar to those of Ralph Cordiner and Harold Smiddy in the 1950s. In fact many of the words of Smiddy and Cordiner could have been said by Welch. The difference is how they were interpreted and implemented. The "Old Way" led to bureaucracy while Welch's new GE led to a lean flexible organization.

Smiddy's rationale for decentralization was:

1. Puts authority to make decisions at points as near as possible to where actions take place
2. Is likely to get best *overall* results by getting greatest and most directly applicable knowledge and most *timely* understanding into play on greatest number of decisions
3. Only works if real authority is delegated; and not if details then have to be reported
4. Requires faith that men in decentralized jobs will have capacity to make sound decisions
5. Requires realization that natural aggregate of many individually sound decisions will be better for the business than centrally planned and controlled decisions
6. Requires understanding that main role for "staff" is the rendering of help through a few experienced people
7. Rests on the need to have general business objectives, organization structure, relationships, policies, and controls known, understood, followed, and controlled
8. Can only work if responsibility commensurate with decision-making authority is truly accepted and exercised at all levels
9. Requires personnel practices based on measured performance, enforced standards, and removal for incapacity of poor performance

Page 82 . . . The CEC helps promote . . . integrated diversity, which is Welch's main political idea . . .

Welch initially talked about Integrated Diversity in terms of GE's hidden values. Two of the slides most frequently used to explain the idea are presented below:

Winning in the 1990s
INTEGRATED DIVERSITY
Earnings Per Share–Accumulated Annual Growth Rate
1986–1989

The second diagram is how Jack Welch presented these benefits to the security analysts in 1989. Note the blend of hard and soft issues.

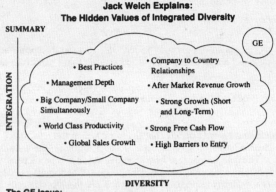

Jack Welch Explains:
The Hidden Values of Integrated Diversity

SUMMARY

INTEGRATION

GE

• Best Practices

• Management Depth

• Big Company/Small Company
Simultaneously

• World Class Productivity

• Global Sales Growth

• Company to Country
Relationships

• After Market Revenue Growth

• Strong Growth (Short
and Long-Term)

• Strong Free Cash Flow

• High Barriers to Entry

DIVERSITY

The GE Issue:
• **Everyone Understands Diversity**
• **Some Understand Integration**
• **Few Recognize the Hidden Values of Integrated Diversity**

Chapter Six: "Kick-Starting the Revolution"

Page 85 ... Trusting his instincts ...

These are four main obstacles to transforming shared values:

1: The lack of clearly articulated and internally consistent shared values.
2: The "do as I say rather than as I do" problem: Failure of role models to live up to shared values creates cynicism in the organization.
3: Pockets of ignorance and/or resistance: Some people remain ignorant of the shared values while others reject them.
4: Overreliance on speeches and one-way communication—the Sunday morning sermon problem:

Values must be built into the everyday fabric of people's lives.

Page 93 ... As a practical matter, though, the earnings goals frequently made job cuts inevitable ...

During this period of time Welch kept track of who was getting cut in businesses that were downsizing, the chiefs or Indians. When the chiefs weren't getting cut as much as the Indians, Welch would send the business leader a note or call them up to discuss why. The message got clearer and clearer over the years: Start cutting at the top.

Page 94 ... He personally answered letters of complaint from laid-off employees ...

Below is a letter from the wife of a laid-off employee, and Welch's personal response, which resulted in the GE business following through on his promise to the spouse to provide relocation assistance.

c.c.: John F. Welch Jr.

August 14, 1985

To:Division Vice-President & General Manager

From:Employee's Spouse

Dear Mr. _____:

I am giving you an opportunity to read this letter and respond before I share my story publicly. I am in a very traumatic situation that I can't fully comprehend. Here are the details:

A man interviews with one of the top 100 corporations in America for a sales position. He is offered the job. The man presently lives in _____, _____, a booming metropolis. The job offer will require him to relocate to _____, _____, a small seaside community. The man and his wife decide that the job is worth the relocation. They arrive at this conclusion based on several facts: 1) The position is with a stable, reputable company. 2) The man knows that he will enjoy the job and be successful at it. 3) He foresees opportunity for upward career mobility. 4) The job offers adequate salary and benefits for family support. The man accepts the job. He sells his home in _____. His wife quits her well-paying job, and they move to _____.

In _____, they rent a place to live and he purchases a company car. Six months pass and they buy a home. The wife becomes pregnant and the couple joyfully await the birth of their first child.

The man works very hard for the company. He frequently works 12 hours a day, arriving home at 7:30 P.M. or later. But he enjoys his job. The hard work pays off, and he meets his sales objectives. He has established new dealers, increased business with old ones and developed large sales with OEM's. After eight months in the field, he reaches 127% of his sales objective. This he accomplished without any hands-on assistance from management. He was an eight-month rookie and he produced! He succeeded in spite of his not knowing how his performance was stacking up by company standards. You see, he was never given a performance evaluation.

Now the man has to sell the home in _____ that he bought two months ago. He and his pregnant wife must prepare to move back to _____, where he will stand a better chance to secure a job to provide for his family.

Why does the man have to move again? He has *just been informed that as of November 1, he will no longer be employed with the company due to "lack of work."* He asks himself, "How can there be lack of work when I could not get the order department to fill a countless number of orders due to product unavailability?" He wonders, "Why me? What about my family? What about my career? I trusted these people."

This is a true story. The man is _____, *my husband.* The company is the General Electric Company, _____ Division. I realize that you may not know my husband, but I was compelled to write this letter because I can't believe that you are fully aware of the effects of your current policies. My husband is intelligent, sharp, ambitious and hardworking. Your _____ management will attest to his attributes on the grounds that they hired him. *It seems to me our family is a victim of General Electric's lack of planning and integrity.* How would you explain this situation?

At this point *I feel that the decent and fair thing for GE to do is to purchase our house in* _____ *and assume responsibility for our moving back to* _____. These requests are quite minimal compared to what we have given you and what we stand to lose because of your actions.

If our experience is indicative of General Electric's regard for the American family, then it's no wonder that the institution of family continues to disintegrate with every height of corporate prosperity.

Sincerely,
Mrs. _____

September 5, 1985

Dear Mrs. _____:
Thanks for your direct and thoughtful letter of August 14.

I wish I could say that no component of General Electric is ever too optimistic in setting its goals, or falls short . . . but clearly you know better. In this case, the _____ industry price collapse was far greater than the management of the business anticipated. In fact, the business will lose more than thirty billion dollars in 1985.

"Fair and decent" is precisely what we want to be to each of the individuals affected by cutbacks in _____, or any of our businesses effecting reduction in force in the struggle to deal with an increasingly competitive environment.

By the time you receive this letter, I believe the _____ program to assist your husband in finding a new job and relocating will be known to you. I hope you both will find it helpful.

Thanks again for your letter. I'm sorry we were so slow in getting our act together.

Sincerely,
Jack Welch

Mrs. _____
_____
_____

bcc: Sector Executive
Division Vice President

Set *D*

Chapter Seven: Nothing Sacred

Page 101 . . . by the end of 1984, the old GE no longer existed . . .

The "Old Way" GE, with sheltering layers of resistance, can be symbolized by its organizational structure:

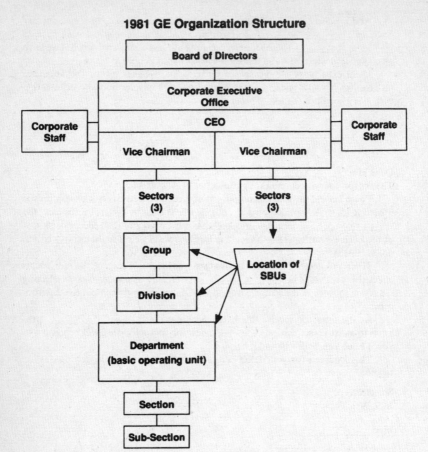

1981 GE Organization Structure

Chapter Eight: Facing Reality

Page 121 . . . Four times a year Richardson would brief union officers . . .

Besides these quarterly meetings, Richardson and Paynter organized:

Weekly dialogue meetings

Monthly operational reviews with 100 to 120 managers

Customer awareness trips—they rented planes and filled them with 150 hourly and salaried employees, to interface with customers

Page 123 . . . Transportation Systems never posted a loss during the 1980s . . .

The effects of Schlemmer's team efforts are shown graphically below.

Earnings Profile—With Cost Reductions

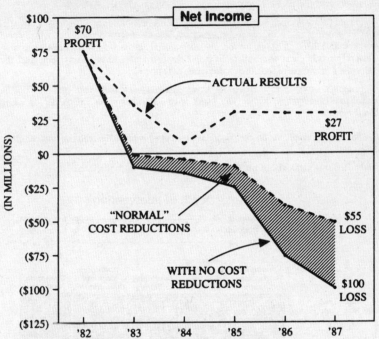

Earnings Achieved Entirely Through Cost Reductions

Chapter Ten: The Turning Point

Page 152 . . . David Letterman has become a regular part of the Crotonville curriculum . . .

Letterman evidently believes he was being courageous by verbally bloodying the GE CEO. Welch spoiled his fun by enjoying the satire. Indeed, several years later Welch tried to return the compliment by personally delivering a fruit basket to Letterman, but the talk-show host didn't seem to get the joke.

Chapter Eleven: Crotonville

Page 155 ... GE's Management Development Institute, overlooking the Hudson River ...

Its forerunner was an organization of top managers called the Electrical Funds Group (ELFUN), who gathered on Association Island in upstate New York during the 1940s and 1950s. Novelist Kurt Vonnegut, Jr., who once worked for GE in Schenectady, lampooned the ELFUN gatherings in his 1958 novel *Player Piano:*

> ... spent a week each summer in an orgy of morale building—through team athletics, group sings, bonfires and skyrockets, bawdy entertainment, free whisky and cigars; and through plays, put on by professional actors, which pleasantly but mistakably made clear the nature of good deportment within the system, and the shape of firm resolves for the challenging year ahead.

In Vonnegut's novel every aspect of these retreats—whether you qualify for the "Green" or "Blue" team, whom you bunk with—signifies one's prospects for rising within the firm.

Page 156 ... The emphasis [in conventional programs] is on skills training and cognitive development ...

We redrafted our ideas about purpose and values for Crotonville into a chart.

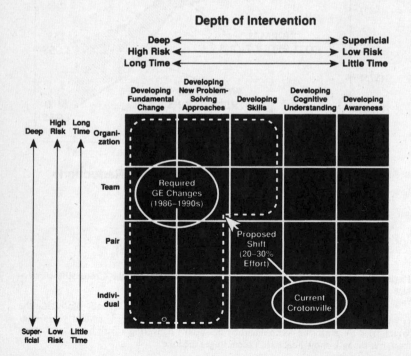

Depth of Intervention

The top line shows each manager's experience. The left-hand axis shows the focus of any particular program. The challenge facing Crotonville was how to move toward the upper left-hand part of the matrix to help deal with the revolutionary agenda of transforming GE.

That analysis helped us define Crotonville's strategic thrusts. The most important of these were:

Serving as think-tank to develop knowledge about organizational effectiveness

Using action learning

Reinforcing the GE values while helping leaders transform the local culture

Bringing GE's top people to Crotonville

Page 157 . . . Welch wanted the final [values] statement to be something all GEers could "own" . . .

The values statement changed dramatically over the years. Some highlights:

Jan. 1981	"fast moving, acting like a small organization even though you're a big organization"
1983	10 major cultural themes: budgets—comparing to our environment; ownership—more delegation; investment—stay number one; lean and agile; excellence; quality; entrepreneurship; reality and candor; communication; stewardship—obligation to take the assets you have, drive them to newer and better heights through excellence
1985	A five-page document on shared values was created
Nov. 1985	The EMS staff created a first draft on GE leadership characteristics, built on the values statement
1986–87	The values statement was discussed at Crotonville by thousands of participants
Spring 1986	25 officers attended a Crotonville workshop to discuss leadership and values
	Image study showed a deteriorating sense of commitment on the part of GE to its employees, to its customers, and to its suppliers
Mid 1987	The feedback from Crotonville on the value statement was pulled together into a document titled *Toward a Shared Vision and Shared Values for GE*
1988	Welch further revised the GE shared values statement to include a list of business and individual leader characteristics
1992	Again, in early 1992 Welch refined his articulation of GE leader characteristics

Chapter Twelve: The Politics of Speed

Page 181 . . . GE had been organized vertically like a many-tiered wedding cake; henceforth it would look like a cartwheel lying on its side . . .

The GE organizational structure when Welch became vice chairman in 1981 is apparently different from that of 1992: [see page 345]

Page 181 . . . GE's thirteen main business units, which would now report directly to Welch or one of the vice chairmen . . .

Several months after Vice Chairman Larry Bossidy took the CEO job at Allied-Signal, Welch added two men to the office of the CEO: Paolo Fresco, now vice chairman, and Frank Doyle, now executive vice president.

Page 183 . . . By the end of 1982, GE had virtually abolished the central strategic-planning staff . . .

Larry Bossidy explained the reasons in a presentation at the Strategic Management Society in Boston, Massachusetts, October 1987:

  a/ it is no longer possible to see that far (three to five years) into the future. Five years is an eternity. In fact, it's two careers in Silicon Valley. We manage GE from the perspective that every cliché about events moving faster and becoming more complex is essentially true.

  b/ strategic planning was reluctant or unable to confront the reality of the need to compete internationally. Planners tended to focus on the more coherent and decipherable U.S. market . . . much like the man who searched for his keys near the lamppost, not because that was where he lost them, but because that was where the light was.

  c/ strategic planning inculcated a preoccupation with precision as well as predictability. Sudden change was viewed more often as threat than opportunity.

  d/ strategic planning—at least at its worst—produced operating management that did not participate in the development of strategy, that did not understand it when developed, and often, when understood disagreed with it.

MOREOVER:

  a separate planning function can undermine the objective because it permits the manager to sidestep the issue, and it promotes isolation. Don't give the manager a planner. Rather demand a comprehensive strategy review within six months of the manager's assignment. This should force a team building, participative process, which combines the analytical process with appropriate communications.

BUT:

  when we deserted strategic planning, we most emphatically did not abandon strategic thinking or strategic management. . . . Strategic thinking identifies and synthesizes the forces which affect your business while strategic management uses strategic thinking to set business objectives and to communicate this direction to the organization. . . . That's [strategic management] what we're trying to spread at GE today.

Chapter Thirteen: The New Order

Page 192 . . . The wide-open debating style that Welch calls constructive conflict . . .

As Karl Weick points out, constructive conflict depends on face-to-face contact. Previously, General Electric had used more formal, less rich channels. Karl Weick:

If you want to be informed in equivocal environments, there is no substitute for face-to-face communication. If you are in a more certain environment, then you can get by with formal media.

Page 194 . . . Sociologist Amitai Etzioni described three methods of organizational control: coercive, utilitarian, and normative . . .

See A. Etzioni. *A Comparative Analysis of Complex Organizations* (New York: Free Press, 1961).

Chapter Fourteen: Getting Excited

Page 206 . . . the company used cross-licensing agreements to form partnerships with competitors . . .

One of these agreements was called "Phoebus." Robert Jones and Oliver Marriott in "A History of G.E.C., A.E.I. and English Electric" in *Anatomy of a Merger* explain:

Phoebus, an allegorical reference to the Sun God, suggesting the necessity of light rather than the morality of the ring. Phoebus was organized through a Swiss limited company, Phoebus S.A. Compagnie Industrielle pour le Developments de l'Eclairage. Its aim was to encourage a complete interchange of patents among members and to fix prices country by country by means of national "Local Meetings."

With one exception, all the world's biggest lamp-makers signed the Phoebus agreement in 1924 and, generally through pressure from Phoebus, a number of smaller producers had fallen into line and signed by 1939. The exception was GE of America, although its subsidiaries in Mexico, Brazil and China were signators.

What finally cemented GE of America's hold on the world ring was its shareholdings. It owned a major shareholding in every one of the leading lamp-producers in the world in the middle of 1935.

Page 208 . . . building the world's first industrial park . . .

It was founded on April 4, 1913, and called "Nela" Park, drawing its name from the initials of the National Electric Lamp Association, an association of smaller companies which pooled their engineering and research. It was formed in 1894 by Franklin S. Terry of the Sunbeam Company of Chicago and Burton G. Tremaine of the Fostoria Lamp Company in Ohio to compete against such giants as GE and Westinghouse. However, they didn't have the capital they needed to grow, so on May 3, 1901, GE's CEO Charles Coffin purchased 75% of NELA with an option to buy the rest. In 1911, the federal courts ordered GE to consolidate NELA. Terry and Tremaine then pursued their idea of moving the division's headquarters to a bucolic, remote surrounding and convinced Coffin and other top GE managers to lay out $1 million for its purchase and development.

Page 213 . . . Stephen Rabinowitz, who was Lighting's technology vice president . . .

He has since left GE and has been hired by Larry Bossidy at AlliedSignal to run one of the Automative Businesses.

GE ORGANIZATION 1981

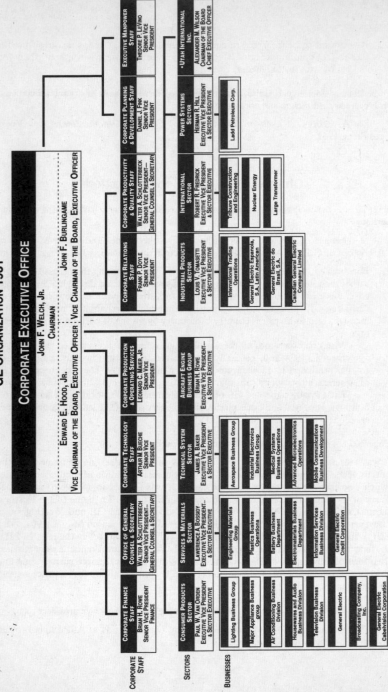

CORPORATE EXECUTIVE OFFICE

JOHN F. WELCH, JR.
CHAIRMAN

EDWARD E. HOOD, JR.
VICE CHAIRMAN OF THE BOARD, EXECUTIVE OFFICER

JOHN F. BURLINGAME
VICE CHAIRMAN OF THE BOARD, EXECUTIVE OFFICER

CORPORATE STAFF

CORPORATE FINANCE STAFF
BRIAN H. ROWE
SENIOR VICE PRESIDENT FINANCE

OFFICE OF GENERAL COUNSEL & SECRETARY
WALTER A. SCHLOTTERBECK
SENIOR VICE PRESIDENT—GENERAL COUNSEL & SECRETARY

CORPORATE TECHNOLOGY STAFF
ARTHUR M. BUECHE
SENIOR VICE PRESIDENT

CORPORATE PRODUCTION & OPERATING SERVICES
LEONARD C. MAIER, JR.
SENIOR VICE PRESIDENT

CORPORATE RELATIONS STAFF
FRANK P. DOYLE
SENIOR VICE PRESIDENT

CORPORATE PRODUCTIVITY & QUALITY STAFF
WALTER A. SCHLOTTERBECK
SENIOR VICE PRESIDENT—GENERAL COUNSEL & SECRETARY

CORPORATE PLANNING & DEVELOPMENT STAFF
DANIEL J. FINK
SENIOR VICE PRESIDENT

EXECUTIVE MANPOWER STAFF
THEODORE P. LEVINO
SENIOR VICE PRESIDENT

SECTORS

CONSUMER PRODUCTS SECTOR
PAUL W. VAN ORDEN
EXECUTIVE VICE PRESIDENT & SECTOR EXECUTIVE

SERVICES & MATERIALS SECTOR
LAWRENCE A. BOSSIDY
EXECUTIVE VICE PRESIDENT & SECTOR EXECUTIVE

TECHNICAL SYSTEM SECTOR
JAMES A. BAKER
EXECUTIVE VICE PRESIDENT & SECTOR EXECUTIVE

AIRCRAFT ENGINE BUSINESS GROUP
BRIAN H. ROWE
EXECUTIVE VICE PRESIDENT—& SECTOR EXECUTIVE

INDUSTRIAL PRODUCTS SECTOR
LOUIS V. TOMASETTI
EXECUTIVE VICE PRESIDENT & SECTOR EXECUTIVE

INTERNATIONAL SECTOR
ROBERT R. FREDRICK
EXECUTIVE VICE PRESIDENT & SECTOR EXECUTIVE

POWER SYSTEMS SECTOR
HERMAN R. HILL
EXECUTIVE VICE PRESIDENT & SECTOR EXECUTIVE

·UTAH INTERNATIONAL INC.
ALEXANDER M. WILSON
CHAIRMAN OF THE BOARD & CHIEF EXECUTIVE OFFICER

BUSINESSES

Consumer Products Sector
- Lighting Business Group
- Major Appliance Business Group
- Air Conditioning Business Division
- Housewares and Audio Business Division
- Television Business Division
- General Electric Broadcasting Company, Inc.
- General Electric Cablevision Corporation

Services & Materials Sector
- Engineering Materials Group
- Plastics Business Operations
- Battery Business Department
- Electromaterials Business Department
- Information Services Business Division
- General Electric Credit Corporation

Technical System Sector
- Aerospace Business Group
- Industrial Electronics Business Group
- Medical Systems Business Operations
- Advanced Microelectronics Operations
- Mobile Communications Business Development

Industrial Products Sector
- International Trading Operations
- General Electric Espanola, S.A. Latin American
- General Electric do Brasil, S.A.
- Canadian General Electric Company Limited

International Sector
- Tribune Construction and Engineering
- Nuclear Energy
- Large Transformer

Power Systems Sector
- Ladd Petroleum Corp.

GE Organization 1992

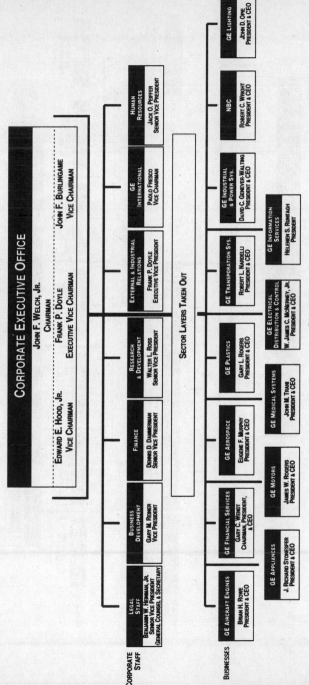

Corporate Executive Office

John F. Welch, Jr.
Chairman

| Edward E. Hood, Jr. | Frank P. Doyle | John F. Burlingame |
| Vice Chairman | Executive Vice Chairman | Vice Chairman |

Corporate Staff

Legal Staff	Business Development	Finance	Research & Development	External & Industrial Relations	GE International	Human Resources
Benjamin W. Heineman, Jr. Senior Vice President General Counsel & Secretary	Gary M. Reiner Vice President	Dennis D. Dammerman Senior Vice President	Walter L. Robb Senior Vice President	Frank P. Doyle Executive Vice President	Paolo Fresco Vice Chairman	Jack O. Peiffer Senior Vice President

Sector Layers Taken Out

Businesses

GE Aircraft Engines	GE Financial Services	GE Aerospace	GE Plastics	GE Transportation Sys.	GE Industrial & Power Sys.	GE Lighting
Brian H. Rowe President & CEO	Gary C. Wendt Chairman, President, & CEO	Eugene F. Murphy President & CEO	Gary L. Rogers President & CEO	Robert L. Nardelli President & CEO	David C. Genever-Watling President & CEO	John D. Opie President & CEO

GE Appliances	GE Motors	GE Medical Systems	GE Electrical Distribution & Control	GE Information Services	NBC
J. Richard Stonesifer President & CEO	James W. Rogers President & CEO	John M. Trani President & CEO	W. James C. McNerney, Jr. President & CEO	Helenen S. Rintagh President	Robert C. Wright President & CEO

GE Organization 1993

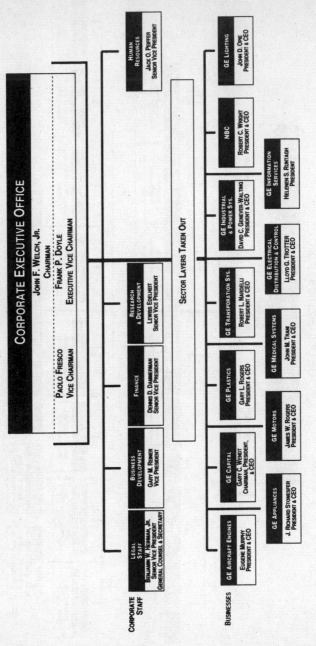

Corporate Executive Office

John F. Welch, Jr.
Chairman

Frank P. Doyle
Executive Vice Chairman

Paolo Fresco
Vice Chairman

Human Resources
Jack O. Peiffer
Senior Vice President

Corporate Staff

Legal Staff
Benjamin W. Heineman, Jr.
Senior Vice President
General Counsel & Secretary

Business Development
Gary M. Reiner
Vice President

Finance
Dennis D. Dammerman
Senior Vice President

Research & Development
Lewiss Edelheit
Senior Vice President

Sector Layers Taken Out

Businesses

GE Aircraft Engines
Eugene Murphy
President & CEO

GE Appliances
J. Richard Stonesifer
President & CEO

GE Capital
Gary C. Wendt
Chairman, President, & CEO

GE Motors
James W. Rogers
President & CEO

GE Plastics
Gary L. Rogers
President & CEO

GE Medical Systems
John M. Trani
President & CEO

GE Transportation Sys.
Robert L. Nardelli
President & CEO

GE Electrical Distribution & Control
Lloyd G. Trotter
President & CEO

GE Industrial & Power Sys.
David C. Genever-Walting
President & CEO

GE Information Services
Helenen S. Runtagh
President

NBC
Robert C. Wright
President & CEO

GE Lighting
John D. Opie
President & CEO

Chapter Fifteen: Globalization

Page 224 . . . International General Electric, which GE disbanded . . .

But in January of 1982 Welch gave a go-ahead to establish the General Electric Trading Company (GETC), which became an independent subsidiary the following July. Its task was to secure GE companies' export orders through countertrade, offset, and bartering.

Chapter Sixteen: Work-Out

Page 245 . . . At first, people spent much of their time griping . . .

To me the evolution of GE's Work-Out efforts follow the phases of a social movement:

Conception Phase: 1987–1989
The launch of town hall meetings and workshops in all businesses.

Pioneering Phase: 1989–1990
During this phase there was no resistnace to Work-Out. It is a social movement that swept GE, reflected in the writings and speeches of the chairman.

Self-Doubt Phase: 1990–1991
In this phase the era of enthusiasm and excitement for the workshops began to wane; in some businesses intense pressures led middle managers themselves to say, "my life isn't any different" and some cynically called this program "Work-In."

Responses to Self-Doubt: 1991–
The responses to "self-doubt" in social movements can be classified as either Maladaptive ("demise by default" or "absorption by default"), or Adaptive. GE adapted and used Work-Out to navigate through the tough recession in the early 1990s.

Chapter Seventeen: The Twenty-first-Century Organization

Page 263 . . . Trani's arrival followed a startling wake-up call . . .

Trani had five strategies to reach his mission of becoming the unquestioned leader in diagnostic imaging:

Globalization:
"I don't think we can win locally without really winning globally and vice versa."

Cost Competitiveness:
"Because that gives us: a) pricing flexibility; b) the low-cost producer wins when the market matures . . ."

Installed base expansion:
"Unless you feed the cow, you can't get the milk out."

Technical preeminence:
"We have technical preeminence in CG and MR and parts of X-ray, but we need to have it everywhere."

Growth:
a) Joint ventures and acquisitions; b) organic growth or increased market share, which among other things means more new products; "we have to turn the line over every three years."

Sources

Personal Interviews

(By Noel Tichy unless otherwise noted)
(Multiple interviews indicated by number in parentheses)

Allen, Jim, Manager, Communication and Community Affairs, GE Appliances.

Andrews, Nigel, Vice President Corporate Development, GE.

Baughman, James, Manager, Corporate Management Development, GE (5).

Bergstrom, Thomas, attorney for Joseph Calabria, by Arathi Krishna.

Bossidy, Lawrence, Chairman and CEO, AlliedSignal, former Vice-Chairman and Executive Officer, GE (3).

Bowen, Bobby, Director, Finance, GE Lighting Europe (2).

Buckley, Larry, former consultant, GE Corporate Human Resources.

Chadwell, Charles, Vice President and General Manager, GE Aircraft Engines Production Division, by Charles Kadushin and MBA Group.

D'Ambola, Toby, Manager, Human Resources, GE Medical Systems (5).

Dillon, Ronald, Manager, Business Development, GE Plastics, Latin America, by Connie Kinnear.

Donovan, Dennis, Vice President, Human Resources, GE Industrial and Power Systems, by Charles Kadushin and MBA Group.

Doyle, Frank, Executive Vice President, GE (3).

Eickert, Stephen, General Manager, Structured Products, GE Plastics, by Connie Kinnear.

Feit, Josh, Media Director, INFACT, by Arathi Krishna.

Frago, Bill, former Vice President and General Manager, GE Lighting Worldwide Marketing, by Connie Kinnear.

Fresco, Paolo, Vice Chairman and Executive Officer (2).

Hamilton, Jack, former Manager of Human Resources, GE Lighting, by Connie Kinnear.

Hiner, Glen, CEO, Owens-Corning Fiberglas, former Senior Vice President, GE Plastics, by Connie Kinnear.

Jones, Reginald, former Chief Executive Officer, GE.

Kane, Donald E., former Manager, Corporate Organization Planning, GE (10).

Klein, Judy L., General Manager, GE Wiring Devices, by Connie Kinnear.

Kline, Jim, Program Manager, Government Practices, GE Aircraft Engines.

LaMadrid, Lorenzo, former Vice President Marketing and Business Development, GE Aerospace.

Madej, John, Manager, Financial Planning, GE Plastics.

McNerney, James, President and Chief Executive Officer, GE Electrical Distribution and Control.

Michaelson, Gertrude G., Senior Vice President—External Affairs and Director, R. H. Macy and Co., Inc., GE Board of Directors.

Modan, Michael, Manager, Licensing/Technology, GE Plastics Legal, by Connie Kinnear.

Mozgala, Robert P., Vice President and General Manager, GE Plastics Americas Manufacturing Division, by Connie Kinnear.

Murphy, George, Managing Director, GE Lighting Asia-Pacific Operation, by Charles Kadushin and MBA Group.

Najhib, Jalal S., National Executive, GE, Iran, by Charles Kadushin and MBA Group.

Opie, John, Chairman and Chief Executive Officer, GE Lighting (5).

Orselet, David K., Consultant, Corporate Human Resources, GE (2).

Pasmore, Carol, Manager, Organization Effectiveness, GE Lighting, by Connie Kinnear.

Paynter, Jim, Manager, Human Resources, Commercial Engines and Service, GE Aircraft Engines (2).

Peiffer, Jack, Senior Vice President, Corporate Human Resources, GE (4).

Reiner, Gary, Vice President, Corporate Business Development, GE.

Rogers, Gary, President and Chief Executive Officer, GE Plastics.

Saline, Craig, former Manager, Human Resources GE CGR (France).

Schipke, Roger, former Senior Vice President, GE Appliances, currently CEO, the Ryland Group.

Schlemmer, Carl J., former Vice President GE Transportation Systems (5).

Schuh, Gary, Manager, Sourcing, Tungsram U.S.A. Ltd., by Connie Kinnear.

Shenian, Popkin, former Manager GE Plastics Ventures Technology, by Connie Kinnear.

Smith, Eva, Executive Secretary, GE Plastics Finance, by Connie Kinnear.

Trani, John, President and Chief Executive Officer, GE Medical Systems (10).

Van Orden, Paul, former Executive Vice President, GE (10).

Welch, John F., Jr.:
(Note: certain of these interviews were attended by Jack Peiffer, James Baughman, or Joyce Hergenhan.)

by Strat Sherman for *Fortune* magazine, 1989: 10 hours
—by Noel Tichy, 1988–91: 45 hours
—by Noel Tichy and Strat Sherman, 1991–92: 55 hours
Williams, Walter, former Vice President and General Manager, GE Housewares and Audio Business Division, currently Chairman of Rubbermaid.
Woodburn, Bill, Vice President and General Manager, GE Lighting Worldwide Marketing.
Wright, Robert, President and Chief Executive Officer, NBC (3).
Wriston, Walter, Retired Chairman of the Board and Former Director, Citicorp and Citibank, GE Board of Directors.

GE Diagnostic and Evaluation Studies

(Conducted by Noel M. Tichy and Colleagues)

Crotonville Needs Assessment Study 1986–87
Personal interviews (35); focus groups (25); surveys of managers (220) in Major Appliances, GE Capital, Plastics, Mobile Communications, and Aircraft Engines (with Professor Charles Kadushin).
Globalization Study of GE Medical Systems 1987–91
Tracking and evaluating the impact of the Global Leadership Program (220 personal interviews, 430 surveys) (with Professor Charles Kadushin).
Human Resources Assessment Survey 1986–87
535 surveys completed by managers across all GE businesses (with Professor Chestor Borucki).
Human Resources Strategy Project 1988–90
Interviews with 55 line and human resource managers on the future of GE Organization and People Systems (with Patricia Stacey).
Organization Diagnostic Studies
(a) *GE Lighting* telephone surveys 1984–86 (430).
(b) *NBC Values Assessment* focus groups and interviews of 135 NBC managers and employees.
(c) *Medical Systems Middle Managers* diagnosis and tracking of the Work-Out process (240 interviews/focus groups).

Internal GE Documents

"Advanced Human Resource Management Program," February 6, 1987.
Andersen, Raymond K. "Dashing Down the Line." *Monogram,* May/June 1980.

Barnette, Carole K. and Rich Fortinberry. "The GE Lighting/Tungsram Acquisition: A Case Profile for Acquisitions," August 9, 1990.

"Career Management," 1990.

CEO and the Executive Management Staff. "CEO's Working Paper on GE Shared Values and Leadership," June 11, 1986.

"Change Acceleration Program," 1992.

"Company Organization for the 1970s," February 26, 1970.

"Company Policies."

"Continuous Improvement Project Report."

Corporate Marketing and Consulting. "Lighting: National Customer Service Center." Working Report. August 25, 1988.

"Crotonville Analysis of Participant Feedback."

"Crotonville Needs Analysis Survey," June 1986.

"Customer Focused Process Improvement."

"DoD Compliance Actions: 1985–1991."

"Ethics Education and Communication at General Electric," January 30, 1987.

"The Evolution of GE Lighting—Some Perspective on the Work-Out! Process," Work-Out! Conference Presentation, June 5, 1989.

Examples of Accomplishment Analyses

Executive Management Staff. "A New Framework for Leadership Development at GE," February 5, 1987.

Freeman, Bennett. "Catalyst for Change." *Monogram,* 1986.

GE Annual Reports, 1970–92.

GE Industry Sales & Services. IS&S Leadership Coaching Workshop: Schenectady, New York, August 26, 1987.

"GE Locomotive Milestone Events."

GE Organization Charts, 1978–92.

GEMS. "Developing Cross-Cultural Teamwork."

GEMS. "Global Leadership Program: Executive Summary" (prepared by Executive Leadership Institute).

GEMS. "Global Leadership Seminar" (handout).

GEMS. "GLP3 Global Leadership Workshop: Workshop 2."

GEMS. "Group Process Mapping: A GEMS Work-Out Tool for Speed, Simplicity, Self-Confidence," 1988.

GEMS. Heritage Reference, 1990.

"General Electric Company Lamp Products Division, Human Resource Index—Results of Survey Administration #1," conducted October/November 1984.

Kane, Donald E. "A GE Case Study: Four Critical Steps to Cultural Change." *Executive Excellence,* November 1984.

Kane, Donald E. "Change and GE," February 1987.

Kane, Donald E. "GE Corporate Management Systems Study," August 5, 1986.

Kane, Donald E. "Multiplying Leadership: A Desirable Next Step in the Evolution of our GE Management System."

Kane, Donald E. "Resizing the Structure." GE Executive Management Staff.

Kane, Donald E., Noel M. Tichy, and Eugene S. Andrews. "A Leadership Development Framework." GE Executive Management Staff, November 1987. OEN-6.

Lake, Dale G., Noel M. Tichy, and Tom Dunham. "Sourcing: New Frontiers for the Boundaryless Organization," July 1990.

"Launching and Leading the Boundaryless Organization: Work-Out Best Practices." Set of papers by Work-Out consultants, 1990.

Lighting. "GE Lighting History."

Lighting. "Introduction to the Work-Out! Process."

Lighting. "Work-Out! Business Component Meeting," June 1989.

Lighting. "World Lighting Markets—Strategies and Challenges."

Lighting. *GE Lighting News,* June 1989, vol. 15, no. 6.

"The Management Development Institute at Crotonville" (brochure).

McKinsey & Co. "Staff Support Needed for Management of General Electric in the 1970s," December 1969.

Monogram. "220 Locomotives," Spring 1984.

Monogram. "Liberating GE's Energy: An Interview with Jack Welch." Fall 1987, vol. 67, no. 4.

"1985 Management Education Catalog" (course catalog).

"Plant Closings and Product Relocations," January 20, 1987.

Plastics. "The GE Plastics Story."

Plastics. "The History of GE Plastics."

"Preliminary Draft: GE Corporate Management System Study," August 5, 1986.

Saperstein, Marc J. "Criteria for Successfully Implementing Significant Organizational Change." GE Executive Management Staff, January 1986. OEN-2.

Smith, Eva M. "How GE Plastics Became an International Business." GEP, May 1986 (updated November 8, 1988).

"Strategic Alliances as a New Way of Life."

Tichy, Noel M. "Crotonville Strategy." February 19, 1986.

Tichy, Noel M. "Global Mindsets: A Model Building Exercise." GEMS Global Leadership Program.

Tichy, Noel, Toby D'Ambola, and Michael Humenik. "The Phases of Organization Development and Work-Out at GE: A Comparative Look," 1990.

"Toward a Shared Vision and Shared Values for GE." Draft, June 10, 1987, June 19, 1987.

Warshaw, David. "Sharing at Every Level." *Monogram,* Fall 1987, vol. 65, no. 4.

"Work-Out Leaders Guide."

"Work-Out! Improving Product Quality," February 12–14, 1990.

General Electric Blue Books:
—Professional Management in GE, 1954
  Book One: History
  Book Two: Organization
  Book Three: The Work of a Professional Manager
  Book Four: The Work of a Functional Individual Contributor, 1959
—Some Classic Contributions to Professional Managing, 1956
  Volume I: Selected Papers
  Volume II: Historical Perspectives
—Manager Development Workbooks, 1956
—Manager Development Guidebooks: Basic Principles and Plan, 1956
  Guidebook I: Managerial Climate
  Guidebook II: Self-Development Planning
  Guidebook III: Manager Manpower Planning
  Guidebook IV: Manager Education
—New Perspectives in Management, Dr. Harry Arthur Hope

Burlingame, J. F. to Reginald H. Jones. May 29, 1980.

Executive Management Staff, handwritten Evaluation of Vice President, 1980.

Fink, Daniel, Vice President of Planning. Re: R. H. Jones' Growth Target. 1980.

Hood, Edward E. to Reginald H. Jones. Re: Success in Self-evaluation. June 3, 1980.

Jones, Reginald H. to J. F. Burlingame, E. E. Hood, and J. F. Welch, Jr. Re: Succession Process—Personal Evaluations. May 8, 1980.

Kane, Donald E. Re: Existing GE Beliefs/Shared Values. October 11, 1985.

Kane, Donald E. Re: Projection of GE 1985 Operating Environment.

Kane, Donald E. Re: Corporate Executive Council. April 1988.

LeVino, Thomas P. to Reginald H. Jones. Re: Vice Chairmen Appraisal Process. May 1, 1980.

LeVino, Thomas P. to Reginald H. Jones. Re: Vice Chairmen Performance Assessment Interview Questions. June 9, 1980.

Peiffer, Jack O. to CEO Direct Reports. Re: Evaluating Leadership of Officers, March 7, 1989.

Trani, John to Group Staff. Re: Global Processes. September 3, 1991.

Welch, John F., Jr., to Corporate Executive Council. Re: Values and Middle Management. April 1987.

Welch, John F., Jr., to Corporate Officers. Re: Shared Values. April 7, 1981.

Welch, John F., Jr., to Corporate Officers. January 14, 1992.

Welch, John F., Jr., to Operating Managers. Re: Values. January 14, 1992.

Welch, John F., Jr., to Reginald H. Jones. Re: Success in Self-evaluation. June 2, 1980.

Speeches/Presentations

Baughman, James, November 1990.

Bossidy, Lawrence. "Some Thoughts on Strategic Thinking." Presented at Strategic Management Society. Boston, October 14, 1987.

Company Officers Speaking at Crotonville, February 2, 1987.

Cordiner, Ralph. Management Conference, 1952.

Fresco, Paolo. "Globalization in GE," October 21, 1988.

Hanson, Kirk O. "Managing Ethics." Crotonville Presentation. Stanford Business School and the Hanson Group.

Lighting. "Lighting Productivity Presentation." Boca Raton, 1989.

Schlemmer, Carl:
  "Excellent Opportunities for the 1980s."
  White Inn Presentation, 1983.

Tichy, Noel M.
  "Creating the Self-renewing Organization." Presentation to the Conference Board, 1986.
  "Strategic Alliances," April 1982.

Trani, John. "1991 Current Business Situation," 1991.

Welch, John F., Jr.:
  "Former Planning Procedures," Question-and-Answer Session with an MBA Class, Harvard Business School, April 27, 1981
  "Audit of Management Systems," 1981
  Closing Remarks at Conference, October 1981
  "Growing Fast in a Slow Growth Economy," December 1981
  Presentation to Financial Community Representatives, December 8, 1981
  Closing Remarks, General Management Conference, 1982
  "The New Competitiveness," June 8, 1983
  "Competitiveness from Within," April 26, 1984
  "Linkages and Leadership," October 17, 1985
  Harvard Business School, October 18, 1985
  Customer Dinner, March 19, 1986

Opening Remarks, Operations Managers Meeting, Boca Raton, January
   1987
Introduction to Security Analysts Presentation, January 1987
Report to Share Owners, April 22, 1987
"Globalization," October 1987
Society of Automotive Engineers, October 9, 1987
Crotonville Faculty Day, September 7, 1988
"GE Growth Engine," December 1988
Boca Raton Remarks, 1989
Aerospace Council Meeting, March 1989
Electrical Products Group of New York, May 10, 1989
"A Boundaryless Company in a Decade of Change." GE Annual Meeting
   of Share Owners, Erie, PA, April 25, 1990
GE OMM, Boca Raton, January 7 & 8, 1991
February 1991
Harvard Business School, November 1991
Speech to Operating Manager, January 1992

Press Coverage

Alexander, Charles P. "Let's Make A Deal." *Time,* December 23, 1985.
Associated Press. "GE to Sell Unit to Black and Decker." *New York Times,*
   December 17, 1983.
Banks, Howard. "General Electric Going with the Winners." *Forbes,* March
   26, 1984.
Barker, Robert. "Commanding General: GE's Management Merits a Premi-
   um—But How Much?" *Barron's,* October 15, 1984.
Barmash, Isadore. "At GE, a Change of Course." *New York Times,* October
   8, 1984.
Bremner, Brian. "Tough Times, Tough Bosses." *Business Week,* November
   25, 1991.
Business Week. "General Electric: The Financial Wizards Switch Back to
   Technology." March 16, 1981.
Carrington, Tim. "U.S. Suspends GE from Defense Work, Asks It, Pratt &
   Whitney for Repayments." *Wall Street Journal,* March 29, 1985.
Cincinnati Inquirer. "GE Fined $10 Million: Two Employees Jailed." July 27,
   1990.
Clayton, Mark. "GE Goes Light Years Beyond the Light Bulb." *Christian
   Science Monitor,* March 23, 1987.
Condo, Adam. "GE's Suspension Called Unfair." *Cincinnati Post,* June 5,
   1992.

Davis, L. J. "Did RCA Have to Be Sold?" *New York Times Magazine*, September 20, 1987.

Davis, L. J. "They Call Him Neutron." *Business Month*, March 1988.

Dentzer, Susan. "GE's New Hi-Tech Boss." *Newsweek*, April 6, 1981.

Dickson, Martin. "Why GE Encourages Lese Majeste." *Financial Times*, October 5, 1990.

Dobrzynski, Judith H., and Russell Mitchell. "General Electric's Jack Welch—How Good a Manager Is He?" *Business Week*, December 14, 1987.

Dumaine, Brian. "How Managers Can Succeed Through Speed." *Fortune*, February 13, 1989.

Egan, Jack. "What Makes Giant GE Keep on Growing." *U.S. News and World Report*, November 23, 1987.

Emshwiller, John R. "Reginald Jones Plans April 1 Retirement from GE—John Welch Will Succeed Him." *Wall Street Journal*, December 22, 1980.

Engelmayer, Paul A. "Black and Decker Agrees to Acquire a GE Operation." *Wall Street Journal*, December 19, 1983.

Feder, Barnaby J. "Companies Find Rewards in Hiring G.E. Executives." *New York Times*, March 9, 1992.

Finn, Edwin A., Jr. "What Will General Electric Eat Next?" *Forbes*, March 23, 1987.

Flanigan, James. "Trading a TV Tradition for Profit Margins." *Los Angeles Times*, July 23, 1987.

Flax, Steven. "The Toughest Bosses in America." *Fortune*, August 6, 1984.

Forbes. "Batter-up." September 18, 1978.

Forbes. "Forbes International 500." July 20, 1992.

Guyon, Janet. "Combative Chief." *Wall Street Journal*, August 4, 1988.

Harris, Diane. "Can GE Shake the GNP Image?" *Financial World*, May 15, 1982.

Harris, Marilyn A., with Zachary Schiller, Russell Mitchell, and Christopher Power. "Can Jack Welch Reinvent GE?" *Business Week*, June 30, 1986.

Holusha, John. "G.E. Inquiry into Diamonds Charge." *New York Times*, April 23, 1992.

Industry Week. "Factories of the Future: A Front-Runner Keeps Pushing." March 21, 1988.

Insight. "After Stagnation's Darkness GE Begins to See the Light." April 6, 1987.

Investor's Daily. "GE to Pay $10 Mil. Fine in Settlement of Lawsuit." July 27, 1990.

Jones, Jack. "Slouching Toward the New Millennium." *Los Angeles Times Magazine*. December 24, 1989.

Kanabayashi, Masayoshi. "Scandal Widens at GE Medical Venture in Japan." *Wall Street Journal,* March 7, 1991.

Kanabayashi, Masayoshi, and Jacob M. Schlesinger. "GE Joint Venture in Japan, Contending with Tough Rivals, Is Hit by Scandal." *Wall Street Journal,* February 22, 1991.

Landro, Laura. "Electric Switch." *Wall Street Journal,* July 12, 1982.

Landro, Laura. "GE's Wizards Turning from the Bottom Line to Share of the Market." *Wall Street Journal,* July 12, 1982.

Landro, Laura, and Douglas A. Sease. "General Electric to Sell Consumer Electronics Lines to Thomson SA for Its Medical Gear Business, Cash." *Wall Street Journal,* July 23, 1987.

Lorenz, Christopher. "GE of the U.S.: Life Under Jack Welch—Opportunistic and Tough." *Financial Times,* May 16, 1988.

Lorenz, Christopher. "GE of the U.S.: Why Strategy Has been Put in the Hands of Line Managers." *Financial Times,* May 18, 1988.

Lueck, Thomas J. "Why Jack Welch Is Changing G.E." *New York Times,* May 5, 1985.

Main, Jeremy. "Managing Now for the 1990s." *Fortune,* September 26, 1986.

Mann, Judy. "Shedding Light on Takeover of NBC." *Washington Post,* December 19, 1986.

McClenahen, John S. "GE's Welch Gambles on Growth." *Industry Week,* April 20, 1987.

Meehan, John. "GE Aims for Nimble Bigness." *International Herald Tribune,* May 5, 1989.

Mitchell, Russell: "Black and Decker in the Kitchen." *New York Times*, January 18, 1984.

Mitchell, Russell, with Judith H. Dobrzynski. "Jack Welch: How Good a Manager?" *Business Week,* December 14, 1987.

Mohl, Bruce A. "General Electric's Man of Action." *Boston Globe,* February 1, 1981.

Morrison, Ann M. "Trying to Bring GE to Life." *Fortune,* January 25, 1982.

Naj, Amal Kumar. "GE Yields to Tiny Rival in Battle over Servicing Medical Machines." *Wall Street Journal,* March 18, 1991.

Naj, Amal Kumar, and Andy Pasztor. "GE Unit Isn't Likely to Feel Impact of Ban." *Wall Street Journal,* June 3, 1992.

Naj, Amal Kumar, and Pauline Yoshi Hashi. "U.S. Broadens Fraud Action Against G.E." *Wall Street Journal,* March 17, 1992.

New England Business. "GE's John F. Welch—General of Excellence or 'Neutron Jack'?" March 1987.

New York Times. "A Change of Course." October 8, 1984.

New York Times. "Mr. Wright? The New Man at NBC." January 19, 1987.

Norman, James R. "Big Changes Are Galvanizing GE." *Business Week,* December 18, 1989.

Norman, James R. "Why GE's Powerhouse Isn't Electrifying Wall Street." *Business Week,* October 31, 1988.

Ottawa Citizen. "Cancer Machine's Malfunction May Cause up to 27 Deaths." February 23, 1991.

Park, Jacob. "Overseas Sales Take Off at Last." *Fortune,* July 16, 1990.

Peters, Tom. "Here's to Another 'Best of Decade' List." *Rocky Mountain News,* December 19, 1989.

Petre, Peter. "GE's Gamble on American Made TVs." *Fortune,* July 6, 1987.

Petre, Peter. "How GE Bobbled the Factory of the Future." *Fortune,* November 11, 1985.

Petre, Peter. "The Man Who Brought GE to Life." *Fortune,* January 5, 1987.

Petre, Peter. "What Welch Has Wrought at GE." *Fortune,* July 7, 1986.

Potts, Mark. "GE Chief Seeks a Strong, Lean Machine." *Washington Post,* May 29, 1988.

Potts, Mark. "GE Sells Consumer Electronics Unit." *Washington Post,* July 23, 1987.

Potts, Mark. "GE's Management Mission." *Washington Post,* May 22, 1988.

Potts, Mark. "GE's Welch Powering Firm into Global Competition." *Washington Post,* September 23, 1984.

Potts, Mark. "A New Vision for Leadership from GE's Visionary." *Washington Post,* March 8, 1992.

Potts, Mark. "Seeking a Better Idea." *Washington Post,* October 7, 1990.

Pound, Edward T. "Charge That GE Conspired to Fix Prices Is Studied." *Wall Street Journal,* April 22, 1992.

Pound, Edward T. "GE Is Expected to Admit Guilt in Dotan Case." *Wall Street Journal,* July 10, 1992.

Pound, Edward T. "Papers Show G.E. Employed Big Guns in Industrial Diamond Market Struggle." *Wall Street Journal,* May 4, 1992.

Pound, Edward T., and Amal Kumar Naj. "GE Launches Internal Probe into Charges." *Wall Street Journal,* April 23, 1992.

Richter, Paul. "GE Selling TV, Electronics Business to French Firm." *Los Angeles Times,* July 23, 1987.

Russell, Mitchell. "GE's Jack Welch—How Good a Manager Is He?" *Business Week,* December 14, 1987.

Sanger, David E. "G.E., a Pioneer in Radio and TV, Is Abandoning Production of Sets." *New York Times,* July 23, 1987.

Sanger, David E. "Pioneers That Grew Up Together into Giants." *New York Times,* December 12, 1985.

Sanger, David E. "Workers at GE Subsidiary Accused by Japan of Bribery." *New York Times,* February 21, 1992.

Schwadel, Francine. "Black and Decker's New Ideas Include Men's Hair Dryers." *Wall Street Journal,* September 14, 1984.

Sherman, Stratford P. "Eight Big Masters of Innovation." *Fortune,* October 15, 1984.

Sherman, Stratford P. "GE's Costly Lesson on Wall Street." *Fortune,* May 9, 1988.

Sherman, Stratford P. "Inside the Mind of Jack Welch." *Fortune,* March 27, 1989.

Sherman, Stratford P. "Today's Leaders Look to Tomorrow: John F. Welch, Jr." *Fortune,* March 26, 1989.

Sherman, Stratford P. "Trashing $150 Billion Business." *Fortune,* August 28, 1989.

Smith, Jim. "GE Admits Guilt, Is Fined 800G Scan." *Philadelphia Daily News,* May 14, 1985.

Smith, Richard Austin. "The Incredible Electrical Conspiracy." *Fortune,* April 1961.

Stevenson, Richard W. "G.E. Whistle Blower Could Face a Suit." *New York Times,* March 17, 1992.

Stevenson, Richard W. "Pentagon Lifts Ban of G.E. Unit." *New York Times,* June 6, 1992.

Stevenson, Richard W. "U.S. Accuses G.E. of Fraud in Israeli Deal." *New York Times,* August 15, 1991.

Stewart, Thomas A. "GE Keeps Those Ideas Coming." *Fortune,* August 12, 1991.

Taylor, John H. "General Electric: Whither NBC's Peacock." *Forbes,* March 4, 1991.

Tetzeli, Rick. "Business Students Cheat Most." *Fortune,* July 1, 1991.

Tully, Shawn. "GE in Hungary: Let There Be Light." *Fortune,* October 22, 1990.

Vise, David A. "GE to Buy RCA for $6.2 Billion." *Washington Post,* December 12, 1985.

Wald, Matthew L. "Four Decades of Bungling at Bomb Plan." *New York Times,* January 25, 1992.

Wall Street Transcript. "Corporate Critics Confidential: Electrical Equipment." July 24, 1989.

Welch, John F., Jr. "Quality Recovery for World Competitiveness." *Financier,* April 1983.

Welch, John F., Jr. "Shun the Incremental; Go For the Quantum Leap." *Financier,* July 1984.

Whitefield, Debra. "Welch: Going for the Leading Edge." *Los Angeles Times,* July 23, 1987.

Wickman, Roy. "Patients Killed by Radiation Blunder." *The European,* March 1–3, 1991.

Young, David. "GM's Rail Unit Chugs Ahead After Lean Spell." *Chicago Tribune,* March 17, 1991.

Books/Academic Articles/Teaching Cases

Auletta, Kenneth. *Three Blind Mice: How the TV Networks Lost Their Way* (New York: Random House, 1991).

Boulware, Lemuel R. *The Truth About Boulwarism* (Washington, D.C.: Bureau of National Affairs, 1969).

Burns, James MacGregor. *Leadership* (New York, Harper & Row, 1978).

Clinard, Marshall B., and Peter C. Yeager (with Ruth Blackburn Clinard). *Corporate Crime* (London, Free Press/Collier Macmillan Publishing, 1980).

Cox, James. A. *A Century of Light* (New York, Benjamin, 1979).

Etzioni, Amatai. *A Comparative Analysis of Complex Organizations* (New York: Free Press, 1961).

Fombrun, Charles, Noel M. Tichy, and Mary Anne Devanna, ed. *Strategic Human Resource Management* (New York: John Wiley & Sons, 1984).

Hall of History Foundation. *The General Electric Story 1876–1986: A Photo History* (Schenectady, NY: Hall of History Foundation, 1981).

INFACT. *Bringing GE to Light* (Philadelphia: New Society Publishers, 1990).

Jones, Robert, and Oliver Marriott. *Anatomy of a Merger: A History of G.E.C., A.E.I., and English Electric* (London: Cape, 1970).

Lydenberg, Steven D., and Alice Tepper Martin, Sean O'Brien Strub, and the Council on Economic Priorities. *Rating America's Corporate Conscience* (Reading, MA: Addison-Wesley, 1986).

Magaziner, Ira C., and Mark Patinkin. "Cold Competition: GE Wages the Refrigerator War." *Harvard Business Review,* March/April 1989.

National Center on Education and the Economy, America's Choice: High Skills or Low Wages (Rochester, NY: National Center on Education and the Economy, 1990).

Neuman, Gerhard. *Herman and the German* (New York: William Morrow, 1984).

Noel, James L., and Ram Charan. "Leadership Development at GE's Crotonville." *Human Resource Management,* Winter 1988, vol. 27, no. 4.

Porter, Michael E. *The Competitive Advantage of Nations* (New York: Free Press, 1990).

Pucik, Vladimir, Noel M. Tichy, and Carole K. Barnett, ed. *Globalizing Management: Creating and Leading the Competitive Organization* (New York: John Wiley & Sons, 1992).

Stewart, James B. *Den of Thieves* (New York: Simon & Schuster, 1991).

Tichy, Noel M. "GE's Crotonville: A Staging Ground for Corporate Revolution." *Academy of Management Executive,* May 1989.

Tichy, Noel M. "The GE Transformation Story." For January 1989 Global Transformation Research Program.

Tichy, Noel M. "Setting the Global Human Resource Management Agenda for the 1990s." *Human Resource Management,* Spring 1988.

Tichy, Noel M. "Training as a Lever for Change." *New Management,* 1986.

Tichy, Noel M., and Mary Anne Devanna. *The Transformational Leader* (New York: John Wiley & Sons, 1986).

Tichy, Noel M., and Ram Charan. "Speed, Simplicity, Self-confidence: An Interview with Jack Welch." *Harvard Business Review,* September/October 1989.

Young, Andrew, Daniel Levi, and Charles Slem. "Dispelling Some Myths About People and Technological Change." *IE,* November 1987.

Harvard Business School Cases

"General Electric Company." 9-113-121. 1964 (Revised 1970).

"General Electric Company: Aircraft Engine Business Group." Case B. 9-183-137. 1982.

"General Electric Company: Aircraft Engine Business Group." Case A. 9-183-136. 1982.

"General Electric Company: Appliance Division Advertising." 9-581-095. 1981.

"General Electric Company: Background Note on Management Systems: 1981." 181-111. 1981.

"General Electric Company: Business Development." 382-092. 1981.

"General Electric Company: Compliance Systems." 1-189-081. 1989.

"General Electric Company: Jack Welch's Second Wave." N9-391-248. 1991.

"General Electric Company: Middle Years." 9-370-160. 1969.

"General Electric Company: 1981 Audit of Management Systems." 181-112. 1981.

"General Electric Company: Origins of Early Development." 9-313-160.

"General Electric Company: Quality of Earnings Analysis." 9-182-243. 1982.

"General Electric Company: Reginald Jones and Jack Welch." N9-391-144. 1991.

"General Electric Company: Role of Staff 1982." 9-182-226. 1982.

"General Electric Company: The Executive Manpower Operation—David Orselet." 9-680-122. 1980.

"General Electric Company: Thermocouple Manufacturing." Case A, B, and C. 9-684-040. 1983.

"General Electric Company: Valley Forge." Case A through H. 1-189-009. 1989.

"General Electric Microwave Oven." 9-579-184. 1979.

Aguilar, Francis J., and Hamermesh, Richard. "General Electric: Strategic Position 1981." 381-174. 1981.

Aguilar, Francis J., Hamermesh, Richard G., and Caroline Brainard. "General Electric: 1984." 9-385-315. 1985.

Collins, Neil, and John Quelch. "General Electric Company: Major Appliance Group: A through D." 9-585-053. 1985.

Hunker, Jeffrey, and Cady, John F. "General Electric: Clock and Timer Market Strategy." 9-582-031. 1984.

Porter, Michael, and Pankaj Ghemawat. "General Electric Versus Westinghouse in Large Turbine Generators." Case A, B, and C. 1980.

Other Sources

Anderson, Eric (MBA Student). "GE: Lighting's Marketing Strategy for Private Label, Consumer Incandescent Light Bulbs." Unpublished manuscript, Nov. 20, 1989.

Baughman, James. "Problems and Performance of the Role of Chief Executive in the General Electric Company 1892–1974." Unpublished manuscript, July 1974.

Charan, Ram, and Noel M. Tichy. "Cracking the Genetic Code for Global Competitiveness: Emotional Energy (E2)." Unpublished manuscript, 1988.

Coakley, Karen, and William Marsh. "General Electric: Strategy and Strategic Planning." Unpublished manuscript, 1980.

Dingell, John D., House of Representatives letter to Richard B. Chaney, Secretary of Defense, June 3, 1992.

Husen, Richard C. "Proceedings: Academy of Management 39th Annual Meeting." University of Georgia, August 8–11, 1979.

JD Power survey, "Customer Satisfaction of U.S. Versus Foreign Auto Companies," July 1992.

Kinnear, Connie. "GE Lighting Case." April 18, 1988.

Kinnear, Connie. "GE Plastics Story."

Kinnear, Connie. "GEMS Case." Unpublished manuscript, 1988.

Smidoly, Harold F. *Address and Papers by Harold F. Smidoly: Outside the Advanced Management Course.* 1958.

Tichy, Noel M., Daniel Denison, Deborah Buhro, Jane Monto, and Patricia Woolcock. "National Broadcasting Company." The University of Michigan Graduate School of Business Administration, Teaching Case, October 1988.

University of Michigan. "General Electric Professional Relations Seminar: May 19–21, 1985."

U.S. Environmental Protection Agency. "Site Enforcement Tracking Report." January 13, 1992.

Wise, George. General Electric's Century: *A History of the General Electric Company From Its Origins to 1986.* Unpublished manuscript, 1986.

HANDBOOK FOR REVOLUTIONARIES

Noel M. Tichy

Introduction

Revolutionary Theater

The GE revolution shows that people can create radical organizational change from within, and they can do it while being financially successful. GE remade itself while earning record profits for over a decade.

Revolution is a call to leadership for all who have a desire to improve the world whether it be to revitalize a major corporation, a department within that corporation, or public sector institutions such as schools and hospitals. It requires taking on the dramatic challenge of creatively destroying and remaking organizations on a continuous basis. Revolution, driven by leaders with ideas and the heart and guts to bring them to life, will become a way of life. It's painful. In all facets of life, including business, one must master change. Faced with increasingly difficult discontinuities, we must redirect life's emotional energies. Leaders of any institution, private or public, are in the business of helping each and every employee generate high levels of positive emotional energy.

1. The Revolutionary Creed

Leaders Add Value to Their Organizations

The ultimate test of leadership is enhancing the long-term value of the organization. For leaders of a publicly held company, this means long-term shareholder value. At every level of the organization, people must understand how their role contributes to value.

Leadership Creates Emotional Energy

One source of competitive advantage is the emotional energy level of the organization. In a fast-moving, complex, changing world, high levels of positive emotional energy lead to faster cycle times, higher quality, lower costs, and the ability to continuously transform.

Corollary: Emotional Energy Is About Ideas

Ideas empower people and provide the fuel for positive emotional energy.

The Goal Is Constant Revolution

The twenty-first-century winners will be those who are in constant revolution: One must embrace every change as an opportunity and not hesitate for fear of being wrong. Being wrong is okay. Change and then get on with it.

Revolutions Have Predictable Patterns

Revolutions follow a predictable set of dynamics. These can be understood and mastered by leaders.

2. The Three-Act Drama: Awakening, Envisioning, and Rearchitecting

Revolutions are predictable. The pain, the resistance, the breakthroughs and joys of successful passage from one phase to another can be understood and mastered.

A corporate revolution is a particular type of drama—a tragedy, perhaps, always with a catharsis and hopefully with a happy ending. For the people involved in the play, it's as gripping and deep as any classical plot. We think of corporations as machines but they are really more like theatrical troupes: Ideas, dialogue, and actions flow among the cast. Managers in the company are part of an ensemble cast demonstrating their skills and magnetism as they perform.

The protagonists of this drama are the people who seek change and set the revolutionary plot in motion. In General

Electric's case, several dozen leaders sought to radically transform the culture. Jack Welch gathered them and came to symbolize their ideas but they all acted as individuals. Inevitably, there are antagonists—people who hold tightly to the company's old ways. The struggle to change involves not just these two opposing groups but thousands of people. They all must deal with grief and deep feelings of loss as the old ways they know disappear. The end of a transformation is exhilarating and leads to a feeling of rebirth. Then the cycle must begin again.

Transformational Leadership in the 1990s

Transformational Leadership: A Three-Act Drama

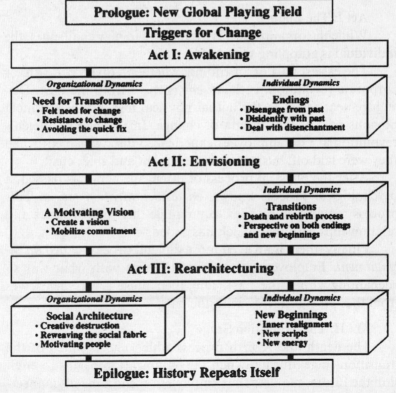

Prologue: New Global Playing Field

Triggers for Change

Act I: Awakening

Organizational Dynamics

Need for Transformation
- Felt need for change
- Resistance to change
- Avoiding the quick fix

Individual Dynamics

Endings
- Disengage from past
- Disidentify with past
- Deal with disenchantment

Act II: Envisioning

A Motivating Vision
- Create a vision
- Mobilize commitment

Individual Dynamics

Transitions
- Death and rebirth process
- Perspective on both endings and new beginnings

Act III: Rearchitecturing

Organizational Dynamics

Social Architecture
- Creative destruction
- Reweaving the social fabric
- Motivating people

Individual Dynamics

New Beginnings
- Inner realignment
- New scripts
- New energy

Epilogue: History Repeats Itself

As the drama plays out in the organization, individual dramas take place within each person. These individual psychological dramas govern the flow of emotional energy in the organization. They are crucial to the success or lack of success of a transformational leader.

3. The Individual During a Revolution

Revolutions are fraught with emotions. Only those who have mastered the emotional issues are qualified to lead. As William Bridges in his book *Transitions* has mapped out, there are predictable and emotional dynamics associated with each act of the revolution.

Act I: The Ending

While the organization is awakening to new challenges, the individual is grappling with loss.

The easiest part of an ending, whether a divorce, death, or corporate revolution, is the *disengagement* from the past. Disengagement refers to the actual physical loss, and is the most obvious part of the trauma of change. In the case of Welch's revolution at GE, employees experienced disengagement when they were laid off, businesses were bought and sold, etc.

After the physical process of disengagement has passed, a psychological process known as *disidentification* starts. This process requires employees to untangle their old loyalties and relationships with that which has ended.

Finally, there is an even more difficult process called *disenchantment*. Employees must come to grips with what was so enchanting about the past, and then must sever themselves from the "enchantment" with the past.

Act II: The Transition Stage

The death and rebirth process which marks much of the transition stage, during which the organization begins to envision the future, requires that employees spend time disconnecting from the past and committing emotionally to the future. Just as in most religions there are processes (funerals, wakes, etc.) designed to aid family and friends of the deceased, employees *must* be given time to gain perspective on both the endings and the new beginnings. Employees of GE had to deal with this in the early and mid-1980s as Welch ended what most viewed as a tremendously successful century.

Act III: The New Beginning

Once employees have moved through the transition stage, they must be prepared for the frustration that accompanies failure as they replace old mastered routines with new ones. Many GE employees have only recently become comfortable with the new precepts at GE—ownership, boundarylessness, etc.

4. The Five Commandments of Revolution

GE's success has been driven by Jack Welch's obsessive desire to win, his ability to stay focused, and his distillation of five core principles that, when taken to heart, will guide any organization through revolutionary change:

1. Know the Business Engine

Have a clear understanding of how an organization's capital and technical resources interact to create value.

2. Understand the Human Connection

In order for the business engine to work, it must be linked with a clearly and carefully articulated vision of how the technical, political, and cultural systems of the organization support one another.

3. Never Compromise on Performance

No excuses. You can make mistakes but you must own them. Take responsibility and move on. Never get stuck in the past.

4. Be Candid and Forthcoming

Use face-to-face constructive conflict as a way to make key decisions.

5. Never Be a Bully

But make the tough decisions that your situation requires. When you cause pain, show others compassion. Be hardheaded and softhearted.

6. How to Use This Handbook

This handbook provides guidelines for applying the powerful ideas from the GE revolution in a variety of situations.

The exhibits and activities are designed to help leaders work through a transformation. These are deep, thought-provoking exercises which provide help for people in various states of revolutionary development. Many of the activities are to be done individually and then discussed by the management team, preferably off-site.

This *Handbook* is designed to help leadership teams plan and guide their work over a several-year period. A corporate revolution is key to the long-term survival and health of the company. As such, it must be treated as the number-one leadership agenda and must draw proportionately on time, money, and leadership focus. Here are some questions and guidelines for leaders to resolve carefully before beginning the revolution:

1. **Time frame for activities**—Both the estimated period for the three acts of the revolution as well as the amount of effort of key leaders.

2. **Roles** of all key leaders—who has responsibility for what.

3. **Task forces**—many of the activities require multimonth task force activities.

4. **Internal staff and external consultant time**—resources, both expertise and facilitation skills needed.

7. Revolutions Take Time—Years

Plan on a multiyear effort. The three acts of the revolutionary drama described in the *Handbook* have already taken over a decade at GE. In preparing to undertake a revolution in your organization it is essential to be realistic about *time*. As you begin the journey, give this careful consideration and set expectations carefully.

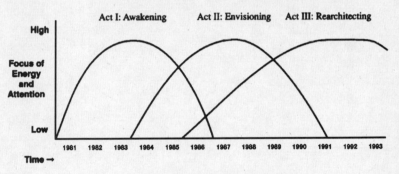

The GE Revolution—The Time Dimension

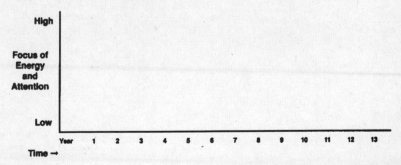

Your Revolution—The Time Dimension

Project what you anticipate to be the time for your revolution and how the three acts of the drama will occur.

WARNING

Do Not Start a Revolution unless you can pass the following test.

ONE

The Organization Test:

How Much of a Revolution Do You Need?

Embracing the Top Line/Bottom Line Paradox

In any organization, there are two kinds of issues: hard and soft. Hard issues include finance, marketing, engineering, and manufacturing. Soft issues concern values, morale, communication, etc. The hard issues generally have the greatest effect on the bottom line (profits), whereas the soft issues have the greatest impact on the top line (total sales).

In the first phase of the GE revolution, Welch moved quickly and aggressively on the hard issues: taking the fat out of the bureaucracy, downsizing, divesting businesses in which GE couldn't win, and investing where he thought they could win. By 1985 the bottom line profitability of GE was positively influenced by Welch's decisive action on the hard issues. Revenue growth and total sales, which are dependent on the trickier soft issues, were progressing at a slower rate.

Paradox of Top Line/Bottom Line Growth

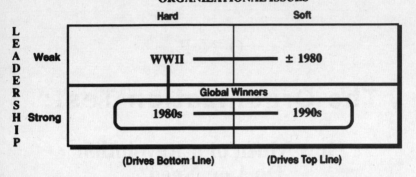

STEP 1: Assess Your Organization: The Top Line/Bottom Line Paradox Test

In order to prepare for the revolution, take time to understand how well your organization is handling this paradox. The activities challenge you to assess:

1. Top Line/Bottom Line trends and implications

2. The capacity for "hard issue" and "soft issue" leadership

This activity provides a catalyst for a lengthy discussion among the leadership team. Have individuals fill out the page individually, then discuss, debate, and draw conclusions.

Results and Projected Results for Your Company
[Fill in the historical numbers and project the future estimates]

	1990	1991	1992	1993	1994	1995
Top Line [Sales]	———	————	————	————	————	————
Bottom Line [Net Income]	———	————	————	————	————	————

What Are the Implications for Your Company?

_____

_____

Assess Your Company's Leadership on Hard Issues:

Below Average For This Industry		Average		Best in Class For This Industry
1	2	3	4	5

Explain Your Rating:

_____

_____

Assess Your Company's Leadership on Soft Issues:

Below Average For This Industry		Average		Best in Class For This Industry
1	2	3	4	5

Explain Your Rating:

_____

_____

STEP 2: Crossing the Gap Between "Old Way" and "New Way"

I like to describe the difference between "Old Way" and "New Way" companies in terms of sports. The old General Electric resembled a football team: Each player had carefully prescribed roles, yielding a carefully orchestrated pattern. The coach called all the plays. Even the strategic-planning guidebooks that governed GE policy were like the playbooks in football. The "New Way" GE is like hockey; roles are blurred, play flows uncontrollably from one side of the rink to the other, there are no timeouts, players adjust to new situations almost every moment and think for themselves while looking out for the team as a whole.

The "Old Way" paradigm of the twentieth-century corporate organization was anti-idea, built on a machine-age mentality. Business institutions created rational, nonemotional, "scientifically" sanitized bureaucracies. People in the organization were not expected to have ideas—the ideas were built into the bureaucracy through a variety of "scientific" practices ranging from time-motion concepts (prescribing how a worker was to do the job down to each physical move) to operations research (a set of quantitative planning tools). At AT&T there were volumes of policy and practice manuals specifying how almost everything was to be done. GE had its five-volume set of Blue Books on how to manage. The larger the bureaucracy, the more ideas were stifled. The focus rapidly became how to perpetuate the technical status quo in the organization, which, in

The Challenge —How Can Your Organization Cross the Gap?
THE TRANSFORMATION

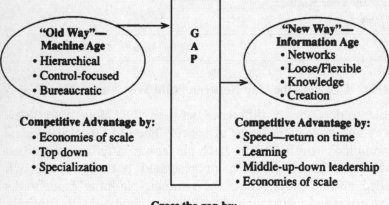

"Old Way"—
Machine Age
• Hierarchical
• Control-focused
• Bureaucratic

G
A
P

"New Way"—
Information Age
• Networks
• Loose/Flexible
• Knowledge
• Creation

Competitive Advantage by:
• Economies of scale
• Top down
• Specialization

Competitive Advantage by:
• Speed—return on time
• Learning
• Middle-up-down leadership
• Economies of scale

Cross the gap by:

• Developing trust
• Empowering All Levels
• Eliminating work
• Architecting the new way—new systems

turn, led people to dwell increasingly on the politics of turf protection and careerism.

The "New Way" organization is built on ideas that provide the energy for breaking frame with the past. Ideas change the direction and provide the emotional energy for moving the organization forward. Ideas are at the core of producing emotional energy for people—ideas about products and services, ideas about customers, ideas about organizations. The challenge for GE and other twenty-first-century winners is to create an environment where many people's ideas can be harnessed.

In order to cross the gap the following conditions are required:

Trust: Downsizing, delayering, and a lack of job security break the feeling of trust between the top and the middle management. It is necessary to rebuild trust in order to take on the quantum leap from "Old Way" to "New Way."

Empowerment: Historically, power is held at the top of the control-oriented, machine-age bureaucracy. Top/down management is still dominant in the United States. As the transformation gap is crossed, this power must be shared with leadership at all levels, up, down, and sideways.

Eliminate Work: People get removed but not work. People are taken out of the organization but time is not taken to remove reports, approvals, meetings, and measurements. To cross the gap work must be taken out.

Vision: In order to have a true quantum change it is necessary to have a "New Way" vision. The social architecture needs to be articulated, those involved must have a clear idea about where they are going.

1. To what extent is there *trust* between the top and middle levels?

Very Low		Moderate			High Level	
1	2	3	4	5	6	7

Comments _____

2. To what extent are middle managers *empowered*?

1	2	3	4	5	6	7

Comments _____

3. To what extent has unnecessary work been eliminated (reports, appraisals, meetings, measurements, etc.)?

Little/No Work Out		Moderate Work Out			Great Deal Work Out	
1	2	3	4	5	6	7

Comments _____

4. To what extent is there a clear vision of the "New Way" organization of work?

No Clear Vision		Moderate Clarity			Very Clear Vision	
1	2	3	4	5	6	7

Comments _____

5. Overall, where would you rate the organization on the transformation from "Old Way" to "New Way"?

Totally "Old Way"		Halfway There			Totally "New Way"	
1	2	3	4	5	6	7

Comments _____

© 1988 Noel Tichy, Ram Charan.

STEP 3: Getting Down to Details—Why Do You Need a Revolution?

These questions help you systematically diagnose why your organization needs a revolution. It may take several months of task force, work, and off-site discussion to reach a final set of conclusions.

1) What is the hand you have been dealt?

GE EXAMPLE	YOUR ORGANIZATION

The Hand Welch Was Dealt—GE in 1980

_____

• A strong balance sheet

_____

• Slow-moving bureaucracy

_____

• Productivity improvements of 1% to 2% per year

_____

• Nonglobal businesses

_____

• Modest technology

2) What legacy is built into your organization's "genetic code"?

<u>GE EXAMPLE</u>   <u>YOUR ORGANIZATION</u>

GE's 100-Year-Old Heritage

GE was always a company of
ideas about management and organization. It grew to be the most diverse company in the United States.

Its culture became very inward-
focused and very bureaucratic
under the fabric of "scientific management." It became the business
school model for financial management, organizational design, strategic planning, development, and
succession planning.

3) What is your bureaucracy like?

<u>GE EXAMPLE</u>   <u>YOUR ORGANIZATION</u>

The Old Bureaucracy

- 9 layers of management from
  CEO to shop floor

- Wedding cake shape of company—
  military-like nomenclature, all the
  same across the company

- Finance mafia—controlled by
  auditing, etc.

- Span-breaker—sector executives
  and staffs putting layers of
  reviews, procedures, etc.,
  between CEO and actual people
  running the businesses.

- Strategic planning process with
  over 100 planning staff at Headquarters producing volumes of
  books and data for presentations.

4) What are the core problems (hard and soft)?

<u>GE EXAMPLE</u>   <u>YOUR ORGANIZATION</u>

The Hard Issues

• Earnings growth was average   ———————————

• Cash flow was a persistent
  problem because of high capital   ———————————
  expenditures and working capital
  expansion   ———————————

• Slow-growing electrical equip-   ———————————
  ment core businesses still
  dominated GE   ———————————

• Productivity growth 1% to 2%—   ———————————
  and the operating margin stayed
  in the 7% to 9% range   ———————————

• Large uncertainties in   ———————————
  —Power systems where the energy
    crisis and Three Mile Island   ———————————
    had devastated backlogs
  —Utah International because the
    Japanese were developing new
    coal supplies   ———————————
  —International mini-GEs
    (Brazil, Canada, Spain,   ———————————
    Mexico), which were high-
    cost entities not ready for the   ———————————
    new emerging global
    competition   ———————————

The Soft Issues   ———————————

• Slow decision making   ———————————

• Turf struggles   ———————————

• Inward focus   ———————————

• Lack of innovation

T W O

The Mirror Test:

Do You Have the Head, Heart, and Guts to Lead a Revolution?

Revolution is a game for leaders. All of us have the capacity to be revolutionary leaders in our own sphere. The question is whether we want to apply our head, heart, and guts to the task. It is not possible to conduct the mirror test alone. Self-perception is always distorted. The steps outlined in this section include self-analyzing and feedback from others.

STEP 1: The Mirror Test—Take Time to Reflect on Your Personal Assessment

	WHAT IS REQUIRED	GE EXAMPLE	HOW DO YOU SEE YOURSELF?
H	Intellectual rigor,	• Ability to	_____
E	understanding of	Conceptualize	
A	business, and ideas		
D	that can win in the	• Knowledge of	_____
	marketplace	Business	
		• A Vision	_____

	WHAT IS REQUIRED	GE EXAMPLE	HOW DO YOU SEE YOURSELF?
H	Compassion, empathy,	• Candor	_____
E	and fairness packaged		
A	in a tough love,	• Integrity	_____
R	absolute candor	• Compassion	_____
T	package		_____
			_____
G	Ability to make the	• Reality	_____
U	tough calls, stand up	• Self-	
T	to unpopular posi-	Knowledge	_____
S	tions, take risks, and		
	have the self-confi-	• Simplicity	_____
	dence to be simple	• Speed	_____

STEP 2: The Accomplishment Analysis

There is more to good leadership than making your numbers. GE uses a powerful analytic tool, the Accomplishment Analysis, to take an in-depth look at a leader's intellectual capability, ability to motivate staff, and capacity for risk-taking. At GE, specially trained members of the Executive Management Staff interview an individual, his subordinates, boss, and peers, focusing qualitatively on accomplishments, strengths, weaknesses, and potential. This activity is best organized by independent human resource staff or outside consultants. They need to interview the individual as well as key stakeholders, boss, subordinates, and customers.

Develop an Action Plan for Accomplishment Analysis

WHO NEEDS TO BE
ANALYZED? (NAMES)   BY WHOM   BY WHEN

1. _____   _____   _____

2. _____   _____   _____

3. _____   _____   _____

4. _____   _____   _____

5. _____   _____   _____

6. _____   _____   _____

STEP 3: Survey of Top Leadership

In 1985, GE developed a Leadership Effectiveness Survey to see how well GE's leaders were adopting the new leadership values Welch advocated. The exhibit below lists the characteristics Jack Welch was seeking in the business and in leadership. The survey captures those dimensions.

Whenever individuals go to Crotonville, ten of their subordinates, peers, and bosses are asked to rate them. The individual also fills out the same survey, providing a self-portrait.

This process is worth developing in all organizations and can be started using a generic leadership survey that can then be customized as the organization clarifies its own set of values. The following page presents examples of ideas from a "Transformational Leader" assessment survey.

GE Value Statement

BUSINESS CHARACTERISTICS

LEAN
What—Reduce tasks and the people required to do them.
Why —Critical to developing world cost leadership.

AGILE
What—Delayering.
Why —Create fast decision making in rapidly changing world through improved communication and increased individual response.

CREATIVE
What—Development of new ideas—innovation.
Why —Increase customer satisfaction and operating margins through higher value products and services.

OWNERSHIP
What—Self-confidence to trust others. Self-confidence to delegate to others the freedom to act while, at the same time, self-confidence to involve higher levels in issues critical to the business and the corporation.

INDIVIDUAL CHARACTERISTICS

REALITY
What—Describe the environment as it is—not as we hope it to be.
Why —Critical to developing a vision and a winning strategy, and to gaining universal acceptance for their implementation.

LEADERSHIP
What—Sustained passion for and commitment to a proactive, shared vision and its implementation.
Why —To rally teams toward achieving a common objective.

CANDOR/OPENNESS
What—Complete and frequent sharing of information with individuals (appraisals, etc.) and organization (everything).
Why —Critical to employees knowing where they, their efforts, and their business stand.

BUSINESS CHARACTERISTICS

Why —Supports concept of more individual responsibility, capability to act quickly and independently. Should increase job satisfaction and improve understanding of risks and rewards. While delegation is critical, there is a small percentage of high-impact issues that need or require involvement of higher levels within the business and within the corporation.

REWARD

What—Recognition and compensation commensurate with risk and performance—highly differentiated by individual, with recognition of total team achievement.

Why —Necessary to attract and motivate the type of individuals required to accomplish GE's objectives. A No. 1 business should provide No. 1 people with No. 1 opportunity.

INDIVIDUAL CHARACTERISTICS

SIMPLICITY

What—Strive for brevity, clarity, the "elegant, simple solution"—less is better.

Why —Less complexity improves everything, from reduced bureaucracy to better product designs to lower costs.

INTEGRITY

What—Never bend or wink at the truth, and live within both the spirit and letter of the laws of every global business arena.

Why —Critical to gaining the global arenas' acceptance of our right to grow and prosper. Every constituency: shareowners who invest; customers who purchase; community that supports; and employees who depend, expect, and deserve our unequivocal commitment to integrity in every facet of our behavior.

BUSINESS CHARACTERISTICS

INDIVIDUAL CHARACTERISTICS

INDIVIDUAL DIGNITY

What—Respect and leverage the talent and contribution of every individual in both good and bad times.

Why —Teamwork depends on trust, mutual understanding, and the shared belief that the individual will be treated fairly in any environment.

The Transformational Leader Survey

(SAMPLE ITEMS)

Act I: Awakening

Getting the organization prepared for the revolution and dealing with the forces of resistance and the psychodynamics of change.

0 Cannot Rate
1 Strongly Disagree
2 Disagree
3 Neutral
4 Agree
5 Strongly Agree

1. Is often first to identify changes in the environment (societal, economic, political) which will impact business 5 4 3 2 1 0

2. In spite of resistance, consistently pursues the need for change 5 4 3 2 1 0

3. Is able to lead *others* to overcome fear and uncertainty in making change 5 4 3 2 1 0

4. Is able to help others overcome organizational resistance to change 5 4 3 2 1 0

5. Avoids shortcuts and gimmicks for achieving organizational change 5 4 3 2 1 0

Act II: Envisioning

Generates ideas for the future success of the company and incorporates them into an exciting and motivating vision and mobilizes others around the vision.

1. Has described characteristics that his/her organization should have in the future 5 4 3 2 1 0

2. Can visualize the business through the eyes of the customer, i.e., is highly customer-conscious 5 4 3 2 1 0

3. Creates enthusiastic commitment for the vision of the business 5 4 3 2 1 0

4. Has a clear vision about the future of the business 5 4 3 2 1 0

5. Is able to help *others* disengage from the past and move into the future 5 4 3 2 1 0

Act III: Rearchitecting

Creatively destroying the old organization and architecting the new.

1. Can dismantle old bureaucracy and can create new organizational forms to fit the vision 5 4 3 2 1 0

Personal Characteristics:

Transformational leadership traits of the person.

1. Has high standards of personal conduct 5 4 3 2 1 0

2. Learns from his/her mistakes 5 4 3 2 1 0

3. Insists on continuous improvement for self 5 4 3 2 1 0

4. Is able to engender a high level of motivation in others 5 4 3 2 1 0

5. Assumes responsibility for own mistakes 5 4 3 2 1 0

6. Is trusted by others 5 4 3 2 1 0

7. Communicates openly and candidly with individuals at lower organizational levels 5 4 3 2 1 0

8. Maintains sound business perspective in the face of dilemmas and paradoxes 5 4 3 2 1 0

9. Builds coalitions and networks across organizational lines to achieve important goals 5 4 3 2 1 0

STEP 4: Selecting the Varsity Team

The mirror test is not just for the top leader. It is a method of evaluating leadership capability at the top of the organization. A leadership team's success depends on the ability of all its members to communicate and cooperate.

Draw a diagram (see below) to assess the communication skills of the senior group: Circles indicate individuals, lines indicate linkages and authority relationships between individuals. Numbers indicate quality of communication: +, -, 0 indicate friendship links. After you identify who belongs in the network, identify each linkage between pairs of individuals. Show who influences whom, the quality of the communication

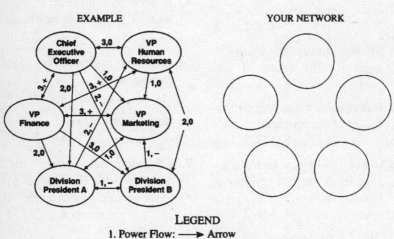

EXAMPLE   YOUR NETWORK

LEGEND

1. Power Flow: ——▶ Arrow
   indicates direction
2. Communication Quality: 1-Poor, 2-Okay, 3-Good
3. Friendship Links: — = Negative
                        0 = Neutral
                        + = Friend

DID YOU PASS THE MIRROR TEST?

(Do you have the head, heart, and guts to lead a revolution?)
If No: Do Not Continue
If Yes: Continue

between the individuals, and the effective links between the individuals—that is, the degree to which there are friendships. There is no room in "New Way" organizations for leaders who don't communicate.

STEP 5: The Idea Test

The fuel for the revolution is ideas because: 1) Ideas give meaning to life—throughout history spiritual ideas, ideas about justice and freedom, have been central to society. People's identities are tied to ideas they consider important. 2) There is nothing like the emotional kick that comes from putting your ideas into action. 3) Empowerment is at the core—the freedom to carry out one's ideas. Have an idea, try it out, and get feedback. It takes an enormous number and range of ideas to transform an organization; ideas about values and strategies, ideas for practical improvements, ideas about how to do small things a little more efficiently and ideas for sweeping change. Ideas get people excited and get people moving. The tremendous energy of many motivated and focused people is what it takes to creatively destroy and rebuild the institution. There must be ideas about the technical system—how the company will make money in the marketplace and organize its resources to do so; the political system—how power, influence, and rewards will be used to energize the organization; and the cultural system—the shared norms and values that hold the people together.

There are two types of ideas vital to revolutionary success. Quantum ideas—the big ideas like No. 1 or No. 2 that throw old habits and techniques out the window—create revolutions. Incremental ideas—the small, evolutionary changes that yield the continuous improvement of "Every day a better way"—sustain them. Companies that master only one type of idea will not be winners. A few years back, Toyota generated the constant flow of incremental ideas necessary to master continuous improvement. Every company in the world wanted its just-in-time manufacturing system to be as lean and flexible as Toyota's. Toyota's bottom line was in great shape but the company wasn't generating the kind of quantum ideas that produce bold new products and top-line growth. Honda, with its innovative Accord and Acura lines, took the lead. A few years later, a wiser Toyota introduced the successful Lexus and Camry lines, proving itself to be a master of quantum as well as incremental ideas.

The table below shows the role of ideas in revolutionary organizations:

**The Paradox of Ideas:
The Twenty-first-Century Winner**

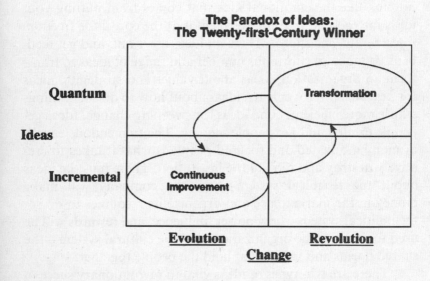

The exercise below is designed to help people understand what happens to ideas in your organization. After doing the individual work, discussion should focus on the analysis of what happens to ideas in your organization and why.

GE Quantum Ideas: • Purchase of RCA • Swap of GE Consumer Electronics for Thomson's CGR medical-imaging business • Product breakthroughs, such as magnetic resonance.

QUANTUM IDEAS	WHO HAD THE IDEA?	WHAT HAPPENED TO THE IDEA?	WHY?

(List one that you or someone in your organization had)

GE Incremental Ideas: • Communication between functions • Improved cycle times in responding to customers • Electronic invoicing.

INCREMENTAL IDEAS	WHO HAD THE IDEA?	WHAT HAPPENED TO THE IDEA?	WHY?

(List at least three incremental ideas)

STEP 6: Ideas for the Revolution

The GE Ideas

Welch led the revolution with three big ideas: The first strategy was to be No. 1 or No. 2 in any GE business and to get there by Fixing, Closing or Selling each of GE's businesses. This was the *technical* idea for GE's revolution. The *political* idea was a corporate structure that pushed most power out into the businesses, giving the businesses control of their destiny while at the same time integrating and holding certain powers at the center of GE. Finally, the *cultural* idea for the GE revolution is captured in Welch's notion of "boundaryless" values and behavior—sharing to gain, partnering across all levels and boundaries within and outside GE. The GE ideas are portrayed in the diagram below:

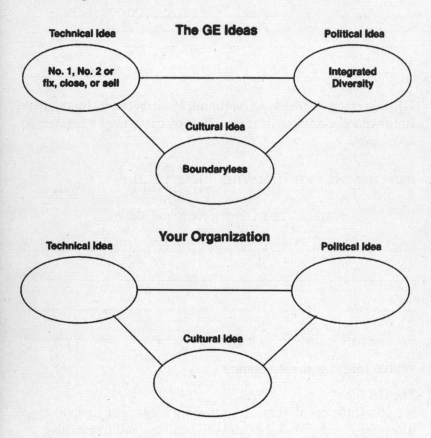

Have you developed core ideas for the 1) technical system, 2) political system, and 3) cultural system? Ideas about the three systems must be interwoven like the strands of a rope, mutually reinforcing each other.

The Technical, Political, and Cultural Building Blocks of an Organization

Ideas Will Create:

A TECHNICAL SYSTEM WITH:

- Extensive shared visions driven at all levels, not just from the executive suite.

- Open, nondistorted flows of information—up, down, and sideways among people at all levels and throughout the organization.

A POLITICAL SYSTEM WITH:

- Total honesty, candor, and willingness to face business reality in the selecting and rewarding of people.

- Decisions made based on expertise, not hierarchical levels.

- Multiple power networks to support multiple tasks.

A CULTURAL SYSTEM WITH:

- Open, candid, reality-focused attitudes.

- Emphasis on both bottom line efficiency needs and top line innovation needs.

- Team values.

THREE

The Readiness Test:

Are You Ready for the Revolution?

Now that you have taken a look at reality, summarize your conclusions below. Note, this is a very serious and critical juncture. Leading a revolution means no turning back. Bridges do get burned and action must be taken.

Summarize your self-evaluation below.

Willingness: The Attitude Toward Revolution

	LITTLE OR NO WILLINGNESS		MODERATE	GREAT AMOUNT OF WILLINGNESS	
You as Leader:	1	2	3	4	5
Your "Varsity Team":	1	2	3	4	5
Your Organization:	1	2	3	4	5

Capability: The Talent, Skill, and Resources for Revolution

	LITTLE OR NO CAPABILITY		MODERATE	GREAT AMOUNT OF CAPABILITY	
You as Leader:	1	2	3	4	5
Your "Varsity Team":	1	2	3	4	5
Your Organization:	1	2	3	4	5

Implications—Should You Start the Revolution?

_____

_____

_____

_____

Act I

AWAKENING

Launching the Revolution

Waking up the organization to the need for change is the most emotionally wrenching and terrifying aspect of a revolution. The protagonists have to shake up the status quo enough to release the emotional energy for the revolution.

Kick-Start the Revolution

The first act of a revolution is creating a sense of urgency and dealing with the inevitable resistance to the new order. This was very tough in GE, as it is in all successful companies. The early Welch years, 1981–1983, were marked by tremendous resistance. Welch was viewed by many as "Neutron Jack" and was named toughest CEO by *Fortune* magazine in 1984. During this phase Welch analyzed the old GE—what was wrong with it, what needed changing, and what didn't. The early articulation of a change agenda, the dynamics of waking the organization, the unfreezing of old mind-sets and cultures are the main scenes of the first act.

STEP 1: Create a Feeling of Urgency

Avoid the Boiled-Frog Phenomenon. The first major test of a revolutionary leader is the speed with which he wakes up the organization. There is an old biological experiment that demonstrates a frog's lack of attention to a changing environment. The first step of the experiment is to place a frog in a pan of cold water. As the water temperature is raised from room temperature to boiling, the frog sits in the water, never jumping out, and is ultimately boiled to death, demonstrating the risk of new organizations that do not attend to their environmental changes. Welch avoided the boiled-frog phenomenon by taking quick, urgent action as the leader of the GE revolution.

Soon after becoming CEO in 1981, Welch gave a speech to his top 100 executives. He was visibly emotionally moved, trying to create a sense of urgency by saying:

> You own these damn businesses. The idea of coming into Fairfield, and Fairfield yells and exhorts and cheers, Big Daddy gets you, and then you come back with another plan a little bit better than the last time. It's an insane system we've built . . . Let's take it away. Number 1, it's ownership, leadership, responsibility—it's yours . . . Our strategic plan doesn't need a book this thick, it's for you to be the leaders in what you're in, to be No. 1 or No. 2 in the business you're in. That's the General Electric plan.

Kick-Starting the Revolution

1) What is the rationale for change?

Start by carefully articulating why change is necessary, make certain the top leadership team is in total agreement.

GE EXAMPLE	YOUR ORGANIZATION
• Increasing global character of markets and competition	
• Slow top line growth of business	
• New growth opportunities emerging	
• Need to be a nimble organization	
• Competitors were speeding up cycle times	

2) How vulnerable to the boiled-frog phenomenon are you?

GE EXAMPLE	YOUR ORGANIZATION
GE was a 100-year-old successful, highly respected corporation in America, coming off a year of record net income with the previous chairman, Reginald Jones, who had been voted *Fortune's* "Best CEO in the U.S." However, there was significant, underlying dry rot in businesses that would rapidly decline if not transformed in the 1980s. Inbred arrogance and complacency at GE made facing reality extremely difficult.	_____ _____ _____ _____ _____ _____ _____ _____

STEP 2: Deal with Resistance

Welch's early exhortations did not result in resistance. In fact, most GE managers responded, more or less, with big yawns. They felt, "Hey, we're GE, we're the best, we've been around for 100 years, this guy Welch is just a lot of talk." But once Welch began to act, resistance started, albeit not for the reasons one might have expected. The nearly $3 billion divestiture of Utah International in 1983 elicited blasé "So what?" behavior on the part of some managers. It wasn't until the Housewares business was sold in 1984 (GE irons, toasters, and other small appliances) that GE managers woke up and figuratively started pointing at Welch and saying, "That son-of-a-bitch is starting to change us, now we have to resist him." And resistance comes in three forms: Technical, Political, and Cultural.

Types of Resistance

Technical resistance includes all of the rational reasons for resisting change: Habit, prior investment, and inertia.

Political resistance is the response to the disruption to the existing power structure. Powerful coalitions are disrupted, resources are limited, and leaders often have to take blame for problems that were created in the organization.

Cultural resistance due to mindsets and blinders built up over the years, resulting in anchors that keep people in the past.

What Are the Major Forces Resisting Change in Your Business?

Diagnose the major forces of resistance: This is a critical step in the process as all of the leadership teams need to agree and work together. There is inevitably a great deal of conflict over resistance. This work often takes a day of intense debate and compromise to resolve.

1. Technical Resistance

CAUSE	GE EXAMPLES	YOUR ORGANIZATION
—Habit and Inertia	GE managers had mastered a set of bureaucratic traditions. Welch's goals required doing things in a different way.	_____ _____ _____
—Fear of the Unknown	GE managers were frightened by Welch's demand to go global. For many managers of traditionally domestic businesses, this caused anxiety and fear.	_____ _____ _____ _____

CAUSE	GE EXAMPLES	YOUR ORGANIZATION
—Prior Investment	A tremendous amount was invested in training people to do things the "GE Way." This investment would allegedly be wasted if everyone changed.	_____ _____ _____ _____

2. Political Resistance

CAUSE	GE EXAMPLES	YOUR ORGANIZATION
—Resource Allocation	Resource allocation tends to be a zero sum game in the best of times. Welch told GEers to get higher productivity and more innovation with less over-head and less headcount. Doing more with less makes the normal politics of resource allocation even tougher.	_____ _____ _____ _____ _____
—Indictment of Leaders	One exception to the "in-dictment of leaders" prob-lem was Carl Schlemmer, the head of GE's Locomo-tive business, who invested $300 million in new plant capacity to overtake its competition, GM. When the bottom fell out of the market, Carl Schlemmer took full responsibility for having misjudged the mar-ket, and said, "I want to stay and clean up the mess."	_____ _____ _____ _____ _____ _____

CAUSE	GE EXAMPLES	YOUR ORGANIZATION
	He went on to lead a very exciting turn-around—he faced his own personal indictment.	_____ _____
—Threats to Powerful Coalitions	The core businesses, such as Power Systems and Light ing, had dominated GE since they were founded: In 1980, 50% of earnings, by 1985 this number had shrunk to 25%. Their leaders resisted Welch as their power (investments, career opportunities, etc.) was threatened.	_____ _____ _____ _____ _____ _____

3. Cultural Resistance

CAUSE	GE EXAMPLES	YOUR ORGANIZATION
—Old Cultural Mind-sets	In Lighting, in 1984 and 1985, people reminisced about Thomas Edison, NELA Park, and the "good old days" of market dominance—while low-cost producers from Korea and elsewhere were eroding GE's market share. A history of dominance precluded Lighting's managers from perceiving a competitive threat. Their mind-sets were often "hard-wired" and immune to retraining.	_____ _____ _____ _____ _____ _____ _____

CAUSE	GE EXAMPLES	YOUR ORGANIZATION
—Sense of Security	Power Systems' several-year backlog of orders, its healthy earnings record, and its traditional technical superiority allowed the business's managers to feel secure even as their business was ending.	_____ _____ _____ _____
—Climate for Change	GE's stable 100-year-old bureaucracy was geared toward doing the same thing, the same way, for the millionth time, thus change was anathema to the organization.	_____ _____ _____ _____

STEP 3: Fighting Resistance

Premise 1: The chain of command is where much of the resistance resides because people's vested interests are at stake.

    a. You must stir up the total populace and begin developing new leaders for the new regime.

    b. You must create a new set of values and templates.

    c. You must invent mechanisms for socializing the work force.

Premise 2: Revolutionaries overturn the current system and replace it with one of their own devising. They do not rely on the chain of command to bring about quantum change—they grab the police, media, and education system. So did Jack Welch.

The Police

GE EXAMPLE	YOUR ORGANIZATION

GE's internal auditing staff, considered by many inside GE as the Gestapo and headed by the top finance executive, was the police. Welch eliminated many measures, created new measures, forced people to look at comparisons to competitors (not just to budgets), and redirected their focus to serving GE's businesses. Thus, rather than controlling it, Corporate audit staff now does more and more consulting to help transform the organization rather than control it.

The Media

Welch took control of all his forms of communication, from board communication to security analyst presentations to using his own words and ideas when writing internal speeches.

The Schools

The GE Blue Books, although not used for fifteen years, had still left their cultural imprint—they were symbolically burned. Welch said there are no more "textbook" answers. Leaders must write their own. Jack Welch took direct control of Crotonville. He continues to

personally appear every two weeks
at Crotonville to interact in classes
and redirect the overall Crotonville
curriculum for everyone, from new
hires to senior executives.

_____

_____

_____

Act II

ENVISIONING

Mobilizing Commitment to a Vision

This is the act of the drama where emotion becomes more positive, where the frustrations and fears get channeled in new and exciting directions. The purpose of the revolution comes into focus.

Revolution requires emotionally exciting visions. The pain of change requires an image of the "New Way." The contemporary problem with vision is that for many leaders it has become a sloganeering "bumper sticker" campaign of platitudes such as "customer-oriented," "fast cycle-time," and "reengineered organization." Without intellectually substantial *ideas* to back these phrases, platitudes quickly become a source of ridicule for the "non-transformational leader." This ridicule leads to deep cynicism and alienation rather than the anticipated liberation of Act II.

In 1981 Welch clearly made this point when he spoke of the importance of having a central idea:

You can express a vision to a broad number of people. People have to want to buy into your vision. You can implement it and together you can all win and reward yourselves and the company. That's what a good leader does. He or she creates an open, caring relationship with every employee. If you can't articulate your business vision, if you can't get people to buy in, forget it. You won't be successful. It won't come from power and title.

The visioning process is a creative, often chaotic, multiple-iteration process. A vision is a group effort. It is what we believe to be important. It is a work in progress, an architectural rendering that constantly gets modified. We need to involve as many people as possible, think "out loud," and get feedback from many different stakeholders.

STEP 1: Preparation for the Vision—A GE Example

Before starting the creative visioning process, take time to carefully describe the current reality. Using the technical, political, and cultural framework, develop a set of summary descriptions for each box in the following chart. Each summary should be the result of intensive examination and discussion of the current organization and the manager who will be involved in the visioning process. The dialogue and discussion will help the teams work through their differences, sensitize each other to assumptions regarding what needs changing, and prepare them to think about the desired future. As soon as Welch took office, he spent six months visiting all corners of GE. These trips were his way of determining GE's reality—the matrix on the following page summarizes this understanding.

Assessing Reality

Another crucial step in creating a vision for your organization is an assessment of today's reality. Before you and your organization can move forward, you need to understand your departure point. An example of GE's reality in 1980 is presented below.

	STRATEGY	ORGANIZATIONAL STRUCTURE	HUMAN RESOURCE MANAGEMENT
T E C H N I C A L	• Diversify • Religious devotion to budgets • Grow high-tech businesses • Strategic planning	• Decentralize • Systematic structuring	• Engineer-dominated professional recruit • One pay system • Formal appraisals, work goals
P O L I T I C A L	• CEO as constitutionalist • Banker role	• Hierarchical • Functional boundaries • Political centralization	• Succession very formal/systematic • Rewards similar/lock step • Approvals boss down
C U L T U R A L	• "Scientific management" • Decentralized philosophy—centralized behavior • Oligopolistic • Stewardship	• GE "way of doing things" • Core business culture dominance	• GE recruits screened for culture • Development used to shape culture • Appraisal and rewards "GE way" driven

Current state of reality: Fill in the TPC matrix for your organization today.

	STRATEGY	ORGANIZATIONAL STRUCTURE	HUMAN RESOURCE MANAGEMENT
T E C H N I C A L			
P O L I T I C A L			
C U L T U R A L			

STEP 2: The Nature of the Visioning Process

An example of this iterative nature of the visioning process at GE is the values statement. Welch was constantly reworking it, asking for feedback from all possible sources. The fundamental ideas remained the same throughout the drafts, but their articulation was reworked for a decade and revisions will continue forever.

1983: Main Points from Speech to Officers on Values

- Lean and Agile
- Excellence
- Quality
- Entrepreneurship
- Reality and Candor
- Communications
- Stewardship

1985: Main Points from Shared Values Statement

- Only satisfied customers can provide job security
- Change is continual; nothing is sacred
- Nothing is secret
- Constructive conflict flourishes
- Dealing with paradox is a way of life

1987: Main Points from Revised Shared Values Statement

- Respect for others
- Openness
- Change is continual
- Dealing with paradox is a way of life
- Constructive conflict
- Resource allocation is dynamic
- Everyone's contribution counts
- Doing the right thing is pervasive
- "Ownership"

1992: Main Points from Revised Shared Values Statement

- Create a clear, simple, reality-based, customer-focused vision and be able to communicate it straightforwardly to all constituencies.

- Understand accountability and commitment and be decisive. Set and meet aggressive targets with unyielding integrity.

- Have a passion for excellence. Hate bureaucracy and all the nonsense that comes with it.

- Have the self-confidence to empower others and behave in a boundaryless fashion. Believe in and be committed to Work-Out as a means of empowerment. Be open to ideas from anywhere.

- Have, or have the capacity to develop, global brands and global sensitivity and be comfortable building diverse global teams.

- Stimulate and relish change; not be frightened or paralyzed by it. See changes as an opportunity, not just a threat.

- Have enormous energy and the ability to energize and invigorate others.

The visioning process is a creative, often chaotic, multiple-iteration process. Brainstorm and organize the ideas around central concepts and then get feedback and think out loud with many different stakeholders. This is akin to the architect doing many renderings, getting feedback, redrawing, rethinking, etc.

The vision must include quantum ideas in the technical, political, and cultural areas. These ideas provide the organizing logic for the transformation. These ideas must also reinforce each other. In order for GE to succeed, each of the three central ideas must contribute to each other. For example, being No. 1 or No. 2 with a very decentralized company could end up with GE as a mere holding company. Instead, Welch always believed there must be synergy between all the companies that make up GE. The political idea came about to provide the freedom for businesses to do their own thing as opposed to meeting the inward bureaucratic needs of the company. The glue that makes it all hold together is the shared values finally articulated under the concept of boundarylessness.

At GE it took Welch a very short period of time to clearly articulate the technical idea of being No. 1 or No. 2. Nonetheless this idea got discussed and revised many times in terms of meaning until it became deeply embedded in the collective mindset of GEers.

The political idea, integrated diversity, with its paradox of decentralized businesses and collective GE action, took a lot longer to come into focus. Welch started with the idea of "ownership" of the businesses; the rendering was too fuzzy, managers misunderstood the concept, and until 1985, when the sector layer was removed from GE and the idea of businesses being directly connected to the office of the CEO occurred, the political idea for GE was not clear. Since that time the idea has been modified to its present articulation of integrated diversity, large freestanding businesses which can also cooperate with each other to accomplish overall GE wins in the marketplace.

The glue to hold GE together is not bureaucracy, but a set of shared values and human networks across its businesses. The most intense of the visioning activities has been the process of articulating the value statement. Welch is constantly reworking it, asking for feedback from all possible sources.

The fundamental ideas remained the same, but their articulation was reworked for a decade and will continue to be revised forever. The technical, political, and cultural matrix provides a systematic framework for ensuring that the architectural rendering is complete, that all the major components of the organization are designed. It is never filled out at once, it is constantly revised and it takes a period of years to get it approximately right.

STEP 3: Creating Your Vision

Remember, visioning is a process. It takes time and multiple iterations. Plan to give individuals time and opportunity to create their own visions of the future organization, then spend adequate time listening and sharing and working to create a common vision. The paradox is that visioning is not a democratic process. All revolutions are led by a minority of leaders, a committed core group. This does not mean they can't be highly participatory, but the top leadership must take a stand and must set stakes in the ground regarding core technical, political, and cultural ideas driving the revolution.

Your leadership responsibility is to create a vision of your organization that is:

- Challenging

- Easy to understand

- Not just one person's dream but indicative of a team's commitment

- Not fixed or static but capable of evolving over time

As you prepare for your vision, articulate a set of assumptions. Take time with the leadership group and develop your assumptions regarding the characteristics necessary for your company to win in the coming years. My personal list for this decade is:

- Marketplace challenges and strategy will be widely understood and provide the context for decision making at all organizational levels

- Efforts will be driven by shared visions and values rather than rules and policy pronouncements

- Command from the top will be replaced by self-direction and teamwork

- Human resources management will be directed toward building an ever-expanding pool of knowledgeable persons skilled in problem-solving and developing others.

The matrix on the following page provides an analytic framework for capturing the creative work.

Do not start by trying to fill out the matrix. Use more creative processes such as having each member of the leadership team write his or her scenario of the future. I frequently have them write a *Fortune* article datelined three to four years in the future in which they journalistically describe where they would like to see the company at that point in time. Journalism requires them to paint a picture and describe in story form the people, corporate culture, and how the transition from today to that time took place.

The stories are then used to generate group discussion. Themes are identified and categorized into agreements and disagreements. This takes a number of days in off-site, open, constructive conflict-type discussions. The next step of working through the differences between group members can take months.

As the process goes along, try and capture the core elements of your vision in the technical, political, and cultural matrix on the following page.

Welch's 1990s Vision for GE

	STRATEGY	ORGANIZATIONAL STRUCTURE	HUMAN RESOURCE MANAGEMENT
T E C H N I C A L	—No. 1 OR No. 2 —high-growth businesses	—13 businesses —share best practices —boundarylessness	—multiple pay systems —new staffing systems —development as a continuous process
P O L I T I C A L	—integrated diversity	—no "wedding cake" hierarchy —cross-functional teamwork —empowerment, decision making pushed to lower levels	—rewards very flexible —appraisals from below as well as above
C U L T U R A L	—speed, simplicity, and self-confidence —ownership —share best practices —Work-Out	—shared values —many cultures —common vision	—human resource systems shape and mold boundarylessness —new staffing and support values

Your Vision

Use this TPC matrix to help articulate your vision.

	STRATEGY	ORGANIZATIONAL STRUCTURE	HUMAN RESOURCE MANAGEMENT
TECHNICAL			
POLITICAL			
CULTURAL			

Act III

REARCHITECTING

Introduction

ARCHITECTURE:
The art or practice of designing and building structures.
(Webster's Collegiate Dictionary)

Why "rearchitecting" when we know this is not a word? Because it captures the core challenge of Act III, the art and practice of redesigning and rebuilding the organization. Architecture is creative; it involves concepts and design as well as the practicality of the structure. Social architecture is the art of designing and building a complex organization. Revolutions require you to creatively destroy, design, and then build the new organization, thus, rearchitecting.

Act III was well underway at GE by the end of the eighties. Welch's vision began to emerge for the twenty-first-century organization, which he characterized with the word "boundarylessness." "Old Way" organizations were all about boundaries and compartmentalization and chains-of-command. The new organization would be free of these increasingly nonproductive strictures. Information would flow freely across functional and business boundaries from where it was developed to where it was needed. The boundaryless corporation would resolve the conflict between organizational size and speed. It would have the might of a large organization and the speed, flexibility, and self-confidence of a small one. Most important of all, it is the only way GE can accomplish the yearly productivity improvements required to span across all the businesses.

The only way to control your destiny is with ever-improving levels of productivity. This is the key portion of Welch's vision. Boundarylessness is the goal: Work-Out is the vehicle for getting there. Welch's statement in 1992, written in the 1991 annual report, defines this challenge well:

> 1991 did once again remind us how absolutely critical productivity growth is in the brutally Darwinian global market places in which virtually all of our businesses compete. We are aware, for instance, that if we had the same productivity growth in '90 and '91 that we had in '80 and '81, our '91 earnings would have been more like $3 billion rather than $4,435 billion. We also are acutely aware that without productivity growth it is possible to lose in 24 months businesses that took a half-century to build. Productivity growth is essential to industrial survival.
>
> But to increase productivity, you first have to clear away all the impediments that keep you from its achievement—primarily the management layers, functional boundaries and all the other trappings of bureaucracy.
>
> We've been trumpeting the removal of bureaucracy and the layers at GE for several years now—and we did take out "sectors," "groups" and other superstructure—but much more remains. Unfortunately, it is still possible to find documents around GE businesses that look like

something out of the National Archives, with five, ten or even more signatures necessary before action can be taken. In some businesses you might still encounter many layers of management in small areas; boiler operators reporting to the supervisor of boilers, who reports to the utility manager, who reports to the manager of plant services, who reports to the plant manager, and so on. Layers insulate. They slow things down. They garble. Leaders in highly layered organizations are like people who wear several sweaters outside on a freezing winter day. They remain warm and comfortable but are blissfully ignorant of the realities of their environment. They couldn't be further from what's going on.

GE Example:

Welch also used the analogy of a house with many floors and walls to represent the "Old Way" GE, pointing out the need to blow up all floors and walls—break down old bureaucratic boundaries—in order to create the new GE.

STEP 1: Access Your Organization on Boundarylessness.

Use the chart below to analyze where you currently are and what you should be doing in the future.

BOUNDARYLESS (type of boundary to remove)	QUESTION (what the boundary deals with)	SOME GE EXAMPLES	YOUR COMPANY
VERTICAL (Floors)	How well have we removed the vertical boundaries in our organization?	• delayering • perks • gain sharing	
HORIZONTAL (Internal Walls)	How well have we removed walls between groups within our business (functions, geographics, product groups, etc.)?	• cross-functional teams • project teams • partnerships	
EXTERNAL (External Walls)	How well have we removed barriers between our business and suppliers, customers, competitors, and other external stakeholders?	• alliances • customer measures • customer teams • customer training	

STEP 2: **Social Architecture at the Top**

Early in Act III, it is critical to start radically changing the way the top of the organization functions. Without this key building block none of the rest of the revolution will succeed. There are two fundamental reasons for this: 1) The top must "walk the talk" and role-model the new values and vision, and 2) The top is usually where a lot of the "Old Way" behavioral patterns are most deeply embedded and thus in great need of change.

Social architecture is a term that refers to the fundamental redesign of how people work together to get things done, who relates to whom for what, and how decisions are made. Examples at the top include all the resource allocation decisions made by top management, i.e., capital allocation, strategic direction, people allocation, as well as the coordination required to transfer technology, managerial learnings, and organizational best practices.

The challenge starts at the board level with a look at the key tasks, and who needs to do what with whom by when. The key conceptual building blocks of social architecture are: *People* (making sure that the right players are selected and put in the right roles); *time* (what goes on the corporate agenda and deciding on the appropriate cycle times—i.e., Should strategic reviews be held every year or on an as needed basis? Should succession planning take place annually or semiannually?); and *space* (where people and activities are physically located, how many hierarchical layers, what people and activities are networked, etc.).

GE Example:

The Corporate Executive Council is the centerpiece of the new GE. The old CEC was a formal monthly session where the heads of the businesses convened with the CEO to review businesses and discuss GE issues. The result was a very stilted, politically charged, "show and tell" session.

Starting in the mid-1980s the CEC began to meet quarterly in off-site settings with total informality. There is one agenda: "How do we, the heads of GE's thirteen major businesses—with Welch and Hood in the CEC, along with key corporate staff executives—team together to be the world's most competitive enterprise." The meeting is designed to share best practices, looking for ways of getting synergy across GE's diverse set of businesses.

The meetings are run in a workshop-type setting. There are no formal presentations. Each of the key business leaders comes with material to share. There is open debate, ties or jackets are not allowed, long coffee breaks are scheduled, and informal time at night is planned so that people can network. There is total sharing of information with Welch acting as a facilitator. This bit of social architecture has now been replicated by GE's thirteen business heads in each of their businesses.

GE's Corporate Management System Study—In 1986 Welch commissioned a study of all the management processes at the top of the company. This study represents one way of doing your homework for social architecture at the top. As with the GE study, assign specific interviews to a key staff individual and/or consultant to collect data from the CEO, his/her direct reports, board members, and select executives one or two levels lower. Be systematic, objective, and dispassionate. This bit of social architecture has now been replicated by GE's thirteen business heads in each of their businesses.

Below please specify your diagnostic questions.

GE Example—Questions Welch used to assess the Social Architecture at the Top.

Vision of what we want an operating business to be: _____

- How much scope? How much autonomy? How much delegation to head of business? Does delegation vary by the nature of   _____ the business, by our comfort with or the degree of tenure of its leader, or by the nature of the contemporary environment?

_____

_____

- How much differentiation are we comfortable in allowing in terms of such factors as organizational structure, nomenclature/officer titles, motivation and reward systems, operating style?

_____

_____

_____

- How much communication laterally between businesses as opposed to vertically (CEO-Businesses)

_____

_____

Vision of what we want the Corporate Executive Office to be:

_____

- What role and scope versus operating businesses?

_____

- What added value should CEO provide over and above the bare minimum necessary to satisfy corporate requirements?

_____

_____

- If operating GE as a classic holding company represents one end of a spectrum and running GE as a highly integrated and centralized company represents the other end, where do we want to be on that spectrum?

_____

_____

_____

_____

- Will "where we want to be" vary with the economic cycle, our comfort level with and trust of our Business Executives or any other factor?

_____

_____

_____

- What decisions do we *clearly* want to make at the CEO level, what decisions *clearly* at the business level, and what decisions require the application of judgment (on whose part) before deciding at which level?

GE EXAMPLE   YOUR ORGANIZATION

Vision of what we want Corporate Staff to be (consistent with the agreed-upon visions for both the CEO and the operating businesses

- What work *must* be done at corporate level to satisfy corporate entity requirements (e.g., financial reporting, tax accounting, shareowner communications, etc.)?

- What work of a "staff" nature does the CEO want done at its behest to help CEO members carry out the vision of what the CEO should be and do?

- What work do we want done at corporate level (in which few areas) that ensures a homogeneous approach across the many and diverse businesses and cultures the company encompasses?

- What work do we want to carry out at corporate level for purposes of taking advantage of critical mass and cost-effectiveness

GE EXAMPLE	YOUR ORGANIZATION

parameters (e.g., Air Transport, Management Education, Pooled Services)?

_____

Given these visions of what we desire in the future insofar as operating businesses, the Corporate Executive Office, and Corporate Staff are concerned, to what extent are the following consistent with those visions:

_____

_____

_____

_____

_____

• Company *Policies* and the *Functional Procedures* which implement those Policies (including the delegations of authority contained therein)?

_____

_____

_____

• Any management *practices* we have installed (whether documented or unwritten) which are *not* in sync with our stated Policies/Procedures?

_____

_____

_____

• The recurrent annual *processes* which we utilize either at Corporate level, at Business level, or at both levels to manage the company.

_____

_____

How can we make the CEO more effective to manage a company one-third larger and significantly more complex than heretofore?

_____

_____

• Should the CEO meet more/less/same as a collective body than at present?

_____

_____

GE EXAMPLE	YOUR ORGANIZATION

- On what things is it critical that we all see the same things/hear the same words? On what things do we trust one another's judgment sufficiently to rely on one individual for sole source inputs on some subject upon which the CEO must make a collective decision?

- What factors seem to be important in reaching timely decisions we feel comfortable with? What factors intervene when we must reach a decision *more quickly* than we're comfortable with? When a decision takes *longer* than we're comfortable with?

- When meeting collectively:
  —Are we too structured or rigid?
  —Too ad hoc and overly flexible?
  —Disciplined and linear or all over the ranch?

- Do we have enough "open" or "white space" days to allow us to carry out our individual responsibilities effectively? Comfortably?

- Are we oppressive, overly lax, or about right in our style of follow-up on operating matters over which we have approval authority?

- How effective are we in utilizing our CEO Staff? What do we need that we're not getting now? Ditto for those Corporate Staff Com-

GE EXAMPLE   YOUR ORGANIZATION

ponents whose role it is to service
the staff needs of the CEO?

- What is the optimum balance
between the CEO interacting
with the company on a hierarchical basis (i.e., through those
reporting directly to CEO members) versus "meeting the people
directly" via appearance at Crotonville courses, Elfun presentations, plant visits, roundtables,
etc.? Are we presently doing too
much or not enough of the latter?

STEP 3: Companywide Involvement in the Revolution

Now that the top has been redesigned, it is time for a multiyear
effort to involve every employee in the revolution. At GE,
Work-Out is the name given to this process. As Welch stated in
1990:

> Work-Out is a fluid and adaptable concept, not a "pro-
> gram." It generally starts as a series of regularly scheduled
> "town meetings" that bring together large cross sections of
> a business—people from manufacturing, engineering, cus-
> tomer service, hourly, salaried, high- and lower-levels—
> people who in their normal routines work within the boxes
> on the organizational charts and have few dealings with
> one another.
>
> The initial purpose of these meetings is simple—to
> remove the more egregious manifestations of bureaucracy:
> multiple approvals, unnecessary paperwork, excessive
> reports, routines, rituals. Ideas and opinions are often, at
> first, voiced hesitantly by people who never before had a
> forum—other than the water cooler—to express them. We
> have found that after a short time, those ideas begin to

come in a torrent—especially when people see action taken on the ones already advanced.

With the desk largely cleared of bureaucratic impediments and distractions, the Work-Out sessions then begin to focus on the more challenging tasks: examining the myriad processes that make up every business, identifying the crucial ones, discarding the rest, and then finding a faster, simpler, better way of doing things. Next, the teams raise the bar of excellence by testing their improved processes against the very best from around the company and from the best companies around the world.

Work-Out sessions should include people from multiple levels and functions, and should be facilitated by trained internal staff and/or external consultants. In order to create trust and positive emotional energy, the process should initially be focused on bureaucracy busting. The following pages present examples from the launch of Work-Out in GE Medical Systems.

STEP 4: Launching a Work-Out Effort—A GE Example

In the fall of 1988 GE Medical Systems (GEMS) launched its Work-Out effort. Even though no two GE businesses approached the launch the same way, there are clearly some fundamental principles of building blocks. Use these case illustrations to think through your own launch process:

GEMS Prework Diagnosis—Work-Out began when some fifty GEMS' employees attended a five-day off-site session. The participants included senior vice president and group executive John Trani, his staff, six employee relations managers, and informal leaders from technology, finance, sales, service, marketing, and manufacturing. Trani selected these informal leaders for their willingness to take business risks, challenge the status quo, and contribute in other key ways to GEMS. We participated as Work-Out faculty members.

The session took place after two important preliminary

steps. First, we conducted in-depth interviews with managers at all levels of GEMS. Interviews uncovered many objections to and criticisms of existing procedures, including measurement systems (too many, not focused enough on customers' cross-functional conflicts); pay and reward systems (lack of work goals, inconsistent signals); career development systems (ambiguous career paths, inadequate performance feedback); and an atmosphere in which blame, fear, and lack of trust overshadowed team commitments to solving problems. Here are some sample quotes from our interviews:

- "I'm frustrated. I simply can't do the quality of work that I want to do and know how to do. I feel my hands are tied. I have no time. I need help on how to delegate and operate in this new culture."

- "The goal of downsizing and delayering is correct. The execution stinks. The concept is to drop a lot of 'less important' work. This just didn't happen. We still have to know all the details, still have to follow all the old policies and systems."

- "I'm overwhelmed. I can and want to do better work. The solution is not simply adding new people, I don't even want to. We need to team up on projects and work. Our leaders must stop piling on more and help us set priorities."

Second, just before the first Work-Out session, Jack Welch traveled to GEMS' headquarters for a half-day roundtable with the Work-Out participants. Here are some sample quotes from middle managers:

- To senior management: "Listen! Think carefully about what the middle managers say. Make them feel like they are the experts and that their opinions are respected. There appear to be too many preconceived beliefs on the part of Welch and Trani."

- To senior management: "Listen to people, don't just pontificate. Trust people's judgment and don't continually second-guess. Treat other people like adults and not children."

- About themselves: "I will recommend work to be discontinued. I will try to find 'blind spots' where I withhold power. Any person I send to speak for me will 'push' peers who resist change."

- About themselves: "I will be more bold in making decisions. I will no longer accept the status quo. I will ask my boss for authority to make decisions. In fact, I will make more decisions on my own."

The Work-Out Session. The five-day Work-Out session was an intense effort to unravel, evaluate, and reconsider the complex web of personal relationships, cross-functional interactions, and formal work procedures through which the business of GEMS gets done. Cross-functional teams cooperated to address actual business problems. Each functional group developed a vision of where its operations are headed.

John Trani participated in a round table where he listened and responded to the concerns and criticisms of middle managers. Senior members of the GEMS staff worked to build trust and more effective communication with the functional managers. All the participants focused on ways to reorganize work and maximize return on organization time, on team time, and on individual time. An important part of the session was Bureaucracy Busting. There are several forms of Bureaucracy Busting. One that we developed is the CRAP detector (Critical Review Appraisal) of unnecessary work. Individuals are asked to look for CRAP, which can be unnecessary plans, approvals, policies, measurements, meetings, and reports. The CRAP detector is presented below and should be used to help identify ways you can begin rearchitecting your job.

Example: The Crap Detector

Critical Review Appraisal—Take Work Out.

**IMPACT ON ORGANIZATION—
HOW MUCH IMPROVEMENT WILL RESULT?**

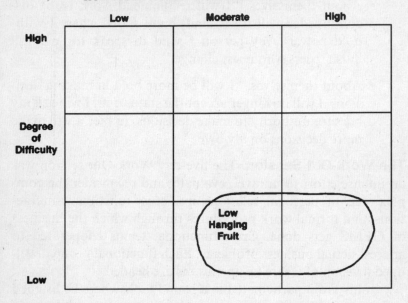

DESCRIPTION: Use the CRAP detector to help individual and group start taking work out.

STEP 1: Review a typical work week—identify activities that do not add value to the customer—look for unnecessary

    meetings
    reports
    measurements
    approvals
    procedures

STEP 2: Determine who needs to be involved to change it (assign a letter to each work elimination item):

    Me alone = M
    A partner = P
    My work group = G

Intergroup (mine and another) = I
Total organization = T

STEP 3: Indicate degree of impact and difficulty of change—place each item in the matrix.

STEP 4: Create an action plan for the "low hanging fruit" items that can be changed quickly and which have impact. Involve relevant parties.

The five-day session ended with individuals and functional teams signing close to 100 written contracts to implement the new procedures. There were contracts between functional teams, contracts between individuals, contracts between function heads and their staffs, and businesswide contracts with John Trani and his staff. This set the stage for phase one of Work-Out in GEMS, a series of similar workshops for hundreds of managers in 1989.

STEP 5: Human Resource Systems to Support Your Vision

Once you have used Work-Out to attain your vision, it is important to change the HR support function. Below are some suggestions:

HR Functions

Selection

Broaden criteria to include not only technical skill but . . .

- Facilitation, problem-solving, and interpersonal skill

- Broad knowledge of the business

- Willingness to teach others

Appraisal Requirements

- Redefine success . . . elevate organizational management above career management

- Make mentoring paramount . . . the key to expanding the organization's expertise

- When weighing results, consider how obtained

- Take a longer-term view when judging an individual's contribution and career potential

Development

Since performance depends on each person knowing more than just his or her job, development is central

Requirements:

- From executive development to organizational development

- From investments in high-potential human resources to investment in *high-leverage* human resources . . .

Let those with innate desire and capacity help to develop others

Rewards

If the many count, then reward structure must reflect this reality

Not just issues of fair play but critical to:

- Attracting the right people

- Keeping them and their accumulated knowledge in the organization

- Providing high degree of stability for boundaryless organization to function effectively

Your Organization

WHAT CHANGES DO YOU NEED TO MAKE TO THE HR FUNCTION?

Selection

_____

_____

_____

Appraisal Requirements

_____

_____

_____

Development

_____

_____

_____

Rewards

_____

_____

_____

STEP 6: Continuous Revolution

In order to institutionalize your revolution's vision and ensure continuous change, it is necessary to make as many people as possible agents of change. At first, you will send people to Work-Out sessions and they will learn to redefine their jobs to meet the challenges of a changing business environment. But change is never finished. You must train leaders to lead their own Work-Out sessions.

After several years of Work-Out using teams of outside consultants as change agents, Welch felt GE was ready to develop its own army of change agents. In 1992 GE started at the top of the organization and started working down. The ultimate result was the Change Acceleration Program, or CAP. As the diagram below shows, CAP was designed to accelerate the rate of change within GE.

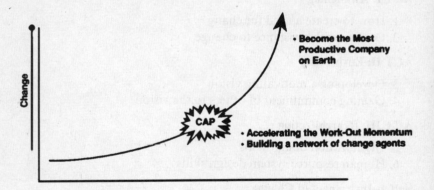

Change Acceleration Program

CAP also allows the top management of GE's businesses to gain valuable leadership skills while simultaneously working on changing their own businesses.

GE Example:

In 1990–1991 GE piloted a process for developing change agents called the Work-Out Leadership Development Series

(LDS). It was designed to provide a means for GE to develop self-sufficiency, that is have a critical mass of internal change agents cutting down on the reliance on external consultants.

LDS was designed to deliver development to individuals and teams from six GE businesses: NBC, Plastics, Motors, Medical Systems, EP&C, and the Audit Staff. Each team had a change project to complete during the LDS and each individual was to be developed as a change agent. The framework for development which guided the effort was based on the Transformational Leader Framework presented below.

Transformational Leader Framework

CHANGE MODEL

ACT I: Awakening

1. How to create a need for change
2. Dealing with resistance to change

ACT II: Envisioning

3. Developing a motivating vision
4. Gaining commitment of others to the vision

ACT III: Rearchitecting

5. Organization design skills
6. Human resource system design skills

Self as Instrument of Change

7. Developing the individual's change agent skill set

Your Organization—What Is Your Model for Leading Change?

Take time to discuss assumption about how to lead change. Lay out a conceptual framework and the rationale as the first step in building a development process for change leadership.

KEY ELEMENTS OF MODEL	BRIEF DESCRIPTION
_____	_____
_____	_____
_____	_____
_____	_____
_____	_____
_____	_____
_____	_____

LDS consisted of three workshops spread over a six-month period. The six change agent teams had five to eight members. The change project constitutes the *action learning* component of the process. In addition, they learned new concepts and skills, and received considerable feedback from the faculty as well as peers and bosses.

The process is presented below:

WORKSHOP I

Facilitation Skills Workshop

- Group Dynamics/Group Development
- Role of the Process Facilitator
- Range of Facilitative Interventions
- Facilitating Work-Out Team Meetings
- Facilitation Lab

Aimed at helping participants learn skills and techniques to assist groups, manage group process, and become self-sufficient.

Process Leadership Workshop

- Transformational Leadership
- Work-Out and Business Process Management
- Team Development
- Process Consultation
- Role of the Change Agent
- Application Planning

Aimed at helping participants learn concepts, skills, and techniques to take a more significant leadership role in the integration of Work-Out within their business; development of a focused, skilled, supportive team of internal change agents.

Organizational Systems Workshop

- Systems View of Organizational Change
- Organizational Analysis & Diagnosis
- Intervention at an Organizational Level (Managing Conflict & Increasing Influence)
- Leading in a Boundaryless Organization

Aimed at helping participants gain the "big picture" view of organizational change and what it will take to reach Work-Out self-sufficiency and organizational "boundarylessness."

Your Organization

As a way of thinking through your own need for a Change Acceleration Program, do an analysis of your company's current effectiveness in each of the aspects of the change model. Use the framework on the next page:

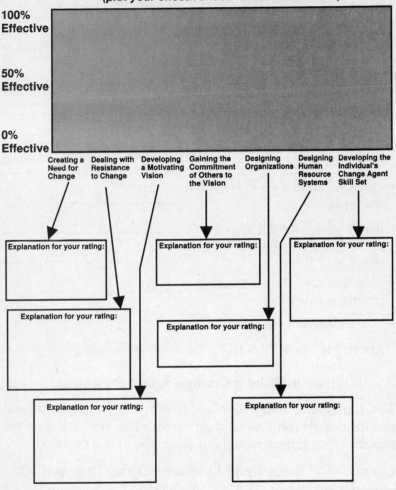

Assess Your Organizations's Effectiveness
(plot your effectiveness for each dimension)

100% Effective

50% Effective

0% Effective

Creating a Need for Change

Dealing with Resistance to Change

Developing a Motivating Vision

Gaining the Commitment of Others to the Vision

Designing Organizations

Designing Human Resource Systems

Developing the Individual's Change Agent Skill Set

Explanation for your rating:

Explanation for your rating:

Explanation for your rating:

Explanation for your rating:

Explanation for your rating:

Explanation for your rating:

Explanation for your rating:

ACT I: Awakening   **ACT II: Envisioning**   **ACT III: Rearchitecting**

Your Challenge

Now specify your goals for designing continuous revolution processes in your organization.

GE EXAMPLE	YOUR ORGANIZATION

- Accelerate Work-Out self-sufficiency efforts

- Forge a true partnership for learning and development between Crotonville and businesses

- Create a critical mass of internal change agents

- Reinforce skill development with active experimentation and coaching on the job.

- Transfer GE Best Practices through site visits

- Position graduates as coaches

- Answer the call for "Act III"

How to Build a Change Agent Program

The top several hundred managers in most companies will require development as change agents. The final steps in the *Handbook* are presented to help guide you in this process.

Example of a Change Agent Program—Change Process (CP):
Over the last five years a set of social technologies has been developed to create a critical mass of change agents in a variety of companies around the world. The CP is designed to accelerate the transformation of companies by producing leadership teams with the necessary skills to integrate various disciplines and programs useful today in successful companies—quality

improvement, work reengineering, process mapping, visioning, cycle-time improvement, and other approaches—into a coherent, integrated agenda for change.

The program focuses on individual skill development *and* organizational change, using a variety of methods to solve important, immediate, critical business issues with leadership and change agent skills.

CP consists of a three-phase, action-learning process, delivered over six months with a combination of on-site and classroom activities to implement needed change in real time. Development of participants occurs both on line and through networking with other executives, interaction with facilitators, and structured learning experiences. The specific objectives are:

1. To build an effective leadership team which will drive the transformation agenda of each company.

2. To develop the individual skills of leaders to diagnose and facilitate individual, team, and organizational transformations.

3. To benchmark the best ideas and practices worldwide in order to accelerate the learning process and transformation of noncompeting consortium companies through creation of a rich learning system.

Fundamental Building Blocks of the Program

Change Process (CP) is both a lever for transforming your company and a powerful leadership experience. A unique set of building blocks, "social technologies," are used to achieve the five primary goals of CP: 1) Deliver on the change projects to make change in the company; 2) Develop change agent mindsets; 3) Develop "change leadership" skills; 4) Develop change team skills; 5) Develop change networks. Each of the major building blocks is described below along with the impact it has on each of the five goals.

The CP is delivered by creating a temporary system, that is building a social organization with its own structure, leadership, and values. Compressed action learning puts individuals and teams under intense time and performance pressures. They must deliver strategic change to their organization while acquiring new skills and immediately using them to deliver on the projects.

IMPACT SCALE
○ = Little or no impact   ◑ = Moderate Impact   ● = Strong Impact

BUILDING BLOCKS	CHANGE PROJECTS	CHANGE MIND-SET	CHANGE LEADERSHIP	CHANGE TEAMS	CHANGE NETWORKS
Top Leadership Team: Ownership of the projects, selection and sponsorship of participants, and full involvement in the commitment process.	●	○	○	◑	○
Expert Faculty: Multidisciplinary faculty leading the process.	◑	●	◑	◑	◑
Coaching Role: Each team has a process consultant, someone selected and trained from the previous CLC who coaches the team.	●	◑	◑	●	◑
Process Learning: Team-building activities including "Outward Bound," learning about high-performing teams, systematic attention to feedback for each other.	●	◑	●	●	◑
Learning Feedback Loops: Collection of data and feedback to participants. 1) Survey pre-CP (self and others ratings of global leader behavior). 2) Team members provide feedback. 3) Coaches give feedback. 4) Another team analyzes and feeds back data. 5) Research team collects data and feeds back as part of program.	◑	◑	●	●	●
Commitment Processes: Throughout CP, individuals, teams, and the total group actively, publicly use processes for contracting and making "who, what, and when" commitments.	●	○	●	●	◑
Concepts/Ideas: The CP faculty present participants with new conceptual tools dealing with global strategy, global operating mechanisms, time-based competitiveness, process loss, change processes, and leadership.	◑	●	●	◑	◑

Design Your Change Process

1. Specify Your Goals. Describe what outcomes you desire.

Mind-set _____

Leadership _____

Teamwork _____

Networking _____

Change Projects _____

2. Identify the Social Technology you will use in the Process.

WHICH BUILDING BLOCKS   DESCRIBE HOW IT WILL BE USED.

1. Top Leadership Team   _____

2. Expert Faculty   _____

3. Coaching Role   _____

4. Process Learning   _____

5. Learning Feedback Loops   _____

6. Commitment Processes   _____

7. Concepts/Ideas   _____

Example of CP

Your Plan
Use the boxes below
to draft your plan.

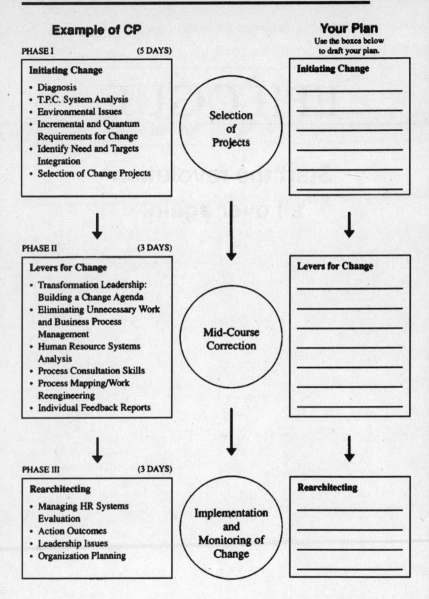

PHASE I   (5 DAYS)

Initiating Change

- Diagnosis
- T.P.C. System Analysis
- Environmental Issues
- Incremental and Quantum Requirements for Change
- Identify Need and Targets Integration
- Selection of Change Projects

Selection of Projects

Initiating Change

PHASE II   (3 DAYS)

Levers for Change

- Transformation Leadership: Building a Change Agenda
- Eliminating Unnecessary Work and Business Process Management
- Human Resource Systems Analysis
- Process Consultation Skills
- Process Mapping/Work Reengineering
- Individual Feedback Reports

Mid-Course Correction

Levers for Change

PHASE III   (3 DAYS)

Rearchitecting

- Managing HR Systems Evaluation
- Action Outcomes
- Leadership Issues
- Organization Planning

Implementation and Monitoring of Change

Rearchitecting

EPILOGUE

Start the revolution all over again.

Index

Accomplishment Analysis, 288–89, 384–85
Advanced Technology process, 274
Africa, 115
Alinsky, Saul, 161
Allied-Signal, 53, 68, 342n–43n
Allis-Chalmers, 46, 132
American Telephone & Telegraph, 74
Anatomy of a Merger (Jones and Marriott), 207, 343n
Andrew, Nigel, 287
Andrews, Eugene, 285
Apollo Computer, 68
ASEA Brown Boveri, 222, 232
Asia, 169–70, 217, 231, 297
Association Island, 340n
Austin, J. Paul, 33
Australia, 34, 64
Austria, 232
Auto Auctions, 29
Avis, 231

Babcock & Wilcox, 35
Baker, James A., 344
Barriers, 285–86
Baughman, James, 39, 85, 94, 156–57, 161–62, 171, 174, 176, 181, 207, 238–40, 244, 251, 255
Bayer, 63, 76
Bellaire, Fla., meeting, 85–86
Benchmarking, 249
Benedetti, Carlo, 226
Benetton, 232
Bergen op Zoom plant, 64
Best Practices, 194, 248–51
Black & Decker, 104, 221

Black Panthers, 161
Boesky, Ivan, 138
"Boiled frog syndrome," 88, 400, 402
Booz Allen, 287
Borch, Fred, 46–47, 69
Borg-Warner Chemicals, 29
Bossidy, Lawrence, 67–68, 92, 139, 163–65, 169, 171–72, 181–82, 186–87, 256, 263, 281, 342n–43n
Boston Consulting Group, 265, 287
Botch, Fred, 40
Boundarylessness, 20, 74, 254, 279, 285–86, 415, 420–23
    Welch on, 246–47, 302
Bradshaw, Thornton, 147
Brazil, 115, 161
Bridges, William, 370
Brimm, Michael, 267
Buckley, Larry, 62, 65, 70
Bueche, Arthur M., 344
Bureaucracy Busting, 433–35
Burlingame, John, 69, 81, 92, 105
Burns, James MacGregor, 158–59
Burton Group Financial Services, 29
Business Development Staff, 287
Business engine, 23–25, 74
Business Week, 53
Bywater, Bill, 302

Calhoun, David, 139
Calloway, Wayne, 191–92
Calma, 29, 110
Canon, 239
Carboloy, 29
Carpenter, Michael, 287

Carter, Jimmy, 33, 115
Cash flow, 299
Catch-22 (Heller), 273
CBS, 147
Central Air Conditioning, 29, 96
Change
  need for, 6, 298
  quantum, 21, 256
  rationale for, 401
  resistance to, 402–8
  teaching at Crotonville, 158–61
  training agents for, 437–47
  Welch's ideas on, 83–84, 256–57
  See also Revolution
Change Acceleration Program, 254,
    437, 440
Change Process program, 442–47
Chapperell Steel, 249
Charan, Ram, 267, 281–82
Chase Manhattan, 74
Chase Manhattan Leasing, 29
Chicago, Global Leadership
    Program meeting in, 270–71
China, 161, 297
Citibank, 46, 74
Citicorp, 19, 23
Clausewitz, Karl von, 63
Cleveland, Ohio, 44, 208. *See also*
    General Electric Lighting
Clinard and Yeager, 127
Coca-Cola, 33
Coffin, Charles, 41–42, 46, 131, 206,
    330*n*, 343*n*
Columbia University, 161
Combustion Engineering, 222
Common Market, 225
Communication, 299
Compagnie des Lampes, 207
*Comparative Analysis of Complex
    Organizations, A* (Etzioni),
    343*n*
Con-Air, 106
Consumer Electronics swap, 29,
    220, 228–30
  under Welch, 66–68
Control, methods of, 194

Cordiner, Ralph, 40, 44–46, 132,
    331*n*, 334*n*
Coronet Carpets, 29, 148, 166
Corporate culture, 37, 82–83
  of General Electric, 38–39,
    83–84, 284
  See also Ideas; Vision
Corporate Entry Leadership
    Conference, 162–66
Corporate Executive Council, 78,
    82, 149, 240, 281, 290
  and corporate values, 195–96
  created, 190
  and globalization, 233
  memo to, 240–42
  operation of, 190–94, 200, 424–25
  and teamwork, 197–200
  women on, 190
Corporations
  and "boiled frog syndrome," 88
  and bribery, 133
  changes facing, 18–23
  earnings of U.S., 35
  emotion and, 77
  employee wrongdoing, 126–28
  and globalization, 79, 297–98
  and ideas, 391–92
  and values, 195
"Cosby Show, The," 147
CRAP detector, 434
Critical Review Appraisal, 434–35
Croton-on-Hudson, New York. *See*
    Crotonville
Crotonville, 3, 12, 39, 78, 86–87, 94,
    105, 136–37, 142, 152,
    182–83, 237–38, 240, 250,
    279, 287, 297, 299–300,
    341*n*, 385
  appraisal sheets of, 167–68
  comments at, 22
  Corporate Entry Leadership
    Conference at, 162–66
  and GE values statement, 171–75
  and globalization, 233
  history of, 158
  purpose of, 340–41*n*

resistance at, 175–76, 185
rounded, 45
success of, 176
and teaching organizational
    change, 158–61
Team Experienced Manager
    Course at, 169–71
Tichy appointed to, 155–57
Welch's goals for, 156–57
and Work-Out, 243–44
Customer satisfaction, 299
Czechoslovakia, 297

Dammerman, Dennis, 49
Dance, Walter, 69
Dash 8 project, 111–24
Deadly Deception, 130
De Beers Consolidated Mines, 129
Decimus, 29
Defense, United States Department
    of, 128
Defense contractors, misconduct
    by, 128, 133–36
Defense Industry Initiative on
    Business Ethics and
    Conduct, 135–36
Depression, 131
Dotan, Rami, 129
Dow-Jones average, 35
Doyle, Frank, 92, 181*n*, 342*n*
Drexel Burnham Lambert, 138
Drucker, Peter, 16, 44, 80, 192,
    331*n*
Dunkirk, N.Y., meeting, 116–17
Du Pont, 76, 130
Dwyer, Jack, 113

Eastern Europe, 225
Eastman Kodak, 5, 19
Edelheit, Lewis S., 345*n*
Edison, Thomas, 5, 41–42, 206
Edison Electric, 207
Effectiveness, assessing, 441
Eickert, Stephen, 60, 64
Electrical Funds Group, 340*n*
Electrolux, 68, 222

Emotion, and corporations, 77
Employee satisfaction, 299, 302
Employers Reinsurance
    Corporation, 16, 29, 102,
    109, 144, 147
Energy, emotional, 21
Environmental Protection Agency,
    130
Environmental standards, 130,
    295–96
Ericsson, 262
Erie, Penn., 44. *See also* General
    Electric Transportation
    Systems
Ethics, survey about, 127
Etzioni, Amitai, 194, 343*n*
Europe, 231, 296
    GE Lighting in, 217
    Welch's 1985 tour of, 226
    See also Globalization
European Community, 225, 296
Exxon, 17

Family Financial Services, 29
Fanuc, 110
Faro, Portugal, workshop, 268–70
Federated Department Stores, 33
Financial Guaranty Insurance Co.,
    29
Financial News Network, 29
Fink, Daniel, 89
Flax, Steven, 103–4
Focus 80 program, 265
Forbes, 17
Ford, Henry, 19, 38
Ford Motor Company, 62, 249
Fortune, 15, 49, 62, 103, 131, 245,
    329*n,* 400
Fortune 500, 87, 127, 148
Fostoria Lamp Co., 343
France, 64, 225
    General Electric in, 79
Frazier, Michael, 249
Frederick, Robert, 68
Fresco, Paolo, 181*n*, 217, 219–20,
    224–27, 230, 342*n*

Frigidaire, 222
Fuji, 231

Gault, Stanley, 53, 68
Geico, 29
General Dynamics, 53
General Electric
  acquisitions/divestitures, 16, 29,
      81, 96, 102
    goals behind, 109
    Housewares, 104–6
    RCA, 146–52, 166, 177
    Thomson, 219–21, 228–30
    Thorn, 217, 231
    Tungsram, 217, 232
  antitrust suits, 131, 207
  Audit Staff, 438
  backlogs at, 88–89
  Blue Books, 45, 61
  boycotts of, 129–30
  business portfolio, 28–29
  CEOs of, 32–37, 41–50
  compensation, 46, 287, 289–90
  computers, 34–35
  corporate culture, 38–39, 83–84,
      284
  cross-licensing agreements, 207,
      343n
  dismissals, 290
  earnings, 16, 21, 31, 34, 330n
  elimination of sectors, 177–89,
      344–46n
  employee misconduct at, 43,
      126–41
  employee statistics, 30.
  ethics stressed at, 126–28, 136–41
  evaluation of managers, 287–91
  Executive Management Staff,
      52–54, 182, 288, 384
  and future trends, 304–5
  and globalization, 34, 79, 207–9,
      217–18, 222–28, 230–33
  history, 5, 41–50
  human resources, 287–89
  importance of ideas to, 74–78
  and insider trading, 138–39
    job-changing at, 284
    job security at, 84, 281–82
    labor relations, 42–43, 119–23,
        338–39n
    layoffs, 9–10, 18, 81, 91–93,
        96–97, 103, 118, 122, 216,
        329n, 335–37n
    leadership in, 277–78
    logo ("meatball"), 104–5
    market share, 16–17, 39–40
    need for growth, 6–7
    1985 problems, 142–46
    and price-fixing, 132
    productivity, 16–17, 31, 33–34,
        329n
    product-management systems,
        284
    promotions at, 284, 290
    recruitment, 286–87, 289
    reorganization of, 19, 30, 40,
        44–45, 47–49, 84, 89–99,
        177–89, 338n, 341–42n,
        344–46n
    revenues, 31
    stock, 16, 31, 35
    strategic planners, 48–49, 95,
        342n
    and Superfund, 130
    technology, 33, 35
    three-act transformation of,
        21–25
    time-card scandal, 126–27,
        133–36, 138
    timetable, 306–27
    training, 290
    and U.S. competitors, 42, 46,
        131–32, 206–7, 343n
    values at, 278–83, 285, 290–93,
        298–99
    values statement, 171–75, 341n,
        413–15
    and Welch's three circles, 107–8
  See also Corporate Executive
      Council; Crotonville;
      Welch, John F., Jr. (Jack);
      Work-Out

General Electric Aerospace, 17, 28, 129, 231, 251
General Electric Aircraft Engines, 17, 25, 28, 34, 36, 90, 109, 129, 223, 231, 245, 286, 295
and Work-Out, 252–54
General Electric Appliances, 28, 44, 226, 231, 245
crisis at, 198–200
Quick Response at, 252
General Electric Audio unit, 262
General Electric Broadcasting Properties, 29
General Electric Company (Britain), 207, 231
General Electric Consumer Products and Services, 99, 179
General Electric Electrical Distribution and Control, 28, 231
General Electric EP&C, 438
General Electric Financial Services, 9, 23–25, 28, 66–68, 77, 90, 112, 231, 286, 304
General Electric Gas Turbines, 34, 90
General Electric Housewares, 108, 221
sale of, 29, 104–6
General Electric Industrial and Power Systems. See General Electric
General Electric Information Services, 28, 231–32
General Electric Large Transformers, 108
General Electric Lighting, 23, 28, 43, 46–47, 66–67, 90, 108, 124, 222–23, 232, 245, 252, 257, 287
acquisitions by, 217
competitors of, 42–43, 131–32, 204, 206–9, 217, 343n
corporate culture, 208

decline of, 209–10
restructuring of, 202–6, 210–18
wages, 209
General Electric Locomotives, 44, 286
General Electric Major Appliances, 66, 99
General Electric Management Development Institute. See Crotonville
General Electric Medical Systems, 9, 17, 28, 77, 90, 112, 233, 244, 258, 438
cultural differences in, 266–67
globalization of, 261, 263–64
and Global Leadership Program, 267–72
as "lab," 260
and market changes, 265
as process-based organization, 272–76
reorganization of, 265–68
technology, 263
and Thomson swap, 219–21, 226–30, 264
under Welch, 65–66
and Work-Out, 431–35
General Electric Mobile Communications, 262
General Electric Motors, 28, 90, 232, 438
General Electric Nuclear Power, 34, 97–98
General Electric Plastics, 9, 28, 34, 36, 77, 90, 112, 166, 169, 223, 232–33, 242, 287, 438
Welch at, 58–65
General Electric Power Systems, 17, 28, 90, 124, 169–70, 222, 232. See also General Electric Turbines
General Electric Re-Entry Systems, 133–34, 138
General Electric Robotics, 167
General Electric Semiconductors, 108

General Electric Services and
    Materials, 182
General Electric Solid State, 29
General Electric Space Systems,
    134, 136
General Electric Trading Company,
    347*n*
General Electric Transportation
    Systems, 28, 232, 257
    earnings, 339*n*
    problems at, 111–24
General Electric Turbines, 34, 44,
    46, 90, 223, 248
General Motors, 4–5, 18, 41, 74,
    112–13, 118, 130
Genever-Watling, David, 187
Genstar, 29
Germany, 64, 133, 225, 232, 296
"Ginza event," 270
Giuliani, Rudolph, 139
Global communication, 270, 272
Globalization
    and cultural differences, 266–67
    and product value, 294
    and U.S. companies, 79, 297–98
    See also General Electric, and
        globalization
Global Leadership Program, 161,
    267–72
Goals, specifying, 442
Gomez, Alain, 219, 226, 230
Goodyear, 53
Gotemba, Japan, course, 169–71
Go-to-Market process, 274
Government regulations, 295–96
Great Britain, 64, 79
Group Operating Council, 274
Grove City, Pa., 114
GTE, 68
Gutoff, Reuben, 59, 61–62, 65

Handbook for Revolutionaries,
    365–448
    how to use, 372–73
Hanford, Wash., 130

Harrods/House of Fraser Credit
    Cards, 29
Harvard Business Review, 281–82
Harvard Business School, 239
Heineman, Benjamin W., 345*n*
Hergenhan, Joyce, 190
Hewlett Packard, 249
Hill, Herman R., 344
Hiner, Glen, 61, 87, 92, 181, 281
Hitachi, 8, 76, 158
Honda, 239, 392
Honeywell, 74
Hood, Edward, Jr., 68–69, 92, 171,
    181
Hughes Aerospace, 129
Human resources
    at GE, 287–89
    and vision, 435–36
Hungary, 209

IBM, 18, 74, 88, 158
Ideas, 299
    cultural, 82–83, 394–95
    flow of, 301
    importance to corporations,
        71–84, 391–92
    importance to vision, 409–10
    political, 81–82, 393–95
    technical, 80–81, 393
Impact program, 215
"Incredible Electric Company,
    The," 131
India, 161, 217, 297
Indonesia, 297
INFACT, 130
INSEAD, 267
In Search of Excellence (Peters), 19,
    104
Integrated diversity, 74, 82, 194
    slides about, 223*n*
International General Electric, 224
International Mineral & Chemicals,
    59
International Union of Electronic
    Workers, 302

Intersil, 29, 110
Israel, 129
Issues, hard versus soft, 375–77
Italy, 225
Itel Containers, 29

Japan, 34, 64, 79, 158, 209, 226, 249–50, 296
course held in, 169–71
GE competitors in, 8, 17
Job security, 281–82
Jones, Reginald H., 39–40, 63, 66, 109, 179, 331n
accomplishments of, 34–36
described, 33
at General Electric, 48–49
selection of successor, 51–54, 66, 68–70, 331–32n
versus Welch, 36–37
Jones, Robert, 207, 343n
Justice Department, United States, 129, 131, 207

Kaizen, 256–57
Kane, Don, 39, 53, 55, 65, 70, 169, 171, 182–84, 188, 285
Kanter, Rosabeth Moss, 80
Kelvinator, 222
Kerr, Steve, 244
Kidder Peabody, 16, 29, 138–39, 287
King, Martin Luther, Jr., 170
Kohl, Helmut, 79
Korea, 209, 226

Ladd Petroleum, 29
"Late Night," 149–52
Lazard Freres, 147
Lazarus, Ralph, 33
Leadership
characteristics for, 383–89
at General Electric, 277–78
Leadership Effectiveness Survey, 385
Lenin, Vladimir, 107

Letterman, David, 149–52, 339n
LeVino, Theodore, 52–55, 68, 70, 92, 332n
LEXAN, 50, 61–63
Loews Corporation, 147
Los Angeles Times, 221
Louisville, Ky., 44, 252, 301. See also General Electric Appliances
Lynn, Mass., 245

M/A-Com, 68
Macy, R. H., & Company, 33, 256
Maier, Leonard C., 344
Malaysia, 232
Management
new versus old way, 19–21
restructuring, 424–30
scientific versus Welch's, 332n
See also Leadership
Management and Technical Services Company, 129
Management Today, 32
Managers
GE's evaluation of, 287–91
GE's recruitment of, 286–87, 289
traits important to Welch, 286–87
Welch's four types of, 279–80
March and Cohen, 145
Marconi, Guglielmo, 148
Marriott, Oliver, 207, 343n
Matsushita, 68, 222, 229
McCabe, Donald, 127–28
McGowan, William, 104
MCI, 104
McKinsey & Company, 47–48, 161
Measurements, 299
Mexico, 115
MGM-United Artists, 147
Michelson, Gertrude G., 33, 256
Michigan, University of, 161
Milken, Michael, 138
Milwaukee. See General Electric Medical Systems

Modan, Michael, 60, 64
Moltke, Johannes von, 63, 72, 228
Monsanto, 130
Montgomery Ward Credit, 29
Morgan, J. P., 41
Morgan, J. P., & Company, 33
Murphy, Eugene, 149

Nacolah Life Insurance, 29, 148
Nader, Ralph, 161
Nardelli, Robert L., 345*n*
National Center on Education and
    the Economy, 19
National Electric Lamp
    Association, 343*n*
NBC, 16, 28–29, 106, 232, 438
    acquisition of, 147–51
    See also RCA
Nela Park, 343*n*
Netherlands, 64
Networks, 390
Newark, N.J., 137
New Deal, 42
"New Way" versus "Old Way,"
    19–21, 329*n*, 377–80
New Way Workshop, 244
New York Times, 105, 221
New Zealand, 232
Nippon Telegraph & Telephone,
    17
NORYL, 60–61, 63
"Number 1 or Number 2," 74, 81,
    86, 108–9, 221, 414–15
    put into effect, 90–92, 96

Offerings Development process,
    274
"Old Way" versus "New Way,"
    19–21, 329*n,* 377–80
Olivetti, 226
Opie, John, 168, 187, 202, 204–5,
    210–16, 218, 222, 245
Order-to-Remittance process,
    274–75
Orr, Verne, 134–36
Orselet, David, 67, 70, 97–98, 190

Osram, 207
Outward Bound, 159–60
Owens-Corning Fiberglas, 53, 281

Paris, France, 266
Parker, Jack, 69
Pathfinder Mines, 29
Paynter, Jim, 117, 120–22, 338*n*
Peiffer, Jack, 156, 171
Peiper, Chuck, 287
Pennzoil, 37
Penske Leasing, 29
PepsiCo, 192
Performance standards, 300
Peters, Tom, 18–19, 80, 104
Philips, 88, 204, 206–7, 209, 216–17,
    222, 231
Phoebus cartel, 131, 343*n*
Pittsfield, Mass. *See* General
    Electric Plastics
Player Piano (Vonnegut), 340*n*
Poland, 209
Polaris, 29
Polyphenylene oxide (PPO), 59
Porter, Michael, 104
Portugal workshop, 268–70
Power, J. D., surveys, 297
Pratt & Whitney, 109
Preston, Lewis T., 33
Pro80 machine, 209–12
*Problems and Performance of the
    Role of Chief Executive in
    GE* (Baughman), 207
Process-based organization, 272–76
Process mapping, 249, 251
Procter & Gamble, 213
Product management, 284

Quantum change, 21, 256
Quick Response, 252, 301

Rabinowitz, Stephen, 213–16, 245,
    343*n*
RCA, 16, 29, 68, 106, 203, 287
    acquisition of, 146–52, 166, 177
RCA Records, 29, 148

Reagan, Ronald, 79
Reed, Charles, 60–62
Reiner, Gary M., 345*n*
Revolution
  creating sense of urgency,
    400–401
  determining need for, 380–82
  emotions associated with, 370
  five commandments of, 371
  ideas for, 393–95
  launching, 399
  readiness for, 396–97
  and "rearchitecting," 420
  as three-act drama, 368–70
  time-frame, 373
  See also Change
Revolutionary creed, 367–68
Richardson, Rick, 113, 338*n*
Richmond, Virginia, 214
Robb, Walter, 92, 263
Robert Bosch, 232
Rogers, Gary L., 350*n*
Rogers, James W., 345*n*
Rohatyn, Felix, 147
Roosevelt, Franklin, 42
Roper, 29
Roper Outdoor Lawn Equipment,
    29
Rowe, Brian, 92, 181, 200
Royal Dutch/Shell, 17
Rubbermaid, 53
Runtagh, Hellene, 190
Russia, 161
Rutgers University, 127
Ryland Corporation, 200

St. Paul, Minnesota, 137
Sands Point School, 158
Schenectady, N.Y., 41. *See also*
    General Electric Turbines
Schipke, Roger, 165–66, 181,
    199–200
Schlemmer, Carl, 185
  and Transportation Systems,
    111–24
Schlesinger, Len, 239

Schlotterbeck, Walter A., 344
Schumpeter, Joseph, 84
Sears, 251
Self-assessment, 383–95
Self-confidence, 75
Service Delivery process, 274–75
Session C, 288–90
Sherman Antitrust Act, 42, 131
Siegel, Martin, 138
Siemens, 76, 204, 220, 222, 229, 265
Silly Putty, 59
Simplicity, 75
Singapore, 232
Sloan, Alfred, 5, 41, 332*n*
Smiddy, Harold, 223*n*, 331*n*
SNECMA, 231
Social architecture. *See*
    Management, restructuring
Soderquist, Donald, 191
South Africa, 129
Soviet Union, 94, 107
Spain, 231
Speed, 75, 301
Standard & Poor's 500, 17, 31, 305
Stewart, Thomas A., 245, 248
Stonesifer, J. Richard, 345*n*
Strategic Management Society
    presentation, 342*n*
Stumberger, Ray, 53
Succession planning, 331*n*
Sunbeam Company, 343*n*
Superfund, 130
Support process, 274
Swope, Gerald, 42–43, 92, 131
Sylvania, 42, 206–7

Taiwan, 209
Takeuchi, Hiro, 170, 267
Team Experienced Manager
    Course, 169–71
Terry, Franklin S., 343*n*
Tests
  idea, 391–93
  mirror, 383–95
  organization, 375–82
  readiness, 396–97

Texaco, 37, 102
Thailand, 297
Thomson-CGR. *See* Thomson S.A.
Thomson S.A., 149, 262
  swap with GE, 29, 219–21,
    226–30, 264
Thorn, 29, 217, 232
Three-act drama, 21–25, 368–70
3M, 251
Three Mile Island, 34, 97
Time, 148, 305
Tisch, Laurence, 147
Tokyo, Japan, 266, 270
Tokyo Electric, 207
Tomasetti, Louis, 119, 185
Top Line/Bottom Line, 376–77
Top Line/Bottom Line test, 376–77
Toshiba, 8, 220, 222, 229–30, 232,
    264–65
Toward a Shared Vision, 341n
Toyota, 239, 391–92
Trani, John, 220, 230, 260–62,
    347–48n
Transformational Leader, 388–89
Transformational Leader
    Framework, 438
Transformational Leader Survey,
    388–89
Transitions (Bridges), 370
Travelers Mortgage, 29
Tremaine, Burton G., 343n
Trotter, Lloyd G., 345n
Tungsram, 29, 217–18, 232
Turner, Ted, 146–47

Union Carbide, 251
United Electrical and Electronic
    Workers, 119–20
United States
  productivity, 18
  wages in, 19
  See also Corporations
United States Air Force, 133–34
United States Department of
    Commerce, 42
United Technologies, 109

Urquhart, John, 185
U.S. Statistical Abstract, 17
Utah International, 29, 34, 81, 96,
    105, 182, 223, 233

Value, product, 294–96
Value Decade, 292, 294, 305
Values
  implementing, 298–99
  importance of, 195, 299
  importance to GE, 278–83, 285,
    290–93
  obstacles to transforming, 335n
Values statement, GE's, 171–75,
    341n, 413–15
Vanderslice, Thomas, 68
Van Orden, Paul, 39, 92, 98–99,
    181, 185
Vision
  articulating, 415–19
  and assessing reality, 410–12
  and human resources function,
    435–36
  importance of, 409
  and values statement, 413–15
  Welch's, 415, 418
Vonnegut, Kurt, Jr., 340n

Wall Street Journal, 186
Wal-Mart, 16, 191
Washington Post, 148
Way, Alva, 66
Weber, Max, 38
Weick, Karl, 343n
Weiss, Herman, 62, 65
Welch, Carolyn, 58
Welch, Grace, 56–58
Welch, Jane, 56
Welch, John, Sr., 56–58
Welch, John F., Jr. (Jack), 111, 114,
    221, 223n, 270, 400–401,
    432. *See also* General
    Electric
  central idea of, 71–74
  on Consumer Electronics swap,
    220

control strategies of, 94–96
on Corporate Executive Council,
191–92, 200–201
at Crotonville, 166–68
and David Letterman, 152, 339n
decision-making of, 60
described, 10–12
on detractors, 305
early career, 49, 52, 58–69
education, 57–58
employee reactions to, 9–10,
101–6
on ethics, 133, 136–38, 140–41
evolution of, 255–57
family of, 56–58
first two years as CEO, 85
on globalization, 222
and hiring of Tichy, 156
and ideas, 71–84
involvement in day-to-day
operations, 96, 98
versus Jones, 36–37
on Lighting, 202–3, 208
management ideas, 66
and negative publicity, 103–4
personal characteristics of, 4–5,
55–56
and "planful opportunism," 63
relations with employees, 75–78,
110, 287–88
on restructuring, 202
and Schlemmer, 117, 119, 123–24
second two years as CEO, 101–10
selection as CEO, 32, 52–54,
331–32n
six rules of, 15
on successor, 303–4
on teamwork, 197
on Thomson swap, 228
three circles of, 107–8
on values, 195
Wendt, Gary C., 345n
Westinghouse, 16, 42, 46, 97, 132,
204, 206–7, 209, 222

Whirlpool, 231
White Consolidated, 222
Wilson, Alexander M., 344
Wilson, Charles (GE CEO), 43, 46,
131
Wilson, Charles (GM CEO), 43
Woodbum, Bill, 205, 208, 216–17
Work-Out, 26, 78, 120, 176, 196,
233, 279, 287–88, 299,
301–2, 421
and Aircraft Engines, 252–54
Change Acceleration Program of,
254, 287
and Critical Review Appraisal,
434–35
and customers/suppliers, 251–52
functioning of, 244–46, 248, 251,
254, 256–57
at GE Medical Systems, 431–35
goals of, 243–44
Leadership Development Series,
437–40
and process mapping, 251
reasons for, 237–42
scale of, 242–43, 248
and social movement phases,
347n
structure of, 430–31
success of, 257–59
training of leaders, 437–42
Welch on, 430–31
and Welch's thinking, 256–57
"Works," 41, 44
Workshops, Leadership
Development Series, 439–40
Wright, Robert, 106, 149, 187, 200
Wriston, Walter, 23, 46, 56

Yohino, Mike, 170
Yokogawa Electric Works, 220
Yokogawa Medical Systems, 220,
229–30, 264

Zenith Corporation, 221

Also by Noel M. Tichy and Stratford Sherman:

"Mastering Revolutionary Change"

This *Fortune* Magazine Video Seminar explains how to lead organizations of any size through dramatic change. It features interviews with GE's Jack Welch and the leaders of three other companies—Allied-Signal, Ameritech, and Tenneco—all distinguished by the determination to control their own destinies.

To order, call:
(800) 227-7703 (in the U.S.A.) or
(617) 247-8890 (overseas)